RESPONDING TO THE CULPABLE STATE

This volume explores ethical aspects relating to claims for mitigation arising from culpable state action (or inaction).

It answers the important and controversial question: to what extent should the state mitigate sentencing for defendants who have been victims of state misconduct?

The volume explores the normative justifications for mitigation and answers many intriguing questions. For example, in terms of the procedural challenges, should the offender have to prove a causal link between state wrongdoing or neglect and the offending? Can a court take judicial notice of state-induced social adversity and apply this consideration to all affected offenders? Other questions relate to the implications for courts and sentencing commissions which issue guidance to courts regarding mitigation at sentencing. To what extent is the offender less culpable as a result of state misconduct, and what are the limits of any resulting sentence reductions? Do sentence reductions for state misconduct undermine proportionality, or deprecate the seriousness of the impact on the victim of crime? Should this factor be included in any sentencing guidelines or possibly even as a statutory mitigating factor?

Each contribution explores a distinct, cross-jurisdictional claim for mitigation on the basis of State negligence or misconduct towards the offender. The chapters all address the appropriate response of courts at sentencing.

Studies in Penal Theory and Ethics: Volume 10

Studies in Penal Theory and Ethics

A Series Published for
the Centre for Penal Theory and Ethics
Institute of Criminology, University of Cambridge

FOUNDING EDITOR: ANDREAS VON HIRSCH

GENERAL EDITOR:
LEO ZAIBERT

The Series publishes cutting-edge work on penal theory and ethics – both broadly construed – and on their intersections. The Series is particularly open to approaches belonging to different intellectual traditions – whether analytical, comparative, or historical – and to interdisciplinary approaches. While the Series's emphasis is theoretical, it is hoped that many of its volumes will highlight some of the ways in which theoretical work relates to practical concerns.

Previous volumes in this series:

Ethical and Social Perspectives on Situational Crime Prevention
edited by Andrew von Hirsch, David Garland and Alison Wakefield

Restorative Justice and Criminal Justice: Competing or Reconcilable Paradigms?
edited by Andrew von Hirsch, Julian Roberts, Anthony E Bottoms, Kent Roach and Mara Schiff

Incivilities: Regulating Offensive Behaviour
edited by A P Simester and Andreas Von Hirsch

Previous Convictions at Sentencing: Theoretical and Applied Perspectives
edited by Julian V Roberts and Andrew von Hirsch

Setting the Watch: Privacy and the Ethics of CCTV Surveillance
Beatrice von Silva-Tarouca Larsen

Criminal Law and the Authority of the State
edited by Antje du Bois-Pedain, Magnus Ulväng and Petter Asp

Penal Censure: Engagements Within and Beyond Desert Theory
edited by Antje du Bois-Pedain and Anthony E Bottoms

Re-Reading Beccaria: On the Contemporary Significance of a Penal Classic
edited by Antje du Bois-Pedain and Shachar Eldar

Criminology as a Moral Science
edited by Anthony Bottoms and Jonathan Jacobs

Responding to the Culpable State: Is Sentence Mitigation Appropriate?
edited by Leo Zaibert, Julian V Roberts and Jesper Ryberg

Responding to the Culpable State

Is Sentence Mitigation Appropriate?

Edited by
Leo Zaibert
Julian V Roberts
and
Jesper Ryberg

•HART•
OXFORD • LONDON • NEW YORK • NEW DELHI • SYDNEY

HART PUBLISHING

Bloomsbury Publishing Plc

Kemp House, Chawley Park, Cumnor Hill, Oxford, OX2 9PH, UK

1385 Broadway, New York, NY 10018, USA

Bloomsbury Publishing Ireland Limited, 29 Earlsfort Terrace, Dublin 2, D02 AY28, Ireland

HART PUBLISHING, the Hart/Stag logo, BLOOMSBURY and the Diana logo are trademarks of Bloomsbury Publishing Plc

First published in Great Britain 2025

First published in hardback, 2025

Paperback edition, 2026

A catalogue record for this book is available from the British Library.

A catalogue record for this book is available from the Library of Congress.

Library of Congress Control Number: 2024946793

ISBN: PB: 978-1-50997-564-8
ePDF: 978-1-50997-567-9
ePub: 978-1-50997-566-2

Typeset by Compuscript Ltd, Shannon

For product safety related questions contact productsafety@bloomsbury.com

To find out more about our authors and books visit www.hartpublishing.co.uk. Here you will find extracts, author information, details of forthcoming events and the option to sign up for our newsletters.

ACKNOWLEDGEMENTS

The chapters in this volume were first discussed at a seminar held at the Institute of Criminology, the University of Cambridge, in December 2023. We are grateful to the Institute and the Centre for Penal Theory and Ethics for financial support. We would like to thank the authors for contributing to this volume. We are also grateful to Hart Bloomsbury for publishing and in particular Verity Stuart for assistance in bringing this volume into print.

Leo Zaibert, Cambridge
Julian V Roberts, Oxford
Jesper Ryberg, Roskilde
15 July 2024

TABLE OF CONTENTS

ABOUT THE AUTHORS

General Editors

Leo Zaibert is Andreas von Hirsch Professor of Penal Theory and Ethics, and Fellow of Wolfson College, both at the University of Cambridge. He is also the Director of Cambridge University's Centre for Penal Theory and Ethics. He has been an NEH fellow, a Humboldt Fellow and an HLA Hart Fellow at Oxford University. He is the author of *Five Ways Patricia Can Kill her Husband: A Theory of Intentionality and Blame* (Chicago, Open Court, 2005), *Punishment and Retribution* (London, Routledge, 2017) and *Rethinking Punishment* (Cambridge, Cambridge University Press, 2018).

Julian V Roberts, KC (Hon) is Emeritus Professor, University of Oxford and Executive Director of the Sentencing Academy. Julian was the 2021 recipient of the American Society of Criminology Sellin-Glueck Award for Comparative Scholarship. His books include: *Sentencing Guidance and Sentencing Commissions: Comparative Perspectives* (New York, Oxford University Press, 2025) (with A Freiberg and R Hester); *Paying for the Past* (Oxford, Oxford University Press, 2019) (with R Frase); *Criminal Justice. A Short Introduction*, 2nd edn (Oxford, Oxford University Press, 2025); *Punishing Persistent Offenders* (Oxford, Oxford University Press, 2008); *The Virtual Prison* (Cambridge, Cambridge University Press, 2004).

Jesper Ryberg is Professor of Ethics and Philosophy of Law, Roskilde University. He is the head of the Research Group for Criminal Justice Ethics. His books include: *The Oxford Handbook of the Philosophy of Punishment* (New York, Oxford University Press, in press); *Sentencing and Artificial Intelligence* (New York, Oxford University Press, 2022) (with JV Roberts); *Neurointerventions, Crime, and Punishment* (New York, Oxford University Press, 2020); *Sentencing Multiple Crimes* (New York, Oxford University Press, 2017) (with JV Roberts and J de Keijser); *Popular Punishment* (New York, Oxford University Press, 2014) (with JV Roberts).

Contributors

Vera Bergelson is a Distinguished Professor of Law and Robert E Knowlton Scholar at Rutgers University School of Law, USA. She specialises in criminal law theory and has written widely about criminal punishment, affirmative defences, sexual offences and victimless crime. Her book, *Victims' Rights and Victims' Wrongs: A*

Theory of Comparative Criminal Liability (Stanford, Stanford University Press, 2009), raises questions about comparative liability in criminal law. Vera Bergelson is a recipient of the Greg Lastowka Memorial Award for Scholarly Excellence.

Thom Brooks is Professor of Law and Government at Durham Law School, Associate Member in Philosophy and the School of Government at Durham University and a Visiting Fellow at Yale Law School. He is former President of the Society of Legal Scholars and executive member of the Fabian Society. He works across law, philosophy and politics with interests in criminal justice, immigration law and jurisprudence. Brooks's publications include *Punishment* (London, Routledge, 2012; 2nd edn 2021); *Rawls's Political Liberalism* (eds with Martha C Nussbaum, New York, Columbia University Press, 2015); *Punishment: A Very Short Introduction* (Oxford, Oxford University Press, 2025).

Netanel Dagan is a Senior Lecturer at the Hebrew University of Jerusalem's Institute of Criminology. His research focuses on penal theory and penology. He has been a senior clerk at the Supreme Court of Israel and an academic visitor at the Centre for Criminology in Oxford and Cambridge.

Antje du Bois-Pedain is Professor of Criminal Law and Philosophy and Deputy Director of the Centre for Penal Theory and Ethics, University of Cambridge. She has published extensively on transitional justice (including the monograph *Transitional Amnesty in South Africa* (Cambridge, Cambridge University Press, 2007)), criminal law theory, sentencing and the philosophy of punishment. Co-edited volumes include *Criminal Law and the Authority of the State* (Oxford, Hart, 2017), *Penal Censure: Engagements Within and Beyond Desert Theory* (Oxford, Hart, 2019) and *Re-Reading Beccaria: On the Contemporary Significance of a Penal Classic* (Oxford, Hart, 2022).

Goran Duus-Otterstrom is Professor of Political Science at the University of Gothenburg and a researcher in the Institute for Futures Studies, Stockholm. Goran works on issues related to the justification of legal punishment, including the role of legitimate authority and political obligation for the state's right to punish. He has published articles in journals such as *British Journal of Political Science*, *Criminal Law and Philosophy*, *European Journal of Political Theory* and *Law and Philosophy*.

Benjamin Ewing is Associate Professor at Queen's University Faculty of Law in Kingston, Ontario, Canada. He teaches criminal law, criminal procedure and criminal law theory. His work has been published in edited books, law reviews (including *Yale Law Journal*, *University of Toronto Law Journal*, and *American Journal of Criminal Law*) and peer-reviewed legal theory journals including *Oxford Journal of Legal Studies*, *Law and Philosophy*, *Criminal Law and Philosophy* and *Canadian Journal of Law and Jurisprudence*.

Hend Hanafy is an Assistant Professor of Criminal Law at the University of Cambridge. She has been the Richard Fellingham Teaching and Research Fellow at St Catharine's College, Cambridge, and previously Assistant Lecturer at Cairo University. Her research focuses on criminal law and penal theory with an interdisciplinary lens that engages with political philosophy and legitimacy, particularly in contexts of social and political injustices, and has published in *Criminal Law and Philosophy*, *Journal of Bentham Studies*, and *Punishment and Society*.

Richard L Lippke is Emeritus Professor of Criminal Justice, Indiana University-Bloomington. His books include *Theorizing Legal Punishment* (New York, Routledge, 2024); *Taming the Presumption of Innocence* (New York, Oxford University Press, 2016); *The Ethics of Plea Bargaining* (Oxford, Oxford University Press, 2011); and *Rethinking Imprisonment* (Oxford, Oxford University Press, 2007).

Marie Manikis is an Associate Professor and William Dawson Scholar at the Faculty of Law of McGill University. She is also a Research Associate at the Centre for Criminology, University of Oxford, and an adviser for the Sentencing Academy. Her research is published in leading peer-reviewed journals including *Oxford Journal of Legal Studies*, *Cambridge Law Journal* and *Modern Law Review*. She has won several awards, including the Canadian Association of Law Teachers Scholarly Paper Award for her article 'Recognising State Blame in Sentencing'.

Matt Matravers is Professor of Law and Director of the Morrell Centre for Legal and Political Philosophy at the University of York. He is the author of two monographs, *Justice and Punishment* (Oxford, Oxford University Press, 2000) and *Responsibility and Justice* (London, Polity, 2007), and of numerous papers in legal and political philosophy. In addition, he has edited seven volumes the latest of which, co-edited with Claes Lernestedt, is *The Criminal Law's Person* (Oxford, Hart, 2022).

Nicola Padfield KC (Hon) is Emeritus Professor of Criminal and Penal Justice at the Law Faculty, University of Cambridge. She was Master of Fitzwilliam College, Cambridge from 2013 to 2019 and is now an Honorary Fellow. She has published widely on criminal law, sentencing and criminal justice. Books include *The Criminal Justice Process: Text and Materials*, 5th edn (Abingdon, Routledge, 2016) (with Jonathan Bild); *Criminal Law*, 10th edn (Oxford, Oxford University Press, 2016); and *Beyond the Tariff: Human rights and the release of life sentence prisoners* (Cullompton, Willan, 2002). She sat as a Recorder (part-time judge) in the Crown Court from 2002 to 2014.

Mojca M Plesničar is a Senior Research Associate at the Institute of Criminology and Associate Professor in Criminology at the University of Ljubljana. Her research focuses on punishment, sentencing and decision-making in criminal justice, exploring themes such as the application of AI, the experiences of marginalised groups, and violent and sexual crime, mainly through a systemic perspective on the design of criminal justice. She has published in national and international journals and contributed to important collective books on these topics.

Andrei Poama is lecturer at the Faculty of Governance and Global Affairs, Leiden University. He works at the intersection of normative theories of punishment, democratic theory and public policy ethics. He is the co-editor of the *Routledge Handbook of Public Policy and Ethics*, and has published in, among others, *Criminal Law and Philosophy*, *British Journal of Criminology*, *Journal of Political Philosophy*, *Social Theory and Practice* and *American Political Science Review*.

Gabrielle Watson is Chancellor's Fellow at Edinburgh Law School. She is the author of *Respect and Criminal Justice* (Oxford and New York, Oxford University Press, 2020) and member of the Criminal Courts Rules Council (Scotland), having been appointed by the Lord Justice General in 2024. Gabrielle was formerly based at the University of Oxford as Leverhulme Early Career Fellow (2017–19) and Shaw Foundation Fellow in Law (2019–23). She has also held Visiting Fellowships at the University of Cambridge (2019, 2021) and the Max Planck Institute for the Study of Crime, Security and Law (2023).

TABLE OF CASES

TABLE OF STATUTES

1

State Misconduct as Sentence Mitigation: Setting the Scene

LEO ZAIBERT, JULIAN V ROBERTS AND JESPER RYBERG

At sentencing, the court's scrutiny falls exclusively on the offender's criminal conduct. From a retributive perspective, the sentencing hearing addresses the nature and degree of harm caused or threatened as well as the offender's culpability for that harm. At no point in the hearing does the state hold up a mirror to examine its own conduct; there is no self-censure or even self-examination.[1] The court assumes the state is blameless. Yet there may be grounds for such an exercise. The state may have acted wrongfully in a manner and to an extent that has consequences for sentencing the offender. This volume examines ethical questions related to whether state wrongdoing should be taken into account when the victim of the misconduct appears for sentencing. Should the state's misconduct mitigate the sentence – and if so, to what extent – for a defendant who is the victim of that wrongful conduct?

The volume explores the normative justifications for mitigation on this ground and addresses many intriguing questions. For example, in terms of the procedural challenges, should the offender have to prove a more or less direct causal link between state wrongdoing or neglect and the offending? That is, must the defendant establish that the state contributed in some material way to the offence? What if the state's wrongful actions were wholly unrelated – or only dimly related – to the offence for which the offender is being sentenced? Can a court take judicial notice of state-induced social adversity and apply this consideration to all affected offenders? Other questions relate to the implications for courts and sentencing commissions which issue guidance to courts regarding mitigation at sentencing. To what extent is the offender less culpable as a result of state misconduct, and what are the limits of any resulting sentence reductions? Do sentence reductions

[1] In this introduction we set aside motions by the offender to dismiss a proceeding for abuse of process. For example, if the court accepts that the evidence adduced by the state was illegally acquired, a common remedy involves discontinuing the prosecution. Here we assume that any such claims on behalf of the defendant have been resolved.

for state misconduct undermine proportionality or deprecate the seriousness of the impact on the crime victim? Should this factor be included in any sentencing guidelines or possibly even recognised by the legislator as a statutory mitigating factor? Certain types of offenders are more likely to be victims of state misconduct. It is now trite to observe that minorities of various kinds (racial, ethnic, immigrant, religious) as well as communities experiencing social and economic adversity are heavily over-represented at sentencing. More broadly, visible minorities are far more likely to be victims of abusive or discriminatory treatment at the hands of state agents, including police and prison officers, sentencers and parole boards. Courts in a number of jurisdictions are now reducing sentences in response to a variety of claims for mitigation arising from racial and other forms of abuse by state actors.

For example, in a Canadian sentencing decision involving a Black offender (discussed in several chapters of this volume), the Ontario Court of Appeal noted that:

> The moral blameworthiness of [the offender] is mitigated by his mental and physical health issues, as well as his educational and economic disadvantages. All of those factors are influenced by the systemic anti-Black racism Mr. Morris has experienced. The factors can only properly be understood, for the purposes of determining the appropriate sentence, by having regard to that context.[2]

A variety of claims for mitigation arise in relation to the state and its duties to citizens, including offenders. Some of these relate to events occurring before, and some after the crime was committed for which the offender is being held to account. They include:

- State indifference to, or neglect of, the social and economic deprivations which give rise to high crime rates – for example, inner cities in the US, or indigenous communities across Canada, Australia and New Zealand.
- State actions which create or exacerbate criminogenic risk factors – for example, the committal of Aboriginal children to state residential schools in Canada
- Direct and indirect discrimination by state agents in the criminal justice system – for example, the over-policing of Black citizens (including 'Stop and Search' and other forms of increased surveillance and control); discrimination by prosecutors, judges, and parole boards or prison officers.
- A protracted delay in judicial proceedings which was harmful to the defendant awaiting trial.
- State-imposed sentences which *increase* the offender's likelihood of reoffending, and undermine the offender's efforts to reform. For example, there is evidence that short-term imprisonment leads to higher reoffending rates than community-based sanctions. Here the offender may claim that had she received

[2] *R v Morris* 2021 ONCA 680 (ontariocourts.ca).

a community penalty, she would have been less likely to commit the current offence. The prison sentence itself contributed to the subsequent offending.

- Mistreatment of prisoners by state officials – for example, racist abuse and mistreatment by other prisoners or prison officers. Here the offender claims that the previous imprisonment was disproportionately harsher than that which the court had envisaged at the time of sentencing. As a result, this additional punishment should now be 'deducted' from the new sentence.
- State-imposed civil restrictions (consequences of the sentence once it has been served) which deprive ex-offenders of opportunities to return to productive and law-abiding lives. For example, the myriad collateral consequences imposed following conviction such as the loss of voting rights; employment and mobility restrictions etc. These restrictions then increase the likelihood of a return to crime.
- Inflexible expungement laws which require an unreasonable period of time to elapse before an ex-offender may have a prior conviction expunged.
- State failure to prevent or address racial abuse and discrimination by elements of civil society – for example, discrimination by private companies and schools (which are more likely to expel minority pupils).

Such circumstances apply to a range of defendants but fall disproportionately on minority offenders and those from lower socio-economic classes. Many forms of misconduct share a common element: the state has to some degree directly or indirectly contributed to the offending (or the reoffending). As such, it carries some liability for it. The state can discharge this liability by awarding mitigation to the offender. Some of the offender's culpability for the offence is shared with the state, and this needs recognition at the time of sentencing. In addition to state misconduct before the crime, the state may maltreat the offender at any point between the detection of the crime and its sentencing. Indeed, mistreatment may even occur long after sentencing (discussed below). This volume is not a collection of unrelated case histories. Instead, contributors explore distinct, cross-jurisdictional claims for mitigation on the basis of state misconduct involving the offender. The chapters all address the appropriate response of courts at sentencing, drawing upon a variety of independent and sometimes overlapping perspectives.

I. Defining State Misconduct

As seen in the preceding examples, the state can act wrongfully in many ways. Courts need a definition of state misconduct in order to determine whether to mitigate sentencing. As this volume makes clear, since misconduct can take so many forms, achieving a precise definition may be difficult. Still, some threshold appears necessary; trivial acts by state agents – for example, verbal abuse by police during arrest or interview – seem insufficient to justify mitigating sentences. The misconduct must attain some threshold of wrongfulness before it will justify mitigation at sentence.

Another definitional question concerns the relationship between the crime and the mistreatment. Is it necessary for the state to have played a more or less direct causal role in the offence? Should the court apply some form of 'but for' requirement before awarding mitigation? Courts in Canada have grappled with this question and concluded that a causal requirement sets the bar too high: few offenders would receive mitigation if they had to prove, even on a balance of probabilities, that the misconduct contributed in a causal sense to the crime. Without some link between the offence and the misconduct, however, the appeal for mitigation may become implausibly loose. The temporal dimension may be particularly important: actions by state officials many years prior to the crime will not sustain a plausible claim in mitigation. Acts occurring immediately prior to the offence will be more significant. If some, even loose, causal or contributory connection is required, this will foreclose claims for mitigation relating to misconduct occurring after the crime (discussed below).

Finally, the nature of the offence for which the offender is being punished will also be an important consideration for a sentencing court. Crimes which relate to the state's wrongful acts in some way will more convincingly justify mitigation. The minority individual who assaults police officers after having been stopped-and-searched many times in the past, may have a convincing claim for mitigation. Yet this same offender's claim for mitigation is less plausible if his offence involves domestic abuse or drug dealing. In addition to the relationship between wrongdoing by the state and the offender, the seriousness of the latter may be a legitimate consideration. If the police assault a suspect who is then convicted of rape or murder, should the assault reduce the sentence ultimately imposed?

II. Calibrating the Level of Mitigation

The calibration problem is likely to prove the most challenging. If the court accepts that mitigation is appropriate, to what extent should the sentence be reduced? Determining the weight of mitigating factors is generally very challenging – for trial courts and for appellate courts which attempt to provide guidance on the issue. Unless the factor tracks some objective dimension (such as the timing of a guilty plea), the impact of a mitigating factor is difficult to determine a priori, in the abstract. Nevertheless, some guidance may be possible; for example, an appellate court could suggest that a given factor may reduce the quantum of punishment but not change the nature of the sanction (from prison to the community, for example).

This challenge resembles the classic problem facing a court which attempts to craft a sentence the severity of which is proportional to the seriousness of the crime. Crime seriousness and sentence severity are two independent scales or dimensions, and there is no obvious way of co-relating them.

Some may argue that the most serious forms of state abuse involving the offender should justify more than mitigation: they should exculpate. The classic argument here, discussed by several contributors, is that the state has lost its authority or legitimacy, not just to impose the fully proportionate punishment, but the right to impose *any* punishment at all.

III. Timing of the Misconduct

All manner of misconduct may therefore be cited to support a claim for mitigation once the offender appears for sentence. Scrutiny of potential state misconduct may not end at sentencing: prison officers may abuse prisoners while they serve their sentences; parole officers may deny a benefit motivated by racism, etc. One obvious remedy for such conduct is a formal complaint by the affected individual to prison authorities. An alternative approach would involve the offender returning to court to seek a reduction in his prison term in recognition of the harm sustained. Few jurisdictions permit such sentence reviews during the administration of the sentence, but when they occur, the arguments for mitigation are the same as in cases where the offender was abused by police during or following arrest. Several contributors address the issue of the timing of the misconduct in relation to the offence.

The timing of the misconduct is therefore another important variable. Misconduct prior to commission of the crime raises questions about the state's contributory role. Did the state misconduct trigger the offending or in some way make the crime more likely? The defence of entrapment is relevant here. If the offender would not have committed the crime without state agents entrapment actions, there is a powerful claim for criminal defences that go beyond mere mitigation, and that may even call for exculpation. Several contributors explore the plausibility of justifying mitigation for temporally more complicated forms of state misconduct, or for state misconduct not already or typically recognised in existing law – say, by the state's participation in socio-economic arrangements that may be in different ways criminogenic.

2

State Illegitimacy and Punishment: Examining the Case for Discounts

GORAN DUUS-OTTERSTROM

When a state acts very unjustly, for example by violating individuals' basic rights, it lacks legitimate authority over at least part of the population it governs and cannot plausibly claim their deference and respect. What consequences does this have for the state's right to impose punishment on lawbreakers? This chapter deals with one aspect of this question: whether a state's lack of legitimate authority ought to count as a mitigating factor at sentencing. Addressing this question is important since the legitimacy of the state seems intimately bound up with its right to enforce the law. Yet, theorists of punishment have tended to neglect issues of legitimacy, preferring 'either to ignore questions of political legitimacy or to stipulate the existence of a legitimate punishing authority' (Ristroph 2016: 82).[1]

I. Overview

I begin, in section III, by offering a retributivist argument for why punishments for offenders over whom a state lacks legitimate authority ought to be less than those imposed on otherwise comparable offenders over whom the state exercises legitimate authority. The argument draws on the claim that breaching one's political obligation – the flipside of legitimate authority as it pertains to the individuals governed by the state – is morally wrongful and something which contributes to an offender's penal desert. Politically obligated persons are those who are under a moral duty to obey the law as a matter of civic respect or good citizenship. The idea is that when a politically obligated person breaks the law, she commits an

[1] When theorists of punishment have addressed state legitimacy in the context of punishment, they have tended to focus on the right to inflict any punishment at all (see eg, Duff 2001: 181–88; Shelby 2016: 238–48; Poama 2021). I return to exemptions from criminal liability in section VII. See also the chapters by Ewing, Hanafy, and Watson in this volume.

additional wrong related to the failure to display civic respectfulness or good citizenship, making the act more wrong than it otherwise would have been.

In sections IV–VI, I turn to the size and nature of the discount in question. One question is whether the lack of legitimate authority should lead to the same penal discount for all crimes. Some would say yes, reasoning that each crime is an act of disobedience, and equally so. However, this leads to the problem that if the discount is to be applied uniformly across all punishments, it would have to be very small and thus make only a trivial difference for severe punishments. I argue that this problem could be overcome by defining the mitigation in relative terms. A second issue is whether the relative discount should be large or small. I argue that since it is implausible that breaching one's political obligation is a significant wrong, the discount to which politically non-obligated offenders are entitled should be modest.

The idea that the lack of political obligation should only result in small sentence discounts would, however, seem to underappreciate the significance of legitimate authority. Intuitively, there is something highly problematic about an illegitimate state holding people accountable for breaching its legal commands since such a state has no right to expect people to comply with its edicts. In section VII, I suggest that this should arguably lead us to consider the idea of legal *exemptions* to in establishing the consequences of illegitimacy for punishment. Yet, as I also argue, the extent to which illegitimacy should lead to exemptions is difficult to assess and defies easy categorisation.

II. Three Preliminary Points

Before I start, it is worth clarifying three points. First, as noted above, I am strictly interested in retributivist arguments for penal discounts, which I understand as arguments that draw directly on moral desert. Non-retributive arguments, such as those a utilitarian might espouse, thus fall outside the scope of the discussion. I shall not engage with, for example, whether penal discounts for the non-obligated would generate, or undermine, respect for the criminal law. This is not because such questions are unimportant, but simply to limit and sharpen the discussion.

Second, though my focus here is on lacking legitimate authority, this should not be read as denying that state misconduct could reduce offenders' moral deservingness of punishment for other reasons. For example, whether or not it is perpetrated by an illegitimate state, it may be that state misconduct can render motives for offending less blameworthy (see the chapters by Bergelson, Ewing, and Manikis in this volume). The claim that politically non-obligated offenders deserve less punishment can be embraced alongside other grounds for sentence mitigation.

Third, the argument I advance does not assume any particular theory of legitimacy or political obligation. All the argument requires is that there are situations in which the state lacks the ability to generate political obligation in the offender. For the purposes of this volume, we can suppose that such situations occur just in case the state has treated the offender seriously unjustly, but the argument I offer is equally compatible with any of the many theories of political obligation that have been proposed. Put differently, the argument does not hinge on the *substantive criteria* for political obligation, but rather on the way the *structure* of this concept relates to moral desert.[2]

III. The Retributivist Case for Penal Discounts Due to State Illegitimacy

Retributivism is a family of views which is notoriously difficult to define. I shall take 'retributivism' to denote any view which accords direct significance to moral desert in the justification of legal punishments, using moral desert to set optimal penalties, penal ranges, or penal minima/maxima.[3] For retributivism understood in this way, the claim that a lack of legitimate authority should lead to penal discounts is, in a sense, already explained by a standard understanding of the central concepts: legitimate authority and political obligation. *Legitimate authority* refers to a state's moral right to rule, where the right to rule entails not only a liberty to issue and enforce legal commands but also a claim to compliance from those ruled by the state (Simmons 2001: 130).[4] *Political obligation*, meanwhile, refers to the duty on part of the individual to comply with the legal commands, ie, a duty to obey the law (Dagger and Lefkowitz 2014).[5] Political obligation, then, is the flipside of legitimate authority. It describes the normative consequences of legitimate authority for the population the state governs.

It is important to note that the duty to obey the law which is the hallmark of political obligation is supposed to be *content-independent*, meaning that the duty does not flow from the particular content of the laws – for example, whether they promote the common good or codify pre-legal moral duties – but instead from the

[2] For a good overview of different theories of political obligation, see Horton (2010). Personally, I find the fair play theory plausible (Duus-Otterstrom 2021).

[3] I write 'direct' significance since it is possible to care about moral desert for indirect reasons (see, eg, Rachels 1997; Robinson 2013). Note that including negative retributivism in the retributivist family, as I do here, is controversial (Duff 2001: 11; Berman 2016).

[4] It is increasingly common to treat a state's liberty to make and enforce legal commands and its claim to compliance as separate issues (see, eg, Buchanan 2002; Applbaum 2010). Shelby usefully calls the former enforcement legitimacy and the latter obedience legitimacy (Shelby 2016: 229). I take legitimate authority to comprise both obedience and enforcement legitimacy. I return to mere enforcement legitimacy in section VII.

[5] Some argue that political obligation covers not only a duty to obey the law but also a duty to cooperate with and promote the interests of the state in legally non-mandatory ways (Parekh 1993; Knowles 2010). I believe this view is correct, but the focus here is the duty to obey the law and I take the liberty of referring to this as 'political obligation'.

fact that the laws are enacted by a legitimate authority. If the state has legitimate authority over us, then we have a duty to obey the law 'because' it is the law and not because of its substantive merits.[6] Joseph Raz famously captures this by saying that the commands of legitimate authorities have 'preemptory force' in that they create a reason to comply with the commands that is not to be simply balanced against other reasons for or against doing what the commands says, but should rather 'exclude and take the place of some of [these reasons]' (Raz 1986: 46).

The idea that states can possess legitimate authority is (to put it mildly) controversial. Certainly, virtually all political theorists reject the thought of an absolute duty to obey the law. They think that the most one could say is that there might be a *pro tanto* duty to obey the commands of legitimate states such that we should typically, but not always, comply. However, even with that qualification there is significant doubt among political theorists whether states can possess legitimate authority. Philosophical anarchists famously maintain that they cannot. They argue that while people often have reason to follow legal commands, this is never because the commands come from the state, as states have no ability to morally bind people.[7] Here, however, I shall simply assume that it is possible for states to have legitimate authority. The analysis I offer is conditional in that it asks what difference legitimate authority makes *if* it is possible that states can have legitimate authority over at least parts of the population they govern. It is obvious that if all states lack legitimate authority, the distinction between politically obligated and non-obligated offenders becomes irrelevant. In such a world, there would only be politically nonobligated offenders.

With this conceptual framework in place, it is an easy matter to argue that the lack of legitimate authority should lead to sentence mitigation. The key idea is that breaching one's political obligation is an additional source of wrongness over and above the other reasons a criminal act was wrong.[8] To illustrate, consider two lawbreakers who, independently of one another, commit two very similar robberies but where only one of them is politically obligated to obey the law. For ease of presentation, let us say that the politically obligated lawbreaker is called Adam, whereas his politically non-obligated counterpart is called Zeke. Since Adam and Zeke commit very similar crimes, they have committed similar wrongs in terms of harm inflicted on the victim, fear aroused in the public, and so on. However, in Adam's case, there is an additional wrong since his act was also a breach of political obligation. We might say that Adam's act displayed *civic disrespect*: a failure to honour the legal commands of the state even though these demands should have

[6] Saying that obedience to the law is owed 'because' it is the law is catchy but slightly misleading, because it is not as though no further normative story can be told. For Raz, for example, the reason we ought to comply with authorities is that this tends to produce better outcomes, as measured by the reasons for which we ought to act, than if everyone were to apply their own judgement (Raz 1986: 53). The definition of legitimate authority adopted in this chapter does not presuppose Raz's or anyone else's account of what Buchanan 2002 usefully refers to as the authoritativeness of political authorities.

[7] For famous statements of philosophical anarchism, see Simmons 1979 and Wolff 1998.

[8] For a similar argument, focusing on reasons for legal compliance, see Ewing 2018: 41–45.

been complied with, at least typically, as a matter of good citizenship. This makes Adam's act more wrongful than Zeke's. Both Adam and Zeke can be condemned for inflicting harm on their victims, but only Adam can be saddled with the further charge that he breached political obligation and thus acted in a civically disrespectful way.[9]

If we allow that Adam's act was more wrongful than Zeke's, it is possible to argue that Zeke is liable to less punishment than Adam's in several ways. One option is to draw on *negative retributivism*, the view that punishments may not be more severe than the offender morally deserves.[10] This allows for the following argument:

(1) The maximally deserved punishment depends on culpability.
(2) Politically non-obligated offenders are less culpable, other things being equal, than politically obligated ones (because their acts displayed no civic disrespect).
(3) Therefore, the maximally deserved punishment will be lower, other things being equal, for politically non-obligated offenders than for politically obligated ones.

Note that this argument does not say that politically non-obligated offenders should *be* punished more leniently. The argument is compatible with the position that both types of lawbreakers receive the same punishment provided that the punishments do not exceed anyone's maximally deserved punishment. This is in keeping with the negative retributivist idea that disproportionately harsh punishments are forbidden whereas disproportionately lenient punishments are permitted. For negative retributivism, then, the difference between politically obligated and non-obligated offenders only matters insofar as the state wishes to inflict maximally deserved punishments. Still, a lower penal maximum is one way to flesh out what it might mean to be liable to less punishment, and so negative retributivism supports a moral difference between politically obligated and non-obligated offenders, even if that difference is not necessarily acted upon.

Another option is to draw on *positive retributivism*, the view that offenders ought to receive the punishment they morally deserve. This allows for a straightforward argument for why someone like Zeke ought to be punished more leniently than someone like Adam. The argument is that since politically non-obligated offenders commit a less serious wrong than otherwise similar but politically obligated offenders, they are less deserving of punishment.

Note that positive retributivism supports sentencing mitigation for politically non-obligated offenders whether we tie it to *comparative* desert (where deserved

[9] The concept of civic disrespect is compatible with different accounts of why it is wrong to breach one's political obligation. On a Razian view, the wrong would go in the direction of some sort of arrogance considering that authorities do not create reasons to act as much as specify them (*cf* Husak 2008: 103–16). However, we can also employ a more directly disobedience-related account according to which the wrong consists in instigating a small-scale rebellion.

[10] Negative retributivism also prohibits punishment of the innocent. See Lippke 2014 for a discussion.

treatment depends on how others are treated) or *noncomparative* desert (where deserved treatment is identified in terms of absolute fit).[11] The argument based on comparative desert runs as follows:

(1) The severity of punishments should respect the difference in culpability between offenders.
(2) Politically non-obligated offenders are less culpable, other things being equal, than politically obligated ones (because their acts displayed no civic disrespect).
(3) Therefore, politically non-obligated offenders should get a lesser punishment than politically obligated ones, other things being equal.

The argument from noncomparative desert, meanwhile, runs like this:

(1) Offenders should get the punishment which they deserve, absolutely speaking, in virtue of their culpable wrongdoing.
(2) Politically non-obligated offenders deserve a lesser punishment, other things being equal, than politically obligated ones (because their acts displayed no civic disrespect).
(3) Therefore, politically non-obligated offenders should get a lesser punishment, other things being equal, than politically obligated ones.

There are, then, several ways in which a retributivist can defend sentencing discounts or at least reduced penal maxima for politically non-obligated offenders. It is worth stressing that these arguments identify a *necessary* connection between penal desert and political obligation. They do not assume, for example, that politically non-obligated offenders find it more difficult or burdensome than others to follow the law. To see the difference, consider Jules Holroyd's (2010) argument that maltreatment by the state may reduce deservingness of punishment by making the offender's *motives* for breaking the law less blameworthy. Holroyd's idea is that an impoverished person who, say, steals to satisfy basic needs is less blameworthy than someone who steals out of greed. In this kind of argument, the effects of distributive injustice on individuals' reasons to offend does all the work. The arguments I have offered, by contrast, put the unjust state's illegitimacy front and centre. They call for sentencing mitigation regardless of the motives that drove someone to offend. So, whereas someone like Holroyd would say that no mitigation should be forthcoming when the state's injustice played no part in explaining why a crime was committed, the arguments I have offered reach the opposite conclusion. They do so by identifying a separate factor affecting an offender's penal desert – political obligation – which is independent of motives for breaking the law.[12]

[11] For the distinction between comparative and noncomparative desert, see Kagan 2012 and Duus-Otterstrom 2020. The distinction sorts under a more general distinction between comparative and noncomparative justice (Feinberg 1974).

[12] Put differently, the reduction would not count as personal mitigation, but would rather flow from the reduced seriousness of the crime (Ashworth 2015).

There are three objections to these arguments which should be immediately addressed. The first is that the arguments rely on the view that political obligation is relevant for penal desert, which is not obvious. Someone might think that although it is more *wrong* to commit a crime when one is politically obligated to obey the law, this does not affect the extent to which one morally deserves to be *punished*. The second objection is that the arguments are irrelevant since it is impossible for a state to wield legitimate authority over some parts of the population but not others. The third is that is that there is no practically feasible way for the state, acting through the courts, to identify whether an offender is under political obligation or not. I discuss the objections in order.

In response to the first objection, I readily admit that it is hard to *prove* that breaching political obligation affects penal desert. It is difficult to see, however, why it would not affect it, and so I would suggest that the burden of proof here rests with the sceptic who claims the opposite. Theorists usually argue that penal desert is a function of the harm or risk brought about by the criminal conduct and the offender's culpability (Duff 2001: 153). The task for the sceptic, therefore, is to show that civic disrespectfulness does not affect culpability. Now, it is true that political obligation is seldom if ever discussed in the context of determining an offender's culpability. Culpability is often associated with a standard list of types of *mens rea* (eg, whether the offender acted intentionally, recklessly, or negligently) and aggravating factors (eg, whether the crime was planned, the victims were especially vulnerable, or the offender abused a position of power), which does not mention political obligation. But the deeper rationale behind assessments of culpability is to do with the offender's blameworthiness, and thus understood it is natural to think that political obligation is relevant, for the point of saying that politically obligated offenders act with civic disrespect is precisely that this renders their acts more blameworthy. Needless to say, any suggestion that the enhanced blameworthiness in question is irrelevant from the perspective of public morality is unpromising considering that political obligation is a paradigmatically public value. My hunch would be that the reason political obligation does not figure on the usual lists over culpability enhancing factors is simply an implicit assumption that offenders are politically obligated.

Consider next the objection that the reduced desert of politically non-obligated offenders lacks practical relevance since no one is politically obligated to an illegitimate state. The thought here is that if the state treats some parts of the population unjustly enough to make it lose legitimate authority over them, then it automatically loses legitimate authority over the entire population.[13] And since this is so, everyone will be entitled to the 'discount', rendering the idea pointless.

The response here is twofold. First, it is not clear that partial legitimate authority *is* impossible. It seems plausible that a state could have such authority

[13] Poama 2021 refers to this as the 'non selectivity objection'.

on a range of standard theories of legitimacy such as consent or reciprocity.[14] Partial legitimate authority does look more problematic in the case of seriously unjust states, but even here we might doubt that a state loses authority across the board as soon as it treats *anyone* unjustly, no matter how few these people are and how impeccably the state treats the rest. Second, nothing crucial hangs on whether a state can possess partial legitimate authority anyway since we can also think about the issue in terms of a comparison between states. Even if we assume that legitimacy is an all-or-nothing thing, so that tolerably just states have legitimate authority over the entire population whereas unjust states have no legitimate authority over anyone, the arguments offered above remain relevant because they imply that unjust states generally ought to punish more leniently than tolerably just ones (or at least that the maximally deserved punishment differs between the two). Indeed, the idea of penal discounts for politically non-obligated offenders would matter even if *no* state had legitimate authority, because then the implication would be that all states must punish more leniently than otherwise.

A third objection is that penal discounts for politically non-obligated offenders is merely a philosophical notion which can never be acted upon. This is so because the state will never be able to determine whether an offender is under political obligation, at least not with the degree of precision we expect from rule of law.

The response is that I do not regard practical implementation as necessary for the success of my argument (but see the chapter by Ryberg in this volume for a different perspective). I have sought to give reasons for why penal discounts in principle ought to be given to politically non-obligated offenders, and the observation that we cannot reliably act on these reasons is neither here nor there for this aim. Keeping that qualification in mind, it is also not obvious that it *would* always be impossible to determine whether an offender is under political obligation. One possibility is that we could establish general rules to draw a line between the politically obligated and others. We might think, for example, that political obligation requires voting rights in political elections. If so, we would extend the discount to any lawbreaker who, say, is old enough to be punished but too young to be enfranchised. Another possibility, which is admittedly more controversial, is to ask courts to engage in individualised assessments of whether the guilty person was under political obligation. More specifically, we might ask courts to assess whether the defendant has been denied basic rights at the hand of the state. This strategy would share some resemblance with the much-discussed Rotten Social Background defence, but it would not require making a judgment of whether the

[14] For theories of legitimacy, see Simmons 1979, Horton 2010 and Knowles 2010. Many such theories permit partial legitimacy since they identify a factor which may be present only in parts of the population. I grapple with this question in Duus-Otterstrom 2021. Worth noting is that partial legitimacy is sometimes seen as a problem for a theory of legitimacy since such a theory is supposed to be general, ie, explain why most people in a state are under political obligation (Simmons 1979: 55–56).

disadvantaged status of the defendant affected their ability to control their actions or understand the law. In this sense, it would be epistemically easier to handle.[15]

IV. A Note on Tourists

Before we continue the analysis, it is worth pausing for a moment to think about whether transient visitors on a territory – paradigmatically, tourists – might also be entitled to a penal discount from the state if they break the law. The idea that the state has an unmitigated right to punish such people is widely accepted by theorists. Indeed, for John Locke, the state's right to punish 'an alien of another country' was a data point he used to infer that there must be a natural right to punish (Locke 2009, chapter 2§9). This seems to speak against the idea of penal discount for non-obligated offenders. We might reason that since tourists lack political obligation to the state they visit, and since tourists may and should be punished equally severely as citizens, it cannot be true that legitimate authority matters for penal severity.

I do not have the space here to engage in depth with the fascinating questions posed by transient visitors when it comes to political obligation, so a few concise remarks will have to suffice.[16] The crux of the matter is that transient visitors might well *be* politically obligated to the state they visit in the sense of having a content-independent duty to obey the law. Indeed, at least on a consent-based theory of legitimacy, it seems *easier* to explain why transient visitors are under political obligation compared to permanent residents since they have voluntarily chosen to travel to the state which subjects them. The reason we fail to see this is that we mix up political obligation with loyalty. This leads us into thinking that political obligation is an emotional bond which strengthens and matures over time. But political obligation can emerge instantaneously, and it does not depend on a psychological attachment to the state. Of course, if transient visitors are as obligated to obey the law as citizens and other residents on the territory, they are liable to similar penal treatment.[17]

Suppose, however, that it could be shown that transient visitors are not politically obligated to the state they visit. Not even this possibility would show that there is anything wrong with the idea that political obligation matters for the

[15] For the Rotten Social Background defence, see eg, Delgado 1985, Morse 2000, Taslitz 2011. It should be noted that from the perspective of practical implementation, the most serious obstacle is arguably motivation-based rather than epistemic in nature. There is little reason to expect unjust states to have a desire to offer sentencing discounts to politically non-obligated offenders even if they knew how to do this. However, this source of practical infeasibility is surely one we should disregard for the purposes of moral theorising.

[16] For discussion, see Wringe 2021 and Coca-Vila and Irarrázaval 2022.

[17] Again, I am speaking about the narrow sense of political obligation here, ie, the duty to obey the law. Some think that political obligation covers a wider set of duties associated with good citizenship (see n 5). These wider duties may well fall exclusively on citizens and other permanent residents.

severity of punishments, for even though states seldom make a distinction in practice between residents and non-residents when they punish, it is possible that they *ought* to do so. There are pragmatic problems with offering penal discounts to transient visitors, but it is difficult to see why this would not be the right thing to do from a retributivist perspective if their crimes do not display civic disrespect.

V. The Nature of the Discount

So far, I have argued that lacking legitimate authority ought to lead to penal discounts on a range of retributivist views. The next set of questions pertain to the nature of the discount itself. How should the discount be designed?

One implication seems to be that the discount should be the same for all politically non-obligated offenders. The reasoning here is that if civic disrespect is the relevant wrong, then the additional wrongfulness will always be the same considering that all crimes are failures to obey the law. However, this would create the problem that it seems impossible to devise a same-sized penal discount for all crimes which does not end up being utterly inconsequential for more severe crimes. Consider, for example, which discount we could reasonably offer to those sentenced to 14 days' imprisonment as well as those sentenced to 18 years.[18] Even if we were to cut the former punishment in half, a reduction by seven days would only make a 0.1 per cent difference to the latter punishment, which is hardly meaningful. It seems odd that civic disrespect halves one sentence but barely moves the needle in the other case.

The solution is to construe the penal discount in relative terms as opposed to absolute ones. More specifically, just as the issue tends to be handled by real-world sentencing guidelines, one option would be to define the discount in terms of a percentage reduction of the punishment that would otherwise be inflicted.[19] Suppose, for example, that politically non-obligated offenders would be entitled to a 10 per cent reduction in punishments. The difference between someone sentenced to 14 days and 18 years would then be meaningful for both types of offenders: the former would spend a day-and-a-half less in prison, whereas the latter would spend 657 fewer days in prison. Obviously, there are several complications, including the possibility of early parole. My point is simply that even if all crimes are owed the same mitigation, 'the same mitigation' should be understood in a relative way.

[18] 14 days and 18 years are the shortest and longest determinate prison terms permitted by Swedish criminal law. Note that for 'whole life' imprisonment, whatever mitigation is owed must be achieved via treatment while imprisoned.

[19] See, for example, the English Sentencing Guidelines on guilty pleas. The Guidelines state that a guilty plea entered at the first court appearance may reduce punishment by up to one-third (Roberts 2013: 114).

Note also that it is not at all clear that all crimes *are* equally civically disrespectful. The reason theorists think so is that they see the duty to obey the law as directed towards the entire legal order. The idea is that if people are expected to obey commands X *and* Y, then it does not matter whether someone breaches command X or command Y since either act violates the injunction to obey the set of all commands (see Duus-Otterstrom (2021) for a discussion). However, although it is true that breaching a legal command is always a failure to discharge one's political obligation, it does not necessarily follow that all breaches are equally grave. From the perspective of civic disrespect, it could well be worse to disobey some legal commands than others.[20]

An analogy to parental authority is helpful here. Parents frequently issue commands to their children and expect[21] them to comply, but they do not take all commands equally seriously: sometimes they really mean it and sometimes they hardly believe what they are saying themselves. Given this, the idea that a child would *equally* challenge the authority of her parents whenever she breaks *any* of their rules is quite odd. Similarly, a state might well take some legal commands – those associated with the basic constitutional order, for example – more seriously than others. It will then be a more grievous breach of political obligation for an offender to disobey these commands.

If one were to adopt such a scalar approach to political obligation – and many things speak in favour of doing so – the same-discount-for-all objection would be avoided, because the penal discount would then no longer be the same for all politically non-obligated offenders. Instead, the size of the discount would be defined by the difference between what a politically obligated and non-obligated offender would deserve for committing the same crime, allowing the difference to vary depending on the type of crime.

VI. The Size of the Discount

Regardless of whether we regard all crime as equal or variable instantiations of civic disrespect, a further question remains as to the *size* of the discount. Are politically non-obligated offenders entitled to substantial mitigation at sentencing, or should the discount rather operate at the margins? The answer depends on how wrong it is for a politically obligated person to show civic disrespect. If it is quite wrong, then a sizeable discount is due as this would mean that politically non-obligated offenders are guilty of much less serious acts. I shall argue, however, that the wrong is not particularly great, meaning that politically obligated offenders are only entitled to a small discount.

[20] And worse the more commands that are disobeyed, other things being equal.
[21] I use 'expect' in a normative sense here, not in a predictive sense!

We can show that the wrong of breaching one's political obligation is not particularly great by making a pair of *reductio* arguments. The first starts out from a comparison between offenders. Consider these scenarios:

(A) Carl is politically obligated to obey the law. Despite this, he steals a sound bar to improve his home entertainment system.
(B) Donna is not politically obligated to obey the law. She steals a whole shipment of sound bars to sell on the black market, thereby enriching herself.

The fact that Carl breaches a political obligation plausibly makes his conduct more wrongful than Donna's in one respect. However, the question is how *significant* this factor is for the overall seriousness of the crime. If breaching one's political obligation were a great wrong, we can easily imagine that Carl's conduct would be as wrong as Donna's and perhaps even more wrong. But this does not seem plausible. Political obligation does not figure so prominently in our judgements about criminal seriousness. If we are unwilling to say that Carl's conduct can be at least as wrong as Donna's, as I believe most of us are, we should conclude that civic disrespect is not a great wrong, at least not in the sense which is relevant for criminal culpability.[22]

The difference between Carl and Donna is of course stark, so one should not overestimate how informative it is to compare them. Just because we can be confident that civic disrespect is not wrong enough to put Carl and Donna's crimes on a par, this does not mean that the wrong is minor. To determine the size of the wrong, we would have to compare pairs of crimes until we reach a level where the absence of political obligation does put a more harmful crime on an equal footing with a less harmful one. My hunch, however, is that this exercise would lead to the conclusion that the wrong is quite minor since, again, political obligation does not register much in our (admittedly unsystematic) intuitive judgements about what makes one crime worse than another.

The case for the same conclusion can also be made on noncomparative grounds. Suppose legal punishment ought to give lawbreakers what they morally deserve. Suppose next that civic disrespect is a major wrong which significantly enhances a person's negative desert. Since all crimes committed by politically obligated offenders are by definition instances of civic disrespect, the implication of this would be that all crimes are major wrongs which call for significant punishments. But we do not think that all crimes are major wrongs, even assuming the breached laws were morally justified or legitimate.[23] Hence, we are once again entitled to conclude that breaching one's politically obligation is not a major wrong.

In light of these arguments, I believe we should say that breaching one's political obligation is, for want of a more precise term, a *minor* wrong. It does make criminal

[22] Husak 2008: 112 comes to the same conclusion in his excellent discussion of *mala prohibita*.

[23] If a law is unjust (or downright silly), we might think that it ought not to be obeyed by anyone in the first place, but my point here is the weaker one that not all crimes against just or sensible laws are major wrongs.

conduct more wrongful than otherwise, but not to a significant extent. What this means precisely is impossible to say, but just to put some ballpark estimates on the table, if one were to express the discount in percentages, I would say that the discount should be closer to 10 per cent than, say, 50 per cent. As noted in the previous section, it might be that some breaches of political obligation are worse than others, so this figure might have to go up or down depending on the nature of the crime. But even if we allow for this quite sensible idea, this will not fundamentally change the conclusion, for there is a difference between saying that all crimes are differently disrespectful and saying that civic disrespect is seriously wrongful.[24]

VII. Exemptions

I have argued that although politically non-obligated offenders are entitled to a penal discount, this discount ought to be slight considering that breaching one's political obligation is a minor wrong. This result, however, is somewhat unsatisfactory. It seems to underappreciate the normative significance of a state's lacking legitimate authority, especially when this lack is due to the state acting in a seriously unjust way. Consider, for example, an illegally invading state which starts enforcing its legal order on the occupied territory firmly against wishes of the local population. The thought that all this means is that the invading state must punish more leniently than otherwise seems to seriously misrepresent the normative position the state finds itself in. More to the point, it seems that we should think about the lack of legitimate authority in terms of *removing* the state's right to punish as opposed to *constraining* it – that politically non-obligated lawbreakers would be entitled to exemptions from criminal responsibility rather than reduced punishments.

The literature on the state's 'standing' to punish has explored the question of exemptions at length.[25] While standing is a broader notion than legitimate authority insofar as a state can conceivably lack standing to punish (or at least to blame) without losing its ability to generate political obligation, it has an equivalent structure in that illegitimate states appear to lack standing to enforce legal commands. We might say that when states lose legitimate authority, they are not morally permitted to punish lawbreakers since they do not have the standing to enforce the laws.

There is much to be said for the idea that legitimate authority may be a precondition of having a moral permission to punish. Clearly, something morally

[24] Crimes whose wrongness is more or less entirely about disobedience, such as pure cases of *mala prohibita*, call for a different analysis. As I argue in section VI, the lack of political obligation in these cases call for exemptions from liability rather than sentence mitigation.

[25] For recent overviews, see Ewing 2018 and Yost 2023. Key texts in this literature are Duff 2001: 179–88 and Tadros 2009. See also the chapters by Bergelson; Roberts and Dagan; Ewing; Manikis; Ryberg; Watson; and Zaibert in this volume.

problematic occurs when a state which lacks a claim to people's legal obedience nevertheless punishes people for legal disobedience. Indeed, legitimate authority appears to offer a more fundamentally correct diagnosis of why seriously unjust states lack standing to punish than the standard accounts found in the literature, because it is not as though the right to punish of such states looks secure even though it cannot be portrayed as hypocritical or inappropriate on complicity grounds. Consider, for example, a seriously unjust state which genuinely condemns murder and wishes to punish a murderer whose crime was committed for reasons entirely independent of the state's unjust laws and policies. In such a situation, punishment would not be hypocritical – it would not seek to protect or promote a value which the state itself does not care about – and the state could not be said to be complicitous in the crime. Yet the intuition remains that the state lacks a right to punish simply because it has treated the lawbreaker seriously unjustly; and the best explanation of this seems to be that it lacks a right to demand legal obedience. To put the argument formally, we might reason that:

(1) The state may only punish people for wrongful acts.
(2) Breaking the law is only a wrongful act if there is a political obligation to obey the law.
(3) Therefore, the state may only punish people for breaking the law if these people have a political obligation to obey the law.
(4) If the state lacks legitimate authority over person P, then P does not have a political obligation to obey the law.
(5) Therefore, if the state lacks legitimate authority over person P, then the state may not punish P for breaking the law.

An obvious response is that many acts are wrongful quite independently of whether they are legally proscribed. In the case of murder, for example, we are dealing with an act which is almost always wrongful and whose wrongfulness has very little to do with it being illegal. So, someone might argue, it is simply not true that political obligation is a necessary condition for the wrongness of breaking the law, at least not when we focus on the content of the law as opposed to the fact of legal prohibition in and of itself.

This response is correct, but it fails to speak directly to someone who endorses the exemption argument from political obligation. The point of the exemption argument is not that murder is wrong because it breaks the law, but rather that the right to *enforce* this (or any other) law against a person requires that she has a political duty to obey it. Put differently, the state punishes people for the *crime* of murder, citing its criminal law statutes and using its institutions of criminal justice. What the exemption argument denies is specifically that people can be liable to such treatment if the state lacks legitimate authority over them. The idea is that although no one ought to break laws against murder, people are not answerable to illegitimate states if they do break these laws. They may well be answerable to other entities, such as the victim or her community, but not to the state or its courts (Duff 2001: 188).

The problem with the exemption argument is instead that it overlooks the important distinction between *obedience legitimacy* and *enforcement legitimacy* (Shelby 2016: 229). Obedience legitimacy has been the focus of this chapter up until this point. It is the kind of legitimacy which entitles a state rightfully to claim legal obedience from the population. Enforcement legitimacy, by contrast, refers to a moral permission to threaten and use force against lawbreakers. Once we bear this distinction in mind, it does not seem true that states lack a right to punish just because they do not possess obedience legitimacy. This is because, as several authors have noted, obedience-illegitimate states may and should still punish lawbreakers insofar as this prevents serious crime in the future, perhaps especially among the disadvantaged parts of the population where the state's injustice is most keenly felt (Duff 2001: 200; Shelby 2016: 233; Duus-Otterstrom and Kelly 2019; but see Yost 2023). To have parts or the whole population act with impunity looks certain to produce precisely the sort of highly harmful social disorder which would give even seriously unjust states a right to enforce the law.[26]

There is little hope, then, in thinking about obedience legitimacy as a necessary condition for the right to inflict any punishment at all. It is more promising to think about whether obedience legitimacy affects the *scope* of the state's right to punish. A natural place to start is the distinction between *mala in se* and *mala prohibita*, where this is understood to track the difference between criminal acts that are wrong independently of their being criminalised and those that are wrong only because they are criminalised (Husak 2008: 103–119; Lee 2022).[27] This distinction seems relevant because one could argue that states lack the right to enforce *mala prohibita* laws against politically non-obligated offenders precisely because such laws prohibit conduct whose wrongness flows exclusively from its illegality (Shelby 2016). More specifically, the idea would be that when a state lacks obedience legitimacy over an offender, the first question to ask is whether the criminal act is wrong because it is illegal or if it is wrong independently of law. If the latter, then the offender is entitled to a penal discount for the reasons explained above. If the former, however, no punishment at all may be inflicted by the state for the simple reason that the conduct is not wrongful. It is not wrong to commit *mala prohibita* offences unless one has a duty to obey the law.

This suggestion has some plausibility. It explains why it would be inappropriate for an obedience-illegitimate state to, for example, enact and enforce laws against a harmless crime like flag-burning. Nevertheless, there are at least two major problems with it. The first is that the distinction between *mala prohibita* and *mala in se*

[26] A further question is whether a state can be obedience-legitimate without having enforcement legitimacy. My inclination is to say that this is at least logically possible. We can imagine a state that has a claim on the population's obedience, but which nevertheless lacks the right to threaten, and use, coercion. This might be the case if, for example, the state is extremely incompetent in the way it goes about enforcing the law.

[27] The category of *malum prohibitum* sometimes raises deep scepticism, but Lee 2022 argues (I think correctly) that the problem lies in classifying offences as either *mala prohibita* or *mala in se* rather than with the distinction itself.

does not exhaust the issues because we also care about the *seriousness* of the conduct quite independently of whether the conduct's wrongness flows from law or morality. The category of *mala in se* no doubt includes the worst crimes, but it plausibly also includes some quite minor ones. Do we really want to say that obedience-illegitimate states have a right to punish such crimes? If the answer is no, the idea of discounts for *mala in se* and exemptions from *mala prohibita* starts to look shaky.[28]

The second and more serious problem is that if the state's right to punish flows from the prevention of very harmful consequences, then it is difficult to maintain any stable account of the types of crime that an obedience-illegitimate state may punish. Consider, for example, a state that enforces a law prohibiting the possession of small amounts of marijuana. Let us suppose that such possession is a *malum prohibitum* and a minor one at that. The problem is that even if the state might lack the right to punish people for breaking this law 'in a vacuum', doing so might be necessary for the sake of preventing serious social disorder. For example, enforcing laws against marijuana possession might be needed to combat gang-related violent crime. If this is the case, then it seems that obedience-illegitimate states have a right to enforce such laws against the politically non-obligated after all.[29]

This is not to suggest that the lack of obedience legitimacy can never extinguish enforcement legitimacy, or that a crime that would have counted as *malum prohibitum* in some circumstances cannot be *malum in se* in others. My point is simply that we should not expect the issue of enforcement legitimacy to be settled in accordance with neat categories over types of crime. For if an obedience-illegitimate state only has a right to enforce laws insofar as enforcement is needed to prevent major societal harm, the prevention of major harms may in turn require the prevention of minor harms. The real questions, in other words, are about social necessity; about the laws that must be enforced to prevent major harms, and about whether only the illegitimate state can realistically enforce these laws.

VIII. Conclusion

This chapter has examined whether lawbreakers are morally entitled to sentence mitigation by lacking any political obligation to obey legal commands. I have argued that, for a retributivist, there is reason to think so. If breaching one's political obligation is an act of civic disrespect which enhances an offender's penal desert, politically non-obligated offenders deserve lesser punishments, or have

[28] Of course, we might also argue that no one should be punished for minor *mala in se*. Compare this with Barry's (2001) argument that rather than granting some people an exception from a legal rule, the better approach is often to abolish the rule entirely.

[29] Note that while this argument is compatible with retributivism, it is not retributivist in nature but rather draws on harm prevention as the crucial consideration.

lower deserved maxima, compared to politically obligated offenders for otherwise similar crimes.

Having established this rationale for mitigation, the chapter then discussed the size and nature of this 'discount'. I argued that even if it turns out that the mitigation should be the same for all politically non-obligated offenders, this does not create a problem if the mitigation is defined in relative terms. However, I also noted that the mitigation should be slight considering that breaching one's political obligation seems only a minor wrong. This led me to investigate whether the lack of legitimate authority might instead play a role at the level of exemptions from criminal responsibility. I argued that although it there is a certain logic to thinking that states should not have *any* right to punish offenders over whom they lack legitimate authority, it is nevertheless plausible that illegitimate states are permitted to enforce laws insofar as doing so is necessary to avert major societal harm. I also noted that it is not easy to determine which crimes obedience-illegitimate states would have a right to sanction on this criterion considering that it might be necessary to enforce laws against minor crimes to prevent major crimes.

The conclusion of this chapter is fourfold. First, retributivists should endorse the idea of a sentencing discount for politically non-obligated offenders. Second, this discount should be small and relatively defined. Third, obedience legitimacy is not a precondition for enforcement legitimacy. Fourth, in exercising its enforcement legitimacy, an obedience-illegitimate state may be permitted to enforce laws which, taken by themselves, could only be issued in a morally binding way by obedience-legitimate states.

3

State Misconduct and Mitigation in Punishment

MATT MATRAVERS[1]

I. Overview

The idea that state wrongdoing and/or state misconduct ought on occasion to result in sentence mitigation has intuitive appeal. In this chapter, I argue that whether it ought to do so is not at all clear (although sentence mitigation may often be the best remedial measure). In particular, I argue that aligning state misconduct with a state permitting chronic social injustice is problematic, and that even if one were to do so, it is difficult to construct an argument from chronic social injustice through state misconduct to individual mitigation. This is significant for many of the debates around the problem of doing penal justice in circumstances of social injustice. In addition, I argue that many familiar arguments that relate state misconduct to individual culpability fail. If we are to defend the intuition, we need to look beyond individual culpability. One, perhaps seemingly unpromising, avenue is that state misconduct diminishes the seriousness of the conduct. Another is that the state has a responsibility to enable its citizens to live non-criminal lives and to respond to the harms inflicted by the criminal justice system.

Thus, section II of this chapter considers the ideas of 'state misconduct' and 'state wrongdoing', and their relationship to questions of criminal justice. The argument is in part that the relationship is more complex than is often appreciated, and that this has implications for the broader literature on the problem of doing penal justice in circumstances of social injustice. Section III surveys some more or less familiar arguments that attempt to provide a ground in state misconduct for sentence mitigation. Section IV considers some less familiar arguments

[1] I am grateful to the editors for the invitation to take part in this project, and to them and the other contributors to the workshop at which initial drafts were discussed. I owe an additional debt to Leo Zaibert for feedback on a later draft. I am also grateful to Vincent Chiao for an invitation to discuss a draft of this paper at a criminal law theory workshop in Toronto, and to the participants in that workshop for their comments. Finally, I would like to thank the Leverhulme Trust for a Major Research Fellowship (award MRF-2020-090) that enabled me to work on this chapter.

that appeal to the reduced seriousness of the crime and the duties of the state to facilitate the living of non-criminal lives. Section V concludes.

To anticipate a little of what is to come, the chapter presents a number of sceptical arguments. On occasion, this scepticism concerns whether the problem – of relating state misconduct and sentence mitigation – can be formulated in any straightforward way. More often, the scepticism is targeted at sentence mitigation as the correct remedy for state misconduct. That does not mean that sentence mitigation is never appropriate; it may be the only thing that can be done in the circumstances. This, it seems to me, is often what we require of sentencing: to try by whatever means it can to make up for the ways in which criminal law, criminal justice systems, and other state institutions fall short of what is properly demanded of them. That is better than doing nothing, but it should not obscure the underlying problems or reduce the anxiety and ambiguity we should feel when implementing penal justice in conditions of profound injustice.

II. State Wrongdoing and State Misconduct

This section considers the problems that arise in thinking about state wrongdoing and state misconduct. The purpose is not simply to try to identify the issues to be discussed, but also to reflect on the ways in which state action (and inaction) is characterised in discussions of the problem of doing penal justice in circumstances of social injustice.

One immediate issue that arises in trying to think about the consequences of state wrongdoing and/or state misconduct is that these are terms without standard definitions. Moreover, people disagree about what is to be included in each category. Thus, someone who favours cosmopolitanism and believes that open borders are a requirement of justice will hold that every state engages in wrongdoing by excluding some people from entering. Others will disagree. Similarly, there are people who think that limited practices of state torture ('enhanced interrogation') ought to be permitted and those who would categorise any such practices by a state as involving both wrongdoing and misconduct.

To add to the difficulty, 'wrongdoing' and 'misconduct' are not synonyms. On the face of it, engaging in misconduct is one way of doing wrong, but not the only way. Someone who legally cuts down the tree in her garden simply to spite her neighbour engages in wrongdoing, but not misconduct. In addition, the relationship between the two concepts is complicated by disagreement over the nature of wrongdoing. Consider, for example, a man who safely breaks the traffic speed limit in order to get his pregnant wife, who has gone into premature labour, to the hospital in time to give birth. One might think that driving in excess of the speed limit is an instance of misconduct, but whether one thinks *this* instance of misconduct is wrongful will depend on one's theory of wrongfulness. A utilitarian might plausibly argue that it is not wrong all things considered, whereas some kinds of

Kantian might argue that it remains wrong, even if excused, in the circumstances described.

In light of these difficulties and ambiguities, for the most part I will focus only on state misconduct. However, even that term is open to disagreement about both its meaning and its application. In addition, the idea of 'the state' as an actor is itself problematic. For example, in 2018, Jamal Khashoggi, a prominent critic of the Saudi Arabian state, was murdered in the Saudi Consulate in Istanbul. It was alleged that the murder was carried out by Saudi operatives at the order of Crown Prince Mohammed bin Salman. If so, the incident certainly involved several instances of misconduct (an extra-judicial killing, the killing of someone by operatives of one sovereign state within the borders of another, and so on), but whose misconduct and in what sense, if any, was it 'the state's'? Assigning misconduct to individuals is (conceptually) straightforward: the Crown Prince ought not to have given the order; the operatives ought not to have killed Khashoggi; the Consulate staff ought not to have helped in covering up the crime; and so on.

So, one way to narrow the scope of the chapter would be to focus only on 'state actor misconduct'; the misconduct of state officials acting improperly in their roles as state officials (and, indeed, examples of just this kind are considered below). However, that might be too narrow. Assigning responsibility and so misconduct to a state is tricky, but of course familiar (as is the assigning of criminal liability to corporations). For example, Agnes Callamard (2019), the UN's Special Rapporteur, concluded of the Khashoggi affair that his death 'constituted an extrajudicial killing for which the state of the Kingdom of Saudi Arabia is responsible', and there were calls from others in the international community for sanctions to follow on the Kingdom (for example, economic sanctions, the breaking of diplomatic ties and the rescinding of invitations to Saudi officials).

This is not hard to explain under international law. Article 7 of the International Law Commission Draft Articles on the Responsibility of States for Internationally Wrongful Acts states:

> The conduct of an organ of a State or of a person or entity empowered to exercise elements of the governmental authority shall be considered an act of the State under international law if the organ, person or entity acts in that capacity, even if it exceeds its authority or contravenes instructions.

There are various reasons why it makes sense in international law for states to be able to be held responsible, but nevertheless in most cases that responsibility is through the actions of its agents. What enables the ascription of responsibility to Saudi Arabia in this case is the identification of a particular act – the killing of Khashoggi – such that it makes sense to ask, 'who did this?'. In this, state responsibility in international law has similarities to the traditional understanding of corporate responsibility in domestic law in that ascribing culpability to a corporation rests on a legal fiction built on the conduct of human agents (for an overview of corporate liability in English and Welsh law, see Child, Simester et al 2022: 302–17).

One comparatively minor implication of this for issues of mitigation is that it raises the question of whether 'acting on orders' ought to provide grounds for mitigation. At least since the trials at Nuremberg, acting on orders has not generally been thought to be an attractive or effective defence, but when it comes to certain states, state agents and sentencing, there may be a case to be made. Consider, for example, a North Korean 'hit squad' acting outside North Korea made up of members who have family relatives still in North Korea. In such circumstances, there might be a case for thinking of their individual actions as resulting from something akin to duress so reducing their appropriate sentence.

The much more important point is that the analysis above casts doubt on, or at least significantly complicates, another sense of state misconduct in relation to criminal law and criminal justice that is prevalent in the literature. This is the well-known and much-discussed problem of doing penal justice in circumstances of social injustice: that seriously distributively unjust states contribute to criminality, in a manner that casts doubt on their capacities to punish justly. This may be because they lack the 'standing' to punish, share responsibility (are complicit) with the offender and so ought to share the blame, or because, in some way, they diminish the capacities of the disadvantaged to obey the law and thus provide grounds for mitigation (for an overview of the recent literature, see Matravers (forthcoming)).[2]

Consider, for example, the clear and influential argument of the 'complicity' kind offered by Victor Tadros (2009: 391):

> For our purposes, it does not matter very much what makes it unjust that the poor are as poor as they are. It only matters, whatever the right view about justice and wealth, that they are worse off than they ought to be, and that this is criminogenic. It also does not matter much why poverty is criminogenic. We need only assume that the state has responsibility for reducing criminogenic social conditions and that, by perpetuating economic injustice, it has failed adequately to achieve this.

As a result, Tadros (2009: 405) argues that 'The state is complicit insofar as the economic injustice it perpetrates creates criminogenic conditions: conditions in which it is more likely that crimes will be committed.'

Let us assume that Tadros is right as an empirical matter that circumstances of economic injustice are criminogenic (the question over whether this makes the state 'complicit' in subsequent crimes is more controversial). Does this mean – as it is often taken to mean – that the state's maintenance of circumstances of economic injustice is an instance of state misconduct? The difficulty is in always identifying a particular act or set of acts through which state responsibility can be constructed. While in some cases that may be easy, in others it will be formidably difficult or impossible. Thus, a state that maintains a system of slavery, or an apartheid state

[2] This chapter does not address issues around the state's standing to hold the accused to account. I have written on this elsewhere (2006). For more recent work on the topic, see Edwards 2019; Lacey and Pickard 2021; Poama 2021; Yost 2023. For a nuanced discussion of the interplay between distributive and retributive justice that avoids matters of standing, see Zaibert's chapter in this volume.

that systematically and formally excludes some citizens from the goods of social cooperation, including political rights, engages in state misconduct in part, but of course not only, because of its contribution to criminality.

However, such formally discriminatory states are not typically the target of criminal law theorists. Rather, a great deal of the literature on the problem of doing penal justice in circumstances of social injustice is aimed at contemporary developed states like the USA and UK. Yet, when it comes to those states, it is much more difficult to sustain an argument of state *misconduct*. For example, the UK is marked by inequality, and indeed poverty, and many years of government spending cuts combined with the COVID-19 pandemic and other external events like the war in Ukraine, mean that its public services are in a dire condition. Thus, the UK meets the description given by Tadros: the poor are worse off than they ought to be, and that is criminogenic.[3] In maintaining these conditions over a considerable period of time, it seems plausible to say that the UK is marked by serious injustice, but it is less clear that we can identify instances of state misconduct.

Consider, for example, the choices made by the UK Chancellor of the Exchequer, Jeremy Hunt, in his so-called 'mini-budget' (more formally, his Autumn Statement) in November 2023. The circumstances were that, for reasons that do not matter here, the Chancellor found himself with what was described as some 'fiscal headroom'; that is, with more money in the public accounts than had been predicted.[4] Hunt could have chosen to spend this money on improving public services, on welfare, directly on crime reduction measures or on programmes for offender rehabilitation, and so on, but instead chose to reduce National Insurance (in effect, a tax paid by both workers and employers) by two pence. Does his choice merit the label of misconduct or wrongdoing? One test might be to ask if it meets Tadros's description of failing in its 'responsibility for reducing criminogenic social conditions'.

However, there are at least two problems with deploying such a test. First, no state could have such a responsibility *simpliciter* because then every state would be failing in its responsibilities every time it spent money on, say, defence or foreign aid. In short, it cannot be a test of public policy generally that it reduces criminogenic social conditions. Second, even if we were to adopt such a test, it is not clear what the timeframe would be, or how we would isolate the necessary variables. Hunt, the Conservative Chancellor, argued that the UK's overall position – including spending on social welfare, education, and so on – could not be improved without both medium- and long-term economic growth and, in particular, an increase in productivity. His argument, if we accept it as made in good

[3] *cf* Howard and Pasternak 2023: 44: 'Social injustices … are prevalent in many real-world democracies, where, despite overall levels of prosperity, parts of the population, and often minorities in particular, experience serious material deprivation, institutional discrimination, social and cultural exclusion, and political marginalization – all of which constitute violations of their entitlements under any minimally plausible theory of justice.'

[4] www.theguardian.com/uk-news/2023/nov/17/jeremy-hunt-autumn-statement-tax-giveaway-polls-economy.

faith,[5] was that the reduction in National Insurance would contribute to both. If so, then the decision – while perpetuating economic injustice and contributing to existing criminogenic conditions in the short term – might enable greater spending to address injustice and reduce criminogenic social conditions in the longer term. However, tracking the effect of a small reduction in one tax on those factors across, say, 10 or 15 years, is not plausible. Thus, the most that could be said of this particular public policy decision is that it did less to address immediate economic injustice and/or to reduce criminogenic social conditions than some alternative decisions would have done. However, nothing follows from that alone that would allow us to determine what decision should have been made or whether or not the decision that was made was an instance of state wrongdoing or misconduct.

Why does this matter? One reason is that it shows how problematic it is to move from general descriptions of states as 'unjust' to specific implications of such descriptions for a given individual who commits a crime. As I have put it elsewhere (Matravers (forthcoming)):

> The state may know that poverty is in general criminogenic, and it may know in general what range of policies would reduce poverty, but the more intimate connection between the state's (lack of) action and any given offence is lacking. The state is not, as Gary Watson (Watson 2015: 179) puts it, 'related to the crimes of the dispossessed literally as accomplice or accessory, aider or abettor.'

Another reason – one that speaks directly to the question of state misconduct and mitigation – is that it shows how problematic it is to move from the state's knowing that poverty is in general criminogenic to its knowing in general what range of policies would reduce poverty and yet not implementing those policies, to the idea of state *misconduct*. In short, there may be arguments from chronic social injustice that suggest either that those who are its victims have reduced responsibility, or that the state's 'standing' to blame is undermined,[6] but it is difficult to see an argument from chronic social injustice through state misconduct to individual mitigation. For that reason, the next section discards the focus on social injustice in favour of considering what connections there might be between state misconduct and mitigation.

III. State Misconduct and Mitigation: Some Familiar Arguments

It makes sense to start with mitigation. If we are asking what the role of x (in this case, state misconduct) is in relation to z (in this case, mitigation), it seems that

[5] Given that the decision was made at most 18 months out from an election, there are reasons to doubt that Hunt's arguments were made in good faith and to assume that his intention was merely to offer a 'pre-election giveaway'.

[6] For reviews of such arguments, see Ewing 2018; Duus-Otterstrom and Kelly 2019; Lacey 2022; Matravers (forthcoming)).

we need to know what z is in order to decide what possible role x might play. Unfortunately, in England and Wales at least, mitigation is a bit of a mess. Or, as the more measured Ashworth and Kelly put it (2021: 157), 'the factors which have been recognised as mitigating sentences in England are a much more heterogenous collection than the aggravating factors'. For example, the Sentencing Council's 'General Guideline' (2019) lists the following 'factors reducing seriousness or reflecting personal mitigation':

- no previous convictions or no relevant/recent convictions;
- good character and/or exemplary conduct;
- remorse;
- self-reporting;
- cooperation with the investigation/early admission;
- little or no planning;
- the offender was in a lesser or subordinate role if acting with others/performed limited role under direction;
- involved through coercion, intimidation or exploitation;
- limited awareness or understanding of the offence;
- little or no financial gain;
- delay since apprehension;
- activity originally legitimate;
- age and/or lack of maturity;
- sole or primary carer for dependent relatives;
- physical disability or serious medical condition requiring urgent, intensive or long-term treatment;
- mental disorder or learning disability;
- determination and/or demonstration of steps having been taken to address addiction or offending behaviour.

And, just in case that were not sufficient, 'any such matters as, in the opinion of the court, are relevant in mitigation of sentence' (§77 of the Code).

The situation in the USA is (as it always is) more complicated given the multiple jurisdictions that exist there, but a survey to identify where there might be consensus on the relevance of factors that mitigate identified the following eight scenarios (Hessick and Berman 2016):

- whether the defendant had an imperfect defence;
- the role played by others in the defendant's crime;
- victim compensation;
- the seriousness of the defendant's criminal conduct;
- the defendant's culpability;

- the defendant's likelihood of recidivism;
- the defendant's acceptance of responsibility or sincere remorse;
- whether the punishment will result in hardship to a defendant or her family.

There is some overlap in the two lists, but little coherence within them.[7] Some factors seem to touch on broadly retributive ideas such as reduced culpability, others to broadly consequentialist ones, such as a reduced need to punish in order to achieve lower recidivism risks, and still others to public policy concerns with the criminal justice system.

To get some kind of grip on this, we might consider the following general categories: assisting the prosecution (eg, a 'guilty plea discount' and cooperation with the investigation); factors indicating a reduction in the (potential) harmfulness of the conduct (eg, little or no financial gain); factors indicating a reduction in the culpability of the offender (eg, little or no planning, involvement through coercion, intimidation or exploitation); and other personal mitigation (eg, remorse, that the offender is the sole or primary carer for dependent relatives).

What is immediately striking about this is that nothing on either list relates in any obvious way to state misconduct. Mitigation seems to be about administrative efficiency, the degree of seriousness of the offence, and the degree of culpability of the offender. Where does state misconduct fit? There are several answers to that question that I want to consider only very briefly as they are familiar and are discussed fully by others in this volume.

A. Mitigation as a Remedy for Reduced Culpability

The first answer is that state misconduct – understood in some general sense of state wrongdoing or state injustice – in some way or other reduces the culpability of the offender. This is an attractive approach given that reducing the culpability of the offender is at 'the core of mitigation' (Ashworth and Kelly 2021: 159). A prime example of this kind of reasoning is raised in the Introduction to this volume in the remarks made in *R v Morris* that 'the moral blameworthiness of [the offender] is mitigated by his mental and physical health issues, as well as his educational and economic disadvantages. All of those factors are influenced by the systemic anti-Black racism Mr. Morris has experienced'. For reasons given at the start of this chapter, I am unsure that such arguments can be tied specifically to state *misconduct*, but insofar as the argument for mitigation rests on reduced capacity it both hangs free from this and is uncontroversial. In any event, this chapter does not pursue these issues further, but rather leaves it to others in the volume.

[7] For an interesting attempt to isolate 'the normative core of mitigation', see Ewing 2019a.

B. Mitigation as a Remedy for State Actor Misconduct

The second familiar argument is clearly related to state misconduct in that it involves state actor misconduct. In her typology of 'state blame and harms', Marie Manikis (2022: 308–21) characterises state actor misconduct as follows:

> [T]he state's role in producing harms that result from its violation of individual rights. More specifically, this would encompass a wide range of violations of human rights, including the rights in the context of a detention, arrest, search and seizure, abusive conditions of pre-trial detention, and the right to counsel.

In certain cases of state actor misconduct, mitigation is offered as a remedy. For example, consider the Canadian case of *R v Nasogaluak*:

> The RCMP received a tip about an intoxicated driver which led to a high speed pursuit of the accused. When the accused's car finally came to a stop, the police had to remove him forcibly. He resisted. One officer, C, punched him twice in the head while wrestling him out of the car. Once the accused was out of the car, he continued to resist. C yelled at the accused to stop resisting and gave him a third hard punch in the head. The accused was pinned face down on the pavement with C straddling his back and another officer kneeling on his thigh. He refused to offer up his hands to be handcuffed, so a second officer, D, punched him twice in the back, breaking the accused's ribs, which ultimately led to a punctured lung …
>
> The accused entered a guilty plea to charges of impaired driving and flight from police. At sentencing, the trial judge held that the police had used excessive force in arresting the accused and breached his rights, inter alia, under s.7 of the *Canadian Charter of Rights and Freedoms*. As a remedy under s.24(1) of the *Charter*, he reduced the accused's sentence below what he otherwise would have imposed and he ordered a 12-month conditional discharge on each count, served concurrently, with a one-year driving prohibition.[8]

Here, perhaps more than anywhere else, is a clear example of state misconduct, on the one hand, and sentence mitigation, on the other. The police officers used excessive force and the court (later affirmed by the Supreme Court) opted for sentence mitigation as the remedy. Again, arguments of this kind are discussed elsewhere in this volume, in particular by Roberts and Dagan, so my remarks here are brief. The puzzle is that the rationale for responding to police brutality by sentence mitigation is not at all clear. On the face of it, the case shows a need for improved police training and for effective disciplinary proceedings for officers who engage in misconduct. The 'windfall' for the defendant requires explanation.[9]

One possibility is that sentence mitigation acts to deter state actors from engaging in misconduct. This is the main argument in Starr's (2009) paper, 'Sentence Reduction as a Remedy for Prosecutorial Misconduct', applied (as the

[8] scc-csc.lexum.com/scc-csc/scc-csc/en/item/7845/index.do. I am grateful to François Tanguay-Renaud for discussion of this case.

[9] The language of a 'windfall' is borrowed from Starr 2009.

title indicates) broadly across categories of prosecutorial misconduct. The issue of whether sentence reductions do in fact deter is an empirical one. However, even if they do, a further empirical question is whether they are the most effective deterrence compared, say, to disciplinary sanctions. Moreover, even if that hurdle is jumped, there is still the question of whether sentence reductions are an appropriate response to state actor misconduct.

A second possibility also considered by Starr is that sentence reductions are 'expressive remedies'. In reducing the sentence, the state acknowledges the wrong it has done *and* seeks 'to "make the defendant whole" in an important sense-to restore full respect for his humanity and his rights as a full member of the community' (Starr 2009: 1534–37). The problem is that, while the idea of expressive remedies is compelling, it is very hard to understand how sentence reduction is the best method of expressing either the wrongness of the state's actions or of showing respect for the humanity and rights of the wronged defendant.[10] Starr's argument is:

> By issuing a sentence reduction, a court would thus measure its response to [state] misconduct in the same currency used to punish the defendant's underlying crime: years of the defendant's liberty. This, in and of itself, might amount to an important expressive signal – it treats [state] misconduct as fundamentally comparable to crime itself and worthy of moral condemnation in the same sense that crime is.

However, this cuts both ways. If state misconduct is 'fundamentally comparable' to crime, then the appropriate response to it is prosecution – or something analogous to prosecution – rather than sentence reduction.

There are an additional two reasons for doubting the appropriateness of sentence reductions as a remedy. The first is that insofar as the idea is that a reduction in sentence is a 'defeat' for the police and so will incentivise different behaviour on the part of officers, the policy rests on, and so legitimises and reinforces, a peculiar and damaging conception of public office-holders as motivated by certain results. For example, a police officer ought to be motivated by professionalism and pride in the job, not by whether this or that alleged offender receives this or that punishment. In criminal justice, 'winning' – understood, for example, as identifying and convicting only the guilty – is a by-product, when it is, of doing one's job properly not an appropriate object of one's job. Reinforcing ideas such as 'us versus them' and that what counts is 'results' is not only bad politics, but corrupts the ideals and institutions of public service. In short, the state ought not to be legitimising police officers thinking, 'we had better not beat him up as he might get off' rather than, 'we had better not beat him up because we are police officers, and it would be wrong to do so'.

The second reason for doubting the appropriateness of sentence reductions as a remedy for state misconduct is that it seems ad hoc and leaves unanswered the question of 'why the windfall for the defendant?'. One possibility is to count the

[10] Although, as noted at the start of the chapter, it will often be better than doing nothing.

excess harm done to the defendant as part of his punishment once convicted and so to be deducted from his sentence. This is often done, for example, when the defendant has been held in prison while waiting for the trial to begin. In such cases, 'time served' is deducted from the sentence on conviction.

Yet, the situations are not analogous. While not straightforward, pre-trial detention is sometimes a justified and legitimate use of state power. It is also (usually) in the same 'currency' as the sanction given to the convicted defendant. Excessive, rights-violating force is by definition not justified or legitimate, and it is not obvious how it should be converted into the currency of penal sanctions. Thus, two problems arise. The first is that the state's 'counting' of the excessive force as if it were part of state punishment lends the use of force a legitimacy it ought not to have. The second is that, even if one were to do this, there is the problem of 'calibration', of how we measure in penal value something. Put starkly, what is a punctured lung 'worth' in sentence reduction?[11]

C. Mitigation as a Remedy for Unjust Criminalisation Practices

Manikis (2022) rightly includes criminalisation practices that unjustly target marginalised groups in her typology of 'state blame and harms', and inapt criminalisation is plausibly an instance of state misconduct. However, once again the appropriateness of sentence mitigation as a remedy is questionable. Take two examples: (i) the criminalisation of consensual adult male homosexual intercourse; (ii) the harsher laws and penalties associated with crack cocaine when compared to its powdered equivalent.

In (i), the law assigns a degree of wrongful harmfulness to conduct that is not in fact wrongful or harmful. That clearly makes the punishment of those convicted under this offence unjust, and mitigation would be better than nothing, but mitigation is nevertheless an inapt response. The correct response is to decriminalise the conduct. Assume, in (ii), that the criminalisation of powdered cocaine is reasonable (so as not simply to reproduce the issues in (i)). The problem then is that, assuming conduct involving crack and powdered cocaine are equivalent (as I do here), then there is an issue of proportionality that needs to be addressed. Again, mitigation is better than nothing for those convicted of crack cocaine-related offences, but it

[11] Of course, the problem of calibration is not unique to this issue, and as Starr 2009: 1541 argues, 'there is also nothing new about the criminal justice system metaphorically "pricing" defendants' rights. Indeed, nearly all such rights are routinely "priced" by the plea-bargaining system, which allows defendants to trade them for reduced charges or sentences'. This is true, but it also lends weight to the worry that much criminal justice has an inappropriate 'transactional' tone. *cf* Rosett: 'One may doubt whether many of the defendants who "cop a plea" on any given day are motivated by this sort of spiritual awakening. In many courts, the guilty-plea process looks more like the purchase of a rug in a Lebanese bazaar than like the confrontation between a man and his soul' (Rosett 1967: 75, as quoted in Brown 2017: 209).

is a second-best option compared to re-legislating to correct the proportionality problem. Thus, in both cases, sentence mitigation might be a remedial step, but only in the absence of the more appropriate, and fundamental, response required from the state.

IV. State Misconduct and Mitigation: Some Speculative Arguments

Section III engaged with some of the more familiar arguments around state misconduct/wrongdoing and sentence mitigation; arguments that are in many cases discussed by others in this volume. This section considers two less familiar arguments, the first based on the reduction of the (expressed) seriousness of the conduct and the second based on the responsibilities of the state to enable its citizens to live non-criminal lives and to respond to the harms inflicted by the criminal justice system. As indicated in the title of this section, the arguments are speculative. This is not for want of trying for more precision. My defence in nevertheless pursuing them is the hope that they are at least suggestive.

A. Mitigation in Response to Reduced Crime Seriousness

That the literature on mitigation has revolved in large part around individual culpability and public policy considerations is not surprising. Not only, as noted above, is individual culpability 'the core of mitigation', but looking at the seriousness of the offence seems a deeply unpromising strategy. After all, first, the seriousness of the offence is given by the relevant laws and sentencing guidelines. Second, in the context of discussions of the problem of doing penal justice in circumstances of social injustice, arguments around the seriousness of the crime seem misplaced. Consider the well-established correlation between male unemployment and impoverishment and domestic violence. That a husband is the subject of distributive injustice does not reduce the seriousness of what he does to his wife when he savagely beats her even if there might be arguments about the degree of his individual culpability in the circumstances. On the face of it, this situation does not change even if the example is one of an economic offence. For example, consider a case in which the husband engages in benefit fraud (that is, he 'signs on' as unemployed to receive benefits while doing undeclared work paid cash in hand). Whatever the seriousness of the crime done by benefit fraud seems unaffected by whether or not its origins lie in state policies of distributive injustice or not.

To motivate the argument, consider the following: a poultry processing plant in 2016 in England adheres to the legal requirements with respect to labour standards, paying the National Minimum Wage, and so on. With the Brexit referendum and then the war in Ukraine, over the following years it comes under increasing financial pressures to the point that it risks bankruptcy. Its owner initially responds by increasing pressures on its employees to be more productive that remain within the law, but incrementally the firm starts to break various employment laws including by failing to pay the National Minimum Wage for all work done. Profits return and the plant continues to operate well below the standards required by the law.

Now add to this example the following: although England has reasonably robust labour laws, the Government has systematically (and wrongfully?) failed to enforce them adequately (the same is true for fraud) and has deliberately made it more difficult for employees to access employment tribunals. In 2013, the Government introduced significant fees for those wishing to take their case to an employment tribunal, which according to some estimates has led to a near 70 per cent reduction in such cases. In 2015, The UK had 0.9 labour inspectors per 100,000 members of the workforce. This compares with 4.6 in Ireland, 5.1 in the Netherlands, 12.5 in Belgium and 18.9 in France.[12] In short, the state has indicated that it does not particularly care about, or take seriously, the enforcement of labour laws.

Is the systemic failure to enforce some laws, which (by stipulation) I am assuming is the case here, an instance of state misconduct? Perhaps not always, but when the state systematically under-enforces laws that protect the most disadvantaged and marginal in society, it seems at least plausible to think of it in that way. Of course, that does not mean that the harms done by the illegal activity decrease. In the example, what happens to the employees – which in addition to being underpaid might include working in appalling and inhumane conditions – does not seem to be any less bad because of it.[13] So, in what way is this example relevant to sentence mitigation?

One way the example might be relevant to sentence mitigation that needs to be mentioned for completeness but is not relevant to the argument in this section, is that there may be a case for sentence mitigation based on reduced culpability. This might arise because of taking into account the stress the owner was under, the threat of bankruptcy, and the mitigating factor in England and Wales that the activity was initially pursued in legitimate ways. In short, the owner started out within the law – she did not always plan to make money by flouting the law – but in response to external factors, and perhaps with her mind affected by stress, she incrementally moved to breaking the law. Such a case for mitigation, though, is based on reduced individual culpability and has nothing to do with state misconduct.

A second, and more interesting possibility that is relevant, is that the defendant might claim that whatever the seriousness of her offences 'on the books', in practice 'everyone knows' – correctly – that the state does not regard protecting workers as particularly serious and that she therefore has a claim to mitigation. Of course, the claim is not about the – as it were, factual – seriousness of what was

[12] www.opendemocracy.net/en/beyond-trafficking-and-slavery/rethinking-recovery-labour-market-exploitation-and-austerity-in-uk.

[13] The example was deliberately chosen because conditions in poultry processing plants that operate within the relevant laws are notoriously awful.

done. Moreover, it is not an instance of the 'everyone does it' defence, although the owner might make that case in explanation of the competitive pressures that motivated her conduct. Rather, the claim is that the state by its acts (and omissions) indicated that these offences are not serious and so she should be sentenced at the very bottom, or perhaps even below, the range of penalties indicated for the offence.

The reason not to dismiss the argument is that the seriousness of criminal offences is not simply given by statutes or sentencing guidelines but constructed not least by the state. The state can of course get it wrong, as most did for many years with respect to, for example, domestic abuse. In such cases, justice overall demands change. However, sentencing is not about the overall justice of the system but about the appropriate response to this or that convicted person. That, encouraged by the state, someone thought – and perhaps most people would have thought – that what she did was not that serious is not obviously absurd as a ground for mitigation.

Nevertheless, this is an uncomfortable argument to make. After all, if a state were to indicate that, for example, it did not much care about criminal assaults on members of minority groups, it would seem odd to propose that those who carried out such assaults merited mitigation. Perhaps, the difference lies in the nature of the offence. Assault, as a *mala in se*, has a seriousness independent of the law that, for example, paying the National Minimum Wage does not. If so, then the argument would have to be limited in that way.[14]

B. Mitigation and the Opportunity to Live a Non-Criminal Life

The final argument depends on a claim that given the awesome and destructive nature of a criminal conviction, the state has a duty to assist those governed by its criminal law to live non-criminal lives.[15] This has positive aspects: the state should design its criminal justice institutions, as well as other areas of public policy, to facilitate the living of non-criminal lives. For example, its criminal laws should be knowable and possible to follow, and it should ensure that its citizens get (some degree of) moral and social education so as to learn how to navigate the social world. Of course, facilitating citizens' living non-criminal lives is not the only, or even the main, argument for rule of law principles or for trying to ensure that children are properly raised, but it is *an* argument (and one that can extend to other

[14] There may also be a form of 'standing' argument. Insofar as crime seriousness is a combination of 'harm/wrong to the victim' and 'harm/affront to the state' (the latter broadly understood in terms such a violation of a public value or a violation of the state's authority), then we might say that what was done to the employees remains the same, but that the state would be acting in bad faith if it pretended that it too the public violation particularly seriously.

[15] The argument in this sub-section builds on Matravers 2023.

institutions including those of the welfare state). It also has negative aspects, in particular that the state ought not to make it harder than it otherwise would be to live a non-criminal life; in short, it should not make things worse.[16]

The implications of this are far-reaching and go well beyond questions of individual mitigation (I have considered some of them in Matravers 2023).[17] Nevertheless, there may be particular instances of the general duty that speak to issues of state misconduct and sentence mitigation.

To motivate the argument, again consider an example. In this case the release of many prisoners in England and Wales as described by the criminologist, Shadd Maruna:

> You're released in the middle of the night … you're on a bus to the inner city where you are dropped off with your fifty quid *which is exactly enough money to score, not enough money to pay for a week's rent* (2021: 47:15, emphasis added).

In fact, the prison discharge grant for people serving over 14 days was raised to £76 in 2021 having been £46 from 1995. It was rebranded as a 'one-off subsistence payment' to cover the period until the person's benefit application is approved despite the government guidance suggesting that approval takes around five weeks. In addition, around one in eight prisoners is homeless when released. The predictable result of these policies is that recidivism rates in the first few days after release are a great deal higher than in countries with different systems.

Two questions arise. First, is this an instance of state misconduct; and, second, is there a case for mitigation for those that offend? The answer to the first is not clear. The arguments that it is not mirror those discussed in the section II. Public policy is a complicated business, and the test of such policies cannot just be that they facilitate the living of non-criminal lives such that any that do not meet that test constitute misconduct. However, there is at least a plausible case that can be made for the opposing view given the specificity of the policy in question. In disregarding the evidence of 'what works', the state expresses a disregard for a disadvantaged and marginalised section of its population to the great detriment of some members of that group. In addition, although more contestable, the policy in question is so flawed that it invites questions around the use of, and accountability for, public money.

Is there a case for mitigation for those that do reoffend? The argument that there is a case rests on something like a fair-opportunity claim. An ex-offender who, having spent his £76, and who is yet to receive a benefits payment, has choices, but those choices are constrained in ways that lessen his culpability should he offend.[18]

[16] 'While a liberal polity should not require specific virtues of its members or enforce some specific conception of how to live, it is also antithetical to the principles of a liberal polity for it to worsen or harm members in known, regular and avoidable ways'(Jacobs 2016: 8).

[17] I am grateful to Jesper Ryberg for pressing me on the possible scope of the argument here.

[18] There is also a potential 'standing' argument (if such arguments can be made to work). The recidivist can respond to being called to account by saying, 'who are you to call me to account, when you left me in a town with insufficient money, no home, etc.'.

Of course, the difficulty is in constraining such an argument. Many ex-offenders suffer from (significantly) constrained choices. Those who have been in prison may be damaged,[19] and even those who are not will often be plagued by the 'after life' of the punished (Flanders and Hoskins 2019).[20] These are reasons to rethink our criminal justice system, not reasons for mitigation. Indeed, there is a sense in which if everyone were to receive mitigation, it would no longer be mitigation.

Thus, we return to where we started, which is that the problem of doing penal justice in circumstances not just of social injustice but of state misconduct is not one that relates easily to sentence mitigation. That said, in the absence of wholesale change, mitigation may be better than nothing, and perhaps in the prisoner release case there is some 'expressive value' in the state acknowledging its part in the recidivist conduct, but if so, its value is remedial.

V. Concluding Thoughts

Elsewhere (Matravers 2021), I have described sentencing as operating a 'pressure release valve' for systems of criminal justice. Pressures build up in the substantive criminal law and in criminal justice over, for example, reduced responsibility that does not meet the threshold for insanity, possible defences that cannot be admitted because they cannot be corralled, or because of the background injustices in which systems of criminal justice operate. Moreover, criminal justice systems cannot afford to be 'fact insensitive'. If they are to be, and to be seen to be, legitimate, they have to attend to facts such as that, for example, many prisons in a given jurisdiction are terrible, or that alcohol and drug recovery services are underfunded and ineffective. When the pressure gets too great, we look to sentencing to find ways to provide relief to the system before it explodes.

A sentencing purist might say that it is not for the criminal justice system to resolve/respond to everything that is wrong in other areas of policy. There is a clarity to saying, 'This is the just sentence. The circumstances of the crime from which it arose, the conditions in which it will be served, and the consequences of it, are matters for others'. Yet even such a purist is likely to accept that the power of being

[19] 'Imprisonment can precipitate a decline in people's ability to interact socially. It can compromise people's capacity to make decisions for themselves, can have a brutalising influence, and can bring about a decline in brain functions connected to self-regulation. Additionally, and most obviously, imprisonment can be traumatising for those subjected to it, precipitating an increase in negative emotions and a deterioration in mental health – something which might, in turn (though the evidence on this is mixed), place these individuals at a higher risk of recidivism and repeat incarceration' (Dore-Horgan 2023: 434, notes omitted).

[20] 'Except for a very fortunate few who have their offenses formally forgiven through pardons or other legal means, individuals with felony records can remain permanently stigmatized, excluded from employment, educational and social opportunities, on the grounds of something they did many years or decades earlier. The resulting cycle of stigma and recidivism is predictable and tragic' (Maruna 2011: 5).

a 'sole or primary carer for dependent relatives' as a mitigating factor may depend on contingent factors; it is one thing to be a primary carer for a dependent relative in a welfare state like Norway, and another in West Virginia.

This does not mean, of course, that we should accept unprincipled sentencing regimes or that the, frankly heroic, work of sentencing theorists, councils and commissions is misguided. However, the criminal justice system is, to switch images, like a wrecking ball at a demolition site: appropriate for the overall purpose of sustaining social order but not always accurate when it comes to knocking out individual bricks. Perhaps, then, we should accept that mitigation is sometimes the best we can do whilst acknowledging the need to work on something better.

4

The State Fault and the Right to Mitigation of Punishment

VERA BERGELSON[1]

On 31 August 2023, Dennis Ray Thompson, a homeless 64-year-old Choctaw Nation citizen from Tulsa, pleaded guilty to aggravated sexual abuse by force in Indian Country. The US Attorney's Office reported:

> In the early morning hours of June 19, 2023, Tulsa Police Officers spotted Thompson on the sidewalk, completely naked, pinning down the victim. They noticed the victim was in distress and crying. The victim, who was homeless and legally blind, informed the officers she 'didn't want this,' and that she had not consented. ('A homeless sex offender pleads guilty to rape' 2023).

In his plea, Thompson admitted to striking the victim in the face, forcing her to the ground and sexually assaulting her.[2] At sentencing, Thompson, who has a criminal record of a prior sexual offence, faces up to life in prison (18 USC §2241). A federal district court judge will determine his sentence after consulting the US Sentencing Guidelines and considering the 'nature and circumstances of the offense' and the 'history and characteristics' of the defendant (18 USC §353(a)(1)).[3]

Pursuant to the US Sentencing Guidelines, the appropriate sentence should: (i) reflect the seriousness of the offence, promote respect for the law, and provide just punishment for the offence; (ii) afford adequate deterrence to criminal conduct; (iii) protect the public from further crimes of the defendant; and (iv) provide the defendant with needed educational or vocational training, medical care, or other correctional treatment in the most effective manner (18 USC

[1] I am indebted to Solo Ye for her excellent research, to Yehudis Lichtenstein and Anna Maria Petracca for their valuable technical assistance, and to the participants of State Misconduct as Sentence Mitigation (Cambridge, Institute of Criminology) workshop and Philosophy of Law (Rutgers, Philosophy Department) seminar for their helpful questions and comments. My special thanks go to Leo Zaibert, Julian Roberts, Jesper Ryberg and Alec Walen for their careful and insightful critique of my work.

[2] Thompson also pleaded guilty to failure to register as a sex offender.

[3] Since 2005, the US Sentencing Guidelines have been advisory rather than mandatory. See *US v Booker* [245]–[246].

§353(a)(2)). These sentencing factors roughly correspond to the traditional justifications for punishment: retributivism ('just desert') and various utilitarian policies (social cohesiveness, general and specific deterrence, incapacitation, and rehabilitation) directed at achieving important societal goals.

The retributivist and the utilitarian policies are not always in accord and may justify different amounts of punishment. The punishment that a defendant *deserves* may not be the same as the punishment best suited for either promoting public safety, social justice and the rule of law, or advancing the offender's rehabilitation and safe return to the community.[4] But despite the lack of consensus on the priority and boundaries of the competing theories of punishment, there has been a nearly uniform agreement that it would be unjust to punish an individual *more* than he deserves. An individual has the right to demand justice. In contrast, mitigation based on furthering utilitarian interests of society does not give the defendant a personal claim. Such mitigation is merely a privilege. A privilege may be asked for but it may never be demanded. This chapter focuses on the first kind of mitigation – the defendant's *right to demand mitigation as a matter of justice.*

The issue that I'd like to explore in this chapter is whether an offender who, like Thompson, is poor, homeless and lacking access to the necessary resources, is entitled to mitigation of punishment due to the state's failure to provide him with his fair share of public goods. To the extent the state owes its members any distributive equality, it may be said that the state has failed in its obligations to Thompson. Moreover, because it is a well-known fact that conditions of poverty, homelessness and deprivation are criminogenic, it may be said that the state's failure to ensure adequate living conditions for Thompson has increased the likelihood of his criminal conduct (Tadros 2009: 391). Should the state failing its distributive justice obligations to Thompson affect the punishment he deserves and give him a normative claim-right to mitigation of his sentence?[5] If so, should that right apply equally to all crimes – victimless crimes and crimes harming identifiable victims?

As a general matter, state failures may, and often do, affect the defendant's criminal liability. For example, state agents' misconduct may result in dismissal of charges, exclusion of incriminating evidence, and reversal of conviction. These remedies have been used in cases of selective and discriminatory prosecution (*United States v Jones* [311]–[313]), racially motivated jury selection (*Batson v Kentucky* [79]), and violation of the defendant's constitutional rights (*Utah v Strieff* [237]–[238]). In other circumstances, state agents' misconduct has served as a complete or partial defence for the crime committed. That misconduct has involved the defendant's entrapment (*Jacobson v United States* [540]) or sentencing entrapment (*United States v Barth* [422]; *Leech v State* [987]; *State v Sanchez* [208]) by the police or breach of the defendant's plea agreement by the prosecutor (*United*

[4] For an illuminating discussion of retributive and distributive justice rationales, see ch 7.

[5] For the normative topology of rights and obligations, See Wesley Newcomb Hohfeld, 'Fundamental Legal Concepts As Applied to Judicial Reasoning' (1917) 26 *Yale Law Journal* 710.

States v Dicus [1162]–[1163]). Overall, criminal process has been sensitive enough to the possibility of mitigation based on certain misconduct by certain state actors. However, so far no court has acknowledged the defendant's right to a reduced sentence due to the state's fault in failing to provide the defendant with the necessary resources and thus placing the defendant in criminogenic circumstances.

In the US, the issue of sentence mitigation has never been as central to punishment as it is now. Historically, sentencing followed a criminal trial, at which the defendant's guilt had to be proven by the state beyond a reasonable doubt. In recent decades, however, trials have been largely replaced by plea bargaining. Today, 'ninety-seven percent of federal convictions and ninety-four percent of state convictions are the result of guilty pleas' (*Lafler v Cooper* [156]).[6] These numbers are likely to be even higher for the poor offenders who have to rely on the court-appointed public defenders. Recent research suggests that, 'the caseload pressures perceived to be a routine part of a court-appointed lawyer's job result in perverse incentives to reduce their caseload by coercing defendants to plea or by refusing to employ time-consuming legal procedures' (Clair 2020: 205).

Accordingly, in most cases, the sentencing stage has become the only opportunity, for the defendant, to have a judge consider the unique circumstances of the defendant's offence and background; and for the judge, to adjust the statutory sentence so that it be just and proportionate, and reflect the broad goals of punishment. If the state's failure of its responsibilities to the offender be relevant to the offender's 'just desert', it is likely to be considered at this stage.

I. Overview

I begin this chapter by comparing certain recognised instances of state misconduct, which usually provide 'just desert' grounds for sentence mitigation, with the state's failure to supply the offender with the necessary public goods (section II). I then continue with a more general hypothesis that distributive injustice suffered by some offenders makes either such offenders less culpable or their lawbreaking less wrongful (section III). In section IV, I explore the claim that, regardless of the disadvantaged offenders' culpability and wrongdoing, the state at fault may have lost or diminished its authority to punish them. Finally, in section V, I consider a retributivist argument for mitigation based on the state's failure to distribute punishment fairly by assigning disproportionately harsh sentences for relatively minor crimes or exacerbating punishment based on morally irrelevant criteria.

[6] The overwhelming majority of remaining cases also result in conviction and sentencing. Meixner 2022: 1403–04.

II. Grounds for 'Just Desert' Mitigation Based on State Misconduct

Intuitively, at least sometimes, state misconduct should have an effect on the punishment the defendant justly deserves. This intuition is stronger when the state misconduct is: (i) proximately related to the crime; (ii) intentional rather than unintentional; and (iii) proactive rather than permissive.[7] Examples of such proximate, intentional and proactive conduct are: a breach of the defendant's plea agreement; crime entrapment; and sentencing entrapment. All three instances involve deception of the defendant by a government agent.

In the case of a breach of a plea agreement, the prosecutor fails to act on the promise to 'seek leniency, probation, a specific sentence, or simply to 'refrain from making any recommendation to the judge' (Khoriaty 1992: 1024). A typical remedy for that failure is judicial withdrawal of a guilty plea. However, other remedies are available too. For example, in *United States v Dicus*, the court mitigated the defendant's sentence, explaining that the sentence should reflect the defendant's 'history', and that history included state misconduct. The judge wrote:

> The defendant's post-plea 'history' presumably includes not only his own conduct, but the conduct of the prosecution toward him. In other words, wrongs done to the defendant post-plea seem to me to be just as relevant to determination of the defendant's sentence as any wrongs done by the defendant post-plea. For that reason, I believe that I could properly consider the prosecution's breach of the defendant's plea agreement as part of his 'history'... in determining the appropriate sentence (*United States v Dicus* [1162]–[1163]).

Crime entrapment serves as a complete defence for an offence committed as a result of the inducement or encouragement by a public official. The inducement or encouragement must be done 'for the purpose of obtaining evidence of the commission of an offense' (Model Penal Code: §2.13(1)), and the defendant must prove that he was not 'predisposed' to commit the offence (*Jacobson v United States* [540]). Entrapment, like any other complete criminal defence, is 'an all-or-nothing doctrine, allowing no subtlety or gradation in the analysis of government behavior or its effect' (Demleitner, Berman, Miller, Wright 2013: 300). It is thus less relevant to the discussion of mitigation of punishment, although it may be argued that courts should allow all defences, which have not been fully successful at the adjudication stage, to be considered again for the purposes of mitigation at the sentencing stage. In fact, some state sentencing statutes allow just that. For example, in Tennessee, the court may reduce a sentence if 'substantial grounds exist tending to excuse or justify the defendant's criminal conduct, though failing to

[7] See ch 6 for more examples of wrongful acts by state actors, such as police or prison officers, committed before, during, and after the offence.

establish a defense' (Tennessee Code: §40-35-113(3)).[8] Under such a statute, crime entrapment may play a role of a mitigator too.

Yet more often, that role falls on the partial defence of sentencing entrapment, which applies when a 'defendant is predisposed to commit a lesser crime, but is entrapped by the government into committing a crime subject to more severe punishment' (*United States v Mejia* [1118]). Sentencing entrapment usually arises in the context of drug offences, whereby, for the purpose of increasing the applicable sentence, the government pressures a suspect to purchase or sell more drugs than he otherwise would (*United States v Black* [310]), engage in a drug transaction in a school zone, or cook powder cocaine into crack (Carter 2009: 137; *United States v Yuman-Hernandez* [474]). The judicial remedy for sentencing entrapment is mitigation of the sentence to the level of the crime the defendant would have committed but for the inducement. To be entitled to this remedy, the defendant must show that he has lacked the predisposition to commit the more serious crime, either through a lack of intent or a lack of capability (*United States v Yuman-Hernandez* [475]).[9]

Of these three mitigators, sentencing entrapment appears to be the closest analogy to the distributional injustice perpetrated by the state on a convicted offender: unlike a breach of the sentencing agreement, it is relevant to the crime itself, not merely its disposition; and unlike crime entrapment, it does not seek to eliminate the offender's criminal liability but merely to reduce it. However, distributional injustice presents a much weaker reason for mitigation than sentencing entrapment: as between the two, the state's misconduct in the case of distributional injustice is significantly less culpable and more attenuated. It is less culpable because, unlike entrapment, which is done intentionally and proactively, the state's failure to provide adequate living conditions to all its citizens typically (albeit not always) comes from unintentional and permissive neglect. It is generally accepted that intentional wrongdoings are more culpable than unintentional, and freely chosen acts are more culpable than omissions.

Additionally, the state neglect is more attenuated from the offender's criminal act than sentencing entrapment. For example, Thompson's crime – rape – is not proximately related to his substandard living conditions; whatever the state fault may be, it cannot be said that the state has tricked Thompson into committing this crime. In contrast, in the case of sentencing entrapment, the state is directly involved in the criminal transaction and plays an active role in inducing the crime. In sum, the analogies with the currently recognised state-misconduct mitigators reveal the weakness of the claim grounded in the state's failure to provide the offender with adequate living conditions.

[8] See also *United States v Whitetail* [857] (battered woman defence); *United States v Cheape* [477] (duress); Demleitner, Berman, Miller and Wright 2013:301.

[9] See also US Sentencing Guidelines Manual 2023: §2D1.1, cmt n17 (instructing federal judges to reduce charges if the government agent set a price substantially below the market, 'thereby leading to the defendant's purchase of a significantly greater quantity of the controlled substance than his available resources would have allowed him to purchase').

III. Less Culpable Defendants

Independent retributivist arguments for mitigating punishment of the disadvantaged or marginalised offenders may be made along several lines. Starting with Judge Bazelon, a number of advocates have argued for a defence based on the 'rotten social background' (*United States v Alexander* [923]). The crux of the argument is that severe socio-economic deprivations lead to volitional deficiencies, and accordingly, seriously disadvantaged offenders are less culpable than those who are not so disadvantaged (Delgado 1985: 9; Lippke 2003: 459). This argument is problematic insofar as it implies that all seriously disadvantaged people lack full volitional capacity and are in fact potential criminals. It is undisputable that poverty reduces one's opportunities and choices; however, most poor people neither commit crimes nor suffer an immanent self-control deficiency. It is also undisputable that a person may sometimes lose self-control in response to unwarranted mistreatment. However, we should distinguish one's situationally specific, *actual* loss of self-control in response to unwarranted mistreatment (eg, provocation) and inherent diminution of *capacity* for self-control. It would be both wrong and condescending to diagnose a whole class of people with reduced volitional capacity based entirely on their disadvantaged socio-economic status.

To avoid these problems, some scholars have argued that the offenders who have been deprived of their fair share of societal resources are less culpable not because they possess reduced moral capacity, but because their motives are not criminal and their acts are not wrongful: by their crimes, they obtain what they have been unjustly denied and thus restore justice (Holroyd 2010: 78). This argument may have purchase when the crime committed is non-violent, such as theft or trespass, and when it is limited to satisfying essential needs (food, medicine, shelter). Indeed, some state statutes explicitly allow for mitigation in these circumstances. For example, under the Tennessee Code, punishment may be reduced when the 'defendant was motivated by a desire to provide necessities for the defendant's family or the defendant's self' (Tennessee Code (2006): §40-35-113(7)). However, most crimes fall outside this scope. It would be hard to argue, for example, that Thompson's motives for raping his victim were non-criminal or that by subduing and sexually assaulting the homeless blind woman he somehow has restored justice.

Another way to assert either the non-criminality of the defendant's motive or the absence of a wrongdoing is by arguing that the criminal act represents, at least in part, political protest. In her book, *In Defense of Looting*, Vicky Osterweil argues that 'rioters who smash windows and take items from stores … are engaging in a powerful tactic that questions the justice of "law and order" and the distribution of property and wealth in an unequal society' (Osterweil 2020). According to this argument:

> [Looting] attacks the idea of property, and it attacks the idea that in order for someone to have a roof over their head or have a meal ticket, they have to work for a boss, in order

> to buy things that people just like them somewhere else in the world had to make under the same conditions. It points to the way in which that's unjust. And the reason that the world is organized that way, obviously, is for the profit of the people who own the stores and the factories. So you get to the heart of that property relation, and demonstrate that without police and without state oppression, we can have things for free (Escobar 2020).

In making her argument, Osterweil resists the objection that 'looters are just acting as consumers: *Why are they taking flat-screen TVs instead of rice and beans?* Like, if they were just surviving, it'd be one thing, but they're taking liquor' (Escobar 2020). Regardless of the merits of her perspective, Osterweil is certainly right to separate the two potential reasons for a defence or mitigation: one, based on necessity, like the reason recognised by the Tennessee statute cited above. For that mitigation, it is essential that the defendant take mere necessities ('rice and beans'). A completely independent argument for a defence or mitigation is that the offence committed is a form of civil disobedience, and in *this* sense, the motive for the crime is not criminal and the nominally criminal act is not wrongful. For that claim, it is irrelevant whether the defendant has taken a flat-screen TV, a few bottles of whiskey, or rice and beans.

And yet, a claim of civil disobedience may not provide a strong retributivist ground for mitigation. It is generally accepted that civil disobedience constitutes an illegal act performed 'within the limits of fidelity to the law' which implies the agent's willingness to undergo the legal consequences by accepting the punishment (Rawls 1999: 322). This willingness separates 'civil' disobedience from other forms of law-breaking conduct and precludes the lawbreaker's *demand* for mitigation. Quoting Justice Fortas,

> Civil disobedience is violation of law. Any violation of law must be punished, whatever its purpose, as the theory of civil disobedience recognizes .... He should be prepared to submit to prosecution by the state for the violation of law and the imposition of punishment if he is wrong or unsuccessful .... And each of us must be ready, like Socrates, to accept the verdict of its institutions if we violate their mandate and our challenge is not vindicated (Fortas 1968: 63).

One may dispute this point of view by insisting that a 'civil disobedient may contest the charges and plead not guilty; he may argue that while he is responsible for disobeying the letter of the law, he should not be deemed liable to punishment (Moraro 2018: 511). However, even if civil disobedience does not preclude pleading 'not guilty' or raising defences, such pleas, by themselves, do not give the defendant any *right* to exoneration from, or mitigation of, criminal liability. As a matter of fact, the majority of the people charged with a crime start with pleading 'not guilty', and some of them do believe that they are entitled to a defence or mitigation. In most circumstances, those beliefs have no mitigating value, as courts have uniformly held that 'exercise of a moral judgment based upon individual standards does not carry with it legal justification or immunity from punishment for breach of the law' (*United States v Moylan* [1008]). Yet, in other circumstances, civil disobedience has been recognised as a mitigating sentencing factor (Chow 2022: 1062).

Usually, such mitigation has been deemed appropriate when the defendants were engaged in the acts of *direct* civil disobedience (ie when the law violated is the subject of the protest) rather than *indirect* disobedience (ie when the law violated is unrelated to the subject of the protest) (*US v Schoon* [193]). Discussing the difference, a US court held in an oft-cited opinion:

> Indirect civil disobedience seeks first and foremost to bring about the repeal of a law or a change of governmental policy, attempting to mobilize public opinion through typically symbolic action. These protestors violate a law, not because it is unconstitutional or otherwise improper, but because doing so calls public attention to their objectives. Thus, the most immediate 'harm' this form of protest targets is the *existence* of the law or policy. However, the mere existence of a constitutional law or governmental policy cannot constitute a legally cognizable harm (*US v Schoon* [196]).

Based on this analysis, looting is an act of indirect disobedience. The protesters do not maintain that a particular law is unjust or discriminatory. According to Osterweil, they attack 'the idea of property', social inequality and the absence of basic universal welfare rights ('the idea that in order for someone to have a roof over their head or have a meal ticket, they have to work for a boss'). Assuming the protesters are right about the state's fault in perpetuating these conditions, should the merit of their allegations defeat, or at least diminish, their culpability or the magnitude of their wrongdoing with respect to an innocent victim? As appealing as this suggestion may seem, we should resist it as a general self-sufficient principle of law, unless we be willing to exculpate, in whole or in part, such crimes as political assassinations and kidnappings committed in the name of long-term social justice goals.

It follows that neither the objectively meritorious allegations nor the subjectively held good-faith beliefs in the justifiability of one's law-breaking conduct should have an *independent* effect on one's criminal liability. In contrast, these factors may become relevant as a part of the multi-factor equation, which includes not only the harms the defendant seeks to avoid, but also the harms inflicted. The latter are relevant because, 'it's not culpability alone that counts in determining desert. … Rather, the amount of harm caused determines the seriousness of the wrong done, and the amount of wrong done does affect desert' (Moore 1999: 87). In fact, many courts have suggested that mitigation, in cases of civil disobedience, may be appropriate when the protestors have behaved 'with a sense of proportion and [have] not cause[d] excessive damage or inconvenience' (*R v Jones* [89]). Quoting a Canadian judge, 'If acts of civil disobedience do not endanger anyone, or damage property, or significantly restrict essential services and processes within society, and interfere in a minor fashion with the rights of others, the State response must be clear but need not be harsh' (*R v Mayer* [7]–[9]).

Applying these principles to a possible claim for mitigation based on the state's neglect of its duties to the offender, it appears that such a claim may succeed if at least two conditions be met. Firstly, the offender's conduct must be in direct response to a need created by the state's failure – for example, trespassing on a governmental office in protest for reduction of public benefits or violating a city ordinance, which prohibits sleeping on park benches after dark, in the absence of available homeless shelters (Heinkel-Wolfe 2018). The direct link between the state's failure of its duties and the offender's violation serves here to reduce both the wrongfulness of the offender's conduct and the offender's shared causal responsibility for the proscribed act.

Secondly, the offence must constitute a victimless crime or at least a crime committed against society in general, not a specific, identifiable victim.[10] This second condition requires some explanation. In the most basic form, it is the following: assuming that the state has failed in its duties to the offender, the offender may be less blamable in failing in his duties against the state (as compared to a perpetrator who has not been similarly mistreated by the state). However, the offender is not less blamable if he has harmed a third-party victim who has not wronged the defendant. Thompson's rape victim has had nothing to do with any state mistreatment he may have suffered. Neither have the mom-and-pop shop-owners in regard to the looters who burglarised their business.

It could be countered that, to some extent, all members of the polity are at fault with respect to an offender who has been denied his fair share of societal goods: in a society of limited resources, the lack of equality in distribution means that anyone who enjoys welfare benefits does so at the cost of someone's deprivation. This argument, however, is flawed in several respects. Firstly, it conflates the cause and effect: one's lack of deprivation is not the *cause* of another's poor living circumstances. The cause is the system of unequal distribution, which has the *effect* that some people suffer from deprivation of resources while others do not. Secondly, it assigns to an individual society member vicarious liability for the culpable conduct of the state, and it does so in the absence of choice or control over the state's conduct by the individual. Finally, it lacks any meaningful line-drawing criteria for determining one's fault.[11] For example, is a newborn baby at fault with respect to the disadvantaged offender? Is the baby's mother who works at a neighborhood grocery shop at fault? Is the elderly couple who own this shop at fault? Whose interests may be fairly discounted as a way of mitigating the defendant's liability for a crime against that person or that person's property? I suggest that any attempt to distinguish between the victims based on their share of collective responsibility would lead to absurd and morally unattractive results.

[10] Other complete or partial defences may eliminate or reduce an offender's punishment for a crime committed against an identifiable victim; however, these defences are based on theories distinct from the state's fault. See, eg, *Commonwealth v Magadini* [1041] (allowing the defence of necessity for trespassing on private property in weather emergency); *People v Fontes* [484] (opining that 'economic necessity may be an important issue in sentencing').

[11] *cf* with the famous line-drawing argument by Macaulay 1874: 528–29: 'Is a person to be a murderer if he does not go fifty yards through the sun of Bengal at noon in May in order to caution a traveler against a swollen river? Is he to be a murderer if he does not go a hundred yards? – if he does not go a mile? – if he does not go ten?'.

There is another, even more essential, reason to hold that the state's fault with respect to the offender may mitigate only victimless or impersonal offences. That reason stems from the political legitimacy of criminal law. Historically, that legitimacy was grounded in the authority of the sovereign, and criminal law was 'conceived of as a system of enforcing the king's peace' (Dubber 2002: 116). That philosophy has withstood centuries of political change, with the 'king's peace' merely having been replaced with the 'state's interests'. Quoting Marcus Dubber,

> Crime, in this model, is an offense to the dignity of the state, and punishment the reaffirmation of that dignity. It is basic blackletter law that criminal law is an exercise of the state's power to police, which is the modern manifestation of the householder's ancient authority to discipline the members of his household (Dubber 2004: 571).

This vision of criminal law, which, with little variations, remains predominant today (Thorburn 2017: 30), leaves little room for individual victims who, at best, play the roles of third-party beneficiaries of the state's prerogative to enforce legal order. The weakness of this model lies in its autocratic nature and questionable source of authority. While sovereigns could rely on a claim of divine provenance, civil governments do not enjoy the same advantage. To be legitimate, they need 'consent of the governed' (Declaration of Independence 1776: § I), which, in turn, presumes that the 'governed' are capable of giving consent by virtue of possessing autonomy and agency. Thus, individual autonomy must precede any civil government and continue throughout political change. To maintain legitimacy, the state must protect the autonomy of its subjects by all means available to it, including its most powerful tool of criminal law. Criminal law carries in itself the state's obligation to enforce individual autonomy in exchange for the citizens' obligation not to use private violence as a method of regulating individual rights. This, competing, philosophy of criminal law has several advantages over the state-centred model: it puts the actual victims into the focus of legal protection; it recognises the equal rights of all society members by conditioning punishment (ie rights deprivation) on the offenders' violation of the rights of others; and finally, it respects individuals as responsible agents, not merely subjects or 'children' of the paternal state (*parens patriae*).

Under criminal law so understood, a state's fault with respect to the offender may not mitigate punishment for a crime committed against an identifiable victim.[12] By committing such a crime, the offender, first and foremost, violates the rights of the victim, and that violation is no less wrongful because the offender has been wronged by the state. It is the state's duty to the victim to prosecute the

[12] Interestingly, due to its largely utilitarian rationale, the defence of entrapment may still be available for non-victimless crimes. Whether entrapment should be an affirmative defence (rather than, say, an evidentiary exclusionary issue) is beyond the scope of this chapter. However, to the extent that defence may shield non-victimless crimes, it is worth observing that cases of entrapment almost never involve real victims – the individuals who might be aggrieved with the crime not being adequately punished – because the victims in such cases are either 'not in being' or played by government agents.

offender for the harm caused by the offender, and it would be disrespectful of the victim to forego some or all of the offender's punishment because of the state's own failure in equitable distribution of societal resources (Duff 2003: 199; Tadros 2009: 410). For example, Thompson's victim would have a legitimate grievance against the state should the state choose not to punish Thompson for raping her, or should it punish him less than a rapist whom the state has not wronged. Discounting Thompson's punishment would symbolically discount condemnation of the harm he has inflicted on the victim's rights and dignity; it would also mean treating her rights and dignity as less important than the rights and dignity of a person who has been raped by a member of a non-disadvantaged class. Considering that, when an offender belongs to a mistreated group of polity, his victim most likely belongs to it too (at least in crimes against person), such mitigation of punishment would create two layers of justice, with the lower one assigned to the victims who have been already mistreated by the state.

IV. The Moral Standing to Prosecute

More recently, the debate about fair punishment of offenders coming from socially disadvantaged groups has shifted from the offender's lesser culpability and wrongdoing to the state's authority to punish (Yost 2022:711; Walen 2024). According to Antony Duff, for instance,

> We should be looking … not for principles that will determine who *is* in some abstract or impersonal sense liable for what, as if criminal liability was a state or condition that we acquire purely by our own efforts; but rather for principles that will help us determine when it is legitimate for some person or body to *hold* someone liable … (Duff 2003: 245).

From that perspective, society that consistently mistreats certain groups of people (identified by race, class or income) by excluding them from the 'rights and benefits that others enjoy in virtue of their membership of the polity – educational or vocational opportunities, welfare provision, political participation, and so on', loses (in full or in part) the right to prosecute them (Duff 2010: 136). According to this belief, to the extent the state has wronged the offender by depriving him of adequate access to societal resources, the state is not in the position to blame the offender.

Proponents of this view maintain that systemic economic and racial injustice deprives the state of the moral standing to punish. The lack of moral standing is usually said to be due to either the state's hypocrisy or to the state's complicity in the crime.[13]

[13] See ch 5 for further discussion of the hypocrisy and complicity arguments.

A. The Hypocrisy Argument

Pursuant to the hypocrisy argument, 'the fact that one person commits the same kinds of wrong as someone else deprives the one of standing to hold the other person responsible for his wrongs' (Tadros 2009: 393). The hypocrisy argument sounds intuitively right when we think about wrongs committed in the *interpersonal* (particularly, bilateral) context. For example, a man cheating on his wife should not hold a grudge against her if she too starts cheating on him – that would be hypocritical. And for the same reason, the man should not criticise those of his neighbours who cheat on their spouses.

However, even in that context, the hypocrisy argument has very limited application: the wrongs committed by the two parties must be identical.[14] Thus, the cheating husband would still maintain the right to hold a grudge against his wife if, instead of cheating on him, she put arsenic in his coffee.[15] He would have an even stronger right to hold a grudge if the wife directed her revenge not at him but at an innocent third party (eg their child). The right to hold a grudge against the wife in that case would be stronger because her retaliation is 'misdirected': the child has done nothing to deserve the harm, whereas in the first case (poisoning the husband), the wrongfulness of the wife's act may be diminished – morally if not legally – by the husband's cheating.[16]

If we translate those insights into the language of criminal punishment, there will be three relevant conclusions. Firstly, the state's own wrongdoing should have no effect on its right to punish the offender for a crime committed against *any third party*, ie anyone but the state. Secondly, the state may lose the right to blame the defendant only when the defendant wrongs the state in *the same manner and same (or lesser) amount* as the state has wronged the offender. This is hardly a realistic proposition: an individual and the state rarely have the capacity to commit identical wrongdoings. Finally, if the offender who has been wronged by the state commits a crime whose sole victim is the state, the state may lose *some* of the moral ground to blame him even when the state's and the offender's mutual wrongs are different, quantitatively or qualitatively.[17] In that case, the deserved mitigation is the difference between the punishment imposed by the state with unimpaired

[14] See Ewing 2018: 47 (holding a similar view); ch 15 (for discussion of other objections to hypocrisy argument).

[15] I agree with Duff 2003: 187 that, even if the injustice suffered by the defendant 'undermines the court's standing to call him to account for *some* crimes, it cannot undermine its standing in relation to *all* crimes'.

[16] For more on the perpetrator's and victim's comparative criminal liability, see Bergelson (2009). It may be true that one's right to hold a grudge for the harm inflicted to self is always stronger than a grudge for the harm inflicted to another or harm that is derivative of the harm to another (eg, the father's suffering because of an injury to his child). What matters here, however, is that, from the perspective of the *hypocrisy* argument, the right to hold a grudge in the second case is stronger.

[17] I agree with the view expressed in chs 5 and 6 that 'standing to punish, properly conceived, is not binary in the simple sense that either a state has standing, or it does not' (ch 5, opening paragraphs), but instead is a matter of degree.

moral standing and the prosecuting state with impaired moral standing.[18] That mitigation may come in the form of a reduced punishment or such punishment that involves no (or less) moral blaming.[19] Even that limited entitlement to mitigation is applicable (just as in the cases of mitigation based on the offender's lesser fault, discussed above) only when the offender commits a victimless or impersonal crime.

B. The Complicity Argument

The complicity argument also has certain intuitive appeal. Pursuant to the complicity argument, 'the fact that one person participates in the wrong of someone else deprives the one of the standing to hold the other person responsible for the wrong. A person cannot act as judge when he ought to be a co-defendant' (Tadros 2009: 393). The state is complicit in the crimes committed by the offenders whom it has deprived of their fair share of societal resources, 'insofar as the economic injustice it perpetrates creates criminogenic conditions', ie conditions in which it is more likely that crimes will be committed (Tadros 2009: 405). However, upon a closer look, this appeal diminishes: creating the conditions for a crime is not enough to make one an accomplice. Criminal complicity, under the predominant view, requires that the accomplice aid the principal with the *purpose* of facilitating the commission of the crime. It would likely be a non-starter to suggest that the state wishes (has the purpose) that its citizens commit crimes. The state certainly had no reason to wish that Thompson rape his victim or looters burglarise small businesses.

Could a lesser degree of culpability result in complicity? The drafters of the Model Penal Code thought so, and the original draft (rejected by the American Law Institute) stated that 'a person is an accomplice of another person in the commission of a crime if … acting with knowledge that such other person was committing or had the purpose of committing the crime, he *knowingly, substantially facilitated* its commission'[20] (Model Penal Code, Tentative Draft No 1 (1953): §2.04(3)(b)). If that standard were applied to the state's exposing the offender to criminogenic conditions, it could be maintained that, by doing so, the state has knowingly 'substantially facilitated' the commission of the offender's crime. The 'knowledge' element in such facilitation could, arguably, be established either by the state's awareness of a 'high probability' (Model Penal Code 1985: §2.02(7))

[18] I agree with the view expressed in ch 2 that such mitigation should be rather small.

[19] See Ewing 2018: 35 (suggesting that, even if the state lacks the standing to *blame* the offender, the offender may not be entitled to reduction in the 'material burdens of punishment' which in principle can be isolated from expression of condemnation).

[20] The 'knowledge' standard has been rejected by the American Legal Institute in favour of 'purpose', and in its final version, the Model Penal Code requires that the actor have 'the purpose of promoting or facilitating' the commission of the crime. Model Penal Code 1985: §2.06(3)(a).

that a crime be committed (due to the strong statistical correlation between the conditions of deprivation and crime) or by 'willful blindness' on the part of the state (Model Penal Code 1985: §2.02). However, even then, it would be hard to argue that the state has exposed a particular offender to these conditions with the knowledge that that offender 'was committing or had the purpose of committing' the *specific* crime for which he was now on trial.

Another theory of complicity that might be invoked to make an argument for state complicity is the 'natural and probable consequences' theory. Pursuant to it, liability of an aider and abettor who intends to encourage or facilitate commission of a crime is 'extended to reach the actual crime committed, rather than the planned or "intended" crime, on the policy [that] aiders and abettors should be responsible for the criminal harms they have naturally, probably and foreseeably put in motion' (*People v Luparello* [832]). Thus, if the state intentionally encouraged or facilitated some wrongdoing by the offender, and that wrongdoing 'naturally, probably and foreseeably' resulted in the offence for which the offender is now being prosecuted, the state could be said to be an accomplice in that offence. This theory of state complicity is lacking too: not only is the doctrine of the 'natural and probable consequences' deeply problematic in itself, but it would also be a huge stretch to suppose that the state 'intended' the offender to commit even some initial wrongdoing. And without such intent on the part of the state, it may not be held to be an accomplice.

Consequently, none of the viable theories of complicity manage to support the claim that the state may not punish an offender because of the state's fault in exposing the offender to criminogenic conditions. Moreover, even if that claim be more successful, it is by no means obvious that the state's facilitation of the crime, in the absence of coercion or manipulation (like in the cases of entrapment), should reduce the culpability or causal responsibility of an autonomous actor.

C. Unfair Distribution of Punishment

There is, however, a strong retributivist argument for mitigation of criminal liability that does not involve the state's standing to punish or the offender's culpability and wrongdoing. It is based instead on the state's failure to distribute punishment fairly. A defendant may have a claim for mitigation when the law, which is *just in principle*, authorises a disproportionately harsh sentence – often, in reaction to a 'moral panic' – for a relatively minor crime or exacerbates punishment based on morally irrelevant criteria. (This situation is different from the one where the law itself is unjust, because it 'further[s] no legitimate interest of the state and because [it] discriminate[s] on the basis of morally impermissible criteria, such as race, religion, and ethnic identity' (Green 2010: 62). A person who violates such a law is not at fault at all and does not deserve any punishment.)

An example of unfair distribution of punishment is the Anti-Drug Abuse Act of 1986, which included a provision that created an enormous disparity between federal penalties for crack cocaine and powder cocaine offences, imposing the same penalties for the possession of one gram of crack cocaine as for 100 grams of powder cocaine (Anti-Drug Abuse Act of 1986 (1986)). Over the years, this 100:1 sentencing disparity has been widely criticised as lacking scientific justification. Furthermore, the crack and powder cocaine sentencing disparity has brought about social inequity as it disproportionately impacted people of colour (Booker 2023).[21] The bipartisan Sentencing Commission[22] has been objecting to the sentencing disparity since the 1990s and has repeatedly called on the Congress to change the law (Fabens-Lassen 2015: 645). Eventually, in 2010, The Fair Sentencing Act reduced the crack and powder cocaine sentencing disparity from 100:1 to 18:1, and in 2023, a bill was introduced to eliminate the federal crack and powder cocaine sentencing disparity and apply it retroactively to those already convicted or sentenced (Booker 2023).

It goes without saying that the primary avenue of changing unjust or unsound laws is by the legislative process. Alternatively, an unjust or unsound law may be struck down by a constitutional court or other supervisory court of the jurisdiction. However, when the legislative process fails or stumbles, and when the flawed law survives constitutional or other substantive challenges, the sentencing judges should exercise any discretion they have to mitigate the unduly harsh penalties. As members of the judiciary, sentencing judges bear responsibility for the proper exercise of justice. They may not boycott or rewrite valid laws, but they may and should strive to avoid injustice within the boundaries of their authority. In fact, the United States Supreme Court has held that departures from the US Sentencing Guidelines were warranted 'based solely on policy considerations, including disagreements with the Guidelines'(*Kimbrough v United States* [110]) as the Court upheld a district court judge's sentence of a crack offender below the Guideline range based on the 100:1 ratio (*Kimbrough v United States* [111]).[23]

Such mitigation should be afforded to any offender convicted of a crack cocaine offence regardless of the offender's race, gender, age, socio-economic status, or other characteristic, even though it is undisputable that young African American men are the group that has been affected the most by the unjustifiably harsh crack cocaine laws.[24] The sentencing disparity between the crack and powder cocaine offences is largely irrational, and thus unfair with respect to any recipient of the

[21] See also Goulian et al 2022. Since the introduction of crack cocaine in American cities as a more accessible form of powder cocaine *c* 1984, the US response to the substance has been framed as an urbanised, racial issue that predominantly involves members of the Black community.

[22] The Sentencing Commission is an independent commission of the US judicial branch charged with ongoing review of sentencing guidelines and recommending appropriate modifications to Congress. United States Sentencing Commission (2012) 28 USC: 1.

[23] See also *Spears v United States* [265]–[266] (*per curiam*) ('district courts are entitled to reject and vary categorically from the crack-cocaine Guidelines based on a policy disagreement with those Guidelines').

[24] A recent US criminal justice system data shows Black offenders were the most common racial group in crack cocaine trafficking offences (77.7%) (United States Sentencing Commission, Fiscal Year 2021 (2022): 14).

crack-related sentence. Accordingly, any defendant sentenced under this law should be entitled to a reduction of the sentence within the judge's authority – to the amount that reflects the actual gravity of the offence.

There may be additional policy reasons for mitigating punishment for representatives of certain social groups, including those that have been historically mistreated or neglected by the state. One such reason may involve disproportionate susceptibility of an offender to a particular form of punishment (Allam, Wahlquist and Evershed 2018). Recognising the offenders' unique susceptibility, a judge, for example, may offer a non-custodial sentence to the very old or very sick, to pregnant women, transgender people, or members of Indigenous populations. The Canadian Criminal Code explicitly directs sentencing judges to consider all available sanctions other than imprisonment that are reasonable in the circumstances, 'with particular attention to the circumstances of aboriginal offenders' (Criminal Code 1985: §718.2(e)). The Supreme Court of Canada has interpreted that directive to mean that 'sentencing judges should pay particular attention to the circumstances of aboriginal offenders *because those circumstances are unique*, and different from those of non-aboriginal offenders' (*R v Gladue* [688]). The Court further explained that the Aboriginal offenders are 'more adversely affected by incarceration and less likely to be "rehabilitated" thereby, because the internment milieu is often culturally inappropriate and regrettably discrimination towards them is so often rampant in penal institutions' (*R v Gladue* [688]).

Another policy reason for mitigation may implicate systemic considerations of social justice, a conscious effort by the judicial branch to mitigate the damage already done to certain communities by disproportionate prosecution and incarceration of its members. Addressing the causes of dramatic overrepresentation of the Aboriginal offenders in prison, the *Gladue* court identified poverty, substance abuse, lack of education and the lack of employment opportunities for Aboriginal people, which arises, at least in part, 'from an unfortunate institutional approach that is more inclined to refuse bail and to impose more and longer prison terms for aboriginal offenders' (*R v Gladue* [688]). The court acknowledged that it is powerless to change many aspects in this sad situation; however, there is something that sentencing judges can and must do to remedy injustice against Aboriginal peoples in Canada (*R v Gladue* [688]). The court explained:

> Sentencing judges are among those decision-makers who have the power to influence the treatment of aboriginal offenders in the justice system. They determine most directly whether an aboriginal offender will go to jail, or whether other sentencing options may be employed which will play perhaps a stronger role in restoring a sense of balance to the offender, victim, and community, and in preventing future crime (*R v Gladue* [688]).

In both instances – when the sentencing judges take into account the special susceptibility of the offender and when they attempt to remedy the overrepresentation of a particular group of offenders in prisons – the judges act within their authority and pursue important social and penal goals. It is worth underscoring, however, that those goals – namely, deterrence, condemnation, social cohesion and rehabilitation – are distinct from the offender's 'just desert'. The *Gladue* court recognises that distinction when it questions whether 'imprisonment would actually serve to *deter, or to denounce crime* in a sense that would be meaningful to the community of which the offender is a member' (*R v Gladue* [688]), and chooses the restorative sentencing principles over the retributivist, 'because the *prevention of crime as well as individual and social healing* cannot occur through other means'. It is a question open for debate whether courts, which are supposed to distribute individual justice, are best suited for solving systemic social problems. However, to the extent judges may be legitimately guided by large-scale considerations, these considerations do not give the offenders themselves any *rights* to mitigation. Unlike the mitigation based on 'just desert', that kind of mitigation is a privilege, which may be asked for, but not demanded, and which may be denied if the desired societal goals can be better served by other means.

V. Conclusion

A significant failure of the state's responsibilities to an offender may provide a retributivist basis for mitigation of the offender's punishment, so long as the crime committed is either victimless or at least directed at the public at large, and not an identifiable victim. A successful claim for mitigation in these circumstances is a claim of right based on the combination of two sets of factors: one, the offender's diminished fault – his subjective culpability and objective wrongdoing – in the commission of the offence compared to an offender who has not been similarly mistreated by the state, and two, the state's diminished moral standing to prosecute the offender. The offender's culpability may be diminished if his wrongdoing lacks malice, as may be the case when the criminal violation is either an act of social protest or is driven by an urgent need of basic necessities. As for the wrongdoing, it may be reduced due to the state's comparative fault in failing its responsibilities to the offender, but only if the state alone (or only the general public) is affected by the offender's criminal act. Thus, such mitigation may be demanded by the offender in extremely rare circumstances of direct civil disobedience or economic, housing, or medical necessity; provided that the offender's conduct has not violated any rights of private parties.

In addition, an offender may have a grievance against the state when the state punishes him too harshly compared to similarly situated offenders. It may be argued, for example, that even though repeat offenders deserve longer sentences than first-time offenders, nevertheless a significant discrepancy between their sentences is unjust.[25] For that reason, Thompson may have an argument that he does not deserve a sentence that is dramatically harsher than a sentence for the same crime committed by a defendant without Thompson's criminal history. Thompson may also argue that, at his age, even an average sentence imposed for a sex crime on a repeat offender (16 years, which in his case, is likely to be much longer due to the aggravated nature of his crime) would effectively mean a life sentence. He could also point out the overrepresentation of incarcerated Native Americans compared with their percentage in the total population. All these arguments offer good reasons for mitigation, and it may be prudent for the sentencing judge to listen to them. However, unlike the first argument, which is a personal claim for justice, the last two are public policy considerations which, at best, can make the defendant a third-party beneficiary. Only an argument based on the defendant's 'just desert', if successful, gives the defendant the *right to demand* mitigation and imposes the *duty* on the sentencing judge to grant it.

[25] Based on a study, an average sentence for a repeat sex offender was 191.7 months compared to an average sentence of 111.2 months for offenders without history of sex crimes. United States Sentencing Commission (1995). The actual sentence for Thompson, recently announced, was 135 months of imprisonment for the sexual act by force and 120 months for failure to register, both terms to run concurrently, followed by lifetime supervised release. Thompson was sentenced to the lowest prison term in the range recommended by the US Sentencing Guidelines for offenders with his criminal history (135–168 months). As a result of a plea deal, the most serious count of the indictment, a sexual act under a threat or fear of death or serious bodily harm, was dismissed. *US v Thompson*.

5

Standing to Punish, Sentence Mitigation and the Applicability Challenge

JESPER RYBERG

The relationship between different aspects of social justice and criminal justice gives rise to a wide range of important ethical questions. For instance, one interesting question is whether the fact that an offender has been exposed to severe social deprivation should be regarded as a mitigating factor at sentencing (see eg Delgado 1985; Lambert 2018; Tonry 2020). Another very different question is whether a state that has maltreated its citizens, or not done what it should to alleviate the plight of citizens living in poverty, has the standing to hold offenders accountable for their misdeeds. This question has usually been considered as one concerning the preconditions for a state to serve as a legitimate punisher (Duff 2001; Beade 2019; Tadros 2009; Watson 2015). Thus, while the first question has been concerned with the severity of the sentences that should be imposed on disadvantaged groups of offenders, the second question has focused on whether the state is in a position to impose punishment on citizens in the first place. But could there be reasons not to separate questions concerning the severity of sentences and the preconditions of legitimate punishment as strictly as has usually been done in the theoretical discussion of these issues?

Suppose that the reasons that undermine a state's standing to hold offenders accountable for their misdeeds are more or less powerful, and that standing to punish, properly conceived, is not binary in the simple sense that either a state has standing, or it does not. In short, suppose that standing to punish is a matter of degree. Could it then be the case that different degrees of standing would manifest themselves in variation in the severity of the sentences that the state can legitimately impose on offenders? That is, does a fully developed account of state standing under conditions of societal injustice provide a framework to justify of sentence mitigation?

The purpose of this chapter is to explore the possibility of an ethical link between considerations of a state's standing to punish and the severity of the sentences that should be imposed on offenders. The motivation behind this investigation is not only that such a link is theoretically underexplored in the literature but, more importantly, that the reasons that have been advanced in the discussion on standing seem to support the view that standing is most properly conceived as a matter of degree. In fact, these arguments do more than support such a view. One of the most thorough recent analyses of the concept of reasons that undermine standing has explicitly underlined that standing is most plausibly interpreted as a scalar concept; that is, as something that comes in degrees (Lippert-Rasmussen 2024). Furthermore, if it turns out that the possibility of connecting considerations of standing and the severity of sentences runs into serious theoretical problems, then this may not only be relevant for the discussion of a possible justification of sentence mitigation; it may also, as will later be argued, constitute a challenge to the traditional idea of applying considerations of standing within the context of punishment. Thus, there are several theoretical reasons in favour of subjecting the relationship between standing to punish and the severity of sentences to a thorough investigation.

I. Overview

Section II of this chapter focuses on the two standard arguments that have been advanced to the effect that wrongful behaviour on the part of the state in its relation to citizens erodes the state's standing to punish offenders. The two arguments concern, respectively, the hypocrisy involved in the unjust state's punishment of offenders and the state's complicity in the offences that are committed. The purpose will not be to consider the plausibility of these arguments, but rather to show how these reasons that undermine standing support the contention that standing should be regarded as something that the state may have to a greater or lesser extent. Section III then considers the relationship between a scalar account of standing and sentence mitigation. The purpose will be to show that even if the idea of connecting degrees of standing and degrees of punishment is plausible in principle, it faces a number of practical problems. The arguments are underpinned by the assumption that the purpose of penal theoretical considerations is not merely to develop theories that are plausible and workable in some abstract reality, but also theories that should be able to guide penal practice. Insofar as a theory fails on this point, this should in itself be regarded as a serious theoretical defect. Section IV then considers two possible objections that might be raised against the arguments presented in the previous section. The objections concern the questions as to whether a scalar conception of standing should be rejected in favour of a binary interpretation, and whether the arguments that have been advanced are based on a naïve and unrealistic view on what we should expect from an ethical theory. Both objections will be refuted. Finally, section V summarises and concludes.

Before embarking upon these considerations, a few comments on the scope of the ensuing discussion are appropriate. First, different arguments have been presented to the effect that a state that treats its citizens unjustly may lose its standing to punish offenders. Whether these arguments for the erosion of standing are plausible, as noted, is not something that will be considered. Rather, the purpose will be to consider whether the arguments, if taken for granted, may provide a basis for a workable theory of sentence mitigation. Moreover, the discussion will be limited to considerations of two reasons that have been regarded as crucial in relation to standing: hypocrisy and complicity. Whether there may be other reasons that undermine standing to punish is not something that will be considered.[1] Second, different interpretations exist regarding the meaning of 'loss of standing'. In the following, I will stick to what could be called the 'moral wrongness account'.[2] What this implies is that a state that imposes punishment on offenders without having the requisite standing to do so will be acting *pro tanto* wrongfully. This does not mean that, all things considered, it would be wrong for the state to punish offenders without proper standing. For instance, it could be held that there are various types of injustice involved in a situation where offenders are not being properly punished for their misdeeds and that these reasons may sometimes outweigh the wrongfulness involved in imposing punishment without the standing to do so. However, it implies that such imposition is wrong unless there are sufficiently strong countervailing reasons. Precisely when possible countervailing reasons should be regarded as sufficiently strong to justify imposing punishment without the standing to do so is a delicate challenge for adherents of the standing position and not something that will be addressed in the ensuing discussion.[3] For reasons of ease in exposition, I will therefore skip the prefix *pro tanto* in the following and simply talk of imposing punishment without the standing to do so as wrongful or illegitimate. Third, the discussion of when a state has standing to punish

[1] Thus, in the following I will not be discussing state exclusion of citizens from the community as a standing-undermining reason (see eg Duff 2001). However, obviously such exclusionary behaviour may indirectly constitute a factor that contributes to state complicity in crime (see also Watson 2015: 179).

[2] For a comprehensive discussion of different theories of what it implies to lose standing as a hypocritical blamer, see Lippert-Rasmussen 2024.

[3] Standing theorists have held somewhat different views of what follows, all things considered, from the conflict between the injustice of imposing punishment without the standing to do so and the injustice of not punishing offenders. For instance, in some of his early writings on this issue, Duff expressed pessimism with regard to the step from theory to practice (Duff 1986: 191–99). However, he also adopted a slightly more optimistic attitude by contending that he found himself veering back and forth between 'on the one hand, a wholly pessimistic view that under present – and foreseeable – conditions criminal punishment simply cannot be or become such a mode of moral communication, and the slightly more optimistic view that, once we grasp the fact "the criminal justice system" is less a monolithic and unitary institution than a set of diverse and partly autonomous sub-systems and practices, we will also see that there may be room, in some contexts, for at least modest efforts at communicative penalty' (Duff 1999: 67). He has also suggested that unjust states should not punish disadvantaged offenders for *mala prohibita* crimes (2001: 200). Tadros, for his part, has proposed that victimless crimes committed by disadvantaged offenders should go unpunished (2009: 413). See also Ryberg 2004: ch 5 and Yost 2022.

offenders instantiates a broader discussion of what it means to have standing to blame. The reason that this discussion has been held to be relevant in a criminal justice context is that punishment is often seen as a way of blaming offenders. In the modern expressivist tradition in penal theory, the fact that a punishment conveys a condemnatory message to offenders is seen as part of the *raison d'être* of the punishment of offenders.[4] However, as has been noted, it could be the case that condemnation could be separated from the hard treatment element of a punishment (see Ewing 2018; Ryberg 2021a; von Hirsch 1993). In the following, I do not consider the possibility of imposing non-condemnatory hard treatment when the state does not have standing to blame.[5] The purpose of setting these limits on the discussion is not to suggest that the outlined issues are uncontroversial or that it would not be worthwhile subjecting them to further scrutiny. Rather, the point is to simplify the discussion by accepting as many as possible of the assumptions usually taken for granted by advocates of standing-based arguments.

II. Diminished Standing and Sentence Mitigation

Why is it that a state cannot always be held to have the proper standing to impose punishment on offenders? Though the arguments in favour of the view that a state may lose standing have been given slightly different expositions, the overall idea can easily be summarised. For instance, according to Tadros, the view is based on two assumptions which he believes are true for many societies. The first assumption is that poor people are poor as a consequence of distributive injustice. This assumption will be shared across many theories of distributive justice. The second is that poverty is a criminogenic factor; that is, it tends to increase the crime rate. The nature of the causal mechanisms behind this assumption is not crucial for the argument.[6] These two assumptions form the background for the view that the state does not have the standing to hold offenders punitively responsible for their misdeeds. More precisely, two different explanations of why the state under these conditions loses standing have often been provided.

The first is that by imposing punishment, the state, on the one hand, blames offenders for their misdeeds, while on the other, by perpetrating injustice against its citizens, it has been engaged in a similar kind of wrongdoing itself. This is the

[4] Many theorists also believe that a 'reprobation requirement' is part of the definition of punishment. See eg Boonin and Ryberg 2020a.

[5] Furthermore, whether there is something a state that has perpetrated injustice and lost standing to punish could subsequently do to regain its position as a legitimate punisher is an issue that has receive surprisingly little attention, but not something that will be considered here.

[6] Despite the fact that the relation between social disadvantage and crime is one of the most discussed topics in crime causation, there is no general agreement on this point. As noted by Wikström and Treiber: 'It is difficult to imagine any criminological topic that is more debated but less scientifically understood than the extent and nature of the relationship between social disadvantage and crime' (Wikström and Treiber 2016: 1233).

hypocrisy argument. In more general terms, the idea is that if you have contributed to a wrong yourself, you will lose standing to blame others for having committed similar types of wrong. The second explanation is that by perpetrating criminogenic injustice, the state has in itself become part of the offenders' crimes. In other words, it loses its status as a judge when it should instead be seen as a co-offender. This is the complicity argument. Let us in the following refer to the fact that a state holds double standards when it hypocritically blames offenders for a wrong that is sufficiently similar to its own wrongdoing, or that it is complicit when it contributes to the offenders' crimes, as 'standing-undermining reasons'. What is interesting for the purpose of the present discussion is that it seems obvious that such standing-undermining reasons must be a matter of degree.

Consider first a case of hypocrisy. Suppose that A is blaming B for not living up to certain standards which A herself is flouting. It seems reasonable to believe that the extent to which A herself has flouted these standards matters for A's standing to blame B. A mild dissociation would not seem to affect A's standing to blame as much as if A has forcefully and persistently violated these standards.[7] Furthermore, it seems to matter how similar the standards flouted by the blamer and the blamed are. In relation to crime, Tadros claims that it is 'especially problematic' when an accuser commits the same wrong as the offender who is accused: 'Thieves have a special reason not to hold other thieves responsible for stealing, a reason that is stronger than that which applies to reckless drivers, even if reckless driving and theft are wrongs of a similar magnitude' (2009: 396). The same picture seems to hold if we turn from hypocrisy to complicity. It is hard to reject that one can be more or less complicit in a particular wrong. Tadros, for his part, underlines this when he contends that the 'seriousness of complicity is sensitive to the degree of involvement and to the mental state of the wrongdoer' (2009: 398).

But if reasons undermining standing come in degrees in the sense that the state can be more or less hypocritical or more or less complicit in crimes that are committed, what does this imply for the degree of blame which the state has standing to impose on offenders? One answer might to be that there is a relation between the degree of blame which someone is entitled to express and the strength of the reasons that undermine standing. In fact, this is precisely the view that has recently been advanced by Lippert-Rasmussen. What he holds is that 'we should think of standing to blame as a scalar matter, where standing and blaming both come in degrees … and where the standing requirement says that for a certain degree of blaming – say, mild censure – a certain degree of standing – say, not

[7] Lippert-Rasmussen makes the same point when he asserts that 'Not only blame but also standing comes in degrees. This should be obvious in light of some of the factors that are said to bear on and undermine standing to blame. Take, for instance, hypocritical blame. There is a scalar difference between people who hypocritically blame others for lying, depending on whether they lied on a particular occasion on a matter that was rather insignificant to the blamee or whether they have massively lied to and deceived their blamee on a wide range of very important matters. Perhaps it is much too simplistic to say that this group of blamers falls into two, mutually exclusive groups, namely those with standing and those without standing to blame' (2024: 52).

strongly objectionable similar faults – is required' (2024: 52). Thus, while the traditional discussion has usually focused only on the polar extremes, namely, those of either having full standing or of not having any standing at all, the more nuanced view that seems to follow from the fact that reasons undermining standing come in degrees is that, in between these extremes, different degrees of blame may require different degrees of standing. However, suppose that this view is combined with the expressivist assumption underlying the discussion: namely, that the severity of a sentence reflects the stringency of the blame that is conveyed to an offender. There may then be cases in which the state, due to some degree of hypocrisy or complicity, is only entitled to punish an offender to an extent that does not reflect the complete blame that is justified by the seriousness of the crime, and which the state should have imposed had its standing not been partially reduced. In simpler terms, suppose that a state has not fully lost its standing, but that, as a result of a mild degree of hypocrisy or complicity, it is entitled to sentence an offender to no more than the blame involved in an eight-month prison term. Suppose, further, that the deserved sentence for a particular crime committed is 10 months' imprisonment. In that case, it would follow that the state would be acting wrongfully by imposing more that the eight months. That is, the offender should receive a sentence mitigation (of two months). Therefore, when it comes to the initial question as to whether considerations of standing could form the grounds for a theory of sentence mitigation, the answer is in the affirmative. In fact, even though it has not been fully acknowledged, this seems to constitute the most obvious interpretation of what a fully fledged account of standing to punish would imply. But if that is the case, then a new question arises: namely, whether these in-principle considerations could also serve as a guide for how offenders should be treated in practice. This is the question to which we shall now turn.

III. Standing, Mitigation and Practical Application

The discussion of reasons that undermine standing in relation to state punishment can take place on many different levels. For instance, we can discuss what constitutes the most plausible interpretation of hypocrisy and complicity, or we can look at what the all-things-considered ethical implications are if a state is hypocritical or complicit in crime. That is, how a loss of standing should be weighed against the injustices of not punishing those who have committed crimes. However, the purpose here, as noted, is more narrowly to consider whether a theory of sentence mitigation based on considerations of standing can provide genuine guidance regarding how severely offenders should be punished in a context where the state does not have full standing to blame offenders. As will now be argued, it is precisely when it comes to giving more detailed content to the outlined idea of sentence mitigation that this justification runs into problems. More specifically, I believe there are two challenges that would have to be addressed to turn the idea into something practically applicable. Unfortunately, as we shall see, these challenges are not easily overcome.

A. Determining Degrees of Standing

If we wish to flesh out the idea that a state that has perpetrated social injustice against its citizens loses standing to blame in proportion to the strength of the reasons that undermine its standing, and to do so in sufficient detail that the view can serve as a guide for the court to the imposition of mitigated sentences, then the first thing that would have to be made clear is to what degree these injustices affect the state's standing. For instance, put in comparative terms, suppose that two offenders O_1 and O_2 have committed equally serious crimes, but that the state has perpetrated one type of injustice prior to the punishment of O_1 and another type of injustice before punishing O_2. In that case, we would need to know whether O_1 should be sentenced more leniently than O_2 or vice versa. However, determining degrees of loss of standing turns out to be a rather complicated task for the simple reason that many elements would have to be considered.

First, consider hypocrisy as a reason that undermines standing. The state will be acting hypocritically by blaming an offender for having acted wrongly if it has itself flouted values that are similar to those violated by the offender. One thing that seems to matter here is the degree of similarity between the wrongs committed by the offender and the state. As we have seen above, Tadros explicitly emphasises the degree of similarity as something that determines the degree of hypocrisy. In general terms, if a 'blamer' has committed the very same type of crime as the one committed by the 'blamee' then the blamer will be more hypocritical than if there is only a weaker affinity between the two instances of wrongdoing. This seems intuitively appealing. However, it may not be easy to determine different degrees of similarity. For instance, if the state has perpetrated economic injustice against groups of citizens, how similar is this to the wrongdoing of offenders who have committed theft, burglary, fraud or assault? Furthermore, suppose that it is made sufficiently clear how relevant similarity should be assessed. This will still not be sufficient to determine how hypocritical the state is. Obviously, another important factor will be the *extent* to which the state has flouted the relevant values. A state may have contributed massively to social injustice and assaulted citizens in various ways, or it may have done so to a more limited extent. If the former is the case, then the subsequent blaming of offenders may well be regarded as more hypocritical. But this complicates the picture. For instance, how should we compare the degree of standing in a case where there is much similarity between the types of wrongdoing committed by the state and by an offender, but where the state has only acted wrongfully to a more limited extent, to that in a case where the similarity is somewhat weaker but the state's involvement in wrongful behaviour is much more significant? It is not easy to see how such a question should be answered. But it may well be the very type of question one would be confronted with in practice if the criminal court is considering a mitigated sentence of an offender on the grounds of reduced standing.

Second, let us turn to the other and allegedly more powerful reason that undermines standing: complicity. As adherents of the relationship between complicity and standing have stressed, complicity is a matter of degree. An agent's degree of complicity depends upon how much the agent has contributed to the crime committed by the principal agent. Thus, following this idea, the state should, *ceteris paribus*, be regarded as more complicit if it has acted in a way that is more rather than less criminogenic. It is remarkable how little has been done to explicate this idea more thoroughly. Much of the discussion considers complicity only in very general terms, or through analogies involving complicity in interpersonal relations. However, it is obvious that if a state's standing is reduced insofar as it has had an impact on an offender's propensity for engaging in criminal conduct, then many types of state decision-making would have to be taken into account. For instance, some people's propensity for crime may be influenced not only by the distribution of resources but also by political initiatives that imply that these citizens lose their jobs. The same is the case with regard to educational policies which result in some groups being less well educated. Furthermore, crime policies may also be relevant in this regard. If it is correct that imprisonment for some people constitutes a criminogenic factor, then the state may be seen as complicit in a crime committed by someone who engages in recidivism after a period of incarceration. Or, what if state regulation prohibits a woman from having an abortion and the child ends up an offender? In this case, it is hard to deny that the state is involved in the simple sense that had it acted (regulated) differently, the crime would not have taken place. The point of these remarks is not to object to the idea of relating the concepts of standing and complicity, but to indicate that the proposal that the degree of complicity is determined (partly) on the grounds of extent to which the state has contributed to the fact that a crime has been committed requires further consideration. The significance of this is something we shall return to shortly.

There is also another important dimension of complicity beyond the degree of state involvement: the mental state of the complicit agent. It seems reasonable to hold that the fault of a complicit agent depends upon the extent to which the agent's mind was focused on bringing about the wrongful result. For instance, Tadros distinguishes between being intentionally complicit, knowingly complicit, recklessly complicit and negligently complicit (2009: 399). It is probably not the case that all of these possibilities are equally relevant to the way in which a state may be regarded as complicit in crime. But even if we disregard the fact that it is always more difficult to determine mental states of collective entities such as states, it seems reasonable to assume that a state may be more or less cognisant of the extent to which it has paved the way for criminal activity. However, if there is both an *actus reus* and *mens rea* dimension of complicity, then it is easy to imagine cases where these dimensions point in opposite directions; that is, where a state has been more involved by perpetrating some sort of injustice but has a lower degree of knowledge. Or, on the contrary, where it is less involved but is more cognisant of the criminogenic effects of its involvement. How one should compare the degrees of complicity and, hence, the degree of reduced standing in such cases is not a question which anyone has yet even attempted to answer.

Third, if one holds, as do Tadros, Beade, and other theorists who have been engaged in the discussion of standing, that hypocrisy and complicity both constitute reasons that undermine standing, then there is a further obvious challenge: that degrees of hypocrisy and complicity need not correlate. Suppose that we have a situation in which the state is only marginally complicit in a crime that has been committed (eg, because of a low degree of *mens rea*), but that it would be rather hypocritical to blame the offender because the state has also contributed to the propensity to various other (sufficiently similar) types of crime. Compare this to an alternative where the state is much more complicit (eg, because of a higher degree of *mens rea*), but would as a blamer nevertheless be less hypocritical than in the first case, because it has only flouted standards relating to this particular type of crime but not to a range of other related types of crime. In which of the two situations would the state have lost more of its standing to blame? Since hypocrisy and complicity, as we have seen, can both come in degrees that need not be associated in any simple way, it is possible to imagine many combinations where these two dimensions point in opposite directions. It will therefore not work as an answer merely to maintain that complicity generally is a weightier reason than hypocrisy. But some sort of answer would be required in order to determine the extent to which state standing in such cases has been lost.

To summarise, it seems reasonable to conclude that attempts at saying something more precise – beyond the claim that a state's standing is reduced, which offers little guidance – about how much it has been diminished prompts a range of theoretically complex and yet unanswered questions. The challenges that have been outlined do not show that there cannot be some cases in which comparative assessments of the degree of standing that is lost can be determined. But they strongly indicate that there are many cases in which such comparisons cannot yet be made and, also, that the challenges do not seem to invite any simple answers. However, this is only one aspect of the challenges prompted by the standing-based view of mitigation.

B. Relating Degrees of Standing and Legitimate Punishment

Suppose that the challenges outlined above have been answered in the sense that some theoretical framework has been provided for making comparative estimates of how much a state's involvement in past and current injustices has affected its standing to punish. The next question that arises then is how should this be translated into an answer to how much the sentence of a crime should be mitigated?

Suppose this time that the appropriate punishment for a serious crime is six years in prison. Suppose, further, that the state has perpetrated injustices in various ways, but only to an extent that leaves it with some degree of standing to punish. Now, how much would the state be entitled to punish the offender? Or conversely put, how large should the mitigation that flows from the reduced standing be? To contend that this is not an important ethical challenge, because all that matters is the purely comparative judgement that the offender should receive a more lenient sentence than in a case where the state's standing is less eroded, and a more severe sentence than in cases where the standing is more eroded, is an unsatisfactory answer. Such a purely comparative (or ordinal) requirement would be satisfied both if the offender gets four years, two years, or a fine, as long as the ordering relative to other situations where the state's standing is more or less reduced is observed. But this cannot be correct. Surely it must make a difference from an ethical point of view whether an offender receives four years in prison or a fine. Therefore, what is required is some sort of theory of how different degrees of standing non-relatively match different degrees of severity of punishment. The problem is that it is very difficult to imagine what such a theory would look like.

A first possibility might be to draw on theories that have been developed in the modern retributivist tradition to handle the more general, but related, question of how severely crimes of varying degree of gravity should be punished. Retributivists have usually strongly emphasised the moral significance of (ordinal) proportionality; that is, the principle that the more serious offences should be responded to with a more severe punishments, while equally serious crimes should receive equally severe punishment. However, this is a purely comparative requirement. It does not say anything about how severely different offenders should be punished (see Ryberg 2004). Thus, in order to answer the question of how crimes of varying gravity non-relatively comport to punishment of different degrees of severity, further theoretical considerations are required. To this effect, several retributivists have defended so-called 'anchor theories' (see eg Kleinig 1973; Scheid 1997). The idea behind an anchor theory is simple: namely, to rank crimes in ascending order of seriousness and punishments in ascending order of severity, and then anchor the most severe punishment to the most serious crime, and the least severe punishment to the least serious crime. All the other crimes and punishments then fall between the extremes. Could a similar idea be applied with regard to the relationship between degrees of standing and legitimate punishment?

The proposal would involve anchoring the fully deserved punishment for a particular crime to the point of full standing, and zero punishment where standing is completely lost, with all the other intermediate degrees of standing and varying degrees of severity of punishment falling in between. Such a scheme would of course provide the correct answers in the extreme cases: if the state's standing is fully intact, there should be no mitigation; if it is completely eroded, the offender should receive full mitigation, that is, no punishment. The problem is what goes on in between these extremes. If it is the case that degrees of standing are only ordinally ordered – that is, if degrees of standing can only be compared in terms of more or less – then the scheme would not provide any guidance, because this ordering can be reflected in the degrees of severity of punishment in endless ways. This was precisely what we saw above. If the fully deserved sentence for a particular crime is six years in prison, then it would be compatible with this scheme to give the offender four years in prison, but also to impose a fine. All that matters is that the relative ordering between other degrees of standing and related degrees of severity of sentence is maintained (ie, that a less eroded standing would give a modest mitigation and a more eroded standing would result in significant mitigation). Therefore, such a scheme would only be workable if it were possible to generate interval matching; that is, if degrees of standing could be compared on some sort of interval scale.[8] However, as we have already seen, this would significantly complicate the task of making comparative assessments of various degrees of standing.

A second possibility could be to invoke another well-known idea in considerations of punishment distribution: namely, that punishment should be imposed parsimoniously. More precisely, the principle of parsimony prescribes that the severity of punishment should be kept to the minimum necessary to achieve the purpose of the sentence. This principle has widespread appeal and has served as a guiding principle in relation to some influential theories of punishment (see eg Lippke 2018; Tonry 2020). Could this principle also serve as a guide for how different degrees of loss of standing should be related to legitimate sentences of varying severity?

It is easy to see that this solution must be refused. If we interpret the principle as suggesting that the state should impose the most lenient sentence possible in cases where it does not have full standing, then the implications are very radical. Assuming that the most lenient punishment is zero punishment, this would imply that in every case where the state does not have full standing, offenders should not be punished at all. This is an extreme view, and hardly one which many penal theorists defending models of standing would accept. The implication is particularly extreme in the light of the fact (underlined above), that a state may in various ways be regarded as at least to some extent complicit in crimes committed by its citizens. Another more plausible interpretation, then, is to keep in mind that the principle is only meant as a supplement to other theoretical considerations outlining the main purpose of punishment. But what does this mean in the present context? If the idea is that the principle should be invoked only in cases where the question of how different degrees of standing should be related to different degrees of severity of punishment has already been determined, but where there is still some zone of indeterminateness left within which the principle should operate, then

[8] This point has also been recognised by retributivists who have defended anchor theories as a way of relating the seriousness of crimes and the severity of punishment. For a discussion of this, see Ryberg 2004: ch 4.

the reference to the principle of parsimony is of little help. It would presuppose that the question of how degrees of standing and severity of punishment should be related has already to a wide extent been answered. That is, this application of the principle presupposes what we are seeking for. Thus, this approach to penal distribution has little to offer in the present theoretical context.

In summary, what we have seen is that even if we assume that we can make some sort of comparative assessments of different degrees of standing, the challenge of how these degrees should be translated into degrees of legitimate degrees of punishment, and thereby show how large the resulting mitigation should be in individual cases of crime, remains genuine. Neither the idea of applying some sort of anchor theory nor the idea of drawing on the principle of parsimony provides sufficient theoretical background for turning the overall idea of standing-based mitigation into something that delivers answers to how one should punish offenders in cases where the state's standing to punishment is compromised. When these considerations are combined with the problems identified above, concerning the possibility of making comparative assessments of degrees of standing in the first place, it seems fair to conclude that the problem facing a standing-based theory of sentence mitigation is not so much that it leads us astray but that is does not lead us anywhere.

IV. Possible Objections

These conclusions may seem premature. The time has come to consider some objections. There are two possible objections which may strike the reader and which concern, respectively, the idea of regarding standing considerations as a way of underpinning sentence mitigation and the underlying expectation with regard to the possibility of delivering genuine guidance. Let us consider each objection in turn.

A. Standing as a Binary Concept

The purpose of the previous discussion has been to determine whether standing to punish should be seen as a matter of degree and that reduced (but non-eliminated) standing would therefore manifest itself in reduced degrees of legitimate punishment. However, if, as argued, it is the case that using considerations of standing to justify sentence mitigation confronts a plethora of theoretical challenges that render the theory practically inapplicable, then there seems to be an easy way out: namely, to abandon the view that standing constitutes a scalar concept. Even though, as we have seen, it is a fact that reasons that undermine standing come in degrees, it does not obviously follow that standing to punish could not be interpreted as a binary concept. As a simple analogy, the level of alcohol in the bloodstream is a matter of degree. If one consumes more alcohol, blood alcohol levels increase. However, this does not exclude the possibility of holding that, once a particular level of alcohol is crossed, a driver will lose the licence to drive. Thus, scalar reasons are fully compatible with a binary view of a licence. Therefore, an obvious reaction to the previous arguments might be to close the whole discussion down by simply rejecting that standing is a question of degree. Either a state has the standing to punish its citizens, or it does not. In fact, I believe that this is precisely the view to which some standing theorists would subscribe. But is this a plausible way of circumventing the theoretical challenges?

Even though the idea of rejecting a standing-based theory of sentence mitigation may seem an obvious reaction, I nevertheless believe that the previous considerations also help us to see that, on closer inspection, a binary interpretation of standing does not afterall constitute an easy escape route. The challenge that this solution is confronted with is, of course, to specify what the relationship then is between the reasons that undermine standing and the state's licence to punish. There are only two possibilities.

The first is to contend that if there are any reasons at all that compromise a state's standing to punish, then the state loses all authority to punish. This is the perfectionist interpretation: only the totally impeccable state has standing to punish. However, in order to determine that a state is not in any way hypocritical or complicit in crime, one still has to engage in conceptual considerations of what precisely is meant by 'relevant similarity' and 'involvement'. But, as indicated above, once one engages in this sort of analysis, one easily ends up with the conclusion that no state will ever be in a position to impose legitimate sentences on offenders. For example, there are probably no states – even among those that treat citizens very decently – that do not sometimes (knowingly) launch initiatives that are criminogenic. As noted, the mere fact that a state imposes lengthy prison terms on some offenders – which is what all states currently do – may increase the risk of (re)offending in some criminals. Thus, the perfectionist interpretation of standing is not a solution to which I believe any standing theorists will adhere.

The second possibility, then, is to hold that it is not any political *faux pas* on the part of the state that eliminates its standing to punish. Rather, it is only when a state has acted *sufficiently* wrongfully against its citizens that its licence to inflict punishment is lost. This is what could be called the threshold interpretation: when a state exercises a sufficient level of hypocrisy or complicity, it loses its standing as a legitimate punisher. It seems that something along these lines is what some standing theorists have in mind.[9] However, this view faces two problems. First, in order not to be totally arbitrary, something needs to be said about why there should be such a threshold. If the reasons that undermine standing, as we have

[9] For instance, Watson contends that: 'As to the question of how criminogenic the unjustified or unjust policies or practices have to be, and how unjust they have to be, it's difficult to say anything general. It seems to me safe to conclude that, on both counts, the criminogenic policies under consideration here exceed any reasonable threshold' (2015: 183).

seen, come in degrees – that is, one can be more or less hypocritical or more or less complicit, then why is it that a state at a particular point moves from being a fully legitimate punisher to one with no standing at all? In the absence of a positive argument to this effect, the suggestion appears somewhat ad hoc.[10] Second, and more importantly, in order to be applicable this proposal will have to say something about where the standing-determining cut-off point should be located. What we have seen above is that there are several theoretical challenges associated with the possibility of determining relative degree of standing. The fact that there are different dimensions of both hypocrisy and complicity that may point in opposite directions, and that hypocrisy and complicity need not correlate, makes it theoretically difficult to make comparative assessments of degrees of standing. However, if one holds that there is a threshold when a state loses all standing to punish, then one will be confronted with precisely the same challenges. In short, if one cannot really tell how much the reasons that undermine standing in relation to a particular criminal case have eroded the state's standing to punish an offender, then it makes little sense to try to locate a threshold. Therefore, the attempt to circumvent the challenges facing a standing-based theory of mitigation by resorting to the idea of a standing threshold does not really meet the challenges that have been identified in the previous discussion. Rather, it presupposes that these challenges have already been answered, which means that this approach does not in itself constitute a genuine solution.

B. Proper Expectations of Action Guidance

A second and very different reaction to the considerations in the previous section might be to question the assumption that seems to underlie the discussion. More precisely, the main point has been to show that a standing-based theory of sentencing mitigation faces massive challenges when it moves from a general idea to application in practice. This move is encumbered with a range of theoretical challenges which, if they are not adequately met, render the idea almost inapplicable in real life. However, perhaps I have simply been demanding more than one can reasonably expect from a penal ethical theory. Perhaps the more apposite picture is that the previous discussion amounts to nothing more than some sort of inappropriate philosophical nitpicking. As some theorists have rightly underlined, one should keep in mind that penal theoretical considerations rarely, if ever, are things that allow for a strict metric or that equal mathematical equations. Thus, can the

[10] It might be held that the challenges I have outlined constitute the reasons that speak in favour of a binary interpretation of standing. However, if the reasons that support the idea that standing can be eroded comes in degrees, then it still seems somewhat ad hoc simply to abandon a scalar interpretation of standing in favour of a binary interpretation just because the former faces challenges. After all, another possibility would be to skip the whole of idea of standing. Thus, in my view some sort of positive argument would be desirable to avoid the accusation that the binary interpretation constitutes an ad hoc manoeuvre.

previous considerations be brushed aside not because they are false, but because they are misplaced?

If this objection is advanced without further qualification, it can easily be dismissed. If we are interested in the question as to whether standing may constitute a basis for a theory of sentence mitigation, then it must be relevant whether (and to what extent) reduced standing can be translated into levels of sentence reduction. If hypocrisy is accepted as a reason that undermines standing, but it turns out to be difficult to determine whether a state is more or less hypocritical, then this is a defect of the theory. The same is the case if complicity is regarded as a reason that undermines standing, but in many cases, for theoretical reasons, it turns out to be difficult to tell whether a state is more or less complicit in a crime that has been committed. Moreover, if one is not able to tell how degrees of standing should be translated into degrees of reduced punishment, then the theory has failed to deliverer the promised goods.

However, perhaps the proper interpretation of the suspicion that the above arguments are dubious does not merely consist of the view that they are misplaced but also of a more positive account of how action guidance can be delivered. For instance, it is a fact that both penal theories and criminal courts in practice operate with many concepts that come in degrees, without having anything close to precise scales or precise methods of measurement. As long as one knows which factors determine offender culpability, it makes perfect sense to hold that one offender is more culpable than another even though there is no exact way of measuring degrees of culpability. Likewise, one crime can be determined to be more harmful than another even in the absence of a strict metric for harm assessment. The same seems to be the case when judgements are made on the grounds of several contributing factors. For instance, in relation to the possibility of comparing crimes in terms of gravity, Ten has suggested that this task is indeed manageable if understood as comparable to evaluations of student essays. He contends that:

> When tutors and teachers rank the essays of their students, they do not have only one relevant feature to look for. There are a number of different features – originality, understanding of the issues discussed, lucidity of presentation, etc. – which each makes contribution to the quality of the essay. An essay may be strong in one dimension but weak in another, and yet it is possible to make an overall assessment of the essay as being better or worse than another' (Ten 1987: 155).

Therefore, could the objection not be raised along these lines that a similar approach should be adopted when it comes to considerations of reasons that undermine standing; that is, that the failure of the previous arguments lies in the fact that they amount to a sort of over-theorizing in an area where all we can do is to listen to what we feel?[11]

The problem with this objection is that it is not entirely clear what it implies. If the idea is that we should draw on intuitive judgement with regard to *general*

[11] For a parallel discussion in relation to the question of how one should compare crimes in terms of gravity, see Ryberg 2004: 85 and Ryberg 2020b.

answers to the different sub-challenges, such as how one should determine degrees of hypocrisy and complicity, and how these judgements should be translated into different degrees of legitimate punishment, then it is far from clear that we possess these sorts of ethical intuition. For instance, do we have an intuitive idea of how one should generally balance degrees of relevant similarity and the extent to which values have been flouted when one makes assessments of how hypocritical a state would be when it sentences offenders? Or do we have an intuitive feeling of how different degrees of state involvement and different degrees of *mens rea* should generally be balanced in assessments of how complicit the state is when offenders commit their crimes? Or do we have a general feeling of how degrees of hypocrisy and complicity should be balanced in cases where these reasons that undermine standing do not correlate? For my own part, I have no intuitive answers to such *general* questions. In fact, it is not even clear to me how a general answer should be articulated.

However, perhaps the whole idea is rather that one should abandon the idea of *general* answers in favour of more case-specific judgments. Such an interpretation seems more in line with Ten's analogy. We are probably unable to present general answers regarding how the various factors that determine the quality of student essays should be weighed, but we are able to make assessments when confronted with individual essays. But even if this is the case with regard to student essays, is it also the case that we have such intuitions in cases of crime in a context where a state has acted with some degree of hypocrisy or complicity? If asked what would constitute the appropriate sentence for a particular offender who has committed a specific crime within a specific political context where different policies have each contributed to some extent to the criminal behaviour of this offender, do we then have an idea of what would constitute the appropriate sentence and, hence, how large the mitigation should be compared to an ideal situation in which the state's standing to punish was not compromised? Once again, for my own part, I am not confident that I would have anything close to an answer. Furthermore, if the idea is that one should draw on case-specific intuitions, such as judgments by individual judges, then does this mean that one should abandon consistency across such judgments? Or can we still maintain requirements of consistency without basing judgments on some degree of generality? What these considerations indicate is that the idea of brushing aside the previously outlined challenges by holding that intuitions will suffice is in itself an answer that prompts a range of challenges.

Thus, the answer to the objection in my view is that, on the one hand, it is reasonable to contend that there are limits to how much guidance we should expect from an ethical theory.[12] To reject a penal ethical theory if it cannot tell whether an offender should be imprisoned for 20 minutes more or less may be to demand too much. On the other hand, it is plausible to regard action guidance as one among several dimensions on the grounds of which the plausibility of ethical

[12] In my view, there is no precise answer to how much action guidance should be expected from an ethical theory. Rather, I believe that action guidance should be seen as one among several virtues which theories should be measured against. That is, everything else being equal, it speaks in favour of one theory relative to another if it is able to provide more precise guidance on how we should act.

theories should be assessed. This, in my view, is sufficient to show that, even if they are insufficient as grounds for an ultimate rejection of a standing-based theory of mitigation, the challenges that have been identified should not be brushed aside as an example of misplaced theoretical pedantry.

V. Conclusion

The discussion in this chapter has assumed that the purpose of engaging in and developing ethical theories is to provide practical guidance. Ethics is not just some sort of theoretical puzzle-solving but a discipline that is supposed to qualify real-life decision-making and behaviour.[13] As Murphy has argued in a classic modern article, it should be regarded a fatal defect of ethical considerations if they fail when it comes to 'the union of theory and practice' (Murphy 1995: 18). Needless to say, this does not mean that one should not engage in abstract principled theorising. On the contrary, such considerations are often highly important if we are dealing with complex ethical issues. But if the connection between such considerations and the reality that should be guided is lost, then so is the point of theorising. As has been argued in the previous sections, this is the sort of challenge that faces a standing-based theory of sentence mitigation. Even if it is taken for granted that hypocrisy and complicity constitute genuine reasons that undermine standing, and that these reasons are scalar and therefore reduce the severity of the punishment which a state has legitimate authority to impose, this still leaves us without a practically applicable theory. As argued, the possibility of turning the idea into practical guidance would require considerations of both the relative strength of reasons that undermine standing and the extent to which diminished standing should be translated into degrees of legitimate punishment and, hence, into mitigation of varying magnitude. The problem, as indicated, is that these challenges have not even tentatively been answered and, more importantly, that even though it is not possible to show that they cannot be met, it seems fair to hold that they do not invite any simple solutions.

Furthermore, it has been argued that the possibility of interpreting standing to punish in strict binary terms, as something a state either has or does not have at all, did not succeed in circumventing all the outlined theoretical challenges. Moreover, that and that the idea that handling the challenges by drawing on ethical intuitions gave rise to several new challenges which meant that this approach should at best be regarded as incomplete. There may be many reasons in favour of sentence mitigation; however, if what has been said so far is correct, the injustices which a state may have perpetrated against its citizens should be excluded from this set of reasons.

[13] For a more comprehensive discussion and defence of the view that the purpose of ethical theorizing is to provide action guidance, see Ryberg 2021b and 2024. For a narrower discussion of applicability in relation to different retributivist approaches to sentence discounts, see eg Ryberg 2014 and 2023.

6

'One Wrong Treads upon the Heels of Another': Mitigating Sentence in Response to State Misconduct

JULIAN V ROBERTS AND NETANEL DAGAN[1]

At sentencing, a court usually focuses exclusively on wrongdoing by the offender – the factors which make the crime more or less serious, and those that affect the offender's culpability or risk of reoffending. This emphasis is reflected in the scholarly literature. Yet in recent decades commentary has paid increased attention to misconduct by the state – on whose behalf legal punishment is imposed. Manikis 2022a: 317, for example, notes that 'state actions are increasingly relevant in sentencing'. This chapter evaluates the claims for mitigation arising from wrongful acts by state actors (such as police or prison officers) which harm the offender. By 'misconduct' we mean unlawful acts, conduct by state officials which rises to the threshold of a criminal offence, or which violates a professional code of conduct. Our focus is on state misconduct occurring after the crime for which the offender is now being punished, although we briefly comment on mistreatment of the offender before the crime has been detected.

We do not address other legal avenues for addressing misconduct by state actors. For example, a defendant may bring an action for abuse of process. In England and Wales there are two grounds for determining whether a stay of proceedings is justified as a result of an abuse of process. The first ground is that the defendant's 'right to a fair trial' has been compromised. That would not appear relevant to, for example, an assault by the police upon arrest. The second, more subjective ground is that the integrity of the justice system would be threatened by continued prosecution (and punishment) (for discussion see Campbell, Ashworth and Redmayne 2019: ch 9). We discuss this latter ground as a justification for sentence mitigation later in the essay.

[1] Our thanks to participants at the Cambridge seminar in December 2023 and in particular Leo Zaibert for his feedback on an earlier draft of this chapter.

When the state has wronged the defendant, the individual appearing for sentence becomes both offender and victim. We expand the traditional retributive focus from merely focusing on the crime as an isolated event – a discrete moment in time and space – to broader societal contexts, including culpable acts or omissions by the state. A wider view takes into account more (albeit within limits) the context of crime. This perspective is more realistic and sensitive to the reality of criminal behaviour, which is not exclusively the result of a rational choice of an individual but often an interaction between the offender and his environment. The chapter examines both retributive and utilitarian arguments for state misconduct mitigation at sentencing, and addresses the following questions:

- If there is a plausible normative justification for state misconduct mitigation, how might this be implemented in practice?
- Are all forms of unlawful conduct by state officials potentially mitigating – or only those directly related to the offence?
- Is there a conceptual distinction between state misconduct occurring prior to the commission of the crime and unlawful acts committed after the crime?
- What are the limits on the power of state misconduct to mitigate sentence?

The state may abuse its power in many ways. State officials who operate the 'machinery of justice' wield great power, exercise wide discretion, and benefit from resources that reflect the state as a 'leviathan' (see Herbert 2008). For the purposes of illustration, in this chapter we use two judgments from the Supreme Court of Canada to explore that plausibility of sentencing mitigation in cases of state misconduct. Courts in Canada[2] have adopted a permissive approach to mitigating sentence based on state misconduct. The Canadian Supreme Court has affirmed that a wide variety of adverse circumstances may reduce sentence, including wrongful acts against the offender occurring before and after the offence.[3] In addition, the Supreme Court has ruled that any harm related to the crime has the potential to mitigate sentence, whether it results from acts by state agents or private citizens. We reject this view, holding it to be too permissive and inconsistent with culpability-based retributivism.[4]

[2] The practice of awarding mitigation for state misconduct appears to be restricted to common law countries. In Germany, for example, misconduct by justice officials or other harms inflicted by a state agent does not mitigate sentence (see Freixo 2019).

[3] 'The sentencing regime provides some scope for sentencing judges to consider not only the actions of the offender, but also those of the state actors … state misconduct which impacts the offender may be a relevant factor in crafting a fit sentence.' *R v Nasogaluak* [3]).

[4] The second author has proposed a normative framework for considering as mitigation a state misconduct even if unrelated to the crime. This account is based on communicative-retributive values that recognise the offender's perspective in the penal dialogue and its subjective experience (see Zimran and Dagan 2023). Here we examine the retributive (culpability-based) and utilitarian justifications for state misconduct mitigation.

I. Two Cases

In *Morris*, the offender had been subject to repeated abuse by police officers on racial grounds.[5] At sentencing, the trial and appeal court judgments both recognised the relevance of this misconduct and mitigated the sentence accordingly. The second offender had been seriously assaulted by police at the time of his arrest (*R v Nasogaloak*). Here the Supreme Court mitigated his sentence to recognise the unlawful acts by state agents. A key distinction between the two cases concerns the *timing* of the misconduct which occurred prior to the offence in *Morris* yet after the crime in *Nasogaloak*. Finally, in *Suter*, the Supreme Court authorised mitigation to reflect the fact that the defendant had been seriously wounded by vigilantes prior to sentencing.[6] One distinction between the third and the previous two cases is that the defendant harmed by non-state actors.

Traditional desert formulations restrict the ambit of mitigation. In determining the offender's level of culpability, the desert lens encompassed events immediately prior to, or at the time of the crime: was the offender provoked? Did he suffer from a mental disorder at the time of the crime? Was the crime premeditated? More distal issues, such as prior offending or childhood poverty, were generally excluded for being unrelated to the offender's culpability at the time of crime (or shortly before).[7] Stricter versions of retributivism focus more on the offender at the time of the crime for assessing the offenders' desert (Moore 2010; von Hirsch 2017). More recently, retributivists have increasingly recognised that a wider range of circumstances – before and after the crime – may be relevant to the level of censure appropriate, and hence the stringency of punishment (Roberts and Dagan 2019).[8]

We seek to introduce some structure and principle into the question of state misconduct mitigation. Without a principled structure, courts are free to consider claims for state misconduct, weigh submissions from counsel and then mitigate according to the individual judge's perspective. The danger is that it risks being, as Nigel Walker describes it, a 'leap into a bog with no boundary'. Individual judges

[5] *R v Morris*.

[6] 'There is no requirement that collateral consequences must emanate from state misconduct in order to be considered as a factor at sentencing.' *R v Suter* [56]. The court ruled that assaults on the offender by vigilantes could justify a sentence discount. The actions of vigilantes and other non-State actors are discussed later in this chapter.

[7] These early works reflect a well-documented phenomenon in the social psychology literature: the *Fundamental Attribution Error* (FAE). This refers to a human tendency to overestimate the importance of personal or dispositional factors relative to environmental influences. This has been demonstrated in a range of contexts. With respect to criminal behaviour, the FAE leads people to overlook environmental influences on the offender and overemphasise the individual's agency and hence responsibility and culpability for the offence (see discussion in Ross 1978: 173, 184). There is also a valence effect. Negative behaviour is more likely to be attributed to the individual rather than the environment; positive actions more likely to be explained by environmental triggers. As in 'he committed the crime out of individual malevolence' but 'he made a charitable donation largely to benefit from a tax credit'.

[8] An important perspective is the subjective retributive approach advanced by Kolber 2009 and other scholars.

will respond differently to claims, and the level of mitigation will vary accordingly. This threatens the principles of parity and proportionality. It may also fail to sufficiently reflect the wrongfulness of the misconduct by state agents, or to deter such actions in the future.

We endorse a more structured approach in which a court applies specific criteria for mitigation. Our model also places limits upon the misconduct which is cited to justify mitigation. This mitigating circumstance should be narrow-tailored. The sentencing hearing should not divert into a bilateral investigation into the relative culpability of both parties. The state is not on trial. An expansive interpretation would shift the censuring vector of the sentencing communication from state-to-offender to offender-to-state. As a result, the sentencing hearing would become a 'trialogue' involving the offender, the state agents and the court. This hearing would engage with broader societal issues, in contrast to the sentencing hearing which focuses on the crime in its communication and dialogue with the offender. The offender is called to account for the offence and should receive a punishment proportionate to the crime. From a culpability-based approach, the scope of the criminal sentencing hearing is limited to the seriousness of the crime. It does not seek to address broad societal problems through sentencing mitigation, unless they are related directly to the individual offender's culpability.

State misconduct is best conceptualised as a specific example of a wider ground for mitigating sentence: diminished culpability – one of the principal components determining the proportionate sentence. This observation highlights the importance of the timing of the misconduct: It excludes misconduct committed after the crime.

The position advocated here may be summarised in the following propositions:

- If the state contributed to the offence, this reduces the offender's culpability and thus justifies mitigation at sentencing. Diminished culpability is a standard mitigating circumstance.
- Clear criteria should guide a court's decision whether to mitigate sentence.
- Some evidentiary burden should be placed upon the defence claiming this form of mitigation.
- From a retributive perspective, state misconduct occurring *after* the crime carries no mitigating value at sentencing; wrongful conduct by state actors does not affect the seriousness of the crime or the culpability of the offender. This leaves utilitarian justifications as the only plausible rationale for misconduct mitigation.
- From an instrumental perspective, we reject vague claims regarding the need to protect the integrity of the criminal justice system or to promote public confidence in justice, unless and until robust empirical evidence demonstrates that mitigating sentence achieves these benefits.
- Mitigating sentence is an inappropriate and ineffective remedy for state misconduct towards the offender which takes place after the crime has occurred.

We see the question of timing as critical. When the wrongful state action follows the crime, it cannot have contributed to the offence and therefore should not affect the sentence imposed. Here we concur with Murphy and Anderson 2014, who discuss what they describe as 'entrapment mitigation'. This refers to mitigation awarded to reflect the fact that law enforcement agents acted in a way which fell short of meeting the test for entrapment, but which nevertheless contributed to, or escalated the offender's illegal acts. If the offender would not have committed the crime without the police actions, there is a case for entrapment. But there are many cases where the police activity merely created the opportunity to commit the offence, which falls short of providing a substantive entrapment defence. These authors argue that courts should mitigate sentence in such cases only where the police actions call into question the extent of the offender's culpability.

Although the principal focus of this chapter is on state misconduct which occurs after the crime, we begin briefly commenting on state misconduct taking place prior to the offence.

II. State Misconduct Occurring Prior to the Offence

The principal justification for state misconduct mitigation relates to the role of the state in relation to the crime. If the state has in some way contributed to the offence, the offender has a colourable claim for a reduced sentence.[9] For example, a visible minority offender subject to repeated and unlawful stop and search may strike out at a police officer. The police misconduct was clearly a contributing factor in the offence. Or a prisoner who had been repeatedly subject to racist abuse and mistreatment in prison subsequently assaults a prison officer after his release. The misconduct reduces his culpability and as such should result in mitigation at sentencing. These claims fall naturally within a broader claim for mitigation on the basis that the offender was not fully culpable. Ryberg (this volume) refers to this as the complicity-based justification for mitigation.

The fact that the state's actions contributed to the crime is analogous to mitigation for any provocation that reduces the offender's culpability.[10] First, when D commits a crime after police provocation through, for example, racist violence, D's actions are not wholly a consequence of his or her 'true' character (Stewart and Freiberg 2008) and 'Actions done in that state do not reflect as badly upon [his or] her settled character as if they had been done whilst calm' (Tadros 2001: 507). Second, when the D commits a crime in such circumstances his or

[9] For discussion of the state's contributory role with respect to the offence see Manikis 2022a.

[10] For example, the Sentencing Council in England and Wales includes in the 'factors indicating lower culpability' 'a greater degree of provocation than normally expected'. See www.sentencingcouncil.org.uk/explanatory-material/magistrates-court/item/aggravating-and-mitigating-factors. The Council does not appear to have considered the issue of state misconduct.

her capacity to refrain from criminal behaviour is impaired either *objectively* (comparing the D's behaviour to a 'morally salient standard') or *subjectively* (considering the D's actual ability to avoid offending). Third, in such a case, D's culpability is reduced as the law recognises the morality of his reasons for committing the crime. These reasons partially justify an inability to exercise self-control (Stewart and Frieberg 2008).

The challenge is to define the kinds of acts or omissions which might legitimately justify mitigation. The sentencing matrix needs limits. These are supplied by a retributive approach: mitigation must reflect the diminished[11] culpability of the offender or the disproportionate impact of the sentence. For example, if the offender is seriously injured by criminal justice professionals while in pre-trial detention in a way that post-conviction imprisonment will be harsher, the prison sentence should be modified accordingly. The proportionate length of sentence has become disproportionate in light of the injuries. But this is a more general claim for mitigation based upon a subjectively calibrated sentence (see Kolber (2009).

A. Limits on the Mitigation[12]

One normative and practical limit is temporal. If as a juvenile D was assaulted by the police, this misconduct cannot plausibly justify mitigation when D is sentenced for a crime committed years later. But at what point does the state misconduct lose its potential to mitigate sentence? This is a matter of debate; there is no magic number. This calculation could be complicated when there has been an extensive history of state misconduct that ultimately triggered a response years later.

The second condition imposes an onus on the defendant to establish a link between the state's misconduct and the crime. In Morris, the Ontario Court of Appeal noted that:

> There must, however, be some connection between the overt and systemic racism identified in the community and the circumstances or events that are said to explain or mitigate the criminal conduct in issue. Racism may have impacted on the offender in a way that bears on the offender's moral culpability for the crime, or it may be relevant in some other way to a determination of the appropriate sentence. Absent some connection, mitigation of sentence based simply on the existence of overt or institutional racism in the community becomes a discount based on the offender's colour.[13]

[11] Would this approach also rule out sentence reductions for a guilty plea? We think not. By entering a guilty plea, a defendant accepts responsibility for the crime and reduces the impact of the crime on the victim who no longer has to testify at a trial. These alone justify the state in expressing less censure for the offence (Roberts and Dagan 2023). However reprehensible, state misconduct which played no role in the offence offers no reason to express less censure for the offence.

[12] Some appellate courts have acknowledged the importance of limits upon state misconduct mitigation. For example, the Alberta Court of Appeal noted that 'a sentence reduction is to be used sparingly, and as a last resort in extraordinary cases.' See *R v Glykis* [38].

[13] *R v Morris* [89]. According to the Sentencing Law in Israel there is a possibility for sentencing mitigation for state misconduct. In this regard the sentencing law distinguishes between two

Such a link demonstrates that the offence does not derive solely from his or her culpable intention, but from other forces. Unless conceded by the state, the legal test would be that associated with any mitigating factor. It would be unreasonable to expect the defendant to have to prove a link beyond a reasonable doubt, but rather to some lower threshold such as a balance of probabilities or an even lower 'air of reality'. Without a link between the misconduct and the crime the mitigation is not based on culpability and could be expanded rather endlessly.[14]

Without some link between the state's offending and that by the defendant, all manner of wrongful actions may be invoked to justify sentence mitigation. Imagine an innocent person wrongfully imprisoned as a result of tampering of evidence by the police. Years after his eventual exoneration, the individual is rightfully convicted of a crime. Should his sentence be mitigated to reflect the state's wrongful actions in convicting him on the first occasion? If so, a wrongful conviction would thus become responsible for a wrongful sentence.

The misconduct must also relate to the specific defendant. Offenders belonging to a community disproportionately targeted by the police or otherwise disadvantaged by state agents may cite this as a 'dirty hands' argument for mitigation. (The lack of standing argument to punish due to 'dirty hands' is discussed later in this chapter.) Sentencing is an individualised exercise. The principal objection to mandatory sentences is that they preclude a court from calibrating the sentence to the specific offence and the individual offender. State misconduct mitigation is subject to the same criticism. Indigenous offenders in Canada, Australia and New Zealand are more likely to have a plausible claim for sentence reductions due to state neglect or overt mistreatment. Such individuals often live in highly impoverished social, educational and economic environments. But the claim in mitigation must relate to the individual being sentenced, and not his community. Put differently, the state's misconduct-based mitigation is not a general entitlement; there is an onus on the offender to demonstrate how it diminished his or her actual culpability for the offence.

A third requirement is that the misconduct must be exceptional in some way, in order to prevent a flood of potentially minor claims. This requirement applies whether the underlying justification is retributive or utilitarian. A sentence reduction should not be awarded for conduct which amounts to no more than unprofessional behaviour by state agents. The misconduct should be considered morally exceptional by criminal law standards to reflect its normative exceptionality.

options based on this crime-related distinction: first, the court determines the deserved sentencing range based on 'circumstances related to the commission of the offence', including among others 'the offender's ability to abstain from committing the act, and his control over his actions, including as a result of provocation' (s 40i(7)); see discussion in Roberts and Gazal-Ayal 2013). In addition, when deciding the appropriate sentence within the deserved sentencing range the court can consider 'circumstances unrelated to the commission of the offence', including among others, the 'the behaviour of the enforcement agencies' (s 40k(9)).

[14] Jurisdictions vary in the legal requirements for establishing mitigating factors (Roberts 2011).

B. Determining the Level of Reduction

There are important practical challenges in determining how much the sentence should be reduced to reflect misconduct by state actors. If the offence warrants a three-year prison sentence, by what quotient should it be reduced? How does a court determine the wrongfulness or harmfulness of the misconduct and then convert this into a sentence reduction? Should the sentence be reduced by the sentence likely to be imposed on the guilty officials? No obvious guiding principle emerges. Some assistance from the appellate courts or a sentencing guidelines authority is necessary. Sentencing guidelines enumerate key aggravating and mitigating factors for courts to apply. To our knowledge no guideline system includes state misconduct as a mitigating factor. Including this circumstance and providing some guidance as to its application would be a useful way of ensuring consistent application. The circumstance would need to be carefully defined and circumscribed.[15]

III. State Misconduct Occurring after the Offence[16]

State misconduct after the crime is a different matter entirely. State officials may act unlawfully in many ways after the offence comes to light. Suspects and defendants may be assaulted at arrest, during interview at the police station, during pre-trial detention by prison officers, or while awaiting trial in the community. Or prosecutors may conceal or withhold exculpatory evidence in violation of their disclosure requirements. None of this misconduct contributed to the offence. As a result, it remains outside a retributive framework. Several rationales have been proposed for mitigating the sentence when the state has acted wrongfully towards the offender:

- As a result of its agents' wrongful acts the state has 'dirty hands' and therefore lacks the full moral standing to punish the offender.

[15] The sentencing guidelines in England and Wales already recognise the relevance of discrimination against minorities as a sentencing factor. For example, the guidelines note that 'Courts should consider that different groups within the criminal justice system have faced multiple disadvantages which may have a bearing on their offending. Such disadvantages include but are not limited to: experience of discrimination.' See Sentencing Council, 'Assault with intent to resist arrest – Sentencing', at www.sentencingcouncil.org.uk/offences/magistrates-court/item/assault-with-intent-to-resist-arrest-2. This guidance seems to suggest that it may be appropriate to mitigate sentence in cases where the offender has experienced discrimination. It is unclear what is meant by the phrase 'have a bearing on their offending', but one reasonable interpretation may be that mitigation is appropriate where the discrimination affected the offender's decision to offend.

[16] In a previous publication we advocated expanding the retributive framework to take into account events occurring after the crime (see Roberts and Dagan 2019). According to this model the state should be responsive to the offender's actions after the crime. Positive actions by the offender diminish the degree of censure appropriate to the crime. The conduct of the state is however out of the frame as misconduct does not diminish the appropriate level of censure.

- State misconduct which harms the defendant constitutes punishment and therefore should be taken into account alongside any court-imposed sanction.
- Mitigating sentence to reflect state misconduct deters criminal justice professionals from violating professional norms.
- Mitigating sentence for state misconduct upholds the integrity of the criminal process and promotes public confidence in the criminal justice system.

A. Lack of Standing to Punish

When its agents have acted unlawfully, has the state lost its standing to punish? It is unclear why wrongful acts by state actors (such as the police) vitiates the state's standing to hold the offender accountable for his crimes. The judgments offer little in the way of justification; the relevance of state wrongdoing to the sentencing exercise is assumed rather than justified (see also Matravers, this volume). For some authors, a lack of standing implies a loss of legitimacy to punish. The concept is woolly.

Why would wrongful acts by the state relieve the offender of any liability for his or her offence? The state's legitimate authority to punish derives from the legitimacy of the criminal law and its fair application – not from the probity of *individual* state agents. If the police retain indecent images following arrest of a suspect for possessing such materials, they are guilty of hypocrisy (see Stark 2024 for a discussion of standing and hypocrisy). By doing so the police officer is demonstrating insufficient commitment to the legal norms which underpin the expression of blame. The state agent demands something from the offender but rejects a similar demand upon him or herself. Culpable state actors fail to recognise that they belong to the same moral community and are thereby answerable to each other. The offender is being treated as if morally inferior to the state agent (see Lippert-Rasmussen 2024: 91, 95–96).

But this does not deprive a court of the standing to impose sentence according to the rule of law. It is the *state*, not the individual judge who is sentencing the offender. As Duff 2005: 400 noted: 'the content of the communication is not "I (the judge, the prison officer, the probation officer) censure your conduct" but "We (the whole community, to which you belong, and by whose laws you are bound) censure your conduct"'. A lawful sentencing provision fairly applied supplies the justification for punishment. The Court can distance itself from the misconduct by police or prosecutors through judicial admonitions of the culpable individuals (see below).

A common criticism of war crimes trials and sentences is that the tribunals sometimes lack the standing to prosecute and punish since the court was established by victorious powers following a war. For example, the sentences of the principal defendants at Nuremberg were criticised by reference to war crimes committed by the Allied belligerents. There may be a claim that these prosecutions reflected a degree of legal hypocrisy, but it would be absurd to mitigate sentence for the Axis combatant who authorised wartime atrocities to reflect an allegation or a finding of war crimes committed by Allied forces. And reducing a sentence for a war crimes conviction by a few years is hardly likely to restore any perceived loss of standing of the tribunal.

Selective prosecution and punishment of war crimes raises another unresolved issue relating to loss of standing. Advocates of the 'loss of standing' also need to explain whether the wrongful acts must relate to the individual defendant. Imagine that the state convicts and punishes two defendants. D1 was treated appropriately; D2 was tortured by police during interrogation. The state has not wronged D1, but it is unable to claim that it has 'clean hands' in its actions. A criminal justice system which tortures defendants surely lacks standing. Should state misconduct mitigate only the sentence imposed on D2? Or should it declare that it lacks the standing to punish D2 while retaining full standing to punish D1? Criticism of the Nuremberg tribunals was not founded on the position that the principal defendants had themselves been wronged by the prosecuting authority.

B. Is the Loss of Standing Full or Partial?

It is unclear who should determine whether the state has lost all or part of its standing to punish. Who should make this determination? If the defence raises an exculpatory claim that the state has no standing to prosecute or punish the defendant, who is to adjudicate the matter?[17] A higher level of court? Is a court required to examine the nature and seriousness of all claims of misconduct and then rule on whether it has lost some, all or none of its standing to hold the offender accountable following a conviction? A higher court has competence to rule on questions of admissibility of evidence or the jurisdiction of the court, but is not authorised to rule on the standing of a lower tribunal.

Ryberg (this volume) addresses the question of whether loss of standing is a binary or continuous variable. If police assault the offender upon arrest, does this extinguish the state's standing to punish wholly or only in part? Surely not the former. What threshold of misconduct would extinguish the state's standing? Does the threshold move according to the seriousness of the crime of which the offender is convicted? That is, might illegal acts by the police vitiate the state's standing to punish relatively minor crimes, but not serious offending? We concur with Ryberg (this volume) that to the extent that the standing to punish may be lost as a result of misconduct, it is a matter of a continuum, from minor to complete loss. As Lippert-Rasmussen argues,

> it is better to adopt a scalar view of standing to blame rather than to think of standing to blame (whatever the degree of blame) as a binary thing … where the standing

[17] It is also unclear how the loss of standing is evidenced in court. The defence can adduce evidence of wrongdoing by state actors, but how does it move from this to demonstrate the court's lack of standing? Call a legal philosopher as an expert witness?

> requirement says that for a certain degree of blaming – say, mild censure – a certain degree of standing – say, not strongly objectionable similar faults – is required (Lippert-Rasmussen 2024: 52–70).

But if standing may be partially lost, on what basis should a court convert a partial loss of standing into partial mitigation? There is no obvious standard to apply.

Nor does there appear to be a methodology for determining the extent to which standing is lost. Assuming the loss of standing is not a binary matter; a sentencing court will have to determine how much to reduce the sentence to reflect the state's misconduct. On one reading, the loss of standing is tied to the seriousness of the misconduct which undermines the standing to punish. Or should there be some proportionality between the seriousness of misconduct and the gravity of the crime?[18] Few would argue that the state has lost the moral standing to impose sentence for murder because the offender was assaulted by police at the time of arrest. These questions need to be resolved if the lack of standing is to serve as a means of justifying mitigation in a criminal court.[19]

Matters are very different for conduct involving individuals. Imagine that A assaults B. Thereafter C assaults D. Person A cannot legitimately censure or punish C because she has no standing to do so, and having committed the same act herself has no standing as an innocent individual. This is the 'let he who is without sin cast the first stone' reasoning. In that Biblical episode, the bystanders' only standing to punish the adulterer sprang from their innocence of similar wrongdoing. They have no institutional authority on which to base their standing to punish. Matters are very different when the state holds offenders accountable.

C. Instrumental Justifications

i. *Mistreatment by State Officials is Part of the Sentence*

Harm inflicted on the offender may be considered part of the sentence – a form of immanent justice or collateral punishment. Some offenders may see no difference between the 'process' and the 'punishment'; both are considered as the 'state' penal intervention.[20] This is then applied to justify reducing the severity of the legal sanction imposed. There are problems of principle and practice with this

[18] Lippert-Rasmussen 2024: 53: 'one's blaming should be proportionate to one's score on standing undermining factors. This is compatible with the view that, in some cases, one has no standing to blame at all, and the view that, in the case of some triplets of blamers, blamees, and blameworthy actions, the blamer has a standing to engage in any degree of blaming of the blamee for the blameworthy act in question. Thus, in a sense, the proportionality view is a threshold view too, but it is a more nuanced threshold view than the simple threshold view.'

[19] See Ryberg (this volume) for the importance of developing theories that are capable of guiding actual practice in the courts.

[20] 'The officer at the street level symbolizes the presence of the Leviathan in the everyday lives of the citizenry'; see Herbert 2008: 171.

position. First, this form of hard treatment is illegitimate. Incorporating it into the sentencing calculus confers some degree of legitimacy – which we would wish to avoid (see below). Second, it is hard to convert the harm sustained by the offender into a portion of a legal sanction. Third, and relatedly, it treats punishment purely as a form of suffering. However, retributivists require that penal suffering be purposefully imposed by a formal legal authority for the proper reasons (see Gray 2010, *cf* Kolber 2009). Some offenders may fail to distinguish between the pain inflicted by the police and that arising from the sentence. Both may be seen as forms of state punishment. This failure to distinguish the two may be understandable, but is misguided from a normative perspective. Offenders, victims and indeed all stakeholders should be encouraged to focus on the court-imposed sentence as the state response to the crime. Only when this occurs will the link between the offence and the punishment be apparent.

ii. Deterring Misconduct by State Agents

It has been argued that mitigating punishment to recognise wrongful acts by its officials encourages compliance with professional codes of conduct. For example, the Supreme Court of Canada noted that: 'provided that the impugned conduct relates to the individual offender, and the circumstances of the offence, the sentencing process includes consideration of society's collective interest in ensuring that law enforcement agents respect the rule of law and the shared values of our society.' *R v Nasogaluak* [49]. The deterrent justification is discussed in the US context in Starr 2009: 1509.

The claim is that criminal justice professionals will be less likely to mistreat suspects, defendants and prisoners if they anticipate that their misconduct may ultimately spare the offender some punishment at sentencing. The justification rests on the implausible assumption that state officials are deterred in this way.[21] Rather than being deterred, they may reason that in light of the uncertain (and possibly lenient) response of the court at sentencing, administering some punishment in advance has merit. The possibility of a criminal prosecution, professional disciplinary proceedings, the potential loss of employment and even the court's recognition of the state's misconduct is likely to be much a more powerful deterrent than the prospect of the offender receiving a discounted sentence.[22] Ultimately, of course, whether state misconduct mitigation serves to deter wrongful acts is an empirical question. To our

[21] A question is also raised with regard to the sentencing court to properly deter such violent police officers in cases of solving serious crimes. See *Gafgen v Germany* [124], where the applicant, charged with murder, disclosed where he had hidden the victim's body after he was threatened by police officers with physical pain. The majority held that the applicant's police investigation had been appropriate, but the police officers' sentence of suspended sentences and fines was 'manifestly disproportionate to a breach of one of the core rights of the Convention' and did not 'have the necessary deterrent effect'.

[22] As acknowledged by Starr 2009: 1527: 'Even more than they fear the sentence reduction itself, Hotshot and Moneybags are likely to fear the professional embarrassment of being found by a court to have committed wrongdoing.'

knowledge there is no direct relevant empirical research on this question. One way of testing the hypothesis would be to measure complaints or findings of misconduct following a well-publicised case in which the offender received a mitigated sentence due to wrongful acts by criminal justice officials.

Is the mitigation awarded to recognise wrongful acts by state officials – whoever they harm – or only misconduct which harms the offender being sentenced? In another Canadian case,[23] the police supplied an illegal drug to the offender. This action was deemed to be reduce the offender's liability for serious drug offences, and he was accordingly awarded mitigation at sentencing. However, Punko's co-defendant received no such mitigation. The difference between the two offenders was that Punko – but not his co-accused – was harmed by the police action because he had been attempting to address his addiction. The court ruled that there had been no adverse effect on the co-accused, hence no mitigation.

The sentencing hearing is not the appropriate means of securing compliance with the law by state officials, especially when the mitigation is awarded long after the misconduct. Finally, considering that many sentences are result of plea bargains – especially those involving law enforcement misconduct – it is unclear how state officials could be condemned through sentencing mitigation in such cases. Caution should, therefore, be exercised before allowing mitigation on this ground.

Other, more appropriate (and effective) mechanisms exist to encourage compliance with the law.[24] The offender can lodge a formal complaint with the professional regulatory authority such as the Independent Office for Police Conduct (IOPC) in England and Wales. Roach 2022: 62 notes that: 'Civil damages against the police can still serve as important marker of injustice'. Defendants can launch individual suits or join class actions. The court can also admonish the state officials responsible for misconduct involving the offender and can direct the prosecution or the regulator to investigate the allegations of wrongdoing.[25]

Allowing judicial disapproval of police or prosecutorial misconduct to mitigate sentence undermines the integrity of the sentencing process. It permits a disproportionately lenient sentence merely to condemn official misconduct. One wrong becomes the trigger for a second injustice.

Sonja Starr 2009: 1565 advocates sentence mitigation because other remedies for prosecutorial (and other) misconduct are ineffective:

> Current remedies for prosecutorial misconduct are strikingly ineffective, largely because courts view them as too costly to grant. Scholars have too often been unrealistic about

[23] *R v Punko*.

[24] If the misconduct involved violating the suspect or defendant's rights prior to trial, the conventional remedy, and the one most likely to deter such wrongdoing is for the court to exclude any inculpatory evidence obtained from those practices.

[25] Murphy and Anderson 2014: 641 conclude that: 'the correct approach is to express judicial censure of law enforcement behaviour through the exclusion of evidence and to recognise the degree of offender culpability through sentencing'.

> this remedial deterrence problem, proposing stronger remedies for misconduct when the more realistic solution might be nominally 'weaker' ones. Adding sentence reduction to current all-or-nothing remedial schemes would help to deter and condemn prosecutorial misconduct.[26]

We reject this view which simply substitutes one injustice (a disproportionate sentence) for another (state misconduct).

D. Ensuring Public Confidence in the Administration of Justice

Perhaps the least convincing rationale for sentence mitigation for misconduct after the crime concerns the general public. It is argued that mitigating sentence in response to wrongful acts by the police or other CJS professionals helps maintain public confidence in the criminal justice system. Again, this too is a claim, not a justification and as such is susceptible of empirical test. Is the awarding of sentence mitigation in such cases really likely to promote public confidence in the judicial process? The claim seems as implausible as the previous ones.

Imagine an empirical test of this hypothesis. Imagine that respondents to a public opinion survey were given a choice between two positions. D is convicted of a serious assault but was himself assaulted by police on arrest. 'Now, should a court: (a) reduce his sentence significantly in recognition of the police misconduct? Or (b) impose the proportionate sentence for the crime and direct the prosecution to investigate the police actions with a view to laying a criminal charge?'[27] It seems unlikely that public would prefer the first option. They may well disapprove of police misconduct and support criminal charges or professional disciplinary action, but would they be happy to see the offender receive a mitigated sentence? The second option seems to be even more implausible from a public confidence perspective in cases of serious offences (eg, sexual or violent crimes) where the public is likely to require deserved punishment regardless of any wrongdoing by criminal justice officials state misconduct. If the offender ultimately benefits from mitigation, the public may also view the state as being complicit causing the victim harm by imposing a mitigated sentence. As with the deterrence claim, this one awaits confirmation by research.

[26] Starr's view ignores a number of points: 1. The reality of plea bargains. 2. That judges focus on the sentencing at the offender not the state official; 3. Sentencing mitigation too can be too costly to grant. 4. Sentencing takes place often years after the misconduct; by which time the police officer can be in another job/promoted meantime. 5. Police officers are never evaluated according to sentences; but per arrests, prosecutions etc. 6. Instead improving police prosecution process it goes to the unrelated approach of offender's mitigation. The is a police-based problem, and not one for a court to address.

[27] A judicial admonition directed at the prosecuting authority is a means to ensure police, prosecutors and others do not violate a defendant's rights. In fact, judges periodically admonish police, prosecutors and other professionals as a means of protecting the integrity of the criminal process.

E. Misconduct by Non-State Agents

Although this chapter focuses on state agent misconduct, the Canadian Supreme Court has also authorised mitigation for wrongful acts by non-state actors. When the Court takes unlawful acts by the state into account at sentencing it inadvertently confers legitimacy on those acts. This becomes particularly problematic in the case of unlawful acts by private citizens. In *Suter*, the defendant had caused the death of an infant through his culpable driving. He was assaulted by bystanders at the crime scene and much later (but before sentencing) seriously wounded by vigilantes. The Canadian Supreme Court approved mitigating sentence in this case on the grounds that Suter's injuries were related to his crime and were therefore appropriately considered at sentencing.[28]

When unlawful acts, defined by the court as 'a brutal act of vigilantes',[29] are folded into the sentencing equation they become part of the lawful sentence, thereby corrupting its integrity and moral standing. State punishment fuses with private vengeance and individual retaliation. Vigilantes may even see the sentence reduction as a form of judicial approval of their actions, in which case it may encourage further acts of vigilantism. Or they may see the state mitigation as an acceptable price to pay for exacting their own wild retribution. The response to one injustice (state misconduct) should not involve a subsequent derogation from justice.[30]

Allowing post-offence misconduct to mitigate sentence blurs the sentencing focus on the offence. The harm experienced by an offender has no affect upon their level of culpability. In short, the principle of proportionality is compromised if all manner of state misconduct after the crime is deployed to reduce sentence.[31] In this respect we concur with Ewing 2019a, who rejects incentivising the state to improve social conditions as a justification for sentence mitigation arising from social adversity.[32]

[28] In *R v Hearns* [20], the court went even further, by noting that 'a sentence may be reduced where it is necessary to denounce state conduct, *or where it is necessary to account for other punitive consequences*, or where the sentence would have a more significant impact on an offender'.

[29] *R v Hearns* [19].

[30] It is always open to a court to exercise mercy at sentencing. The vigilante-inflicted harm sustained by *Suter* was truly exceptional and may well merit an exceptionally merciful sentence from the court.

[31] Although rejected by the court, the Crown's position in this litigation captures the argument well: 'the discretion to reduce a sentence would undermine the principles of proportionality and parity. It would also impermissibly shift the focus of the sentencing process away from the culpability of the offender and the gravity of the offence to the conduct of state officials'. R v Nasogaluak [28].

[32] There is a halfway house position. The court could consider imposing the sentence proportionate to the offence, and then suspend the sentence in whole or in part. The court could calibrate the degree of harm inflicted on the offender applying some living standard analysis, and then suspend the appropriate portion of the sentence. This option is preferable to breaking the proportional model wide open in response to state misconduct. Yet a suspended or partially suspended sentence does not carry the same penal weight as a term of immediate imprisonment and accordingly there will be an inevitable dilution of the proportionality principle. For this reason, we do not endorse the use of suspended sentences in this way.

F. Mistreatment which Affects the Onerousness of the Sentence

Finally, one form of post-offence misconduct should be considered. Defendants detained in pre-trial custody are often subject to adverse treatment which may rise to the level of unlawful acts. The prison service may fail to provide adequate conditions, may permit or facilitate abuse or assaults of various kinds in a way that is demonstrably unlawful (and not merely below declared standards). This form of misconduct is straightforwardly incorporated into the sentencing decision. When a court imposes a sentence of immediate imprisonment it is normal practice to deduct any time served in pre-trial detention. When prison conditions are particularly or unlawfully adverse, courts award enhanced credit for the time served. This simply ensures that the prison sentence served is not disproportionate.[33] This reasoning also justifies mitigation when the state is responsible for an unreasonable delay in bring the case to court.[34]

G. The Crime Victim's Perspective

Padfield (this volume) urges greater attention to the interests of crime victims. Their perspective has largely been overlooked in the discussion of this issue. Mitigation for state misconduct after the offence will likely engender opposition from crime victims who hold the offender accountable and will not welcome a dilution of punishment as a result of the state's actions. Victims may well disapprove of the offender evading full punishment due to police transgressions, particularly if the offence is serious. If an offender convicted of manslaughter or rape receives a much-reduced sentence to reflect the fact that he was assaulted by police while in custody, bereaved relatives of the direct victim are likely to criticise such mitigation. As von Hirsch (2017) has noted, the sentence communicates a message of censure to the offender as well as a message to the victim. To the latter the court is acknowledging that they have been the victim of a criminal wrong, not merely adventitious harm. The stringency of the sentence reflects the court's calibration of the wrongfulness of that harm.[35] Mitigating sentence to reflect the state's mistreatment of the offender disregards the interests of the victim. Finally, the offender's

[33] 'Hardship in serving a jail sentence has always been a proper consideration in crafting an appropriate sentence.' *R v Kandhai* [7].

[34] In *R v Foster and Rex* [31], the English Court of Appeal ruled that 'where there has been an unreasonable delay in proceedings since apprehension which is not the fault of the offender, a court may take this into account by reducing the sentence if this has had a detrimental effect on the offender'.

[35] In one case the Israeli Supreme Court was divided with regard to the degree of reduction for *state* misconduct in a way that implies a similar logic. An offender, convicted for murder, complained that his co-offender had not been indicted at all based on an inappropriate promise to assist the police. Justice Amit held that while this result is disturbing, considering the mandatory life sentence for murder,

level of risk may also be a concern. Reducing sentence to reflect wrongful acts by state agents also disregards the question of risk of reoffending. The offender may receive a mitigated sentence which fails to reflect his true risk of reoffending, and this too may infringe the interests of the crime victim.

IV. Summary and Conclusion

The expanded scrutiny of state agents' treatment of the offender is a welcome development. It recognises the reality that criminal offending is not wholly a consequence of individual decision-making; environmental influences also contribute to the offence. A sentencing court should be alive to all potential sources of legitimate mitigation. Once an individual has contact with the criminal justice system, its officials must comply with the laws which they enforce. If the offender is victimised by state agents or receives unlawful treatment, remedies are necessary. If the state misconduct makes the sentence harsher, the court should mitigate punishment in order to ensure proportionality. But the sentencing process should not be highjacked, and proportionate sentencing abandoned, in order to respond to, or prevent wrongdoing by the state or private citizens. The legitimate response to one wrongful act is not to derogate from a standard of justice, creating another injustice – unless there are powerful countervailing arguments which justify such a derogation.[36]

At sentencing, the court should focus on the individual offender. Unlawful state acts which have no bearing on the offender's level of culpability should remain outside the retributive framework.[37] And nor can the mitigation be justified on utilitarian grounds in order to ensure state compliance with the law or public confidence in the administration of justice.

'it is inappropriate that the appellant would enjoy it and will receive a sentencing "discount", and even more for murder, the most serious crime'. He stressed that 'even if a mistake was made …. we cannot remedy one mistake with another and one injustice with another injustice … as justice for one (the defendant) can cause injustice for others (such as the crime victim or his family' (emphasis in original). In contrast, Justice Barak-Erez held that while the state's misconduct was unintentional, considering its discriminatory result, and the 'feeling of injustice' of the 'individual offender', a mitigation by reducing the conviction from murder (mandatory life sentence at that time) to manslaughter should be offered. *Agbaria v State of Israel*.

[36] Substantial mitigation for offenders who offer testimony against other offenders is an example where an injustice (a less than proportionate sentence) may be justified in order to secure justice through the conviction and punishment of other offenders. There may be examples where such mitigation is necessary to ensure successful prosecution of others. Without the testimony of the co-operating defendant, no additional prosecutions will ensue. Organised crime is one example where prosecutions are sometimes only possible with the testimony of co-operating defendants – who then demand sentence reductions for their co-operation. In the present context, however, the preventive claims are exactly that: mere claims.

[37] A court may always exercise mercy in exceptional cases. For example, Ashworth and Kelly 2023: 182–83 note a judgment in which the court reduced the sentence of a householder who caused grievous harm to the offender who had broken into his home. This case could also fall into the category of mitigation for precipitating acts which reduced the offender's culpability.

7

Sentence Mitigation as a Response to Intrinsic State Injustice

LEO ZAIBERT

In the sadly neglected essay, 'An Eye for an Eye', Simone de Beauvoir explains her refusal to join the noted intellectuals who signed a petition to have the French Government pardon the Nazi collaborationist Robert Brasillach. Not only did she not sign the petition; she vehemently defended the view that Brasillach ought to be executed (as he was). Interestingly, de Beauvoir contrasted her position regarding Brasillach with her abolitionism regarding ordinary criminals. She claimed never to have endorsed the punishment of the latter, because she

> would not have dared demand respect for our lives from those whose misery, whose very birth, place them outside of the human community. Conscious of our privilege, we forbade ourselves to judge them. And we would not have wanted to align ourselves with tribunals that persisted in defending an order we disapproved of (De Beauvoir 2004: 245–46).

French society, in her view, was far too unjust – too *intrinsically* unjust – for her to support its criminal justice system.

De Beauvoir's position is as flawed as it is interesting. The flaw strikes me as obvious: surely some 'ordinary criminals' commit serious wrongs independently of whatever injustices can be attributed to the French – or to any other – government. The fact that a certain government is unjust (or permits injustice, etc) does not seem to provide enough reason for thoroughgoing abolitionism. Unless a given government is systematically and extraordinarily unjust, and similarly systematically itself to blame for crime in general, it seems exaggerated to endorse the view that no particular token crime – regardless of its gravity and its genesis – is ever to be punished. But at a deeper level, and putting aside both utterly unjust societies and complete abolitionism, the relationship between the overall level of justice in general in a society and that society's criminal justice system in particular is complicated and it deserves attention. For this reason (amongst others), I find de Beauvoir's position very interesting. No society I know of is completely just, and thus, even if we distance ourselves from de Beauvoir's radical (albeit evidently selective) abolitionism, the extent to which such social injustice may impact our allegiance to any criminal justice system remains a penetrating question – much more so when the social injustice can be tied to state *misconduct*.

I. Overview

In this chapter, I pursue the distinction between justice in general and justice in particular in three ways. In section II, I discuss the fundamental distinction between distributive justice and retributive justice. A state in which the poor get taxed more than the rich, or the rich have exclusive or even preferential access to basic goods and services, is prima facie unjust. All of these would be instances of *distributive* injustice. *Retributive* justice, in contrast, is not concerned with socioeconomic matters, but with responses to specific human actions: rewarding a particularly meritorious action, or punishing a blameworthy one, are matters of retributive justice. A state can be just in a retributive sense without being just in a distributive sense (and vice versa). In section III, I explore the relation between justice as the name of a particular moral virtue (on a par with other moral virtues, like courage, generosity, etc) and justice as signalling the possession of many individual moral virtues to a high degree. A person who is courageous, generous, just (in the first sense), temperate, etc, is called just in the second sense. Something similar can be said of the state: a state can be just in the narrow sense without being just in the general sense. In section IV, I discuss the tension between the value of justice (in any of its meanings) and the value of mercy (or forgiveness).[1]

States can of course misbehave in myriad ways. Some instances of state misconduct already give rise to specific defences in the criminal law: malicious prosecution, entrapment, evidence tampering, coerced confessions, etc. But states whose criminal justice is stipulated to be free from these vices can also be said to engage in misconduct along distributive justice lines. Some discrepancies between distributive and retributive justice, or between justice the individual virtue and justice the sum of many virtues, or in fact between a zeal to punish disconnected from a certain openness to forgive can also be seen as forms of state misconduct. These are interesting forms of state misconduct that de Beauvoir's position foregrounds. My main goals here are, first, to shed light on forms of state misconduct that are not already well-recognised in the criminal law; second, to suggest that some of them are cases of *intrinsic* injustice; and third, to explore whether sentence mitigation (of individual defendants) can be seen as a proper response to these (usually systemic) forms of injustice.

[1] I use 'mercy' and 'forgiveness' interchangeably.

II. Distributive and Retributive Justice – And their Circumstances

Much has been written by political theorists regarding the so-called 'circumstances of justice'. Rather than on an analysis of justice itself, this more fundamental concern focuses on what may be termed the *preconditions* of such an analysis. As the slogan has it, these are the preconditions that render the very talk of justice 'both possible and necessary'. As with much in contemporary Anglophone political philosophy the *locus classicus* for the idea has become the work of John Rawls, although he himself credits Hume, Hart and others with having searchingly explored the idea (which is not surprising, since the idea has been discussed by many) (Rawls 1999: 109–12). Rawls usefully divides these circumstances into objective and subjective – and amongst the former he focuses on two: a certain 'moderate scarcity' and a certain 'similarity in physical and mental powers'. If goods to be distributed were either massively over-abundant or drastically scarce, there would be no point in schemes of cooperation; if one person were immensely superior to others, she would, likewise, have no incentive for cooperating with others. Subjective circumstances revolve around the idea that we all have (and value) our own life projects. Since our projects can conflict with others', resource allocation affects which projects are likelier to succeed, or even to be attempted.

This admittedly sensible and fruitful investigation has attracted attention mostly – if not only – regarding *distributive* justice. As Rawls himself puts it, by 'justice' he means essentially a scheme for 'human cooperation', or a 'cooperative venture for mutual advantage' (Rawls 1999: 109). It would be a mockery of retributive justice were I to be given an award for being the best footballer in the Premier League, or if someone was served a very severe punishment for a minor infraction, etc. Furthermore, it is plain that doings – either reprehensible or admirable (or indifferent) – can occur both in situations of scarcity and of abundance, in situations in which participants are similarly powerful and in which they are not. Interestingly, while the existence of this other form of justice is hardly ever denied (surely in part because it is in some ways more fundamental than its distributive counterpart), I know of no explicit effort to examine the circumstances of *retributive* justice, in a way similar to the examination of the circumstances of (distributive) justice: what are the preconditions that make retributive justice 'both possible and necessary'? And I think that this contrast between the study of the preconditions of each of these two types of justice is worth some attention.

It may perhaps be tempting to assume that the question of circumstances really is not very useful when applied to retributive justice, since, as I have just suggested, wrongdoing (and with it retributive justice) seems to be possible in all sorts of contexts, not only in those in which distributive justice would have a point. But I wish to resist such (rushed) assumption, for the assumption may be taken to entail that the primordial circumstance of retributive justice is wrongdoing itself. After all, without (wrong)doing retributive justice is not possible – much less necessary.

But if this is so, then the assumption conflates the preconditions for the analysis with the analysis itself: that retributive justice is a response to (perceived) (wrong) doing is a matter of its definition, not of its preconditions.[2]

More substantively, the assumption would also fail if it were taken to entail that insofar as wrongdoing is potentially omnipresent, the talk of preconditions has no role to play at all within the context of retributive justice. Thus, on this interpretation there are *no* preconditions of retributive justice, or no preconditions of retributive justice worth our attention. But this move fails too: that wrongdoing is potentially omnipresent would at best obviate the question concerning the *objective* circumstances of retributive justice. This would still leave open the possibility that the subjective circumstances of retributive justice are as important as those of distributive justice.

I think that they are indeed. But I will not articulate their importance by suggesting that some facts about our psychology make the talk of retributive justice 'both possible and necessary'. This risks smuggling, I think, too much of the 'scheme of cooperation' framework of distributive justice. Retributive justice is not 'necessary' in the same sense in which distributive justice may often be; and retributive justice is 'possible' in ways that are very different, too, from those that render distributive justice 'possible'. Humans are so psychologically constituted that they may yearn for retributive justice absent any cooperative scheme, but it would be odd (and perhaps even unreasonable) to yearn for distribute justice absent any cooperative scheme. An imaginary superhuman, who is astronomically superior to all other humans in every possible way, may indeed have no incentive for cooperating in ways conducive to distributive justice (as Rawls and others have surmised) – but this superhuman may still feel the pull of retributive justice just as much as non-superhumans do.

Endeavouring to lay bare the subjective circumstances of retributive justice is a theoretically risky enterprise. One risk would be to fail to move beyond platitudes: to claim, for example, that a subjective circumstance of justice is that sentient beings exist. This would be as true and as perfectly uninteresting in this context as in the context of distributive justice. Another overly general suggestion would be to say that a circumstance of (distributive) justice is that material things (to be distributed) exist: again, this is true but perfectly uninteresting. Yet another risk would be to simply notice widespread human psychological preferences and uncritically take them as data points without questioning their genesis and continued existence.

Consider an admittedly preliminary sketch of how the talk of 'possible and necessary' so common in the literature on the circumstances of (distributive) justice would play out in the context of retributive justice. Take necessity first. Given the circumstances of distributive justice, it is clear that *society* itself would

[2] For ease of exposition, but also because it is my focus here, I will talk about retributive justice in connection to wrongdoing and not to 'rightdoing', although 'retributive justice' in general covers both good and bad deeds.

be jeopardised absent an attempt to abide by defensible, efficient and rational schemes of cooperation. The necessity invoked here is linked to the (perfectly legitimate) goal of living in (a good) society: distributive justice is necessary for (a good) society, and arguably for the continued, prolonged existence of such (good) society. This does not apply to retributive justice.

The most immediately attractive suggestion as to what would count as a circumstance of retributive justice, it seems to me, is the existence of beings that seek meaning in the world. I hope that it is obvious that being the sort of creature that seeks meaning in the world is different from being sentient: my cat is obviously sentient, but I doubt she seeks meaning in the world. Moreover, while I cannot here fully unpack 'meaning-seeking creature', the concept is not as general – or as inert – as merely being sentient.[3] And this highlights an important difference between distributive and retributive justice: our meaning-seeking nature does not play as prominent a role within the context of distributive justice as it does within the context of retributive justice.[4] Mere sentient beings (ie, those who are not meaning-seeking creatures) can indeed enter into (incipient, tacit, etc) schemes of cooperation – just watch any David Attenborough nature show. But they cannot value retributive justice for its own sake – this is something reserved for rational beings capable of finding and creating *deep* meaning in their worlds.[5]

The sense in which retributive justice is rendered *possible* by its circumstances also seems importantly different from the sense at play in distributive justice. In the latter case, the talk of possibility seems to relate to a certain sense of *having a point*: the phrase 'both possible and necessary' could be replaced with 'sensible' without much loss. Imagine a state of affairs in which every being can, without any effort, procure whatever she needs and wants. Here it may indeed be pointless to care about distributive justice. In fact, there are isolated situations in which we disregard a certain distributive injustice, since our share in that *ex hypothesi* unfair distribution happens to be sufficiently abundant nonetheless. Pointlessness, however, does not entail impossibility, neither does lack of necessity. The circumstances of distributive justice render distributive justice 'possible and necessary' merely in the sense of rendering it important, or useful.

There is no equivalent sense of retributive justice being possible. Distributive justice is necessarily a matter of cooperation; retributive justice is not. When we think that someone has done wrong, and we seek to punish them (or wish that

[3] I have tried to sketch some of what is involved in seeking meaning in Zaibert 2018 and Zaibert 2021.

[4] Alexandra Giannidi, Jesper Ryberg and Anna Schur have, independently, pushed back on this point by insisting that rational beings like us can also seek meaning in schemes of distributive justice, and that deeply unfair schemes of distributive justice can disappoint rational beings as much as deeply unjust retributive justice schemes do. Their point is well taken. But I still believe that rational beings would only (or much more) find intrinsic value in retributive justice, as opposed to distributive justice.

[5] Clutton-Brock and Parker 2013 explore the possibility that animals punish. But their sense of 'punishment' is (appropriately) very thin, and essentially linked to instrumental aggression – aggression to secure dominance, mating partners, etc, but not (it seems to me) to realise the intrinsic goodness of retributive justice.

the state would punish them, etc), we do not *need* to be seeking any cooperation whatsoever. Of course we *may* be doing just that: it may be the case that in order for society to function, some regime of retributive justice must be in place, but this is but one of the possible goals of the criminal justice system. The criminal justice system plainly seeks to attain a plurality of goals, some of which conflict with each other. To restrict the goals that the criminal justice system seeks to attain to those linked to the well-functioning of society is reductive to a fault.

Furthermore, given the sort of complex meaning-seeking creatures that we are, we need not commit to achieving retributive justice on every occasion – though we are committed to achieving it on *some* occasions. Unlike the circumstances of distributive justice, the circumstances of retributive justice do not render it *necessary* in the same way in which moderate scarcity and rough equality of power render distributive justice necessary. Granted, a world with wrongdoing in it but without retributive justice – understood as a type – seems uninspiring; but failing to bring about retributive justice – understood as a token – need not be uninspiring at all.

Thus, the ways in which the two forms of justice can coexist is not immediately obvious. I do not mean to suggest that there is any particular impediment for the two forms of justice coexisting – what I mean is quite literally that the exact nature of the interaction between the two forms of justice is not obvious. To the extent that I am right in seeing retributive justice as not essentially a matter of cooperation, then it is theoretically possible that a particular realisation of retributive justice may be at odds with whatever cooperative goals distributive justice may pursue. In some contexts, of course, the linkages between the two types of justice can be quite close: deterring wrongdoers (or others) from acting wrongly again, or teaching (via punishment) this or that important lesson, etc, may be very closely connected to some of the cooperative goals that one's favoured distributive justice cooperative scheme may seek. But, in some other contexts, the two sorts of goals may diverge.

To deny that the goals of retributive justice and the goals of distributive justice may diverge risks eroding the very difference between these two types of justice. If, say, the only (or main) point of retributive justice were to advance whatever scheme of cooperation distributive justice may recommend, then retributive justice would not really be an independent form of justice, but an appendix to distributive justice after all.[6] If, on the other hand, the only (or main) point of distributive justice were to realise the fit between what people get and what people deserve, this 'distributive' justice scheme may be very problematic. Even those of us who see desert as crucially important within the context of retributive justice, can see the unattractiveness of a system of distributive justice built around the notion of desert.[7]

[6] Under this light some versions of retributivism – say, Herbert Morris's 'unfair advantage' approach – may be revealed as ultimately not about retributive justice after all. See Morris 1958.

[7] Rawls's rejection of the system of natural aristocracy is very helpful here – see Rawls 1999. See also the recent assaults on merit and meritocracy in Markovits 2019 and Sandel 2021.

The connection between this general discussion of the circumstances of justice and the issue of sentence mitigation for state misconduct should have, by now, begun to emerge. Conceding that the main candidate for a circumstance of retributive justice is the fact that we are complex, meaning-seeking creatures makes it easy to understand how odd – not to say morally obtuse – it would be to insist on the attainment of retributive justice within hypothesised deeply (distributively) unjust societies. A deeply (distributively) unjust state that, despite this injustice (to which it has contributed at least in the sense of not correcting it when it may have been incumbent upon it to have done so) zealously sought to realise retributive justice seems worse than hypocritical. And perhaps one way in which the government of this state may seek to avoid this charge of at least hypocrisy – one way, that is, in which it may seek to avoid the disconnect between these two dimensions of justice – is to mitigate sentences. As this volume make abundantly clear, this is a very difficult matter. All sorts of details need to be worked out. But for the state to mitigate on account of its own misconduct is *intrinsically* valuable. It is not just that in and of itself this mitigation sends a message that is salutary to meaning-seeking creatures; it is also that to *some* extent sentence mitigation improves a state of affairs that is in and of itself objectionable to meaning-seeking creatures.

The consideration of what the circumstances of retributive justice may be has led us to focus on the fact that we are complex, meaning-seeking creatures. This in turn has led us to see that creatures like us have prima facie reasons for welcoming modifications to retributive justice resulting from (seemingly unrelated) deficiencies within distributive justice. One such modification would be sentence mitigation – and at least part of its value would be intrinsic.

III. Justice and Other Virtues

In addition to the potential complications arising from the existence of (and the interplay between) the two senses of justice discussed above, ever since Aristotle, the term 'justice' has been notoriously ambiguous in another way. For, as sketched at the outset, we deem 'just' both the person who displays the specific moral virtue of 'giving everyone their due' and the person who displays many individual moral virtues to a high degree. While the person in the latter case a fortiori possesses several virtues in addition to (and perhaps even independently of) the specific virtue of justice, the opposite is not necessarily true: a person can possess the specific virtue of justice without possessing too many of the other virtues.

Something similar holds for the state. In a narrow sense, a state can be said to be just when its criminal justice system functions well. But a state can only be said to be just in the broad sense when *several* aspects of its functioning (distributive justice, healthcare, educational system, migratory system, etc, and *also* its criminal justice system) – work well. And while a state that is just in the broad sense is presumably also just in the narrow sense, the opposite is not necessarily true: a state can be just in the narrow criminal justice sense without being just in the broader sense. The latter case is presumably what de Beauvoir thought of French society.

There is, however, an interesting disanalogy between the personal and the political. That someone can be just in the narrow sense without displaying any of the other virtues (in very high degree, etc) seems odd. Purely in terms of moral psychology, it may seem unrealistic that someone who has developed her character so as to be just (in the narrow sense) at the right times, and in the right ways (etc) would not *also* be generous, and temperate and so on at the right times and in the right ways (etc). In other words, moral conscience, it may be thought, is not likely to be so compartmentalised. It seems too psychologically dissonant for someone to be virtuous only regarding this or that virtue, and not regarding the others: while the specific virtues are evidently different amongst themselves, they nonetheless seem to come together as some sort of (rational) package deal.

I am not sure that I share the scepticism at the root of this view about psychological dissonance – surely we are not always perfectly coherent and perfectly alike in the development of every aspect of our character. Indeed, many of us are virtuous in some ways and not in others. But we can side-step that discussion. For what seems obvious is that in the context of the state, these sorts of discrepancies between different areas of governance can occur without anything resembling psychological dissonance even insinuating itself. In fact, not only are these discrepancies possible: they are quite common. Aspects of the US or UK Governments, for example, are eminently just, while other aspects are scandalously unjust, etc. Similar 'dissonances' can be detected in other countries – now and throughout history.

The disanalogy between the personal and the political cuts even deeper. While it is relatively easy to see how someone can be, say, generous but cowardly, it is much harder to see how someone's generosity could be the *cause* of his cowardice. Within the context of the state things are dramatically different. The state's power and reach are truly awesome, and thus the state can effectively mould certain lives, severely limiting genuine paths and choices. The state, moreover, to a very large extent gets to declare what wrongdoing is (or what the wrongdoing that it deems its business to punish is) to begin with, and what its punishment should be. Finally, and most importantly for current purposes, the state's lack of virtue in this or that dimension – say, concerning distributive justice – is often at least a contributing cause to crime. These ways in which the state and the individual differ render the assessment of the *overall* justice of the state (and not just the internal workings of its criminal justice system) all the more important.

Imagine a case in which a person behaves justly by giving a wrongdoer their due (that is, a case of a person acting justly in the narrow sense). We respect this person's behaviour – or at least we find it justified. Imagine further, however, that this *ex hypothesi* just punisher deliberately created the conditions that gave rise to the wrongdoing, so that she could then administer this punishment 'justly'. We no longer respect this person's behaviour – there is something perverse about it – even if the 'giving their due' bit can perhaps still be isolated and considered 'justified' in a narrow sense. We would not, I think, see this situation – once described more fully – as one in which the person has behaved justly *overall*, even if we stipulate that she behaved justly in the narrow sense.

Admittedly, this case is different from what typically happens in the context of the state, even in the context of a state that misbehaves. While I think that, scandalously, sometimes the state *deliberately* puts people in situations in which it may be very difficult for them no to do wrong, I will leave that possibility aside: the state does not typically deliberately cause people to commit wrongs in order to then 'justly' punish them. Consider a case in which a person gives a wrongdoer their due; that is, she behaves justly in the narrow sense stipulated. But imagine that she non-deliberately contributed to the person behaving wrongly in the first place. I take it that this is more akin to what typically happens regarding actual criminal justice systems. It may be wrong to still claim that this person is perverse or that the infliction of *ex hypothesi* (narrowly) justified punishment is a perversion. But, still, not to take into account that this punisher (justified in a narrow sense) partially contributed to (even if unintentionally) the wrongdoing which she now punishes is a form of self-imposed blindness. We certainly do not respect this person as much as we would have had she had nothing to do with the wrongdoing in the first place. Even if perhaps just in the narrow sense, neither this person nor this state of affairs are just in the broad sense.

Similarly at the level of the state. If the improper functioning of a certain aspect of the state's functioning contributes to someone committing a crime, then this state is simply not just in the broad sense, even if we stipulated that it is just in the narrow sense. If, as is often the case, remedying this improper functioning is itself the responsibility of the state, then our condemnation of that state is even greater. The least that justice (in the broad sense) would demand in terms of ameliorating the situation – both at the level of the personal case and at the level of the state – is that the punishing agent (stipulated to be just in the narrow sense) somehow took into account its own involvement in the occurrence of the wrongdoing.

The relevance of sentence mitigation for state misconduct should by now be downright obvious. When the state's involvement in the occurrence of the crime is deliberate, then its taking this involvement into account may perhaps go as far as refraining from punishment altogether. But when the state's involvement is less than deliberate – less perverse – then its taking its involvement into account may underwrite a downward deviation from what the proportionate punishment may have been (ie, from the punishment that would have been just had the punisher not been involved in the production of the wrong): it may involve mitigating the sentence.

The point of the mitigation here is not related to standing (or legitimacy, authority, moral authority, etc): it is not merely an application of the 'let he who is without sin cast the first stone' line. Such considerations matter.[8] But even if we put those considerations aside, there is something *intrinsically* bad – ranging

[8] As several chapters in this volume – especially chs 5 and 10 – show.

from full perversity to admittedly much less than that – in the state of affairs in which someone who has somehow contributed to the occurrence of a punishable wrong punishes that wrong as if she had had no involvement in it at all. When the punishing agent is normatively involved in the genesis of the crime (even if she did not intend to be involved), there exists – strictly as a matter of justice (both in the broad and the narrow senses) – a prima facie case for punishment to be mitigated.

Part of the problem here is that justice is, of course, not the only thing that matters. There are occasions in which we ought to punish quite severely even if we have been somehow involved in the genesis of the wrongdoing. Imagine a very dangerous criminal out on a rampage and imagine that we are somehow responsible for his having turned out the way he did. Still, society needs this dangerous criminal apprehended and prevented from killing more innocent people. So important is to apprehend him that who does the apprehending, and what her virtues or other moral credentials may pale in comparison. But what is happening here is largely a matter of expedience, of societal risk and threat management – and not, strictly speaking, of justice (or even of *punishment*).[9]

By no means do I wish to deny the pluralism at the heart of both penal theory and the criminal justice system. What I wish to highlight is how, already from the theoretical perspective of justice as such, a case for mitigation regarding state misconduct – even of unintentional state misconduct – is, although admittedly not quite dispositive, surprisingly strong.

Consider one infamous contemporary case of social injustice: the treatment of African Americans in the US. (It takes no great perspicacity to suspect that other groups are also treated unjustly both in the US and elsewhere, but one example suffices for my purposes here.) It is well-known that the Thirteenth Amendment to the United States Constitution abolished slavery and involuntary servitude. Much less known is the fact that this abolition was never *tout court*, for it prominently includes a disgraceful exception: slavery was abolished 'except as punishment for a crime' (US Constitution amendment XIII). In other words, someone could – strictly speaking – still be enslaved in the US, provided that this is a punishment for a crime for which he was duly convicted. The fact that the US's abolition of slavery has never been complete, and that the US continues to explicitly permit slavery as a punishment, even if only 'in the books' and not in terms of real practice is, of course, a scandal. And it speaks volumes as to the US's anachronistic and harsh understanding of wrongdoers, of their rights, and of penal theory itself. The US recognises that committing some crimes may render their perpetrators not merely liable to undergo considerable punishment, but liable to forego the *totality* of their rights, including, a fortiori, all of their human rights.

In *Slavery by Another Name*, Douglas A Blackmon points out:

> Beginning in the late 1860s [on the wake of the passing of the Thirteenth Amendment] and accelerating after the return of white political control in 1877, every southern state

[9] For a fuller explanation, see Zaibert 2018 and Zaibert 2013.

> enacted an array of interlocking laws essentially intended to criminalize black life. Many such laws were struck down in court appeals or through federal interventions, but new statutes embracing the same strictures on black life quickly appeared to replace them (Blackmon 2008: 53).

Blackmon's Pulitzer-winning book amply – and depressingly – documents how these efforts to persevere in enslaving African Americans continued, with remarkable 'success', long after slavery was 'abolished'. While, as its title suggests, Blackmon's book documents developments until the Second World War, these practices have continued.[10] Michelle Alexander's term to refer to African Americans in the U today as a 'racial undercaste' is not an exaggeration (Alexander 2012: 17). The sheer demographic composition of the US's bloated prison population today – where African Americans are extraordinarily over-represented – serves as a shameful reminder of the persistence of the problem. The social injustice that renders African Americans in the US an undercaste, that renders them much more likely to commit crimes than members of other groups, and that in fact contributes to keep some of them de facto *enslaved* should not be morally inert.

One could react to the US's reprehensible treatment of African Americans in at least two importantly different ways. One could claim, plausibly, that this treatment casts doubt on the US's standing (or authority, or legitimacy, etc) to punish members of a segment of the population it has so consistently mistreated throughout history. Again, I have nothing against this perfectly legitimate reaction. But one could also register the *intrinsic* injustice of this punishment. This is also a perfectly legitimate reaction – and it is the one on which I focus here. Both reactions need to be alive to the considerations that stem from pluralism: just as de Beauvoir favored Brasillach's execution despite what she saw as a profoundly unfair French legal system, there may be an African American serial killer who poses serious risk to innocent members of society who simply needs apprehending, independently of both matters of standing and matters related to intrinsic injustice. Reasons for mitigation may, of course, be outweighed – as in these two cases. Nonetheless, the independent prima facie reasons for mitigation exist there before they are (sometimes) defeated by other considerations.

IV. Mercy and Mitigation: Moving beyond Reasons of Justice

Let us take stock. Thus far we have seen how both the tension between retributive justice and distributive justice and the tension between justice understood as an individual virtue or as the sum of many virtues create theoretical space for thinking

[10] An inmate in an Alabama prison (serving a life sentence for involvement in a murder committed when he was 14) was denied the right to read Blackmon's book, insofar as the prison's authorities considered the book an incitement to violence. See Robertson 2011 and Washington Post Editorial Board 2011.

about sentence mitigation as a possible response for state misconduct. I now want to turn our attention to a much more fundamental tension, and suggest that it, too, is amenable to creating space for sentence mitigation for state misconduct. This is the tension between punishment and its merciful remission. This more fundamental problem was, during periods of human history, *the* central problem concerning proper responses to wrongdoing, whether the responses were those of ordinary people, rulers or deities. In fact, this was Seneca's central worry as he sought to instruct Nero on the craft of governance (Seneca 1995). It was also one of Anselm's main preoccupations in his *Proslogion*, which although much better known for its championing the ontological argument for the existence of God, another (much less discussed) key topic therein is the complicated relationship between God's justice and God's mercy (Anselm 2007). For reasons I cannot address here, the Enlightenment brought with it a certain dismissive attitude regarding mercy, but attuned to the Enlightenment's ethos, contemporary penal theory tends to be inimical to the role that mercy may play in our thinking about punishment.[11]

A central worry is that mercy appears hard to institutionalise: it is hard to fit it within the strictures of government functions. For example, to the extent that mercy shares the phenomenology of gifts, it seems to fly in the face of the sort of procedural justice – the sacrosanct Enlightenment principle of treating like cases alike – that is taken to be a crucial element of the rule of law. Just as a gift-giver gives gifts whenever she wants (for if she were 'required to gift', then she would no longer be gifting), someone granting mercy does it whenever she wants. And the setting of a modern courtroom seems inimical to this sort of freedom. Mercy, in other words, seems to leave too much to the *discretion* of whoever grants it.

I admit that this is a problem. And although I have elsewhere attempted to show that it is less of a problem than customarily assumed, I do not have a solution for it. But the fact that it is a problem does not license us to simply ignore that mercy exists. In fact, very few people deny that to act mercifully is sometimes the right thing to do; very few people deny that merciful acts can be virtuous. The standard position, however, is that, despite mercy's goodness, it just does not belong in the criminal justice system. But if it is granted that mercy is sometimes admirable – sometimes contributing to justice in the broad sense – then why not grant that it may sometimes play a role within the criminal justice system? It is not that mercy would be the only occasion for discretion within the criminal justice system.

A related problem with mercy – perhaps the most famous problem – is that it seems very difficult to explain what reason we could possibly adduce for ever granting it. This is because if there were good reasons to treat a wrongdoer with more leniency than initially suspected, then these would be the sort of reasons that – necessarily – are already countenanced by the discussion of justice, by the usual arguments and defences of the criminal law. So, if I do something wrong,

[11] See Bull 2019, Tuckness and Parrish 2014, Campagna 2023, Zaibert 2024.

but the state later discovers that I was acting under duress, or that I had a justification, or that my judgement may have been impaired because I was afflicted by immense sorrow, etc, then the state will likely punish me less severely than in the standard case (in which these circumstances do not obtain). But there would be nothing *merciful* about doing that: this is exactly what *justice* would demand. Mercy, however, is supposed to only come into play – if ever – *after* the considerations pertaining justice play themselves out. But those considerations of justice offer all the reasons we may need, or, in fact, that can possibly exist.

A similar sort of scepticism concerns the idea of sentence mitigation for state misconduct. Either the misconduct is already covered by garden-variety criminal law defences against prosecutorial misconduct, entrapment, evidence-tampering, etc, or we end up with too diffuse and unmanageable a notion of mitigation. I think that such scepticism is overdone. Granted, the alleged reasons of mercy which are not reasons of justice are indeed elusive (hence the tendency to 'reduce' mercy to something else more at home in the realm of justice, such as equity).[12] But that they may be elusive does not entail that they do not exist. Unless you belong to that very small minority of thinkers who deny that merciful acts are ever justified or admirable, you should be able to identify reasons in those cases in which you grant that mercy is indeed justified or admirable. Of course, perhaps you also believe that such cases never obtain within the context of criminal justice, but that is a different matter: the fact that there are cases of mercy that you find justified or admirable is enough to show that there are reasons for mercy that do not belong within the realm of justice – *mutatis mutandis* for cases of sentence mitigation for state misconduct not already covered by criminal law defences.

Once again, concrete examples may help. I offer two, neither one directly connected to state misconduct, or even to mercy as such, but rather to leniency/generosity, and to the elusive types of reasons that we may mobilise as we think about mercy and about sentence mitigation for state misconduct. I choose these examples because they are helpful in pointing to that liminal space where the reasons for mercy live – and where some of the reasons for sentence mitigation for state misconduct (of the sort not already covered by established defences in the criminal law) may live too.

The first example is of an experience I had when teaching an evening mega-course on 'Introduction to Philosophy'. I had a student who sat on the front row, and who essentially spent the entire term – class after class – sound asleep. Not surprisingly, she failed the class. The following year, as I was teaching another iteration of the course, I saw the same student again sitting on the front row. I then informed her that she had already taken this class (and failed) – to which she replied that she knew, but that she was planning on doing better this time. As it turned out, she did remarkably better: she was the best score (amongst more than 100 students) in the multiple-choice mid-term exam, and also in the final exam.

[12] See Nussbaum 1993; for illuminating criticism see Tasioulas 2003.

She really tried very hard, visiting me frequently during office hours to discuss philosophy and to seek help with her term paper. I was in awe of her commitment, her rigorous mind, and how much she was learning. During these many visits I learned a lot of her life: she was a single mother, mightily struggling to make ends meet and to support her three young children; she was raised by a destitute single mother herself; she had always lived in very dangerous neighbourhoods, etc. She worked as a nurse; during the term in which she first took my course, she came to class immediately after working a rather brutal many-hours stint at her hospital – no wonder she was sleepy. Despite her remarkable mind, writing did not come easy to her. As much as we worked on her term paper, in the end she produced a one-page 'paper'; this was much shorter than required, and not very good. Since the term-paper constituted 40 per cent of the mark, technically speaking, she deserved a failing mark again. But it seemed clearly wrong for me to give her the same failing mark as the year before. So, I gave her a very high mark – the second highest mark possible.

When I shared this story with other students (at a different institution), their reaction was rather uniform. The majority commented that I should have failed this student; several students quipped (in a smart-alecky way) that they too had problems, and that I should make sure that I bump up their marks accordingly.[13] Their tacit invocation of the treating like cases alike principle did not move me. In any case, I stand by my decision. The point I wish to highlight with this story is that, clearly, there was no reason of justice that generated an obligation to be extra lenient with this student. The fact that I treated this student the way I did, does not commit me to treating similar students in similar ways.

The suite of reasons connected to this student's personal circumstances, socio-economic background, and so on may not all belong to the usual reasons of justice: the student was clearly not *entitled* to – or *deserving* of – my extra leniency. And yet it is *possible* that my decision was correct, and that it was supported by reasons. These reasons strike me as akin to reasons of mercy (even though this may not be a proper case of mercy, since it is unclear what the wrongdoing was, if anything) and to the reasons for sentence mitigation in the context of non-intentional state misconduct. (If the misconduct is intentional, then reasons of justice may be enough.)

The second example concerns Gary Watson's insightful reflections on the case of Robert Alton Harris. Watson's article revolves around the life of this ruthless offender, who was despised (and feared) even by his hard-boiled companions on death row. Although Watson describes the horror of Harris's crimes in hair-raising detail, he also describes the remarkably miserable and brutal existence Harris had had ever since the moment he was born. Watson not only grew up in an utterly

[13] One student suggested that I should have given this student the highest mark, not the second highest. Interestingly, this was the only student whose socio-economic background resembled that of the protagonist in the story.

dysfunctional home, and saw mostly violence, cruelty and ugliness all around him, but he was himself abused and indeed hated since he was a toddler. Watson's goal is not to exculpate (or excuse, or justify, etc) Harris, but to compel us to see the whole story of his life. This story 'forces us to see him as a *victim*' as well as a wrong-doer (Watson 2004: 227). The fact that someone – even someone who committed extraordinarily grave crimes – can himself be seen as a victim of terrible circumstances and upbringing should not be morally inert: it matters. Now, how exactly it matters is a very complicated question, but it is a question that commands our attention.

The main purpose of these examples is to signal to another entry point into the discussion of social injustice and state misconduct – and into the role that sentence mitigation may play therein. If someone belongs, say, to a group that has been systematically discriminated against, whose members are customarily denied opportunities that are commonly available to members of other (dominant) groups, this fact should not be morally inert: it, too, matters. Again, we do not know exactly how it matters, but it better matter somehow. This is admittedly vague – but it already highlights the intrinsic appeal of sentence mitigation for forms of state misconduct not already (fully) recognised by the criminal law. The alternative is to give up the search for a fully morally defensible way of dealing with these admittedly very difficult problems. The alternative entails, to echo Watson's perceptive way of putting it, interacting with the world around us from an overly 'detached and austerely objective standpoint' (Watson 2004: 227).

Consider a contrasting example. In his (partial) dissent to the landmark *Lockett* decision – which allowed for expansive consideration of mitigating circumstances *in capital cases* – Justice Rehnquist claimed that the decision fails to offer a 'coherent doctrine' of mitigation, and that it 'completely sacrifices' 'reasonable predictability'. He further bemoaned that the decision would force judges and juries to 'receive in evidence [for mitigation] whatever the defense attorney wants them to hear' (*Lockett v Ohio* [629]). And he approvingly cites another United States Supreme Court decision in which it is asserted that the law 'does not guarantee trial procedures that are the best of all worlds, or that accord with the most enlightened ideas of students of the infant science of criminology, or even those that measure up to the individual predilections of members of this Court'. What the law does require is 'no more than that trials be fairly conducted and that guaranteed of defendant be scrupulously respected' (ibid [632]–[633]). Rehnquit's position strikes me as problematically austere. (It is worth noting that Lockett involved a defendant – an African American woman – convicted to death for a homicide she did not commit nor intended to commit.)

How could the fact that, in the second decade of the twenty-first century, slavery-as-a-punishment is still permitted by the United States Constitution *not* be part of the discussion of how to achieve retributive justice?[14] There better be,

[14] It is hard not to be reminded of Leonard Cohen's lamentation 'Everybody knows the deal is rotten; Old Black Joe's still picking cotton; For your ribbons and bows' (Cohen 1988).

within the broad discussion of justice as a whole, theoretical space for taking matters relating to social injustice into account. The ways in which the US continues to treat African Americans is but one example (albeit a particularly depressing one). The fact that slavery-as-a-punishment is still permitted in the US should at least be *part* of the conversation amongst specialists. And it belongs there even if *some* of the reasons that may underwrite this or that sentence mitigation for this or that defendant turns out to be not wholly based in diaphanous 'reasons of justice'. To close ourselves off to these considerations is to embrace the uninspiring austerity of which Watson speaks, which Rehnquist exemplifies, and which clings to a reductive understanding of the demands of justice.

It goes without saying that the vast majority of African Americans in the US do not commit crimes – just as it goes without saying that the vast majority of people who suffered horrible upbringings do not commit the crimes Harris committed. And it may appear as if these undeniable facts would bolster the view that it cannot be an excuse (much less a justification) for Susan to claim that she belongs to this or that state-disadvantaged group if Linda and many others who also belong to the same group do not commit the wrongs that Susan committed. But the fact that someone similarly situated – or even the majority of those similarly situated – would not do wrong, does not quite warrant the conclusion that social injustice (or awful upbringings, etc) or state misconduct are *irrelevant*. That a fact does not quite fit one of the standard, enumerated, defences of the criminal law is insufficient, I think, for concluding that this fact is of no concern whatsoever. Surely *some* ameliorative state responses – including sentence mitigation – vis-à-vis particularly egregious forms of state misconduct may be underwritten by garden-variety 'reasons of justice'. Just as clearly, however, other ameliorative responses require creatively exploring those more elusive reasons that are foregrounded when we reflect on the tension between justice and mercy, or about the disconnects between different senses of justice.

V. Conclusion

There is at least one commonality amongst the focus of the preceding three sections. Rather than idle exercises in theoretical boundary allocation, each of the sections offers an unusual vantage point for thinking about sentence mitigation for state misconduct. Furthermore, each suggests prima facie reasons for the normative defensibility of sentence mitigation for state misconduct. Admittedly, these reasons are not always the usual 'reasons of justice' typically (and appropriately) at play in the context of criminal justice. But they are reasons, nonetheless. Finally, the reasons that have been sketched above all point to the (prima facie) *intrinsic* desirability of sentence mitigation in connection to state misconduct. In my reading of de Beauvoir, she saw something intrinsically bad about punishing ordinary criminals in France, and she saw something intrinsically good about executing

Brasillach. Independently of de Beauvoir, the discussion above leads me to suggest that there is something intrinsically good about sentence mitigation in the face of state misconduct.

My emphasis on this intrinsic goodness is not meant to deny the importance of other, consequentialist rationales for (or against) sentence mitigation – but it is indeed meant to highlight that already at such an abstract level of reflection sentence mitigation for state misconduct appears attractive. The details as to the exact type of crime and the exact type of misconduct (and the relationship between these two) at play in any given case would of course matter considerably. Surely the final case for mitigation will be stronger when the crime is directly caused by – or directly responsive to – the misconduct, or when the misconduct directly affects the specific defendant in question. Surely comprehensive solutions to some forms of state misconduct involve structural change in policies and institutions rather than sentence mitigation. But even when the connections between the misconduct and the crime may be indirect or diffuse, and even when mitigation cannot plausible be seen as a solution to the problem of state misconduct, the force of the intrinsic reasons I have identified here would remain. These reasons may not always (or even frequently) prevail, but they will always matter – and even when they do not prevail, their importance will not thereby disappear.

8

Sentence Mitigation for Unjustly Disadvantaged Offenders: Some Hard Questions

RICHARD L LIPPKE

The fact that a disproportionate number of the people who are arrested, convicted and punished for crimes are poor, and sometimes desperately so, has long troubled scholars who write about the criminal law and its enforcement.[1] It might be that the crimes of the socially deprived are easier to detect or that the authorities invest more of their resources in policing and prosecuting them (Stuntz 1998). In that case, the poor who commit crimes are disproportionately arrested, prosecuted and punished, even if better-off citizens commit perhaps as many, if not more, crimes as members of society who struggle to survive and flourish. Such enforcement practices would seem in conflict with societal commitments to equal treatment by and before the law. Yet many who have examined the issues point to another and seemingly more profound problem with the high number of socially disadvantaged persons who cycle through the criminal justice system. They argue that severe forms of poverty and social exclusion are criminogenic and thus that societies marked by them are, in effect, pushing their least well-off members towards wayward lives that will, more or less inevitably, result in their coming into contact with the criminal justice system. A variety of explanations of the ways in which social disadvantage produces criminal offending have been advanced by scholars.[2] These explanations are typically combined with the assumption that such deprivation is unjust and that such injustice is a wrong perpetrated by state officials, or the polity on whose behalf they act. If all of this is correct, the question that follows is what should be done about it.

The obvious solution would appear to be that societies marked by unjust disadvantages ought to undertake measures to substantially reduce, if not eliminate them. Only by doing so will they create social orders in which all citizens are

[1] See, among others, Murphy 1973; Bazelon 1976; Morse 1976 and 1998; Duff 2001; Tadros 2009; Lippke 2011 and 2014; Bagaric 2015; and Ewing 2018, 2023 and this volume.
[2] For an especially useful discussion of recent attempts to do so, see Ewing 2018.

given fair opportunities to pursue their chosen aims and interests without being tempted, or so strongly tempted, to commit crimes. The problem with this obvious solution is that it is apparently not in the offing in many existing societies, ones in which there is little widespread or deep societal commitment to addressing the problems raised by social and political inequality, higher rates of crime by the least well-off among them.[3] A number of scholars who write about the problems posed by unjust social deprivation for the legal punishment of offenders implicitly recognise this lack of commitment and thus propose an alternative, one that consists of having judges consider unjust social deprivation as a mitigating factor as they determine the sentences to be meted out to those convicted of crimes (Morse 1998, Lippke 2014, Bagaric 2015 and Ewing 2023). If the state treats some of its citizens wrongly by not ensuring that they have genuine opportunities for decent, responsible lives, then its officials should acknowledge this and reduce the criminal sentences imposed on the affected members of society. I believe it is fair to say that this alternative has more often been proposed without being explored carefully. My aim in this chapter is to take it seriously and raise a variety of difficult questions that would have to be addressed if we were to go forward with such a proposal. In doing so, I will mostly assume that unjust social disadvantage is linked to higher rates of criminal offending without trying to explain why that is. My primary focus will be on how sentence mitigation might be implemented.

I. Overview

In section II, I discuss what I believe is an odd, if not paradoxical, feature of the proposal to have sentencing judges weigh unjust social disadvantage in determining the sentences of offenders. Again, the context, we should presume, is this: we are considering societies in which some members are wrongly disadvantaged but also ones in which there seems little recognition of that wrong or a commitment, on the part of most citizens and either elected or appointed public officials, to do much about reducing or eliminating it. In such a context, would not sentencing judges either be puzzled by or resistant to suggestions that they should reduce the sentences assigned to the relevant offenders? After all, the broader society in which they operate is not, apparently, moved by the plight of the unjustly disadvantaged to do anything more systemic about it. Even if some judges were tempted to mitigate the sentences of the unjustly disadvantaged, they might reasonably wonder whether they would be acting appropriately (ie within the law) by doing so. Would they not, in effect, be imposing their idiosyncratic views on the majority of their fellow citizens who are sceptical about or actively opposed to those views?

[3] Some scholars also question whether the state has the moral authority to punish those to whom it fails to provide decent lives. See Duff 2001; Tadros 2009; and Duus-Otterstrom and Kelly 2019. I shall ignore this line of argument in my discussion.

In section III, I discuss some of the challenges posed by operationalising sentence mitigation for unjustly disadvantaged offenders. For instance, how would we determine who is eligible for the mitigation? One possibility is that we might make eligibility depend on the income level of an offender's family of origin. But would differences in socially deprived family incomes be taken into account, such that those who came from comparatively poorer families would be eligible for more sentence mitigation? Or would the number of dependents in a socially deprived family unit be factored into eligibility decisions? Further, there are questions about how substantial such sentence mitigation should be and whether it should be weighed in determining sentences for all crimes of which individuals have been convicted or only some of them. There is unease in the literature about extending sentence mitigation to individuals who have been convicted of serious crimes, especially ones inflicting violence, injury or death upon their victims (Duff 2001: 199; Bagaric 2015: 37–39; Bergelson (this volume, 45)). But how do we make sense of excluding socially deprived offenders who commit such crimes from receiving mitigation? Finally, what should we make of the fact that many socially deprived individuals do not commit crimes at all or very often, and certainly not very serious ones (Bagaric 2015: 12)? Is it social deprivation alone that is criminogenic? Or is it, perhaps, social deprivation combined with other factors (eg, youthfulness) that is criminogenic?

In section IV, I raise and discuss questions about how unjust disadvantage should be weighed in determining sentences for the crimes of which individuals have been convicted. Is such mitigation supposed to be conceived as one mitigating factor among many other factors that might be taken into account by sentencing judges, including aggravating ones? If so, might not even severe social disadvantage in an offender's life be outweighed by the aggravating factors of his or her crimes? Or should we conceive of social deprivation as grounds for a kind of exceptional sentence mitigation, one that comes into play only once all of the other mitigating and aggravating factors of an offender's criminal misconduct have been weighed and a presumptive sentence has been determined? And how would we make sense of such an elevated mitigation status?

In section V, questions concerning the duration of the proposed sentence mitigation for socially disadvantaged offenders are examined. Should such offenders continue to receive mitigation if they persist in offending? It might be argued that the unjustly disadvantaged should not receive recidivist premiums when they persist in offending, since they have already endured enough burdens in their lives from state failures to address the systemic problems that precipitated their criminal misconduct. Perhaps so, but might they not progressively lose their claims to sentence mitigation if they continue to offend (Wasik and von Hirsch 1995)?

I conclude that the many challenges posed by sentence mitigation for unjustly disadvantaged offenders ought to leave us somewhat sceptical about it as a remedy for state failures to do what it really ought to do about endemic poverty and social exclusion in society. Some form of sentence mitigation for the socially disadvantaged might be defensible, but the far more sensible approach, all things considered, would be to work towards achieving and acting upon a broader societal consensus about social and economic equality and its necessary conditions. We might also work to make criminal sanctions – imprisonment foremost among them – less damaging to individuals' life prospects and reduce the other burdens imposed on individuals who have fully served the sentences for their crimes (Matravers, this volume).

II. The Viewpoint Problem

It seems fair to say that proposals to implement sentence mitigation for unjustly disadvantaged offenders are mostly made by scholars of the criminal justice system, or the legal system more broadly, who embrace forms of welfare liberalism or egalitarianism.[4] Welfare liberals and egalitarians are a diverse lot, but in general they endorse fairly robust social welfare measures that would not only provide all individuals with decent starts to their lives (ensured by the provision of adequate nutrition, housing, healthcare and education) but also (at least typically) some floor below which they would not be allowed to fall due to bad luck or even their own bad choices. Theorists in these two camps also endorse state measures to keep social and economic inequalities in check, although some urge more robust measures of these kinds than others. When those who embrace these kinds of state social welfare and equality-preserving measures examine societies that leave a subset of their citizens struggling mightily to provide for their own basic needs, they are not surprised to find that some of them resort to criminal offending not only to make ends meet, but also because they feel alienated from or resentful towards the social order that seems indifferent to their life prospects. Sensing, perhaps, that such social orders will do little to rectify the criminogenic conditions which they wrongly tolerate, or worse, encourage, it is natural for theorists who worry about unjust social disadvantage to propose that something be done at the sentencing of those marginalised by the prevailing social order to recognise or compensate them for the ways in which the state has wronged them. This is where a paradox, or at least a tension, rears its head in these scholarly accounts.

In many, if not most, of the societies that fall well short of the ideals to which welfare liberal or egalitarians subscribe, there is unlikely to be a society-wide consensus in support of those ideals (von Hirsch and Ashworth 2005: 72). Indeed, there might be more of a consensus in support of libertarian or neoliberal ideals that tend to place more emphasis on individuals fending for themselves when it comes to meeting their basic needs and supporting their families (Nozick 1974, Narveson 1988 and Barnett 1998). Granted, theorists who eschew state social welfare measures might admit that there are other kinds of state wrongs that

[4] Representatives of the former camp include Rawls 1971; Ackerman 1980; and Dworkin 2000. Representatives of the latter camp include Sen 1992; Anderson 1999; and Cohen 2008.

judges should take into account as they sentence those convicted of crimes. For instance, suppose that the state has wrongly confiscated the property of individuals who, in their resultant desperation to survive, resort to minor forms of criminal offending. Or suppose that the state refuses to accord some citizens property rights at all or only very dilute forms of them. Libertarians or neoliberals might concur with proposals to mitigate the sentences of such citizens when they commit and are convicted of crimes, in recognition of the ways in which their lives are made difficult by their limited abilities to acquire and enjoy property. But such theorists are likely to balk at proposals to reduce the sentences of less well-off individuals in the absence of what they regard as state wrongs against them. And state officials in some existing societies are apt to concur with libertarian or neoliberal assumptions about the nature of the just society, ones that give little weight to the promotion of robust social welfare measures. Even if such officials are sympathetic to state efforts to reduce unjust disadvantage, they likely cannot be understood as authorised to support and uphold public commitments to doing so, for such commitments do not seem to exist within the relevant polities.[5] After all, if such commitments exist, why is the body politic not insisting that efforts be undertaken to reduce social deprivation, rather than waiting for its criminogenic effects to take hold and precipitate crime? Perhaps liberal and egalitarian scholars should be understood as encouraging state officials, and in particular sentencing judges, to act in defiance of the prevailing norms of the societies in question and reduce the sentences of offenders whose lives have been marked by societal neglect and injustice. But not only would such officials have dubious authority to do so in otherwise democratic societies, they would likely incur criticism from other state officials and members of the public. Their acting in defiance of broader social and political norms might spur efforts to either bring them back into line with prevailing ideologies or have them removed from office. Moreover, if state officials were, somewhat miraculously, inclined to forge ahead with such contrarian (to the public) sentencing policies, one wonders why they would not at least try to do more to get at the root of the problem, so to speak, which would involve acting summarily to reduce unjust social disadvantage at its source.

Things would be different if scholars of the criminal justice system pointed to injustices within the system that a given society's operative political ideals seem to effectively condemn. For instance, suppose that police and prosecutors routinely arrest and prosecute crimes by the poor while largely ignoring similar or worse crimes committed by the better-off. Assuming that a commitment to equal treatment by and before the law is a value of the relevant political order, scholars could point to unequal treatment of some citizens and plausibly insist that it is a wrong that should be rectified. Such a critique would appeal to values 'internal' to the relevant society and its political order, and so might have some traction with the

[5] As Bergelson (this volume, 45) notes, mitigation based on social deprivation is not recognised in the US legal system.

public and with state officials authorised to act on its behalf. Proposals by welfare liberals and egalitarians that sentencing judges act to mitigate the burdens of legal punishment because society has failed some of its members are different. Such proposals derive from external and somewhat alien normative political ideals and thus are likely to fall on deaf or sceptical ears in social orders in which there is little commitment to social and economic equality, or even to maintaining a welfare floor below which no one in society should be allowed to fall (Matravers, this volume).

III. Eligibility for and Magnitude of Sentence Mitigation

Suppose that we set to one side the paradoxical character of calls to mitigate the sentences of the wrongly disadvantaged in social orders that seem largely indifferent to such wrongs or their effects. If we are determined to go forward with sentence mitigation, we will have to address an assortment of questions, the first of which concerns how to determine who would be eligible for it. Unjust social disadvantaged might seem to be one of those 'you know it when you see it' phenomena, but something as vague and subjective as this will not work for the purposes of sentencing. Judges must be given some criteria with which to work in sorting out which of the convicted who appear before them should be given special consideration because of their backgrounds or living circumstances, and which should not. It is natural to focus on such things as the income of those convicted, or perhaps of their families if they are still living with them, the kinds of neighbourhoods in which they grew up and continue to reside, the quality of the educational opportunities afforded them, the jobs, if any, available to them, and their access, if any, to mental healthcare, if that is something they need. We should probably add to the preceding evidence concerning the existence of forms of racial, ethnic, gender or religious bias that can not only limit the options of individuals but also leave them feeling dispirited about their life prospects and resentful towards the larger social order. Still, listing these factors is one thing; defining and refining them so that they can sensibly be used by sentencing judges is another. Also, the existence of such negative influences in the lives of individuals need not be due to state wrongs. People can find themselves in difficult life circumstances, ones that might incline them to commit crimes to escape them, for a variety of reasons – their own or others' previous bad choices among them. Suppose an offender about to be sentenced grew up in a social order that provided for everyone's basic welfare needs at fairly substantial levels, but the offender's parents frittered away the state income support by gambling, using drugs or engaging in conspicuous consumption. Should the resulting hard early life of such an individual make him eligible for sentence mitigation premised upon the existence of state wrongs? It would seem not.

Even if we focus on one of the factors that would seem to determine whether individuals about to be sentenced for their crimes should be eligible for mitigation – the income of their families of origin, for instance – there will be complications to address. Would the cost of living in the area in which the offender resides or grew up need to be taken into account? Seemingly, it might, since such costs can vary widely, and what might be an adequate individual or family income in one area could be quite inadequate in another. Would the number of individuals dependent upon the earnings of parents or other caregivers in offenders' families of origin be taken in account? Again, it might seem that it should, since the more dependents there were, the greater the challenges faced by those who tried to provide for them. An adequate income for three or four members of a household might be considerably less than adequate for a household with seven or eight members. And what if an offender grew up in an impoverished neighborhood but with parents or caregivers who provided a stable, nurturing environment sustained by better than average (for the area) collective income? Should such an offender be deemed less eligible for mitigation at sentencing? Last but not least, how would we have sentencing judges treat offenders who otherwise satisfy whatever criteria they are to employ in allocating mitigation but who are, at least in part, disadvantaged because they (or perhaps their parents) entered the country illegally? The problem such cases raise is that it might seem less clear whether it is state wrongs that undermine such offenders' opportunities to have and live decent lives or their own (or their parents') choices that have done so.

Supposing that we can devise plausible answers to the preceding kinds of questions in determining who should or should not be eligible for sentence mitigation, others will have to be faced. First, would anyone who satisfied the relevant eligibility criteria automatically be granted sentence mitigation? Second, how would we determine the amount of mitigation to which those deserving of it should be provided? Third, and related to the preceding question, should the amount of mitigation for which an offender is eligible be fixed or variable, perhaps depending on how far he falls below whatever is deemed the relevant baseline for a decent living in the area or region? Lastly, and perhaps most importantly, would some types of offences render those who commit them ineligible for sentence mitigation, no matter how unjustly disadvantaged their lives have been?

Allow me to elaborate on the issues these questions raise and offer some tentative answers to at least some of them. In response to the first question, it might seem that all of the individuals facing sentencing for their crimes who satisfy whatever criteria we devise for guiding judges' decisions about eligibility for sentence mitigation ought to receive it. Individuals whose lives are hard because of state failures to provide them some adequate baseline of social welfare will all be sorely tempted to commit crimes to escape their difficulties. They also might understandably be profoundly alienated from a social order that seems to care so little about them. While such an approach seems plausible, it is important to raise a problem here that few who urge sentence mitigation for the wrongly disadvantaged have squarely addressed. As one advocate of such mitigation, Mirko Bagaric, notes, many if not most wrongly disadvantaged individuals refrain from crime and especially the more serious kinds of it (Bagaric 2015: 12; see also von Hirsch and Ashworth 2005: 68). And they do this despite the fact that they endure very difficult lives, perhaps for years on end. Even with the stresses and strains of their lives, they soldier on, earning what income they can, struggling to make ends meet, while abiding by the law. Indeed, many of them manage to live responsible lives despite the fact that one or more of their family members or friends resort to crime, seemingly in response to the challenging lives and circumstances that they face. What are we to make of all of this?

Bagaric sensibly stipulates that to be eligible for sentence mitigation, wrongly disadvantaged offenders should have to demonstrate a link between the injustices they have endured and their specific crimes (Bagaric 2015: 41–42; see also Roberts and Dagan, this volume, 84). This approach tacitly seems to recognise that not all crimes flow directly from individuals' unjustly difficult lives. As a result, individuals about to be sentenced should (perhaps through their lawyers) have to convince sentencing judges that they are deserving of mitigation (see Matravers, this volume). While such a requirement seems sensible, we might wonder whether many offenders will be able to satisfy it. Individuals who have credible stories linking their histories of unjust social disadvantage to their crimes might face scepticism from judges who insist that they probably had other options besides offending. Might there not be charitable organisations, for instance, to which those struggling to make ends meet might have turned? Judges might also point to the many other unjustly disadvantaged individuals in society who refrain from committing crimes. Why should not those who committed crimes be held to the same public standards of conduct that their unjustly deprived fellow citizens have managed, through arduous efforts, to meet?

In response, it might be claimed that no one should have to struggle mightily to have and live a decent life. Those who succeed in hewing to the legal straight and narrow despite the obstacles in their paths are admirable, but they should not have to be. Richard Frase notes that the criminal law incorporates what is termed the 'person of reasonable firmness' standard in determining whether those accused of crimes should be held accountable for them if they face particularly difficult choices (Frase 2013: 229). Individuals can be fairly held responsible for their failures to resist all sorts of the more ordinary stresses and temptations that might lead them to commit crimes. But the criminal law (eg, in allowing excuses based on duress) also recognises that individuals can find themselves in especially trying circumstances, through no or little fault of their own, where declining to commit crimes will be extremely hard. We might believe that the unjustly disadvantaged continually find themselves in such challenging circumstances (Lippke 2014). Even if we are unwilling to fully excuse them for their crimes, we might believe that they should be given some consideration for the challenging lives they face in the form of sentence mitigation.

Although this line of argument appears convincing, one concern about it should be noted. The 'person of reasonable firmness' standard implicitly acknowledges that there might be some persons who resist even the most powerful temptations or pressures to commit crimes (Frase 2013: 229). Yet, the criminal law requires only 'reasonable firmness', not 'extraordinary firmness'. However, as we have seen, it is not simply a small minority of unjustly disadvantaged citizens who manage to refrain from offending; it is the majority of them, and perhaps a substantial majority of them. Are we to therefore conclude that many if not most of the unjustly disadvantaged are (or are close to) individuals of extraordinary firmness?[6]

Perhaps it might be useful, in this context, to remind ourselves of one of the other factors that, in addition to unjust disadvantage, is linked to criminal offending. It is well established that most crimes are committed by young people, and more specifically, young males (Steffensmeier et al 1989). Once individuals who have engaged in offending reach their late twenties or early thirties, they tend to 'age out' (Nagin 1998: 364; Laub and Sampson 2001). What this suggests is that crime might not simply be a product of unjust disadvantage, but also of the well-known factors that incline young people, and especially young males, to engage in deviant behaviour: impulsiveness and the risk-taking that goes with it, along with greater responsivity to peer pressure, including the kinds that encourage criminal (and other) misconduct. Add to the preceding the ways in which socially deprived neighbourhoods are more disorganised, lacking in the kinds of informal monitoring and social control that exist in more affluent neighborhoods, or worse, dominated by gangs or other groups that encourage criminal offending, and we have a potent mix of criminogenic forces that push young people in the direction of crime (Clear 2009). Again, despite all of this, many who come from such social backgrounds refrain from crime, but arguably we should have sympathy for the youthful among them who succumb to the warping effects of such backgrounds and grant them some slack when it comes to sentencing them for their crimes. This conclusion might seem more compelling if we believe that such challenging social backgrounds or circumstances should have been addressed by the state in the form of robustly ameliorative social welfare measures. Still, should we have less sympathy for the poor who refrain from offending when they are young but, somewhat unusually, start to commit crimes when they are approaching middle age? That might seem to be an implication of the preceding line of argument.

This brings us to the questions of how much 'slack' we should grant the wrongly advantaged and whether it should vary with the extent of their disadvantage.[7] It seems plausible to give an affirmative answer to the second question, even if

[6] It should be noted that many of the unjustly disadvantaged might refrain from offending not solely because they are sufficiently moved by the moral reasons against doing so. They, like others in society, might refrain from crime because they fear the consequences of arrest, prosecution, and punishment.

[7] It is worth noting that many of the crimes for which persons are sentenced will not be serious ones. In the US, for instance, an estimated 80% of the crimes processed by the criminal justice system are classified as 'misdemeanors', which means that many of them will be punished by something other than imprisonment (Natapoff 2012). As a result, fines, community service and terms of probation will typically be the sanctions imposed, perhaps in some combination. This will complicate efforts to mitigate the sentences of the unjustly disadvantaged by some percentage amount.

we are unsure of how to answer the first one, which I suspect we might be. In his thoughtful discussion of sentence mitigation for the socially deprived, Bagaric suggests sentence reductions of 'no more than 25%' (Bagaric 2015: 42). He warns against more mitigation on the grounds that it might signal to offenders and the public that their crimes are less serious than they really were. His emphasis here seems to be on what legal punishment communicates about crimes, rather than its deterrent effects. Indeed, he is doubtful that further mitigation would encourage more offending, given the lack of empirical evidence linking punishment severity and either general or special deterrence (Bagaric 2015: 42–43).

It is unclear how Bagaric arrives at the 25 per cent figure. We might worry that such a percentage approach to mitigation leaves out other ways in which punishment can be reduced to accommodate unjust disadvantage (see Matravers, this volume; and Hanafy, this volume). For instance, we might think it appropriate, presumptively at least, to assign unjustly deprived offenders non-custodial sanctions rather than custodial ones, at least when their crimes are not too serious. Simply put, 'less punishment' could entail different kinds of sanctions, not just less enduring ones. More to the point, there is an argument that might push us towards higher levels of sentence mitigation than Bagaric countenances. We might not think that the unjustly disadvantaged should be eligible for excuses under the criminal law. Their difficult lives and the choices they face are not like those of individuals who act under duress, for instance. Still, Bagaric's 25 per cent mitigation cap suggests that the circumstances of the unjustly disadvantaged are only modestly-to-moderately trying. Might it not make sense to urge mitigation in the 50–75 per cent range if we think that the lives and the choices foisted on them are at least 'in the vicinity' of duress? Bagaric's recommended cap might seem to underestimate the challenges of the unjustly disadvantaged. Granted, he could concede this point and rest his case for less mitigation on the worrisome messages that more of it would convey.

Setting the magnitude question aside, Bagaric's account does seem to imply that there should be some variation in the mitigation sentencing judges grant to the unjustly disadvantaged. After all, whatever baseline of a decent standard of living that we employ in determining eligibility for sentence mitigation, it is likely that some individuals will fall farther below it than others and thus face more challenging lives. Perhaps we shall have to grant sentencing judges considerable discretion in factoring unjust social deprivation into their decisions, just as we do in expecting them to take a variety of other mitigating and aggravating factors into account.

This brings us to another important issue. There is discomfort expressed in the scholarly literature with having the unjustly disadvantaged who commit more serious crimes be the recipients of mitigation (Bagaric 2015: 3; see also Bergelson, this volume, 51). Bagaric, for instance, claims that the 'manifest wrongness' of crimes like murder, aggravated assault resulting in grave bodily injury, and rape is or should be abundantly clear and should, I take it, give considerable pause to anyone who contemplates them and who is at all responsive to moral considerations. One slight difficulty with this is that the wrongness of less serious crimes, such as thefts of smallish amounts of property or assaults that injure others in mild to moderate ways, ought also to be at least somewhat clear to those who are responsive to moral considerations, as we should assume most offenders will be. Also, the same criminogenic factors that precipitate many of the more minor criminal offences will likely play some role in precipitating more serious ones. It is not as if unjust social deprivation's distorting or stunting effects on the capacities of persons to have and live moral lives simply leave off as they contemplate or engage in more serious crimes. This suggests that even those who commit more worrisome crimes should be eligible for some mitigation of their sentences.

If we are to resist this conclusion, as I suspect we should, we may have to bring in other considerations besides the obviousness of certain kinds of criminal wrongs. Recall that Bagaric rejects sentence mitigation of more than 25 per cent because of what it will communicate about the relative seriousness of offences. We might similarly draw on the expressive character of legal punishment to mount an argument against sentence mitigation for more serious crimes. As Jean Hampton (1991) and Anthony Duff (2003) have argued, individuals who have been victimised by crimes, and especially serious crimes, look to the state to respond to the wrongs done to them by arresting, prosecuting and punishing those who wronged them. By doing so, the state validates and stands for victims and the importance of their lives and interests. If we accept something like this, then one problem with mitigating the sentences of the unjustly disadvantaged is that it might seem to devalue the lives or interests of their victims, at least when compared to the punishment meted out to offenders who are not unjustly disadvantaged. And the greater the mitigation, the more symbolically devalued will be the lives and interests of the victims of the unjustly socially deprived. We might therefore hesitate to mitigate the sentences of socially deprived offenders whose crimes have clear victims, and the more so the graver the harms done to them. By contrast, for crimes without victims, the victim-affirming aspect of legal punishment would seem to have less pertinence; this might leave us more room for sentence mitigation.

There is a further complication here that should be noted. Many of those who are victimised by the unjustly disadvantaged will themselves be unjustly disadvantaged. This, in turn, likely means that the criminal harms they suffer will tend, in various ways, to be somewhat greater or more enduring than the harms that better off victims suffer, all else being equal (Frase 2013: 221–22). For instance, the poor are more apt to be living at the margins, such that thefts of or damage to their property will leave them in more difficult straits compared with other, better-off members of society. Similarly, if the disadvantaged are caused physical or emotional injury by the crimes against them, they might lack the resources to get full or speedy medical and psychological treatment. Yet, if crimes against the impoverished generally do more harm, as well they might, then on accounts of legal punishment that link the kinds and quantities of it to the harms wrought by criminal offences, it would seem to follow that those who victimise the poor ought to receive somewhat more punishment, not less. Or perhaps any mitigation to which they are thought entitled due to their unjustly hard lives ought to be weighed against the greater harms they cause their unjustly disadvantaged victims. One way out of this seeming difficulty might be for the state to step in and do more to help the victims of crimes, and especially poor ones whose lives are already challenging. If it were to do so, that might leave us with more room to argue that those who criminally victimise the poor should not receive longer or harsher sentences. But would it leave us room to argue that unjustly disadvantaged offenders should receive shorter or less burdensome sentences? That seems a bit unclear. Also, whether the state will be inclined to help victims, or help them very much, will depend on a variety of factors, at least one of which is likely to be prevailing views about the injustice of social disadvantage.[8]

IV. How Significant of a Mitigating Factor?

Suppose that we endorse sentence mitigation for unjustly socially deprived offenders whose crimes are not too serious. A further question must then be addressed: is such mitigation to be counted as simply one among the many mitigating and aggravating factors that judges routinely weigh before reaching decisions on the sentences for those convicted of crimes? Or should such mitigation have elevated significance, such that it would be 'applied', so to speak, after judges have considered other mitigating and aggregating factors and arrived at something like presumptive sentences for the individuals who appear before them? If the latter option seems preferrable, what is it about unjust social deprivation that merits such elevated status in the sentencing process? I would note that a similar question might be raised about calls for offender remorse to be counted as an elevated mitigating factor in sentencing (Maslen 2015; Proeve and Tudor 2016). Even assuming that we are prepared to count 'genuine remorse' as a mitigating factor, is it to be counted as one among many relevant sentencing factors or as one that has elevated significance? I have argued that the latter option seems a dubious one in relation to mitigation for remorse (Lippke 2022). Why should how individuals react and feel after they have committed crimes matter more than the various factors that determine their degree of culpability for their crimes or the kinds and degrees of harm their crimes inflict? This is not to claim, of course, that remorse should have no role in sentencing – just not a special one. But notice, if remorse is treated as only one mitigating factor among a host of other mitigating and aggravating factors, there is no guarantee that it will exert much influence over ultimate sentencing outcomes, which seems at odds with the enthusiasm for counting it evinced by some of its supporters. Something similar would presumably be true if unjust disadvantage

[8] Still, victim compensation programmes are widespread in the US, despite its minimal and inconsistent commitment to the basic social welfare of its citizens. See 'US Resource Map of Crime Victim Services and Information', Office for Victims of Crime, at www.ovc.gov/map.html.

was to be regarded simply as one mitigating factor among a host of other factors, some of which might be mitigating while others are aggravating.

It might be possible, in the case of unjust disadvantage, to construct an argument for giving it elevated status. Unlike some of the more standard aggravating and mitigating factors, it is not one whose significance seems confined to events close in temporal proximity to the commission of criminal acts. For instance, an individual who is slightly provoked might overreact and violently attack his provoker, inflicting some injury upon him. Even if the attacker ought to be officially reprimanded for his attack by state punishment, we might reasonably believe that the provocation should work to mitigate the punishment he receives. Similarly, if someone steals or otherwise illegally appropriates some property from someone over whom one is acting as an appointed guardian, we might believe that the fact of that guardianship really should have made the thief think twice before she acted as she did. Hence, we might count her special responsibility for the victim as an aggravating factor in her sentencing.

Unjust disadvantage seems different in its impact on the perpetrators of crimes because its existence is typically more foundational in their lives. By this I mean that, in significant ways, it profoundly shapes their values and their abilities to make moral choices.[9] As a result, the unjustly disadvantaged might be more drawn toward crime than other, better-off citizens, or more prone to dismiss its harmful effects on others than other, better-off citizens, or both. Layered over this might be the perception that society does not care enough about the disadvantaged to give them a fair chance to have and live decent lives – itself, one suspects, a crime-precipitating outlook on things.[10] Of course, as we have seen, many of the unjustly impoverished will nonetheless refrain from offending. But it makes sense to view the lives of the socially deprived as generally 'hard'. They do not face occasional temptations or provocations, ones that, we should assume, they are well-prepared, as moral agents, to deal with. Instead, they face them continually and might be a bit less capable of responding as they really should. If something like all of this seems correct, then we might be persuaded to view unjust social deprivation as a special kind of mitigating factor at sentencing, one that should enjoy elevated status.[11]

[9] In a similar way, severe childhood abuse or neglect might play a foundational role in shaping the personal and moral development of individuals and thus merit elevated mitigation status when it comes to sentencing individuals for their crimes (see Bagaric 2015: 10–13).

[10] Add to this the anger that members of socially and economically marginalised racial or ethnic groups might feel towards the police who routinely target them for scrutiny, stops and arrests, especially when such interactions are marked by forms of derision or abuse. Such official misconduct is, in principle at least, distinguishable from wrongful neglect of the disadvantaged but it will often go hand-in-hand with it.

[11] There might be the concern here, noted by von Hirsch and Ashworth 2005: 63 that if the socially disadvantaged are cast as less responsive to moral considerations than other citizens whose lives and circumstances are less trying, it might seem advisable to employ various 'civil' measures to limit their freedom.

Despite this, there seem at least some grounds for doubting that unjust social deprivation should be treated as different in kind than other factors at sentencing. We have already seen a bit of this when the focus is on serious criminal offences, ones with victims whose lives are damaged or destroyed by the crimes committed against them. Suppose that not only was there a victim whose life was ruined, but several of them, and that the perpetrator both carefully planned his attacks and publicly reveled in the harms he did after the fact. In such a case, it might seem difficult to defend the claim that his unjustly disadvantaged background ought to have any status in determining his sentence, let alone an elevated one.

In response, it might be conceded that unjust social deprivation should not serve as a mitigating factor in sentencing when the crimes involved exceed some specified level of severity. The more pressing question, it would seem, is whether such disadvantage should always serve as an elevated mitigating factor when crimes are less serious. Perhaps so, but what if the disadvantaged offender who is facing sentencing for her relatively minor offence is a repeat offender, one who has a substantial history of mostly minor skirmishes with the law for which she has previously been convicted and punished? This brings us to the question of how sentence mitigation for the unjustly disadvantaged should be seen as interacting with the well-known phenomenon of recidivist premiums in sentencing.

V. Mitigation and Recidivist Premiums

It is common throughout the world for individuals with previous criminal records to incur recidivist premiums when they are convicted and sentenced for further crimes. Such premiums include such things as larger fines, longer terms of probation or more onerous forms of it, or longer custodial sentences (Roberts 2008). What typically distinguishes various legal jurisdictions in this regard is the magnitude of such premiums, with some countries – the US perhaps foremost among them – prone to levying premiums that are quite substantial. Suppose that we decline to go in that direction and instead keep recidivist premiums modest in character, as seems more defensible (Frase 2013: 189–98). Should we impose them on repeat offenders who are unjustly disadvantaged?

It is tempting to argue against doing so, perhaps on the grounds that such individuals have already suffered enough due to their impoverished upbringings or stations in life. Alternatively, and more convincingly it seems to me, it might be claimed that the unjustly hard lives of some individuals have made it too difficult for them to refrain from further offending. As we saw in the previous section, unjust social disadvantage shapes its victims' lives in foundational ways, ones that do not simply disappear once they have been convicted and punished for one or more crimes. Add to this the likelihood that the prior criminal records of such individuals will further compound their woes by weakening their abilities to find work or earn enough income from it to sustain themselves and those dependent upon them (Frase 2013: 219–20). Especially if such individuals refrain from committing serious criminal offences, we might be persuaded that assessing them recidivist premiums amounts to unconscionably 'piling on' to the unfair challenges in their lives.

That being said, should we also believe it appropriate to continue assigning repeat minor offenders reduced sentences based on their unjust disadvantages? Or should we consider gradually reducing such mitigation, eventually eliminating it altogether, if individuals persist in offending (Wasik and von Hirsch 1995)? As we have seen, even the socially deprived should be understood as somewhat responsive to the moral reasons that exist for refraining from minor criminal offences, ones that might victimise others (including other disadvantaged members of society) in modest ways or manifest defiance of reasonable *mala prohibita* upon which society relies to reduce risks, fund the government, or coordinate activities of various kinds. Even if we are doubtful that the longer sentences that repeat offenders would thereby accrue would effectively strengthen their incentives to desist from crime, we might think it useful to reduce mitigation for another reason – to communicate more firmly to repeat offenders, and the larger public, that the relevant criminal actions flout defensible (let us suppose) standards of conduct.[12] Indeed, the law-abiding public, including other unjustly disadvantaged citizens who hew to the legal straight and narrow, might grow increasingly impatient with repeat offenders and look to the state to more forcefully convey its disapproval of them and thus solidarity with the defensible public norms of conduct embodied in the criminal law. Again, most individuals who become involved in crime in their youth gradually desist from it. But what if some persist in offending, perhaps in mostly minor ways, well into their adulthood? Might it not be reasonable to gradually reduce, if not eliminate, any sentence mitigation they once received out of recognition of their unjustly disadvantaged backgrounds? Others like them seem to have gotten the message that their conduct is unacceptable, not to mention that many like them never needed to receive that message in the first place.

Granted, if we were to go down the preceding path, as I believe we probably should, it might become difficult to explain why, after the lapse of all mitigation for unjust disadvantage, we should not, at some point, begin to assess repeat offenders more ordinary (but let us assume modest) recidivist premiums, regardless of the trying circumstances of their lives. And it will be more difficult to explain why we should not do so if the crimes being committed by them appear to be gradually increasing in seriousness. This will especially be true in sentencing regimes that accord some weight to the incapacitation of offenders, perhaps within broader sentencing limits determined by proportionality.[13]

[12] The view that legal punishment expresses public values concerning permissible and impermissible conduct has been defended by many. See Hampton 1991; Duff 2001; and von Hirsch and Ashworth 2005, among others.

[13] We might also wonder how sentence mitigation for the unjustly disadvantaged would work for offenders being sentenced for multiple crimes. A variety of approaches to sentencing so-called

Importantly, we might be more inclined to reduce sentence mitigation, or even levy recidivist premiums on unjustly disadvantaged repeat offenders if society undertook some of the reforms in legal punishment that social welfare liberal and egalitarian theorists are apt to support – reducing the harms of imprisonment and helping those convicted of crimes to acquire education, job training, and gainful employment, among them. If society were to do these things, then its responsibility for having wrongly saddled some of its members with challenging lives would be somewhat reduced. Still, some individuals might persist in offending, and it will become increasingly difficult to defend going easier on them at sentencing than we do with recidivists who were never wrongly disadvantaged.[14]

VI. Conclusion

My aim in this chapter has not been to build a strong case against sentence mitigation for the wrongly disadvantaged. Instead, it has been to highlight the various challenges that proponents of such mitigation will have to face, ones that, I believe, have heretofore gone largely unaddressed. I have suggested what I believe are plausible responses to at least some of these challenges. However, I also believe that much work remains to be done and I am not certain, ultimately, that sentence mitigation for such offenders can be coherently defended, especially in its more robust forms. Substantial sentence discounts, awarded to offenders based solely on their unjustly disadvantaged backgrounds, without regard to the seriousness of their crimes, and regardless of their criminal histories, seem to me rather difficult to defend. By contrast, modest mitigation, granted to youthful individuals who have only recently begun to engage in minor forms of offending, who can demonstrate to the courts that their unjustly disadvantaged lives played significant roles in precipitating their wayward conduct, seems more defensible. Still, implementing mitigation for the unjustly disadvantaged in social orders that do not appear to recognise any special state moral responsibilities towards those deprived of opportunities for decent and law-abiding lives seems something of a lost cause. But I am open to, and even hopeful of, being persuaded otherwise.

'multiple offenders' have been proposed (Ryberg, Roberts and De Keijser 2018), the most prominent of which decline to simply aggregate the sentences for their several crimes. Yet if we decline to do so, it will seem that we are already mitigating their punishment and the question might be raised whether they should receive further mitigation based on their unjustly disadvantaged lives.

[14] Even in Scandinavian countries that do more than many others to reduce the negative effects of legal punishment and prepare offenders to resume law-abiding lives, recidivism persists although there is debate about the rate at which it occurs (see Andersen and Skardhamar 2015).

9

The Relevance of State Misconduct for Mitigating Punishment

THOM BROOKS[1]

Two offenders might have in common their conviction for the same crime, but each may receive very different punishments. For example, this could be justified if there were aggravating or mitigating factors, such as intoxication or provocation among others, that could make the amount of punishment more or less than if no such factors were present (Roberts 2011). Normally, these factors centre on an offender and any relevant relation to victims. Where an offender has been provoked or suffers from a mental illness, it could justify mitigation and a less severe punishment (Sentencing Council of England and Wales 2024). However, we may question whether other factors external to the offender might apply for mitigation.

This chapter examines the relevance of *state misconduct* as a factor for mitigating individual sentencing. This analysis is more theoretical than doctrinal in considering what we have normative reason to approve or disapprove. Of course, such judgements may have a bearing on how we view the justification of relevant practices relating to a criminal justice system, as will be explained below.

I. Overview

The chapter begins with preliminary remarks defining state misconduct and clarifying my focus on the relevance of state misconduct for mitigating sentences rather than other kinds of cases. I then consider the ways in which state misconduct may justify mitigation as a form of provocation. The chapter concludes surveying different penal approaches to demonstrate that the view of state misconduct as mitigation defended here is coherent with a wide variety of penal approaches.

[1] This chapter has benefited enormously from comments received from the editors – Julian Roberts, Jesper Ryberg and Leo Zaibert – on previous drafts.

My conclusion is that the relevance of state misconduct for sentencing mitigating might apply directly to individual sentencing decisions where some connection can be demonstrated between the state misconduct and the offender either as systematic discrimination or deliberate bad faith. Whether or not the mitigation is justified is to be assessed by taking the full circumstances into account on a case-by-case basis by the sentencer and where evidence of this connection is compelling. And, where it is found, the state should be compelled to ensure such misconduct is addressed so it is no longer a factor.

II. Preliminaries

State misconduct is defined as wrongful acts by state actors. This may include the unlawful actions of the police, prison officers or other state officials. State misconduct might consist of unlawful arrest or detention and unlawful discriminatory treatment amongst other forms. It may arbitrarily target some or non-arbitrarily impact all.

In this chapter, I will exclude such cases in order to focus more narrowly on the relevance of state misconduct for sentencing mitigation for any liberal democratic state, such as the US, UK and others. These are states governed by the rule of law that can and do have the legitimacy to convict offenders and impose punishments and they can and do recognise when misconduct by the state or its officials has occurred. It is readily acknowledged that while these states can and do acknowledge their own state misconduct, they may do so imperfectly and not every example may be so recognised.[2]

This focus leaves out non-liberal democratic states, such as authoritarian regimes (Arendt 2017). These are polities where state misconduct occurs but not acknowledged by the state. For example, there are reports of serious human rights abuses in countries such as North Korea. These include alleged unlawful killings perpetuated by the Government, forced disappearances, political prison camps with life-threatening conditions and families punished for the alleged offences of an individual. Yet, in all these cases, the state has not accepted its responsibility for misconduct.[3]

These are not regimes that would recognise any mitigation for state misconduct whenever it does occur. Therefore, it is impractical to consider the possible role for mitigation in regimes that deny any such possibility.[4] Moreover, there may

[2] In *Storey v Lumpkin*, the state failed to disclose evidence favourable to the defence in a murder trial where the defence did not become aware until it was too late to make an appeal and so the defendant remained liable to execution despite what Justice Sotomayor describes as 'serious claims of prosecutorial malfeasance in federal habeas proceedings'. See *Storey v Lumpkin* [2577].

[3] See US Department of State (2022).

[4] It is not my argument that any consideration of mitigation in sentencing within such regimes lacks merit, only that any such view is impractical as these regimes deny acknowledging any relevant state misconduct that might justify mitigating sentences.

be foundational issues relating to the legitimacy of authoritarian states governing through oppression that undermines the legitimacy of its criminal justice system more broadly.[5] This is especially the case if we accept that the justification of any punishment is intrinsically linked to the justification of the relevant criminal law that was breached (see Brooks 2021b: 3).

Nevertheless, it is clear that instances of state misconduct happen and too often in modern liberal democratic states. Consider the examples of the UK and US, for instance.[6] The UK's Criminal Cases Review Commission (2022) reported there is 'one miscarriage of justice overturned every week this year'. These cases related to historical racist and corrupt practices, for example, of the British Transport Police involving the use of fabricated evidence, the destruction of witness statements and failure to report it, and convictions for theft and false accounting prosecuted by the Post Office that were based on a faulty computer system in the most widespread miscarriage of justice in British history.

In the US, the National Registry of Exonerations (2002) reported 1,733 exonerations between 1989 and 2015. Official misconduct was found to have contributed to more than half (54 per cent) of all wrongful convictions, including the creation of false evidence or concealing evidence of innocence. The report found state misconduct more likely in murder cases than for most non-violent crimes. Neither the UK nor US is alone in having these problems. In some of these cases, innocent defendants have been wrongfully convicted (Monaghan 2015). The question of whether mitigation should apply does not arise because no punishment is warranted.

However, in other cases of state misconduct, defendants who *did* commit criminal acts or omissions *are* relevant for considering if the presence of state misconduct can have a mitigating impact on their sentence. As a result, this chapter will assume that we are only considering the punishment of defendants who are guilty of their crimes. We will focus on the issue of whether state misconduct justifies mitigation for offenders who are liable for punishment by the state.[7]

I acknowledge that these assumptions exclude other issues. One is the relevance, if any, of any plea bargaining or guilty plea discounts influenced by some form of state misconduct (Brooks 2023; Roberts and Ryberg 2023). There may be state misconduct relating to those matters in how a decision is made about whether a plea should be made and its impact on any sentencing.

A second assumption is that convicted offenders *are* guilty. This is intended to exclude issues of whether individuals are wrongfully convicted and innocent, or

[5] While not explored here, it could be argued that significantly endemic state misconduct might undermine the justifiably of the criminal justice itself, not just the distribution of punishments (see Green 1988).

[6] While my comments are intended to relate to other jurisdictions, most of my examples will be drawn from the UK and US, the legal systems I know best.

[7] This discussion brackets the issue of whether punishment may happen outside the state. For discussion on these points, see Zaibert (2006:195–202).

whether they are guilty but charged with the wrong crime, perhaps a more serious offence than was actually committed (see Scheck, Neufeld and Dwyer 2000). There can be state misconduct in such instances. However, state misconduct leading to a wrongful conviction warrants exoneration and what is needed is the quashing of any conviction for a crime that was not committed. There is no question arising about whether mitigation of punishment is justified in such instances. State misconduct may play a role in someone's being convicted of a more serious criminal offence than was committed. But the issue, as I see it, is not so much whether punishment should be mitigated for the criminal conviction, but reassessing what is the more relevant crime committed before turning to considering sentencing options and whether any mitigation might apply.

To conclude these preliminary remarks, my focus in this chapter is on how we might justify mitigation at sentencing for state misconduct. It is restricted to its possibility in liberal democratic states that might acknowledge state misconduct where it occurs and not for illiberal regimes that do not. It is important because it happens across states both liberal and illiberal. I assume that the punishment of crimes is for crimes the offender did commit. Other implications that go beyond this chapter would follow if the offender did not. I further assume that any state misconduct is unrelated to any guilty plea discounts. This would also open other implications beyond this paper as well.

III. Mitigating Individual Sentences

An increasing number of jurisdictions use sentencing guidelines for deciding whether and how much to punish in what we might call a *standard case*. These guidelines typically spell out factors that may justify mitigation with less severe punishments than would be enforced in a standard case.[8] The relevant guidance regarding sentencing factors tends 'to be modest' where most schemes 'generally adopt a laissez-faire approach' (Roberts 2011: 5). For example, someone whose crime was racially or religiously motivated or whose offences targeted victims deliberately because of their perceived vulnerability may be aggravating factors leading to a more severe punishment than would be otherwise justifiable.

Similarly, there are also other kinds of factors that, where present, may justify mitigation and a less severe sentence than in an otherwise standard case. Possible mitigating factors might include where there was a degree of higher provocation than might be normally expected, a mental illness or incapacity or one's age where relevant to affecting an individual's responsibility. Where present, these factors can also justify different sentencing outcomes than if they did not obtain. The relevance

[8] On aggravating and mitigating factors in England and Wales, see Sentencing Council of England and Wales (2024). For their relevance in the US, see US Sentencing Commission (2023) ss 3B1.1 and 3B1.2.

is that where harm and culpability play a key role in making proportionality judgements about sentencing that mitigating factors may provide evidence for less harm or culpability than in a standard case (see Ashworth 2011: 25).

The list of mitigating factors provided in guidelines is usually shorter than aggravating factors. Martin Wasik (2014: 65) argues that 'this is probably because the majority of mitigating factors in sentencing related to harm or culpability are offence-specific, rather than … generic factors' applied more generally.

Notably, factors may often pertain to how an offender responds to a situation. The focus is on *his* reaction to provocation or *his* age, for example.[9] It would appear that we decide whether any such relevant factors might obtain by looking at the offender and their response to a situation and, if so, these factors might less culpability or harmfulness (Ashworth 2011: 25). These situations are often understood as fundamentally individual-to-individual as they concern the interactions of individuals as individuals.

State misconduct is a different kind of consideration as it is about the relationship between the state and the individual. State misconduct is not itself listed as an explicit mitigating factor for sentencing guidelines. However, it may be relevant for those that are listed. For example, the courts may consider any factors deemed relevant for mitigation: the Sentencing Act 2020 states that courts are not prevented from 'taking into account any matters that, in the opinion of the court, are relevant in mitigation of sentence'.[10] This can include cases where state misconduct is a mitigating factor.

Where state misconduct is relevant, it can often lead to the dismissal of charges or quashing of convictions, as well as lead to a retrial. In *Smith*, the Supreme Court of Maryland noted that 'the most severe sanction "typically" observed' in such cases is 'a new trial', and so not mitigating of a sentence.[11] The Court notes 'the following standard' that 'where a defendant shows wilful misconduct by the State, dismissal is appropriate only when (1) the misconduct results in irreparable prejudice; and (2) no less drastic alternative is available'.[12] This is a common effect of state misconduct findings.[13]

Similar outcomes may occur in cases of entrapment, where officials incite, instigate, persuade or pressurise an individual to commit an offence.[14] In these cases, if entrapment is proved, the defendant has an excusatory defence removing liability. Part of the reason for this is, as Andrew Ashworth (2009: 225) observes, it helps 'to protect the integrity of the criminal justice system' maintained by the state officials where state misconduct is found. Markus D Dubber (2015: 189) claims the Model

[9] I use the pronoun 'his' as the overwhelming majority of offenders are men.
[10] See Sentencing Act 2020, s 77.
[11] *Smith v Smith* [13].
[12] ibid, citing *Smith v State*.
[13] Banks and Harris (2013: 325) claim that while individual circumstances may justify mitigating a sentence, this can often 'make little or no difference'.
[14] See *R v Looseley*.

Penal Code's acceptance of entrapment as a defence 'is designed "to deter wrongful conduct on the part of the government"'.[15] In these cases, the effect of state misconduct is to limit, if not exclude, the admissible evidence in a trial (Monaghan 2015: 23). This may include removing any basis for conviction whereby the defendant is unpunished because of state misconduct, but not out of mitigation as there is no sentence to reduce.

So, how might state misconduct mitigate individual sentences? We have already noted that 'any matters that, in the opinion of the court, are relevant in mitigation of sentence' may be taken into account, including cases of state misconduct.[16] This raises a concern about how this might be applied fairly. As Lord Justice Rose has said, 'Consistency of approach by sentencers is essential to maintain public confidence' (Sentencing Guidelines Council 2005: i).

This concern is exacerbated by the fact that there is a burden of proof on defendants to claim state misconduct as mitigation in sentencing, common to other mitigation factors. Thus, it is crucial that same kinds of judgements are made about when state misconduct is relevant for mitigation. It is noteworthy that evidence may not always be available to defendants to prove state misconduct, especially in cases relating to terrorism charges.[17]

The first reason why state misconduct might mitigate sentences is where there is *systematic discrimination*. Everyone should be treated equally before the law. In *Wehr v Burroughs Corp*, the Third Circuit of the US Court of Appeals found wilful misconduct by the state involves conduct that is 'intentional, knowing or reckless'.[18] As Kate Warner (2011: 125) observes, 'we should strive for equal impact of sanctions on different offenders and different groups of offenders'. But where these impacts are different on account of a protected characteristic, such as race, sex, sexual orientation or disability, the systematic discrimination of offenders may not remove their having liability to be punished but may justify mitigation.

The US Supreme Court case of *Furman* is well known for invalidating capital punishment as unconstitutional, albeit temporarily.[19] It is a lesson for some in how the death penalty was briefly stopped, but I argue it has a continuing relevance for one important way we might think about state misconduct as mitigation. In *Furman*, the Court held capital punishment unconstitutional. In the lead opinion, Justice Douglas argued that the use of death as a punishment constituted cruel and unusual punishment that was constitutionally prohibited. He claimed that 'a penalty … should be considered "unusually" imposed if it is administered arbitrarily or discriminatorily'.[20] And this was how the Court found the death penalty administered. Justice Douglas said 'it would seem incontestable that the death penalty inflicted on one defendant is "unusual" if it discriminates against him by

[15] Citing American Law Institute (1985) §2.13, at 406.
[16] See Sentencing Act 2020, s 77.
[17] See *Secretary of State for the Home Department v CC.*
[18] *Wehr v Burroughs Corp* [281].
[19] *Furman v Georgia.*
[20] See ibid [249] (Douglas, J, concurring).

reason of his race, religion, wealth, social position, or class, or if it is imposed under a procedure that gives room for the play of such prejudices'.[21] The evidence before the Court was that African Americans were far, far more likely to be sentenced to death than white Americans for the same crimes (Baldus et al 1998).

The *Furman* decision found the administration of capital trials run by the state to have discriminatory impacts by race. The Court found that it rendered unsafe the condemning of offenders, but not their guilt for serious crimes like murder. The effect was that sentences were mitigated from death row to life imprisonment.

Furman's prohibition of capital punishment was short-lived. The main issue relating to misconduct arising from maladministration was addressed in *Gregg*, which reopened the use of the death penalty through new sentencing procedures aimed at addressing the systematic discrimination found in *Furman*. For example, the US Supreme Court held that

> *Furman* mandates that where discretion is afforded a sentencing body on a matter so grave as the determination of whether a human life should be taken or spared, that discretion must be suitably directed and limited so as to minimize the risk of wholly arbitrary and capricious action.[22]

The *Furman* issue was that conviction for a capital crime might mandate a death sentence and this was shown to be applied in a discriminatory way in sentencing. In *Gregg*, the procedure was bifurcated into a finding of innocence or conviction first, followed by a second process to determine the sentence where there was a choice of death or life imprisonment. While this has since been held a satisfactory approach for mitigating discriminatory sentencing outcomes, there are serious doubts about its operation and there is evidence that racial discrimination continues to impact the likelihood of whether offenders are sentenced differently because of their race that is deeply concerning (see Death Penalty Information Centre 2024).

State misconduct is present where offenders committing the same crime are treated differently due to their race or other protected characteristics.[23] This may be justified through finding discriminatory sentencing outcomes are 'unusual' punishments violating the Eighth Amendment or a breach of the Fourteenth Amendment's equal protection clause in the US Constitution, or similar prohibitions on unlawfully arbitrary sentencing legislation in other jurisdictions.[24] The argument here is not about the *content* of penal severity per se, but about considerations relating to *proceduralist* justice (see Zedner 2017). *Furman* found capital punishment unconstitutional because of its maladministration, specifically its systematic discrimination based on race, not that punishment could not include

[21] ibid [242].

[22] *Gregg v Georgia* [189].

[23] For a list of protected characteristics, see UK Government (2024).

[24] See Brooks (2015) and Nathanson (1985). On capital punishment, see *US v Quinones* [264] and *State v Santiago (Santiago II)*.

execution under any circumstances. State misconduct as systematic discrimination of offenders does not negate the fact that offenders have committed crimes nor need it require that convicted offenders are unpunished for their crimes. But the maladministration of punishing some differently for reasons that breach the equal protection of citizens should be remedied by correcting this difference so that there is equal treatment.[25]

A similar position is reached in the Canadian case of *Morris* where an offender was subjected to racism which was found to have 'a profound and insidious impact' more widely.[26] This view was based on earlier findings that an offender's relevant circumstances are 'tied to overt and *institutional* racism and its multi-faceted effects'.[27] *Morris* held that state misconduct in the form of systematic racial discrimination does not impact the gravity of an offender's crime, but it does mitigate the degree of responsibility the offender has for the crime.[28] The finding of state misconduct does not mean offenders cannot be punished, only that we may accept it as mitigation.

All this rests on establishing 'some connection' between overt and systematic racism with the circumstances involving state misconduct relating to the criminal conduct.[29] Where any systematic discrimination of state officials is not so related, this connection is either absent or too weak to justify mitigation on this basis. Consider the presence of unemployment in society. Unemployment is a known risk factor for offending. Moreover, unemployment is a risk factor that can have 'a disparate impact, *albeit indirectly* on non-white offenders' in countries like the US (Frase 2013: 36).

It should not be controversial to concur with Richard Frase (2013: 36) that 'steps must be taken to mitigate' the racial disparities in how unemployment impacts individuals differently. These impacts 'can, and must, be eliminated' (Frase 2013: 226). However, as Frase (2013: 226) argues, 'these problems [of unemployment] seem to lie outside of the criminal justice system and the mandate of sentencing commissions'. The issue is not whether there is a need to tackle unemployment and its '*collateral* consequences': we should tackle it (Frase 2013: 226).[30] Instead, the issue is whether merely being unemployed is sufficient to be viewed as mitigation for state misconduct.

For Frase, the answer is no. As Odudu (2003: 418) observes, 'The moral blameworthiness of the deprived is different because the choices the deprived face and

[25] The maladministration of sentencing that systematically discriminates against underrepresented groups typically results in punishments that are more severe than for those in groups that are not discriminated against. I note that maladministration may, at least in theory, extend to a discriminatory use of pardons as well as overly severe punishments although I will not comment on the relation to the practical uses (or misuses) of pardons here for want of space. On pardons generally, see Brooks (2021b: 153) and Perry (2021).

[26] *R v Morris* [1].

[27] ibid [4]–[5] (emphasis added). See *R v Borde* and *R v Hamilton*.

[28] ibid [149]–[153].

[29] ibid [97].

[30] Emphasis added. See Tonry (1995: 44, 127, 191).

what motivates their action is different'. Thus, someone's being unemployed (or otherwise disadvantaged) need not be a product of anything but an individual's choices independently of any activities by state officials. In these cases, there may be risk factors for future offending present, such as unemployment, but without a proven connection with protected characteristics then misconduct due to a failure of equal protection is not established. We may live in a 'left behind' community that suffers from social and economic deprivation (Norris and Inglehart 2019). It might be argued that the state should do more to enable these communities to prosper. If the state did so, it would make crime much less likely than at present. It might be claimed that any offenders within these communities were more likely to become offenders through no fault of their own and that the state has some responsibility.

But the mere fact of deprivation does not demonstrate that an offender's punishment should justify mitigation. Not everyone living in a deprived community reoffends. Some choose to stay within the community when they had opportunities to leave, while others choose to join when they could have lived elsewhere. Simply being left behind in a community is not necessarily evidence of state misconduct and, as noted above, it is for the defendant to establish that state misconduct is relevant to their circumstances. The discriminatory environment must be a product of state misconduct to have contributory connection to the criminal circumstances to have relevance.

An illustrative analogy is the relation between climate change and extreme weather (Brooks 2021a: 78–79). Climate change contributes to more extreme weather events such as hurricanes and tsunamis being more powerful and more frequent than if no human-caused climate change was present. This does not mean that every extreme weather event is a direct product of climate change. These events occurred long before there were human beings. However, it is undeniable that climate change has potentially catastrophic effects if not mitigated. But it is also true that not every event has a human cause.

The analogy with punishment is as follows. Our community may be deprived. This deprivation may create a social *environment* where crime may become more likely. What matters is showing that state officials bear sufficient responsibility for this environment and that this environment has had some negative impact on my blameworthiness. If my criminal decision-making is a *collateral* consequence of being unemployed, for example, then perhaps there should be mitigation, *but not for state misconduct*. For there to be mitigation for state misconduct, the consequences must be more direct and not merely a side-effect. Furthermore, I may be discriminated against on account of my race; however, if this racism impacting my criminal activity is not by state officials, then it must be shown to connect more directly with them to prove state misconduct is relevant beyond reasonable doubt, rather than some other form of racial discrimination which might warrant mitigation *but not as state misconduct*.

In these cases of state misconduct, there is no systematic discrimination. However, establishing evidence of a sufficiently satisfactory connection may appear elusive. I would argue that this connection required to demonstrate state misconduct might be established through proving the state or its officials had *deliberate bad faith* in its relevant relation to a defendant, an admittedly high bar. This bad faith might not be enough to quash a conviction, but, if proven, it may mitigate punishment.

For example, in *Samir*, the Crown Prosecution Service (CPS) recommended charges relating to one Act of Parliament, but the police incorrectly charged the defendant on that Act, plus another two Acts.[31] When the CPS reviewed the case, they found no evidence to support the incorrect charges wrongly brought by the police and withdrew then. The court found that while much of the conduct here was 'incompetent', 'it seems wholly impossible to see how bad faith could be inferred'.[32] The court claimed that there was no 'state misconduct' because 'there was no evidence whatsoever of any form of deliberate conduct, let alone any conduct evidencing bad faith on the part of either the CPS or the police' to suggest that there was.[33]

We find similar views elsewhere. In *Warren*, the deliberate bad faith is described as 'a sustained, deliberate … and cynical act of law breaking' by the state.[34] That the state, if not systematically, has deliberately impacted me in bad faith in such a way as to create a provocation is a serious occurrence. In such cases, where I have committed a crime, the state's deliberate bad faith towards me can, if proven, provide the required connection for mitigation on account of state misconduct.

There is no one-size-fits-all approach. We must always seek evidence of some direct connection on a case-by-case basis where sentencers assess whether state misconduct is relevant depending 'on the specifics of the individual case'.[35] When making each assessment, it may be that, for example, we find evidence an individual has mitigation because of provocation by a private individual's actions (see Sentencing Council of England and Wales 2024).

My argument is that we might also find provocation by state misconduct where we can show that: (1) we were subjected to systematic discrimination by the state or its officials relating to a protected characteristic (and so potentially without any malintent); or (2) the state or its officials have some more direct connection with our becoming provoked, such as acting in deliberate bad faith.

A final question to consider here is whether provocation by *some private individual* is as or more relevant than provocation by *state misconduct*. First, I am in agreement with other contributors to this volume, such as Ryberg and Roberts and Dagan, that state misconduct as a form of provocation is neither small nor large, but of varying gradients along a continuum. More significant provocations can have a strong impact on the mitigation of punishment for reduced responsibility for criminal offending (Brooks 2021b: 143–79).

[31] *Samir v Crown Prosecution Service.*
[32] ibid [12].
[33] ibid [15].
[34] *Warren et alv Attorney General of the Bailiwick of Jersey* [2011] 3 WLR 464 [63].
[35] *R v Morris* [4].

Secondly, provocation by state misconduct seems to me both more difficult to prove at times and more significant where proven. While it may be difficult to demonstrate complex systematic discrimination or the deliberate bad faith of the state against an individual, it is a major event for a state to recognise that state misconduct has happened – and hold itself to account. Not all states can bring themselves to do so and those that do arguably might not do so as often as they should. Moreover, state misconduct in evidence-gathering, in trial conduct and more can contribute to the innocent convicted, to those guilty of no crime or minor offences becoming imprisoned overly harshly and more. Or where state misconduct is acknowledged, it can lead to cases dismissed, convictions quashed, defendants retried and the guilty punished less.

IV. Sentencing Policy Aims

In the last section, I examined how state misconduct might mitigate individual sentences. I have argued that this can take two forms: either as a systematic discrimination or arising from deliberate bad faith. While state misconduct may be relevant for mitigation, I have not addressed the question of whether this view is compatible with most broad penal aims. For example, if my account of state misconduct as mitigation was only consistent with general retributivism, then it could be problematic for consequentialist theories. So, is my view of state misconduct acceptable to most penal theories or only a few?

I will argue that state misconduct is a problem for any the main penal theories defended by most theorists. However, it is a problem for each in different ways. Notably, state misconduct is not only problematic as a form of misconduct, but because its presence can undermine, in different ways, the different penal aims. While these aims do not share the same arguments, they share the same conclusion that state misconduct is problematic, undermining whatever leading penal aim is defended. My analysis is not exhaustive, but wide-ranging considering retribution, deterrence, rehabilitation and mixed theories of punishment.

In his classic article 'Marxism and Retribution', my former mentor Jeffrie Murphy (1973: 218) discusses Karl Marx's concern about states with a 'system that breeds … crimes' in a criminogenic society. If we should punish the deserving, how should we act when conditions are such that some individuals may be more likely to engage in crime because of their social environment?

For Murphy (1973: 223–24), it is vital that 'my undesired suffering of punishment at the hands of the state' is reconciled in some substantive way with my autonomous choice bringing such suffering onto myself. If a significant factor separating offenders from others is that the former are more likely to live in criminogenic communities than the latter, then some may become more likely to receive punishment based on where they happen to live, which may be their home arbitrarily through birth or upbringing. Any policy aim based on desert will be concerned about cases like these where my location counts more than my responsibility.

We may find it compelling that someone's social deprivation could justify mitigation because of reduced culpability. For example, von Hirsch and Ashworth (2005: 63) argue:

> Under the principle of proportionality, an offender's sentence should be reduced if the circumstances render the offence less serious, with seriousness being a matter of the conduct's degree of harmfulness and of the offender's culpability.

But they note that any 'reduced-culpability' approach is fraught with risk because it is unclear that individuals act less culpably, even 'where his incentives for offending may admittedly be stronger' (von Hirsch and Ashworth 2005: 66). They are also sceptical about simply leaving to sentencers to decide individually on a case-by-case basis. They argue: 'Merely authorizing sentencing judges to decide when an offender qualifies as being sufficiently deprived would lead to highly variable results, given judges' differing outlooks on this highly charged question' (von Hirsch and Ashworth 2005: 71).

However, if, for example, state misconduct created a discriminatory environment that could be evidenced as playing some part in provoking an offender to engage in criminal activity, this would surely impact that offender's culpability for the crime as is the case with provocation. In fact, provocation is widely seen as reducing an individual's desert. So, while it may be difficult to evidence in some cases, retributivists should care about state misconduct as a form of provocation where they are concerned about provocation more generally.

Von Hirsch and Ashworth make a good point that it is difficult to establish that *general* social deprivation can form grounds for mitigation. Not all socially deprived individuals engage in crime, and those that do might have done so anyway. But where my deprivation is linked to *state misconduct*, then this is a different case as the state should be protecting my rights rather than putting them at risk – and my engagement with the criminal justice system is with a system run by a state whose misconduct has a connection to the crime. Retributivists can accept state misconduct as mitigation on grounds of desert.

Consider the use of deterrent punishments. General deterrence aims at reducing crime by dissuading people from the threat of punishment (Ellis 2003). This is expressed by David Hume (1978: 410) as:

> 'Tis indeed certain, that is all human laws are founded on rewards and punishments, 'tis suppos'd as a fundamental principle, that these motives have an influence on the mind, and both produce the good and prevent the evil action.

Deterrence proponents claim a criminal justice system aimed at deterring others operates through clear motives to act lawfully and avoid criminality, in part, through punishment for the latter. A deterrence-based criminal justice system is undermined through state misconduct. The state cannot provide consistent motives to deter from crime if its misconduct guides its decision-making. A discriminatory or wrongful distribution of punishments based on factors other than what is required to reduce crime generally may prove counterproductive.

This is because the threat of punishment is not directly primarily towards deterring crimes in future.

While state misconduct may undermine macrodeterrence (or general deterrence), it might also undermine microdeterrence (or specific deterrence) (see Brooks 2021b: 45). Microdeterrence is where the target of our deterrent effect is an individual, not the general society. To be successful, microdeterrence is aimed at deterring the individual from future criminal activity. However, if the punishment is set at a different amount and different way in order to treat the individual with some degree of state misconduct, the deterrent goal of the punishment can be thwarted. And where an offender is provoked to criminality, at least in part, by state misconduct, the need to deter is less – as the activity is in part caused by the state misconduct. Thus, deterrence theories can accept state misconduct as mitigation on different grounds than retributivists.

Let us consider where the aim of punishment is the rehabilitation of offenders. Perhaps we view this aim as when we morally educate offenders in the wrongness of their crimes so they avoid criminal activities in future (see Hampton 1984). To succeed, this view requires that our punishment is what is needed to rehabilitate the offender so that they decide against future offending. But if there is state misconduct present as a provocation, then offenders require less such reform as their actions were stirred by the wrongful treatment of the state. This is especially true if they face overly harsh punishment because of systematic discrimination. In these cases, their required rehabilitation is reduced on account of their punishment being arbitrarily high because of discrimination. Proponents of rehabilitative punishments can accept state misconduct as mitigation, too.

This also holds for those who argue that punishment's reformatory aim is to communicate censure in some form (Duff 2001, von Hirsch 1993). These views are often modelled on the need to respect persons as persons. But where state misconduct is a factor in provocation, this respect is lessened and so too the need for punishment. This is also the case if misconduct contributes to systematic discrimination as this breaches the equal treatment of persons that communicative and censure views hold undermining their penal aims (see Manikis 2022a). Communication's 'authoritative' character is critically undermined where state misconduct is present and provides grounds for mitigating in sentencing (von Hirsch and Ashworth 2005: 19).

Finally, hybrid or mixed theories bring together multiple penal purposes in a single approach. They might claim we set punishments with a view towards the future as deterrents, but distribute them where deserved (see Rawls 1955). But this only combines concerns addressed above. If punishments are not fully deserved or if they fail to deliver deterrent effects because of the arbitrary or discriminatory way they are applied, any such approach collapses under the weight of state misconduct. Similarly, if we held the view that punishment's aim is to restore and maintain a system of rights where crimes are seen as infringements of rights, this system cannot be sustained where the state is engaged as a rights violation, not a rights preserver (see Brooks 2021b: 143–79). My rights-based unified theory of punishment can justify mitigation for state misconduct for this reason.

In summary, this section surveyed several key penal theories. The aim was not to defend any of them. Instead, this discussion has tried to show that idea of state misconduct as provocation justifying mitigating in sentencing is compatible with any of these broad approaches to justifying different penal theories. Noticeably, each theory can accommodate state misconduct as mitigation, but in different ways, and I bracket which may (or may not) be preferable to others. My purpose is not to settle fundamental disputes between different penal approaches, but to show that whatever our preference among these leading views, that the argument for mitigation can be accepted and for reduced culpability.

This is not merely a matter of trying to satisfy the interests of academic colleagues who defend a wide range of different penal approached between them. Instead, my interest is the more practical issue that the ever-growing prominence of sentencing guidelines and their common acceptance of what I call 'penal pluralism' in supporting multiple purposes for justifying punishment make necessary, to my mind, the need to ensure that any compelling view is coherent with the penal pluralism we find in our sentencing systems if it is to be practical (see Brooks 2021b: 143–49).[36]

V. Conclusion

I have focused on the possible relevance of state misconduct for mitigating individual sentences. I argued that state misconduct *can* justify mitigation where a sufficient connection is made between the state misconduct and the offender in one of two ways. First, this may take the form of systematic discrimination whether or not intentional where offenders are subjected to overly harsh punishments as a result of bias against their protected characteristics, like race. Secondly, this may take the form of deliberate bad faith that may not be systematically applied, but no less problematic.

I have argued that state misconduct matters for mitigation as a form of provocation that impacts culpability. This might be understood differently by different penal theories, whether desert-based or consequentialist. Either way, I have tried to show that this view of mitigation is coherent with a variety of very different penal theories even if each might justify mitigation in different ways.

This view rests on an important assumption that it applies to states that can and do acknowledge when they, as a state, have engaged in state misconduct. State misconduct happens and too often. But no view of mitigation is possible where it is impossible for the state to recognise its shortcomings. And, where it is found, the state should be compelled to ensure such misconduct is addressed so it is no longer a factor.

[36] See Sentencing Act 2020, s 57.

10

Sentence Mitigation as a Remedy for the State's Legitimacy Deficit

HEND HANAFY

To what extent does the state's misconduct towards an individual or a group of individuals justify mitigation in the sentence imposed on them for committing a criminal offence? To answer this question, one must engage with three interrelated issues: what kind of misconduct has the state committed; how has the misconduct affected the relationship between the state and the individual; and why should the remedy be found at sentencing? In exploring these issues, penal theory has traditionally focused on state misconduct in relation to socio-economic inequalities and how these affect the state's moral standing to blame and punish the offender. The remedy was rarely found in sentence mitigation. This chapter aims to broaden the discussion to reflect on serious political as well as socio-economic misconduct, to reframe the nature of the relationship from moral standing to political legitimacy, and to discuss how and when sentence mitigation might be an appropriate response to remedy the fractured legitimacy of the state.

I. Overview

My starting point in this chapter is to identify the nature and terms of the relationship that governs the state's authority and its normative bind on the individual. Section II discusses legitimacy as a key governing framework. Legitimacy, as a multi-dimensional concept, includes necessary pre-conditions that govern the foundation of the relationship and continuous functional conditions regarding how authority should be exercised. The impact of the state's misconduct and its remedy depends on which dimension is affected. The chapter differentiates between foundational misconduct, which threatens the pre-conditions of legitimacy, and functional misconduct, which violates how the authority should be legitimately exercised. Section III addresses serious political misconduct as foundational misconduct and clarifies why sentence mitigation would not be an appropriate remedy to the state's illegitimacy. Section IV moves to functional misconduct, exploring its nature and relevance to offending and sentencing. Finally, section V argues why desistance-driven mitigation from custodial to non-custodial sentences can offer an appropriate remedy to the state's functional misconduct.

II. The Relationship between the State and Offenders

In exploring the nature of the relationship between the state and offenders, and the impact of state misconduct, one finds two approaches in penal theory. The first conceptualises the relationship on the basis of 'juridically imagined interpersonal moral relationships' (Lacey and Pickard 2021: 265). The state stands as a moral desert agent that judges, condemns and has a duty to impose deserved punishment on the offender for moral wrongdoing (Walen 2021). The state's standing as a desert agent is compromised if it engaged in misconduct through claims of hypocrisy or complicity in the offender's wrongdoing.

However, these accusations rarely successfully translate into grounds for undermining the relationship, either in depriving the state of the basis on which it punishes the offender or mitigating the kind or degree of deserved punishment. Ewing, in his contribution to this volume, offers insightful analysis concerning why claims of hypocrisy and complicity face difficulties in justifying sentence mitigation. More importantly, as Lacey and Pickard argue, conceptualising the criminal justice system on the basis of interpersonal relationships stands in tension with the criminal law's distinctive practical role in regulating harmful conduct (Lacey and Pickard 2021). This tension leads to a common conclusion that even if the state loses its moral standing, punishment, though imperfect and 'morally tainted', is still possibly 'the best we can do' in a morally problematic situation, given the need to protect victims of crime (Duff 2001: 199; Tadros 2009; Watson 2015).

A second recent approach conceptualises the nature of the relationship based on the state's regulatory functions and its position as a political authority in 'what is often referred to as a "political" or "public law" turn in criminal law theory' (Chiao 2016; Thorburn 2019; Lacey and Pickard 2021: 275). The criminal law and the authority to punish represent integral parts of the state's political authority; they stand at the heart of the state's powers in rule determination, enforcement, and control over the organised means of coercion. Such powers are justified to the extent that the state's authority is and remains legitimate. According to this approach, 'The question is … not how standing is lost, but rather what conditions must be met if the authority to regulate behaviour … is to be legitimate' (Lacey and Pickard 2021: 273). Yet, the conditions of legitimacy and their implications for state misconduct are still underexplored. To develop this approach further, one must discuss the conditions of legitimacy that the state must meet in its relationship with the offender and how the state's misconduct might undermine its legitimacy.

Legitimacy is a multi-dimensional concept, and in exploring its multiple dimensions, I rely on an amended version of Beetham's framework for the legitimation of power (Beetham 2013). Beetham's original framework aims to offer a social sciences approach to legitimacy with a view to measuring and assessing the degree of legitimacy within a given society. He argues that

> Power can … be legitimate where it does not breach established rules; where its acquisition and exercise are normatively validated in terms of socially accepted beliefs about rightful authorisation and due performance; and where it is confirmed through appropriate acts of recognition and acknowledgement (Beetham 2013: xiv).

Hence, he offers three dimensions to legitimacy (Beetham 2013: 16). The first dimension is legality in terms of conformity to established rules. The second dimension is the state's compatibility with acceptable social beliefs concerning two aspects: rightful authorisation and due performance. The state must acquire its powers from a valid source of authority and should exercise them to serve 'some general interest or social purpose' (Beetham 2013: 70). Finally, the third dimension is evidence of consent to the power relation by those subject to the state's powers.

The second dimension represents 'normative justifiability' and 'the core of legitimacy', with legality acting as a precondition, and acts of consent as a reinforcement of legitimacy (Beetham 2013: 293). Beetham later supplements this framework with normative considerations that transcend shared values and beliefs within a given society by identifying principles that are qualitatively superior to others in terms of their ability to break the self-confirmation cycle of power relations of dominance and subordination and, hence, are 'more emancipatory than others' (Beetham 2013: 112).

In reorienting Beetham's framework from a social sciences perspective to a normative philosophical one, and for the purposes of this chapter, I introduce two modifications. The first modification is to focus on legitimacy as a normative concept by reference to rationally justified principles, rather than based on empirical shared values and beliefs within a given society. The second modification is to reorient the focus of the first dimension – the pre-conditions of legitimacy – to include not only legality, but also part of Beetham's second dimension, which is rightful authorisation or a valid source of authority. Arguably, one cannot fully consider the first dimension of legality – that the state exercises its powers according to established rules – without reflecting on whether these rules emanate from a normatively valid source of authority. The first dimension of legitimacy would thus focus on the conditions necessary for a valid foundation of the relationship. The second dimension, by contrast, would focus on the functionality of the state's exercise of authority to serve common general interests. Finally, for the purposes of this chapter, which focuses on the conditions of legitimacy and the impact of state misconduct in this regard, it is unnecessary to discuss the third dimension of reinforcing legitimacy through acts of consent.

Accordingly, the state's relationship with the offender is legitimate to the extent that the state satisfies two dimensions. The first dimension is composed of two conditions: legality and validity; that power is exercised according to established rules, and these rules emanate from a valid source of authority. The second dimension is that the state must exercise its powers to serve common general interests. In identifying the nature of these general interests, Beetham refers to two broad interests: the provision of physical security; and the necessary conditions for material welfare (Beetham 2013: 138).

The impact of the state's misconduct on its legitimacy differs according to which dimension is compromised. Serious political misconduct that threatens the first dimension of legitimacy 'has more profound, because more all-pervasive, consequences for legitimacy than some breach or contravention in its exercise' (Beetham 2013: 16). Such misconduct is more impactful in terms of the pressure it places on the legitimacy of the state. It usually includes 'manifest illegality', 'definitive breaks' from the acceptable framework, and its remedy is more difficult to pursue and succeed (Beetham 2013: 206). Violations of the first dimension, thus, threaten to erode the foundation of the relationship, rendering the state's authority illegitimate.

In contrast, serious state misconduct that threatens the second dimension of legitimacy, where the state fails to at least serve the general interests of security and material welfare, leads to a 'legitimacy deficit or weakness' (Beetham 2013: 18). The foundation of the relationship of legitimacy remains in place for the state has acquired its authority from a valid source and is largely abiding by the rules; however, the strength with which it can claim individual compliance, cooperation and answerability weakens. The functional misconduct builds up pressure on the state's legitimacy as it diverges from the minimum functions that it should be pursuing. The extent of the pressure depends on the extent of the state's failures. In certain contexts, the chronic persistence of functional failures can lead to a complete erosion of legitimacy and transform into foundational failures, leaving the authority illegitimate, such as in grave military defeats, or persistent manifest partiality in using power for private gain or advantaging one part of the population at the expense of the rest. However, more commonly, functional misconduct leads to legitimacy deficits and its remedy requires less extensive efforts than that of remedying foundational misconduct and carries more chances of success.

Such differences in the ways in which the legitimacy of the state is lost or weakened have consequences for how we think about appropriate remedies. Foundational misconduct that renders the state's authority illegitimate cannot typically be remedied by a change in sentencing. The framework that binds the individual to accept the state as the legitimate authority to impose punishment and choose a sentence is broken. It must be remedied by re-establishing an acceptable framework of legality and validity. Mere changes in how the state exercises its authority, ie by a change to the quality or quantity of a sentence, do not address or remedy the illegitimacy problem.

Functional misconduct, in contrast, assumes that the foundation of the relationship between the state and the offender is acceptable. The state's authority to punish and impose a sentence has a normative bind on the individual. Yet, the state has committed serious misconduct in exercising its authority by failing to serve common general interests. This weakens the strength of its normative claims, causing a legitimacy deficit rather than breaking the legitimacy framework. To remedy such deficit, the state must change how it exercises its authority. However, the most pressing question becomes why a change in exercising its authority to sentence particularly would be an appropriate remedy. Within this framework, the following sections address sentence mitigation in relation to foundational and functional misconduct.

III. Foundational Misconduct

The relationship between the state and those over whom it exercises its authority is founded on legality and validity. Legality dictates that the state does not acquire legitimacy unless it acts in compliance with known and established rules. Beetham argues that even in the absence of control over the law's content and what the rules dictate, the exercise of authority according to established rules serves what one can categorise as three legitimating functions. First, it restricts the arbitrary exercise of power, where the powerful must respect the rules themselves to sustain legitimacy (Beetham 2013: 68). Second, there is the essential protection of individuals represented in 'the protection of due process when they fall foul of the powerful', and third is predictability and an element of 'settled expectations into our lives' (Beetham 2013: 65, 68).

Serious state misconduct that breaches legality includes arbitrary arrest and detention, forced disappearances, executive manipulation of the decision to prosecute, executive control of the judiciary and directed verdicts. Such serious misconduct usually involves the deprivation of liberty without a legal basis or using the criminal justice system to prevent the exercise of civil and political rights, usually as a tool for silencing opposition and imposing control and repression. Many states engage in such serious misconduct, some more systematic than others (Working Group on Arbitrary Detention 2023).[1] For instance, Amnesty International report on Venezuela documents patterns of

> arrests without warrants … short periods of enforced disappearance … charging of crimes using a wide margin of discretion; limitations on access to the right to defence; use of torture or other cruel, inhuman or degrading treatment; undue delays in investigations (Amnesty International 2023: 4).

In another report on Hong Kong,

> The evidence leaves little room for doubt [that] … Hong Kong's security forces have engaged in a disturbing pattern of reckless and unlawful tactics against people during

[1] For instance, the UN working group on arbitrary detention identified violations in 50 countries in 2022.

> the protests. This has included arbitrary arrests and retaliatory violence against arrested persons in custody, some of which has amounted to torture' (Amnesty International 2019).

In respect of Egypt, the UN Human Rights Committee highlighted its concerns over 'reports of arbitrary detention, systematic use of pretrial detention and the recycling of charges to avoid statutory limits on the length of pretrial detention' (United Nations 2023). Regarding Gambia, a Human Rights Watch report documented 'human rights abuses by state security forces and pro-government paramilitaries, including arbitrary arrest and detention, torture and other ill-treatment, enforced disappearance, unlawful killing' (Thompson 2015: 1). These are but a few examples to indicate the kind of serious misconduct that breaks the legality condition.

Such serious misconduct is usually – though not always – entangled with a breach of validity; that the state must acquire its authority 'from a valid source of authority' (Beetham 2013: 17). It is not enough for the foundation of the relationship that the state exercises its authority according to established rules, but also the rules of power themselves must be justified; that is, the rules which specify who has the right to govern and how to acquire such right. The state must have acquired its right to govern from a justified and valid source of authority.

The justification and validity of the rules of power, for Beetham, emanate from conformity with constitutional arrangements that reflect 'established beliefs about the proper source from which power should be derived' (Beetham 2013: 126). While compatibility with the constitutional arrangements would work well in most situations in identifying violations of legitimacy, it poses problems if the constitutional arrangements themselves establish inequality between individuals or deny representation to certain groups in society. Therefore, one must supplement the understanding of validity as a condition for legitimacy by insisting that the constitutional arrangements must guarantee equality and minimum conditions of popular sovereignty, that is, 'some element of popular representation by electoral process, even if this is complemented or qualified' by other sources of authority (Beetham 2013: 132).

I do not aim to offer a complete defence of equality and popular sovereignty as part of the legitimating principles, but for the purpose of this chapter, there are at least two main reasons for their importance as minimum conditions. The first is derived from a tension in political philosophy between authority and autonomy. Part of the state's normative claims of authority is a command or expectation of submission, obedience or at least non-resistance from individuals by reason of the state having the authority. In other words, 'the mere utterance of an instruction by a recognized authority is supposed to be a sufficient reason for compliance' (Bird 2006: 156). However, individual autonomy necessitates freedom from another's will and being able to act according to one's independent reasons. There is a tension then between the normative bind of authority and respect for individual autonomy.

One of the traditional ways in which political philosophy aims to overcome this tension is by grounding the source of authority in popular sovereignty through some form of democratic representation. The state aims to represent the common will of members of the society; hence, when it exercises its authority, individuals are not bound by the will of others, but by themselves. This way, individuals preserve their autonomy while accepting the authority claims as binding. Thus, a valid source of authority must reflect some form of popular sovereignty in which members of the society are equally represented. Otherwise, the state cannot acquire a legitimacy that normatively commands individuals' compliance.

The second reason is derived from Beetham's observation that while different societies may have different arrangements for the rules of power, ranging from the divine right to rule to popular sovereignty, the principle of popular sovereignty deserves special attention as a legitimating principle. First, popular sovereignty has played a central role in the history of the contemporary world as a legitimating principle, even when qualified or supplemented by other principles (Beetham 2013: 128–29). Secondly, some legitimating sources of authority are qualitatively more emancipatory than others in their ability to break relations of dominance and subordination in different power relations in societies. These legitimating principles are equality and popular sovereignty. Beetham argues that:

> Together, then, the principle of equal opportunity to acquire positions or means of power, combined with the equal right to take part in determining the rules that define what the necessary positions and inequalities in the general interest should be, and what should be the limits of power associated with them – these two principles allow the possibility of a legitimacy that is not constructed or reproduced by the established rules of power (Beetham 2013: 113–14).

On this basis, serious state misconduct that violates the validity dimension of legitimacy includes acquiring authority in violation of recognised constitutional arrangements such as *coup d'états* and military dictatorships, or governing on the basis of an invalid source of authority such as colonial authorities or totalitarian governments.

Serious state misconduct that violates legality and validity often involves – as can be seen in the examples mentioned – a broad use of the criminal justice system. It involves targeted use of the state's authority to punish, engagement of the police in repression, use of the prosecution powers to limit liberties, and influence over the judiciary through special courts or direct executive involvement. Such infringements often undermine or deny equality altogether and reduce any principles of popular sovereignty to meaningless assertions.

The authority of the state, particularly its authority to punish, turns into an illegitimate use of power and holds no genuine normative hold over individuals. The foundation of the relationship that governs the state and the individual is eroded. The best we can ascribe to such states is a functionalist de facto authority. The state's exercise of authority is justified by its necessary role in ensuring the flow of essential functions, but it lost its genuine normative power over individuals. This kind of authority is best described by Bottoms and Tankebe as 'dull compulsion', a

> type of de facto authority … frequently found in contexts (… such as military dictatorships) where there is a radical power differential between rulers and the ruled. In such situations, the powerless typically have mixed emotions: they feel that someone has to hold power; that the current authorities do hold effective de facto power and are therefore useful in ensuring a basic flow of essential services; that in consequence the power-holders are, in Weber's terms, a minimally valid authority; that powerless people have no way of challenging this de facto power anyway; and yet that it is impossible to accord to the power-holders any genuine normative authority or true respect (Bottoms and Tankebe 2012: 148–49).

The effect of this illegitimacy is pervasive and extends to the population at large. The impact undermines the state's authority over all offenders, not only those who infringe the rules which intend to silence political opposition and curtail the exercise of civil and political freedoms. The state authority is also illegitimate over offenders who commit other types of crimes as they live in fear and repression, are silenced, and suffer from the absence of any guarantees of due process, being denied their equality and autonomy. In these contexts, the state holds de facto authority over the population. It performs essential functions but does not normatively command the compliance of those over whom it exercises its authority due to the invalid and illegal form of authority that it wields. The foundation of the relationship that enables the state to make a normative claim of legitimacy is demolished.

The absence of a proper foundation cannot be remedied by a change in how the illegitimate authority exercises its functions, including in sentencing. A mitigation of the sentence imposed, a change to detention conditions, or even reigning in the security forces' abuse of authority cannot remedy such extensive damage to legitimacy. The remedy can only be a rebuilding of the foundation by an equal systematic return to the rule of law and respect for the constitutional arrangements and principles of popular sovereignty and equality so that the state can once more command the respect of its members and demand legitimate compliance.

Thus, even though the state commits such serious misconduct using the criminal justice system, it cannot remedy it by changing how it operates. The abuse of the criminal justice system becomes just a symptom of illegitimacy. The true problem created by state misconduct is the serious destabilisation of the legality and validity of political power, and it can only be remedied in the political sphere. Mitigation becomes thus a misplaced response to symptoms of foundational illegitimacy.

IV. Functional Misconduct

The second dimension of legitimacy focuses on the functionality of the state in exercising its authority to serve common general interests. As Beetham observes,

'Unless we are anarchists, most of us take it for granted that the justification for the state lies in its provision of physical security and of the conditions necessary to material welfare' (Beetham 2013: 138). Thus, if a state meets the pre-conditions of legality and validity, the sustainability of its legitimacy becomes dependent on the extent to which the state is seen to provide at least physical security and necessary conditions for material welfare to those over whom it exercises its authority.

The impact of the state's serious misconduct in failing to protect or provide conditions for material welfare is to weaken its legitimacy. While foundational misconduct leads to illegitimacy as the framework of the relationship breaks down at the root, as it were, functional misconduct can 'be described as examples, not so much of illegitimacy, as of legitimacy deficit or weakness' (Beetham 2013: 18). The state still holds its legitimate normative bind over individuals, although the strength with which it can claim individual compliance, cooperation and answerability weakens.

Functional misconduct includes failure to provide essential services necessary for material welfare, prolonged deprivations and poverty in whole communities, and experiences of repeated victimisation and lack of protection. We can see rampant forms of functional misconduct, especially concerning basic conditions of material welfare, in countries which operate primarily within a framework of legality and validity. For instance, a recent UN report on human rights and poverty in the UK highlights that:

> Although the United Kingdom is the world's fifth largest economy, one fifth of its population (14 million people) live in poverty, and 1.5 million of them experienced destitution in 2017 … Close to 40 per cent of children are predicted to be living in poverty by 2021. Food banks have proliferated; homelessness and rough sleeping have increased greatly; tens of thousands of poor families must live in accommodation far from their schools, jobs and community networks; life expectancy is falling for certain groups; and the legal aid system has been decimated (United Nations Human Rights Council 2019: 1).

A similar report concerning poverty and human rights in the US indicated that 'About 40 million live in poverty, 18.5 million in extreme poverty, and 5.3 million live in Third World conditions of absolute poverty' (United Nations 2018: 3). Similarly, in the EU:

> One in five people – totalling 91.4 million people, or 20.9 per cent of the population – are still at risk of poverty or social exclusion in the European Union. Inequality levels have remained virtually static or even worsened in some cases since the 2008 crisis. A total of 17.9 million children, or 22.2 per cent, are at risk of poverty or social exclusion across the European Union (United Nations Human Rights Council 2021: 4).

These inequalities and deprivations are the direct result of state policies that fail to extend basic conditions of material welfare to all those over whom the state exercises its authority. In the UK, it is the accumulative result of the austerity policies since 2010 (United Nations Human Rights Council 2019). In the US, 'the policies pursued … seem deliberately designed to remove basic protections from the poorest, punish those who are not in employment and make even basic health care into a privilege to be earned rather than a right of citizenship' (United Nations Human Rights Council 2018: 4). In the EU, it is the result of policies that are 'too narrow to be deemed appropriate for the scale of the problem' (United Nations Human Rights Council 2021: 4).

How does such functional misconduct impact the relationship between the state and the wronged individuals? It is helpful here to think of legitimacy in terms of Bottoms and Tankebe's dialogic approach to legitimacy. They argue that:

> [L]egitimacy needs to be perceived as always dialogic and relational in character. That is to say, those in power (or seeking power) in a given context make a claim to be the legitimate ruler(s); then members of the audience respond to this claim; the power-holder might adjust the nature of the claim in light of the audience's response; and this process repeats itself. It follows that legitimacy should not be viewed as a single transaction; it is more like a perpetual discussion, in which the content of power-holders' later claims will be affected by the nature of the audience response (Bottoms and Tankebe 2012: 129).

If we follow this dialogic logic, the state can claim to the wronged individuals that it has acquired its authority rightly and is largely abiding by the established rules. However, the state has a much weaker claim in justifying its powers by reference to successfully securing basic conditions of material welfare. These millions of individuals have not witnessed or experienced the state's function in providing conditions of material welfare. Further, not only are they experiencing deprivations of basic conditions of material welfare, but they are also placed under a criminogenic disadvantage; the socio-economic deprivations increase the likelihood of committing a crime.

According to situational action theory, 'criminal behaviour is the result of the interaction between who individuals are (characteristics and experience) and where they are' (Wikstrom 2006; Schepers 2017: 144). Both of these questions – *who individuals are* and *where they are* – are shaped by experiences of poverty and deprivations resulting from state policies. Rivers, Gibbs and Paternoster point to 'accumulated evidence in the medical literature that poverty serves essentially as a neurotoxin for cognitive development, particularly in the area of working memory and executive functioning, and that the greater the economic disadvantage the greater the neurological damage' (Rivers, Gibbs and Paternoster 2017: 87). Further, 'environments of concentrated disadvantage are fertile soil for the development of decision-making styles and practices that frequently result in behaviors that are neither in the actor's short- or long-term interests, including crime and substance use' (Rivers, Gibbs and Paternoster 2017: 86).

Such experiences, of course, impact individuals differently, and even though 'many "truly disadvantaged" … individuals manage to avoid it … social injustice is a key cause of crime' (Lacey 2022: 11). The concentration of criminal behaviour among individuals who experience poverty and deprivations has led social scientists to 'time and again empirically confirm … their conclusion that social inequality in the world outside the prison strongly predicts the distribution of inmates inside it' (Muller and Wildeman 2013: 169).

How can the state then remedy this legitimacy deficit that is created by its functional failures? At this stage, one has to distinguish between the affected communities that suffer from the state's policies, and individuals who committed crimes in the context of these deprivations and are held accountable as offenders for their criminal conduct.

Addressing the affected communities is a more straightforward task. The appropriate remedy has to engage with the reasons that created the deficit in the first place. The direct response to strengthen the state's normative claims is a change in the state policies in the socio-economic sphere, redistributing resources, improving conditions of material welfare, and reversing harmful policies. The state would have to show these communities that its powers are justified by its function in serving the general interest and providing conditions of material welfare.

The response to offenders, by contrast, is more complex. On the one hand, the increased likelihood of offending caused by poverty and social deprivation does not necessarily absolve individuals from responsibility for their crimes. The state also owes a response to crime victims, demonstrating how it is successfully protecting them from victimisation by addressing the harms they suffered and holding the guilty accountable. On the other hand, the legitimacy deficit towards offenders who suffered from the state's functional failures grows as a result of other state policies which alienate those who engaged in criminal behaviour from being part of the general interest served by the state. States commonly adopt policies which are designed to deprive offenders, especially those who spent a term in custody, from the basic conditions of material welfare. For instance, Muller and Wildeman indicate that

> A former inmate whose poor economic prospects might have influenced his path to prison may therefore find himself with even worse prospects upon release. Legal bans on voting and the receipt of welfare, public housing and financial aid might further impede his chances of success following a spell of incarceration (Muller and Wildeman 2013: 170).

Hoskins 'distinguish[es] three general ways in which governmental policies may contribute to burdensome restrictions on offenders' (Hoskins 2019: 22). First, the state may impose specific restrictions, such as voting bans. Second, the state may explicitly permit public authorities and private individuals to restrict offenders' access to employment, public housing and financial aid. Third, there are policies which 'facilitate informal restrictions, as with rules that make criminal histories publicly accessible and thus facilitate employers and landlords in denying offenders' (Hoskins 2019: 22).

I share Hoskins' view that these policies are mostly unjustified. Hence, they would be fairly characterised as state misconduct. Hoskins argues that:

> [W]e should take seriously the idea of punishment as the institution by which offenders pay their debts to society, and that it follows from this that imposing additional

> burdensome measures beyond the scope and duration of punishment is presumptively unjustified. Those who complete punishment should be regarded as having regained full, equal standing as citizens, with the same rights as everyone else (Hoskins 2019: 30).

Criminal behaviour does not deprive offenders of their status as equal autonomous individuals who have the right to ask the state to justify its powers over them. The justification offered by the state only answers to its rightful authority and conditions of legality, which legitimise, in principle, holding the offenders accountable for their criminal behaviour. However, the state's legitimacy still suffers from weakness in justifying itself to these equal autonomous individuals in terms of its function to provide basic conditions of material welfare. How can the state address this legitimacy deficit vis-à-vis these offenders, and could mitigation be an appropriate remedy?

V. Mitigation

Let's consider mitigation in terms of reducing the sentence imposed on an offender who has suffered from the state's functional misconduct. It is unclear how such a reduction constitutes an appropriate or relevant response to the legitimacy deficit. From the offender's perspective in the legitimacy dialogue, although the state, in principle, holds a legitimate authority to punish her, it has a weakened normative claim given it adopted policies that deprived her of the basic conditions of material welfare. When the state offers a sentence reduction, the state fails to engage with the expressed grievance and ignores the reasons that created the legitimacy deficit in the first place. The reduction does not address the state's functional misconduct and does not change, in any meaningful way, how the state exercises its authority. At best, the reduction can be characterised as a declaratory remedy that perhaps acknowledges that the state has wronged these individuals with its policies. Such a declaration might have some value but fails to remedy the legitimacy deficit.

To strengthen the state's normative claims and remedy the legitimacy deficit, the state must respond in a way that engages with the reasons for the deficit. It must change how it exercises its authority and offer alternative policies that guarantee basic conditions of material welfare. Some of these policies will naturally take place outside the criminal justice system, such as reversing policies that hinder offenders' access to basic goods and services such as housing, employment and financial aid. Still, other policies that can remedy the deficit should occur in the criminal justice system, particularly in sentencing.

In showing how sentencing can contribute to remedying the state's legitimacy deficit, one has to start by highlighting that it is common for states to accommodate various aims and policies in sentencing offenders which are not directly relevant to either harm or culpability for the crime committed. Most common among these are policies which aim to save costs and enhance the smooth running of the criminal justice system, such as discounts for guilty pleas. This also includes policies which aim to limit the collateral consequences of punishment on individuals other than the offender, such as dependants. Thus, sentencing is an arena in which the state exercises its authority for purposes beyond responding to the harm, culpability and nature of an individual's crime. Therefore, in principle, there is no objection to accommodating the aims of remedying the state's legitimacy deficit at sentencing. Further, the expressive nature of sentencing carries the potential to contribute meaningfully to the legitimacy dialogue by offering responses that engage with the reasons for the deficit. The more difficult question is what form sentencing should take so it can reasonably contribute to remedying the legitimacy deficit.

The deficit that the state aims to remedy is that it has failed in its function to provide basic conditions of material welfare and excluded these offenders from being part of the general interest served by the state. So, the logical correlation would be a move towards sentencing them in a way that balances holding them responsible for the crimes they committed and remedying the failed state function by enhancing access to basic conditions of material welfare. Such an aim can hardly be achieved by custodial sentences because custody in itself – even without state policies that deprive those who served their term from accessing material goods and services – hinders basic socio-economic prospects. Custody

> could reduce the skills inmates already possess or would have developed absent confinement. Prisoners likewise might adopt survival techniques inside prison that work at cross purposes to their desire to find work upon release … for example, … cultivate unpredictability inconsistent with the sort of routine necessary to maintain stable work (Muller and Wildeman 2013: 175).

Custody also 'inserts a large gap into one's resume' and hinders professional and educational attainment (Muller and Wildeman 2013: 175). Custodial sentences are the least compatible sanction to remedy the deficit resulting from functional failures to provide basic conditions of material welfare.

Mitigation in the form of a move towards non-custodial sentences for offenders who suffered from the state's functional misconduct carries the potential to mend the relationship between the state and the offender if it was desistance-driven. Desistance is leading a life without engaging in criminal activity. It depends on individual agency and the decision-making process to not engage in criminal behaviour, so it emphasises individual responsibility. At the same time, desistance is 'extremely difficult' to achieve without state policies to support it socially and economically (Shapland 2011: 74). Shapland offers an illustration of how desistance-driven mitigation would work as part of sentencing. She argues that the sentencing process would combine a focus on individual decisions towards desistance and reparation and state policies that support 'offers of employment, agreement to participate in substance abuse programmes, skills training (particularly learning to drive – a driving licence seems currently to be the key to less skilled employment for men), seeking out help, [and] participating in debt advice' (Shapland 2011: 77).

If the state adopted and implemented desistance-driven mitigation, including wider policies concerning offenders' access to basic conditions of material welfare, it would offer an appropriate response to its legitimacy deficit. It would engage with the reasons for the deficit, justifying how the new policies remedy the previous misconduct. It would chart a new claim of legitimacy built on the state's function in successfully offering basic conditions of material welfare to all its members equally.

Implementing this form of mitigation in sentencing is not practically difficult. It requires a step in the sentencing process which offers information about the offender's socio-economic conditions and whether they suffered deprivations from essential services such as housing, education and employment. For instance, a similar step exists in England and Wales in the pre-sentence reports, which should ideally give a fuller picture of the offender's life and circumstances.

Ideally, the sentencer would take into consideration individual factors such as remorse and willingness to make reparation and potentially support and encourage such willingness through restorative justice initiatives. The sentencer should be strongly encouraged to mitigate the sentence from a custodial to a non-custodial sentence to support the offender's desistance in recognition of the deprivations that this individual has suffered due to the state's policies. I emphasise *ideally* because, in practice, Jacobson and Hough's research indicates that:

> [S]entencers appear to be somewhat deaf to claims of disadvantage … There is a simple reason for this: the vast majority of defendants are disadvantaged in one way or another (and often in many ways), which effectively rules out special treatment on these grounds. As one respondent dismissively noted, 'There is a sob story in everyone' (Jacobson and Hough 2011: 157).

It seems that the prevalence of the state's functional failures towards millions of individuals, the criminogenic impact of such functional failures, and hence the concentration of criminal behaviour in disadvantaged communities have impacted how sentencers approach sentence mitigation for disadvantaged individuals. Addressing this problem requires a political will to change the way the state exercises its authority, including in sentencing, and a genuine concern for remedying its defective legitimacy.

Two final points are worth clarifying given their recurrence in discussing mitigation for disadvantaged offenders. The first is why this mitigation should apply only to those who suffered from the state's functional misconduct and not everyone; indeed, all offenders should be able to benefit from state policies that support desistance. Legitimacy's relational character illuminates the response to this problem. While the state might have independent reasons for adopting desistance as an aim of sentencing, the proposed mitigation is justified principally on the basis of remedying the state's legitimacy deficit towards a particular audience: offenders who suffered from the state's functional misconduct. By contrast, the state holds a valid, legitimate authority towards offenders who were served by the state as part of the common general interests.

In practice, it seems that the proposed mitigation is adopted more for relatively advantaged offenders, such as in mitigating a sentence from custodial to non-custodial based on one's employment. Jacobson and Hough's research indicates that such mitigation is informed by assumptions that

> the relatively advantaged defendant poses little risk of reoffending or has good prospects for reform. Sentencers may also assume that the advantaged defendant has more to lose than other defendants and will therefore suffer more – and be disproportionately punished – if a custodial sentence is passed' (Jacobson and Hough 2011:158).

So, the practical problem, counterintuitively, is offering a justification to sentencers for why there are stronger reasons to apply this mitigation to disadvantaged offenders. While advantaged offenders can and do benefit from mitigation, the state has stronger reasons to address its legitimacy deficit and guide sentencers to give due weight to the deprivations as a reason for mitigation.

The second issue is that proposing mitigation for disadvantaged offenders usually faces the hurdle of answering the question posed by Matravers in his chapter – borrowing from Starr – 'why the windfall for the defendant?'. Mitigating a sentence from custodial to non-custodial can be characterised as a windfall only in terms of the traditional ways in which we think about the scale of punishment severity where custody imposes more burdensome treatment than community-based sentences, for example. Still, as Freer puts it, the criminal justice system 'assumes that any person will experience more 'punishment' from a custodial sentence than a community order ('CO'), and from a community order than from a fine [however] The common-sense conclusion, supported by research, is that this is not correct' (Freer 2021: 28). The punitive impact of a sentence differs according to individual circumstances, so that a fine might feel more punitive for a person with very little money as opposed to a community order

> which would cost them nothing and give them a short-term purpose. Similarly, some offenders say that they find a prison sentence 'easier' than a CO … as it just requires them to wait out their time in prison, as opposed to actively engage in a programme or keep commitments (Freer 2021: 28).

Therefore, moving from custodial to non-custodial sentences for offenders who suffered from the state's functional misconduct does not necessarily offer them an easy path or a windfall, especially if it is desistance-driven and dependent on the individual's willingness to change their life towards a pathway out of crime. It is a complex process that is unlikely to succeed without state policies to support it, and a state that pays attention to its weakened legitimacy – as it should – would have strong reasons to put such policies in place.

VI. Conclusion

This chapter aimed to move the discussion about sentence mitigation for state misconduct beyond focusing on individual culpability and blameworthiness towards considering the nature and terms of the state's authority. It discussed legitimacy as a key governing framework which should inform our understanding about the impact of the state's misconduct. Serious foundational misconduct that violates the conditions of legality and validity threatens to render the state's authority illegitimate. Such misconduct typically cannot be remedied by changing how the state exercises its authority, including sentencing. Instead, rebuilding the eroded legitimacy framework is necessary for the state to claim a valid normative authority. By contrast, functional misconduct resulting from the state's failure to perform one of its primary functions in providing basic conditions of material welfare leads to a legitimacy deficit. Such deficit can be remedied by changing how the state exercises its authority, including sentence mitigation. The chapter argued that desistance-driven mitigation from custodial to non-custodial sentences would offer an appropriate remedy and enable the state to offer a reasonable response that can address its legitimacy deficit.

11

The Relevance of State Misconduct in Sentencing: Distinguishing Justifications

MARIE MANIKIS[1]

The role of state misconduct in sentencing is an area that has produced few scholarly and case law discussions to date yet warrants analysis in both sentencing theory and practice. While some scholars and courts have started considering certain forms of state misconduct as relevant to sentencing, its conceptualisation, justifications, and limits remain underdeveloped in academic and judicial discourse.

I. Overview

This chapter conceptualises state misconduct in ways that encompasses various dimensions of the 'state' and 'misconduct'. Misconduct can be systemic and/or individual and imply various forms of blameworthy conduct notably, intentional, negligent and wilful blindness. Relatedly, the state can also take many forms, including state actors, institutions or decisions/processes that relate to criminalisation, the criminal justice process, and punishment.

This chapter proposes and explores three distinct theoretical justifications for recognising state misconduct as relevant mitigation (or sentence reduction) in sentencing. It does not aim to address how much punishment is adequate to reflect sentence mitigation or reduction for state misconduct. A terminological

[1] The author is most grateful to the co-organisers/editors Leo Zaibert, Julian V Roberts and Jesper Ryberg as well as participants of the workshop at the Institute of Criminology, University of Cambridge for their invaluable comments on a preliminary draft of this chapter. A sincere thanks to Beverly Osazuwa for her invaluable research assistance as well as the William Dawson Scholarship, McGill University, and the Social Sciences and Humanities Research Council for their generous funding. Any errors remain my own.

distinction is made between the language of sentence mitigation and reduction, suggesting that mitigation relates to desert-based underpinnings while a sentence reduction would be underpinned by broader penological purposes (Manikis 2022a).

The first justification for considering state misconduct in sentencing is based on just desert-based proportionality. It highlights the relevance of state misconduct as a source of mitigation when it affects the offender's volition. The mitigation then communicates a lower level of blameworthiness and censure for the offence. The second is justified under a wider communicative theory of sentencing that considers censure as dynamic and relational, suggesting that state misconduct which is criminogenic should be relevant at sentencing to communicate the state's responsibility in contributing to the offence. The third justification argues that some forms of state misconduct, even if not necessarily criminogenic, can still be relevant in sentencing within a rationale that seeks to communicate state wrongs/harms that contribute to creating excess harms from what would be considered legitimate punishment in criminal justice. This third justification can be divided into two: state wrongs/harms that can be understood as excesses of legitimate punishment, which typically refer to conditions of imprisonment or the sentence that occur during the administration of the sentence; and those that exceed legitimate state harms that take place before sentencing. Distinguishing between these rationales and related forms of misconduct is key to establishing the relevance, scope and limits of various misconduct in sentencing.

II. Desert-Based Rationales for Mitigation

The justification for punishment within retributivism flows directly from the person's desert relative to the offence (Manson 2001; Kant 1887). Rooted in this framing, just deserts theorists have highlighted that punishment must censure the offence in a proportionate way, by reflecting the gravity of the crime and the offender's culpability for the offence. (von Hirsch 1992: 57–58; Manson 2001; von Hirsch and Ashworth 2005; Ashworth 2011; Manikis 2022a).

Can state misconduct affect either component of proportionality and individual censure? This chapter contends that while the gravity of the offence (harm) is typically unaffected by state misconduct, certain limited forms of state misconduct can affect the offender's level of blameworthiness.

These forms of state misconduct would need to be criminogenic and affect the offender's degree of volition in specific ways – notably by either affecting their mental state/decision-making processes by limiting their ability to make choices in offending or by creating incentives/reasons for offending.

State misconduct that affects mental state and decision-making processes includes those that contribute to various forms of traumas which impact the emotional regulatory system, such as a series of chronic systemic discriminatory practices as well as physical abuses by state agents in criminal justice. Studies in neuroscience, social psychology and trauma have made clear that the state's infliction of trauma on an individual can be criminogenic; it may affect the person's degree of volition and decision-making. It may also incite violence. These studies have shown that exposure to extreme adversity or toxic stress, including physical abuse and other chronic exposure to violence, can induce significant and long-standing, yet reversible, alterations in the brain's structure and neurotransmission pathways (Mervyn and Ashton, 2023) that govern judgement, impulse control, empathetic responses, emotional regulation, threat perception and social cues. These alterations have been associated with a greater risk of maladaptive actions and behaviours, less impulse control, challenges with deciphering when danger is truly present, and a quickly activated fight/flight stress response system (Aiyer et al 2014; Bremner 2006). Nevertheless, considering the brain's adaptability and spasticity, alterations can be reversed through an adapted relational environment (Coppola 2021). This is significant in that it suggests the importance of adequately adapted responsive sentences that consider this lower level of blameworthiness.

Moreover, state misconduct that also affects volition can include situations that create reasons/incitements for individuals to commit offences. An individual's past traumatic experiences can provide reasons that may fall short of necessity or duress exculpatory defences yet still be relevant to the degree of moral blameworthiness (Lippke 2014; Ewing 2021). Additionally, contexts typically understood as police entrapment, where state agents offer strong incentives to marginalised groups who may have important unmet needs to commit offences may be read as criminogenic state misconduct warranting reduced blameworthiness. The need to consider this form of criminogenic state misconduct as an element of the wider social context becomes important within a desert-based framework to understand the offender's level of culpability and give effect to mitigating practices and responses that recognise this reality.

To be considered relevant to desert-based mitigation, the criminogenic state misconduct would need to precede, and its impact be present, during the commission of the offence. This makes sense from a perspective under which state misconduct under a desert-based justification would need to affect volition and decision-making, creating reasons for committing the offence and/or creating inducements present at the moment of the offence to affect culpability. Depending on whether state misconduct is an isolated event or a series of misconducts across a longer timeframe, such as systemic forms of violence or harms, the proximity to the actual commission of the offence may vary. In this sense, unless post-offence misconduct is used to illustrate a wider pattern of state practices that continue to occur after the commission of the offence, it would not be relevant in the determination of the level of blameworthiness. We suggest that state misconduct that occurs after the commission of the offence for which the person is sentenced cannot be a relevant mitigating factor under a desert-based rationale and thus would need to rely on a different justification.

The focus of the analysis under this rationale relates to the degree to which state misconduct affects one's mental state/decision-making process rather than the severity of state misconduct. Relatedly, the level of mitigation due to lower culpability would depend on the degree to which misconduct is criminogenic and the extent to which individual volition is affected by this criminogenic state misconduct. As suggested by Morse, contrary to the 'all-or-nothing doctrines' relating to capacity for rationality, control and hard choices, agency and mental state should be understood as concepts arrayed on a continuum (Morse 2002: 296). While Morse suggests this applies across the criminal justice process, we contend that this framing is particularly important in sentencing, since this stage of the process, within desert theory, is meant to welcome various degrees of mental states relating to rationality and agency as part of a continuum.

Regarding evidence, it is worth highlighting that state misconduct's effects on one's volition can be evidenced in different ways. These include expert evidence which can take various forms, including sociological and criminological expert reports, studies on criminogenic conditions, as well as social neuroscience, psychological studies and background-cultural assessment reports (*R v Ipeelee*) that examine the impact of state misconduct on individual volition. Experiential evidence can also be useful but would need to be complemented by scientific research on the specific criminogenic nature of conduct and its effect on volition. Since we are within such a complex field with interconnected variables that may affect levels of volition, evidence should be admitted with flexibility to draw a fuller portrait of the situational context between this misconduct and its impact on bringing the individual to offend.

A challenge within a desert-based framework of proportionality remains the unresolved question of weight and relationship between the gravity of the offence and the level of blameworthiness of the offender. On this point, we agree with Ashworth that the degree of responsibility towards the offence should take precedence over the objective gravity of the offence, which focuses on results, since the primary aim for the criminal law under a desert-based perspective is to reflect the offender's individual and moral responsibility vis à vis the offence (Ashworth, forthcoming). Ashworth highlights that

> all that a person can and should be blamed for is the exertion, for that is all that lies within their control: to allow results to determine blame is to place weight on chance or luck, and that is an inappropriate basis for a rational and proportionate system of public censuring.

Underpinning this argument is the notion that offenders should not be blamed for actions that they do not control. Within proportionality, if state misconduct has impacted the degree of control a person has towards their actions, this should be considered to mitigate their degree of responsibility and not ignored or lessened by the harm caused by the offence. Finally, since the rationale for mitigation in this chapter is desert-based and relies on reduced blameworthiness, we do not foresee any problems of 'norm and exception' raised by desert theorists in contexts of compassion-based rationales (von Hirsch and Ashworth 2005: 70).

While most jurisdictions have yet to recognise desert-based arguments for justifying the mitigating role of state misconduct in sentencing, various upper-level courts in Canada have recognised the relevance of this factor in cases of systemic state misconduct that relate to anti-Black racism and Indigenous colonialism (*R v Morris*; *R v Anderson*; *R v Ipeelee*). While these decisions do not explicitly employ the language of criminogenic effect of state misconduct, they nevertheless recognise the systemic and background factors 'which may have played a part in bringing' the offender before the court (*R v Ipeelee* [59]). Recognising the effects of colonialism and anti-Black racism on offending, courts have started laying the ground for this form of mitigation.

For instance, the Ontario Court of Appeal's decision in *Morris* (2021) recognised that anti-Black racism partly created by police and other state agents can partially explain the offender's offence of possessing an illegal firearm. This type of state misconduct would be relevant to understanding the level of blameworthiness as part of a desert-based framework if there is sufficient evidence to suggest that this has affected the offender's volition/decision-making.

The following passages by the Court capture the potential for anti-Black racism misconduct by the state (police), as a form of criminogenic misconduct, to be adduced as relevant mitigating evidence at sentencing that serves to reduce the offender's moral blameworthiness. The Court highlights:

> [99] The social context evidence may offer an explanation for the commission of the offence which mitigates the offender's personal responsibility and culpability for the offence. Mr. Morris's strong and ever-present fear of many people around him in his community, including the police, was offered as an explanation for his possession of a loaded gun. The information in both reports supported the inference that Mr. Morris's fears were real, justified and existed, in part, as a result of systemic racism that played a role in shaping his perception of his community, his relationship with others in the community, and his relationship with the police.
>
> [100] … That state of mind offered a mitigating explanation for Mr. Morris's possession of the loaded, concealed handgun. Looked at in this way, evidence of anti-Black racism, which played a role in generating the fear that helps explain why Mr. Morris had a loaded gun, is akin, for the purposes of sentencing, to evidence that Mr. Morris had been terrorized by somebody in the community and had armed himself because he genuinely feared that person. In either scenario, the offender offers an explanation for possessing a loaded gun, which, to some extent, ameliorates the offender's moral responsibility for that choice.
>
> [101] It must be stressed, however, that Mr. Morris's genuine fear, regardless of its cause, is only a limited mitigating factor. He still chose to arm himself in public with a concealed, loaded, deadly weapon. As indicated above, Mr. Morris's reasons for choosing to arm himself do not detract from the seriousness of the crime he committed. Even if his conduct is made somewhat less blameworthy by the explanation offered for possessing the loaded handgun, Mr. Morris's conduct still put members of the community, and police officers engaged in the lawful execution of their duties, at real risk.

The Court considers social context evidence relating to anti-Black racism as a credible explanation for the offender's possession of a loaded firearm, which is relevant to understanding and assessing his level of culpability. Importantly, it also highlights that its mitigating effect is limited and does not absolve all responsibility for the offence, nor does it diminish the second component of proportionality, namely the gravity of the offence.

The evidence in this case, which draws connections between anti-Black racism and its impact on the offender, was adduced by referring to reports that include sociological, experiential and psychiatric knowledge. One was prepared by a clinical social worker working on a doctorate with a research focus on education and social work, with extensive clinical experience, and who conducts workshops on the ways systemic anti-Black racism impacts Black youth in various contexts. Drawing connections between systemic factors and the commission of the offence, the reports also contained experiential information provided by Morris about his perceptions of how he has been treated by the police and correctional authorities over the years. This evidence was deemed admissible and relevant by the Court. Specifically, in light of the report writer's academic and clinical experiences as a social worker, she was deemed competent to offer an opinion as to the connection between anti-Black racism and Morris's involvement in the criminal justice system. However, the Court noted the limited qualifications in providing information on the offender's state of mind (emotional difficulties/diagnosis of PTSD, which was complemented by the psychiatric report) and the physical injury suffered by Morris.

A similar perspective on reduced moral blameworthiness was articulated in *R v Anderson*, as well as the aforementioned Canadian cases relating to systemic discrimination towards Indigenous offenders. As articulated by the Supreme Court of Canada in *R v Ipeelee* [85], 'unless the unique circumstances of the particular offender bear on his or her culpability for the offence or indicate which sentencing objectives can and should be actualized, they will not influence the ultimate sentence'.

These judgments posit that state misconduct in the form of discriminatory practices by the state (and others), such as anti-Black systemic racism and colonialism, does not need to be causally connected to the commission of the offence to affect the degree of blameworthiness. Indeed, as highlighted by the Aboriginal Justice Inquiry of Manitoba and reaffirmed in *Ipeelee*, 'cultural oppression, social inequality, the loss of self-government and systemic discrimination, which are the legacy of the Canadian Government's treatment of Aboriginal people, are intertwined and interdependent factors, and in very few cases is it possible to draw a simple and direct correlation between any one of them and the events which lead an individual Aboriginal person to commit a crime or to become incarcerated' (Public Inquiry into the Administration of Justice and Aboriginal People, 1991: 86; *Ipeelee* 2012 [83]). In this sense, due to the complexity and impossibility of making a direct and sole causal link between the state's misconduct and the commission of the offence, it is worth relying on this evidence as circumstantial, which should be sufficient in such contexts to illustrate the impact on the offender's degree of volition and culpability.

In brief, a desert-based framework provides justifications for treating state misconduct as mitigation that communicates individual censure. The key dimension within this framework would be an analysis that focuses on the degree of moral impairment that this misconduct has had on the individual's volition. It may indeed be that in certain contexts the degree of impairment rises to the level of a defence where the person's responsibility is not engaged. In such contexts, this dimension can be brought forward even prior to sentencing and can affect the verdict. The next frameworks provide justifications which rely on censure but from a wider communicative perspective that expands censure to the state.

III. Communicating State Censure and Relational Responsibility for Criminogenic State Misconduct

The previous section outlined a framework rooted within desert for considering forms of state misconduct affecting one's degree of volition. The framework in this section suggests that state misconduct which is criminogenic is relevant in sentencing, not only under a desert-based rationale, but to ensure that the enterprise of criminal law and punishment serves its overall function of assigning accurate responsibility for public wrongs committed and enable responses to this responsibility. Indeed, when the state is involved in criminogenic misconduct, which contributes to one's commission of the offence, the individual should not be the one who bears all responsibility and blame whether the state created conditions that contributed to or facilitated this offence. Although this communicative process may also take place at other stages of the criminal justice process, sentencing is a relevant place to do so considering its communicative function and analysis of level of blameworthiness. This dimension would be an additional and complementary dimension from sentencing's desert-based function and would be rooted within a wider communicative theory of punishment.

In some contexts of state misconduct, the state and its agents can be responsible for creating conditions where the offence is more likely to occur (referred to as criminogenic). This reality suggests that the state is also a contributory agent of criminality or in some way complicit to the offence. This contributory role is part of a relational understanding of responsibility, which recognises responsibility for the offence not just as the doing of one person, but at times the doing of others – including the state.

Importantly, this recognition and rationale is not intended to absolve the offender from responsibility for the crime committed nor necessarily remove the state's standing to recognise and legitimately sanction individual wrongdoing (Duff 1988; Duff 2010). Rather, the framework expands communicative theory by also recognising the state's role and duties owed to the offender, the offence, and accurate punishment – suggesting that the state should also be the subject of censure and held accountable for its contribution to the various harms relating to criminality, criminalisation, and punishment (Manikis 2022b).

Under this relational/contributory responsibility framework, state misconduct would need to be criminogenic since the underpinning of this rationale is based on a shared/complementary, yet different form of responsibility for the offence as the wrongdoing (rather than another separate form of wrongdoing).

In such situations, building on communicative theories of responsibility and punishment, we suggest that sentencing should recognise and communicate censure for state wrongdoing that relates to the creation of criminogenic conditions. This requires that the state can be considered a wrongdoer – partially challenging the traditional conception in criminal law that the state is the victim and that the individual is the wrongdoer. In addition to contributing to a more fulsome and accurate understanding of responsibility, this form of relational state censure also legitimises and strengthens the communicative endeavour of punishment by recognising, communicating and responding to contexts where the state shares part of the blame.

Within this relational framework of responsibility, the focus of state misconduct is to communicate/censure the degree/type of wrongdoing and harms by the state. While desert theorists have rejected this rationale on the basis that 'it would not be easy to develop doctrines or theories which enable one to identify when this kind of fault is present' (von Hirsch and Ashworth 2005: 69), we think that this endeavour can begin by articulating conceptions and typologies of criminogenic wrongdoing/harms by the state.

The state's relational responsibility relating to criminogenic conditions, which are relevant to communicate at sentencing, can be divided into two categories. The first category (type 1) relates to the state's criminogenic creation and maintenance of societal inequalities. This type of state misconduct is predominantly systemic, consisting of state policies that promote various forms of inequalities that are *known* by the state to perpetuate criminogenic conditions.

This criminogenic type of state wrongdoing closely aligns with some of Duff and Watson's scholarship (Duff 2001; Watson 2015) which primarily engages with socio-economic injustices as forms of systemic wrongdoing to suggest a form of responsibility and complicity by the political community/state in the crime. They highlight the importance of listening and answering to the offender, collectively, by taking responsibility for the collective wrongdoing as part of the trial to gain legitimacy to punish socio-economically deprived individuals. Similar arguments in the context of social deprivation suggest the relevance of recognising the state's relational responsibility alongside a duty to punish (Tadros 2009). Tadros discusses this type of relational responsibility in the context of the state's contribution to economic injustice (2009). He argues that the state is blameworthy through complicity where the economic injustice it perpetrates by distributive injustice creates criminogenic conditions. In such instances, although the state cannot specifically identify who will commit crimes, it knows that the crime rate will increase in conditions of economic inequality.

Manikis (2022b) has expanded this framing to other forms of state-produced criminogenic inequalities and practices, such as those rooted in state colonialism, gender/patriarchal structures, anti-racism, anti-Semitic, anti-Muslim and other power imbalances, known by the state to be criminogenic and produce related harms through documented studies on inequalities. She highlights the importance of censuring the state as part of punishment's communicative endeavour, as it shares part of the blame for the offence. While there is an underlying legitimacy-based rationale in this argument, it relates to attributing a more accurate and nuanced responsibility for the offence.

Concrete situations where communicating this type of state misconduct would be relevant in sentencing are cases of gender-based violence, including sexual assault and domestic violence, particularly within marginalised communities. To do so, the state's contribution to the creation of inequalities should be discussed and analysed separately in judgments, in addition to desert-based rationales, to highlight the state's role in creating criminogenic conditions and the extent of related harms. This approach allows for a more thorough and nuanced communicative endeavour about responsibility and related responses instead of promoting a one-way message that contributes to defective practices of responsibility by assigning blame solely to the offender.

An example where this type of state blame/harm would have been relevant to communicate was the case of *R v LP*, where an Indigenous person with a long history of violent domestic abuse recidivated against his partner while heavily intoxicated. In its decision, the Quebec Court of Appeal gave priority to objectives of denunciation and deterrence on the legislative basis (718.201 Criminal Code) that consideration needs to be given to the 'increased vulnerability of female victims in cases of abuse, with particular attention to the circumstances of Indigenous female victims'(*R v LP* [76]). The interpretation of victim vulnerability favoured an approach that emphasised the offender's individual blame and harms suffered by the victim instead of engaging in a wider censuring approach that also examined the causes of this vulnerability, which can be traced to the state's contribution.

More specifically, the disproportionate rate of domestic violence and harms suffered by Indigenous women was attributed to the individual offender without a separate focus of the state's criminogenic contribution to this wider issue. While the Court referred to reports and evidence (National Inquiry into Missing and Murdered Indigenous Women and Girls 2019) that point to systemic blame, notably by highlighting the way social and economic marginalisation of Indigenous people is criminogenic, it used these reports to suggest that the blame should be focused on the individual offender (*R v LP* [85]). This was also the case when the Court identified colonialism as additional state criminogenic conduct, including the insufficiency and credibility bias of institutional response to all forms of interpersonal violence suffered by Indigenous women and girls, notably from law enforcement.

Although these statements seem to point to the state's relational contribution in creating criminogenic conditions, the Court in *R v LP* ultimately avoids framing it as such, and instead considers these harms as 'suffered at the hands of her spouse' (at [101]), relevant to the offender's blame and proposing imprisonment as a response. Further, the offender's drinking problems are attributed to himself whereas a separate additional analysis of state blame focusing on its criminogenic contribution to colonialism would have allowed a more nuanced understanding of blame and state-induced harms that have contributed to alcoholism within Indigenous communities (Ross et al 2015). This example highlights the prominent role that desert-based reasoning plays in Canada.

In addition to this first type, criminogenic state misconduct can also derive from the state's more concrete Criminalization Policies and Practices that Target or Affect Marginalised Groups (referred to as type 2). This type of state misconduct and related harms is also predominantly systemic but directly linked to the criminal justice process, since the state's criminogenic relational responsibility is engaged by specifically resorting to criminal law policies and practices that target or affect marginalised groups which generate crimes. This second type includes two possible scenarios of state criminogenic misconduct: (1) through criminalisation policies and practices that directly target and/or intend to harm members of marginalised groups; and (2) through criminalisation policies and practices which the state does not intend but knows are more likely to criminalise and impact members of marginalised groups.

State misconduct is more reprehensible in scenario (1) since knowledge and intent (including targeted misconduct) are directly involved. Notable historical examples in England and Wales and Canada can fall into the first subcategory, including the criminalisation of sodomy (eg Buggery Act of 1533; Blackstone 1765), of self-liberated people of African descent (Maynard 2017; Dugas 2020), and of certain Indigenous cultural practices (Monchalin 2016). Current examples also include the criminalisation of refugees through migration policies (Criddle 2020), and the crime of gender fraud in England and Wales (*R v McNally*). They can also include law enforcement policies that knowingly target certain groups, including the consideration of certain criteria in carding (when police officers randomly stop and question someone and collect information about them) and stop and frisk policies (*Luamba v Québec (AG)*), as well as direct and intentional actions by state agents, such as violence or other forms of intentional human rights breaches in the context of the criminal justice process that are criminogenic in light of the social context and situation of the accused. An example of this scenario's state intentional/targeted wrongdoing that benefits from sentence reduction can include cases that fall short of entrapment in which police targeted a person addicted to heroin to commit drug offences (eg *R v Kirzner*).

In scenario (2), although the state does not know who will commit crimes and does not intentionally target members of marginalised groups, it does know or ought to know through documented research as well as training, that some of its criminalisation and punishment policies and practices towards marginalised groups are criminogenic. Current examples include state practices that disproportionately enforce criminalisation upon certain groups for certain offences, contributing to the revolving door phenomenon (Petrich et al 2021). For instance, the phenomenon of over-policing, over-prosecution (National Council of Welfare 2000), and harsher punishment (Cardoso 2020; Manikis 2022a) that disproportionately affect certain marginalised groups and give rise to the revolving door phenomenon in contexts relating to drug offences, and contexts of mental health involvement or indigence would need to be accounted for as part of a relational responsibility rationale within a sentencing process that sees its role as communicative.

Relatedly, in Canada, the Court of Appeal of Ontario in *R v Morris*, recognised that 'sentencing judges must acknowledge societal complicity in systemic racism and be alert to the possibility that the sentencing process itself may foster that complicity' (2021 [86]). Nevertheless, while acknowledging this wider complicity, the Court rejected the idea of relational responsibility in sentencing, highlighting that allocating responsibility for crimes as between society and the individual offender should play a role in fixing the appropriate sentence as it is currently not a justified objective in sentencing. Interestingly, in *R v Nasogaluak*, a context of state misconduct that involved police brutality upon arrest, the Supreme Court of Canada also posited that:

> S. 718 of the *Criminal Code* describes the fundamental purpose of sentencing as that of contributing to 'respect for the law and the maintenance of a just, peaceful and safe society'. This function must be understood as providing scope for sentencing judges to consider not only the actions of the offender, but also those of state actors. Provided that the impugned conduct relates to the individual offender and the circumstances of his or her offence, the sentencing process includes consideration of society's collective interest in ensuring that law enforcement agents respect the rule of law and the shared values of our society (2010 [49]).

Building on components of *Nasogaluak* and as a response to *Morris*, we suggest that criminogenic state misconduct rooted in various dimensions of systemic inequalities, discussed in this section, ought to be reflected in communication about responsibility and sentencing in a way that understands responsibility as relational, which is rooted in values of substantive equality.

A justificatory rationale would highlight that this type of recognition of the state's relational misconduct and responsibility in sentencing sits within a communicative theory of punishment, since ascription of responsibility, blame and punishment needs to attribute responsibility for the offence in an accurate qualitative fashion that also promotes dialogue and legitimacy within the process. If the state is partly responsible for the offence, state actors would have a moral duty to recognise this reality, communicate it within the public process, and respond as part of the overall sentence. For instance, sentencing judges, who are also agents of the state and part of a state decision-making process should recognise their own potentially criminogenic role and relational responsibility in sentencing and as part of this recognition, respond to these forms of systemic misconduct in sentencing.

It may be that in some contexts, judges can craft sentences that partly address such criminogenic realities or at least aim to limit them. Depending on the type of state misconduct/wrongdoing, its nature and gravity, responses at sentencing might entail a recognition of this type of systemic state misconduct, an apology, a stay of proceedings, sentence reduction, a sentence that ensures an appropriate environment for the offender – such as avoiding imprisonment with adequate support systems – or a consultation/delegation to or with Indigenous communities or other recognised entities that would have legitimacy and responses in such instance. Sentencing judges can tailor their responses in ways that recognise individual blame and address wider systemic dimensions such as colonialism. For instance, consulting with or delegating to Indigenous and Black-led groups when community-based approaches are available may be relevant responses in sentencing that can address the criminogenic root cause of crime.

These types of responses can advance various victim interests, particularly by contributing to approaches that value long-term safety and reduction of criminogenic conditions (Krinsky and Komar 2021). This, ultimately, will lead to fewer victims. It is particularly relevant to address some of the root causes of crime for victims and address criminogenic conditions as most are part of marginalised communities and are themselves criminalised by the criminal legal system (Sered D et al 2014).

With this form of communication in sentencing, sentencing judges, who are agents of the state within criminal justice, also communicate messages to other state agencies about their relational role in the creation of criminogenic conditions that may have a seemingly more direct impact on redressing such systemic and criminogenic injustices (Chan 2010). This signalling may give rise to concrete actions by these branches of government that are outside the criminal justice process, yet attentive to the criminogenic effects of certain policies or actions.

Criminogenic state misconduct that engages the state's relational responsibility would need to precede the offence. The key dimension in relational responsibility is to determine whether the state's misconduct can be considered criminogenic and if so, finding ways to communicate this form of state misconduct by using the terminology relating to responsibility, along with its relevant responses/effects on sentencing. Evidence of what is considered criminogenic can include expert reports, social science research and the range of knowledge discussed earlier in this chapter. As such, there may be forms of state misconduct that are closer in timing of the offence, while others may have occurred before (or are systemically ongoing). While it may be that certain forms of criminogenic misconduct that occur closer to the offence are easier to prove in terms of criminogeneity, it may not always be so and studies on trauma discussed above as well as social science knowledge suggest that systemic events that are ongoing and have occurred years prior can also be criminogenic (Gibbons et al 2020). In this sense, state misconduct that occurs after the offence and/or is not criminogenic may be best captured under different justifications, such as those discussed below.

IV. Communicating State 'Excess Harms' that Exceed Legitimate Punishment

This third justificatory rationale for considering state misconduct in sentencing relies on communicative theories of punishment that articulate the relevance of sentencing for communicating and responding to state-created wrongs/harms that exceed what would be deemed legitimate punishment. We propose an analysis of forms of state misconduct that relate to the administration of the sentence. Such misconduct can be two-fold and include misconduct that is considered foreseeable during the administration of the sentence (scenario 1) and misconduct which has already affected the offender during the administration of the sentence (scenario 2) and requires a form of sentence review.

This third rationale is relevant to the enterprise of criminal law and punishment since it is premised on the notion that the state, as part of the administration of the sentence, should not cause greater harm to individuals than the level that is proportionate and legitimate for punishment. Any additional harm caused by the state during the administration of the sentence, whether it has already occurred, whether it is foreseeable or unforeseeable at sentencing should be a relevant element to communicate and address within sentencing as part of a reciprocal communicative endeavour. This type of rationale for considering state wrongdoing as relevant in sentencing is different to the one discussed above – the latter being premised on relational responsibility for the offence. While within a relational responsibility framework, discussed above, the state's degree of wrongdoing is measured by looking at the degree of criminogenic impact/state contribution to the offence, state wrongdoing within this third rationale relates solely to the type of wrongdoing and degree to which it creates excessive and thus illegitimate harm and does not need to be criminogenic. It therefore needs to clearly articulate the type of wrongdoing the state is involved in (foreseeable/known excess harms, intentional, etc) and then compare the level of excess with what is considered proportionate/legitimate punishment.

This third rationale is rooted within communicative theories of punishment and relies on the notion that communicating censure is a dynamic process (Dagan and Roberts 2019), where the offender/citizen should be heard as part of the censuring exercise. This includes instances where the offender/citizen brings dimensions of state wrongs/harms as 'excess' from punishment that can or has taken place during the administration of the sentence. A dialectical process of censure requires listening to the offender/citizen to recognise, communicate and respond within sentencing to instances of state failures to the wider public, the offender, and victims, as state-produced harms that exceed legitimate punishment.

State misconduct as excess harms under this rationale can take various forms. They include state-created ancillary harms that occur during the administration of the sentence, state abuses/violence during the administration of punishment, and various harmful prison/sentencing conditions in the context of imprisonment/sanction that exceed legitimate punishment. These situations are typically *known* by the state or *foreseeable* at sentencing through empirical evidence on prisons or reports. To this end, counsel may need to familiarise themselves with the world of corrections in order to supply the requisite evidentiary foundation to sentencing judges. For instance, sentencing judges could require prosecutors to provide plans for a proposed sentence, including the expected level of security, institutional setting and available programming. Relevant evidence can also come from probation officers, academic researchers, correctional watchdogs that have drafted annual reports, correctional officials, or offenders with experiential knowledge on local realities.

Moreover, certain forms of state wrongdoing may only arise during the administration of the sentence/punishment and thus may be unforeseeable at sentencing. In such contexts, the sentencing process would require a mechanism of sentence review during the administration of the sentence to ensure that such excess harms are recognised, communicated and responded to throughout the administration of the sentence (Manikis and Matheson 2024; Manikis and Doiron 2023).

This rationale recognises the duty of sentencing judges, as state actors, equipped and aware of what is considered legitimate punishment[2] to recognise, communicate and respond to excess harms that can foreseeably occur or have already occurred during the administration of the sentence in a public way in order to acknowledge and address state failures as part of its role in the wider administration of punishment.

Responses that relate to the administration of justice can take multiple forms and depend on circumstances. In contexts of foreseeable excess harms, such as scenarios in which judges would be brought evidence of problematic prison conditions, it may be that imprisonment or certain forms of punishment would be judged unacceptable for certain offenders in specific contexts of state failures and alternatives to imprisonment would be warranted. Suspended sentences may also be considered to communicate misconduct regarding excess harm. Sentence reduction can be sufficient to censure the state and respond to the misconduct, but the signalling would need to be clear to highlight the reasons for the reduction. In most cases, appropriate responses would entail other state entities making minor or wider systemic changes within prisons or as part of sentences in the community to reduce or remove these exceeding harms. In such scenarios, sentencing judges would need to be clear about these wider failings in their judgment and signal these potential responses to the relevant state branches. As such, communication of state censure may serve as an opportunity for sentencing courts to send wider messages to separate, yet related state agencies, such as probations, prisons or other government bodies to introduce better conditions, services and programmes within prisons, or as alternatives to incarceration. These responses can take place at sentencing or during sentence reviews.

[2] The development of sentencing guidelines to delineate what is considered normatively proportionate and legitimate as punishment would need to be developed. State-imposed excessive punishment would arguably be considered as harm above and beyond the accepted level of punishment.

Responses as remedies offered during sentence review would arguably be more precise since they would relate directly to excess harms that have already occurred rather than foreseeable harms. In contexts of prison conditions that are not considered legitimate punishment by initial sentencers, responses can include terminating detention and opting for alternatives or requiring that certain prisons introduce relevant changes prior to incarcerating additional individuals. The sentence review process can have important systemic transformational potential that takes the communicative endeavour beyond mere individual censure.

This third justification should not be analysed within the proportionality/experiential punishment framework but rather as a standalone analysis of state censure after having decided what would otherwise constitute a proportionate punishment. Proportionality communicates a legitimate degree of censure to the individual offender (and society) for one's level of blameworthiness for the offence rather than drawing any mutual responsibility and censure towards the state (von Hirsch and Ashworth 2005; Manikis 2022a). Analysing this matter as part of proportionality and experience of punishment limits the analytical endeavour that relates to communicating and responding to state misconduct. It also can legitimise certain excess harms by increasingly normalising them as part of inevitable components of punishment.

Indeed, the principle of proportionality, which has a longstanding history rooted in just deserts theory comprises dual components, namely the gravity of the offence and level of blameworthiness. Proportionality serves to communicate a legitimate degree of censure to the individual offender (and society) for the individual's level of blameworthiness for the offence rather than drawing any mutual responsibility and censure towards the state (von Hirsch and Ashworth 2005; Manikis 2022a). As part of the proportionality analysis, the system focuses on determining the type of sentence and its duration. When a type of sentence is considered proportionate to communicate individual censure, proportionality rests on an assumption that conditions under the responsibility of the state are reasonable. In this sense, proportionality should maintain this specific and limited rationale related to censuring individual desert with legitimate sanctions rather than seeking to communicate state censure or respond to the potential excess harms related to the sentence. Since the rationale proposed in this section is rooted within a wider communicative framework that seeks to censure and respond to state excess harms from a proportionate sentence, we suggest that this sentencing assessment would be part of a consequentialist rationale that is different, yet complementary, to desert-based retributive proportionality. Lumping this rationale into proportionality risks undermining that principle and limiting the wider communicative potential of censuring the state.

This framework offers a wider and conceptually different communicative perspective than proportionality, rooted in Manikis's framework of 'state blame' (2022b), which shifts the gaze onto state misconduct and engages with censuring the state.

Within this wider communicative framework, if conditions exceed what are normatively[3] considered proportionate/legitimate conditions at sentencing, serving penological legitimate aims, these harmful conditions, if caused by the state, should be considered state wrongs referred to as excess harms and responded to as part of sentencing within a separate framework than just deserts-based proportionality. Referring to such excesses as 'punishment' should be avoided as it can serve to legitimise this misconduct, which sends a problematic message to society and citizens. Moreover, as highlighted by HLA Hart, legitimate punishment requires key elements, including the *intentional* administration of consequences considered unpleasant to an offender for his offence by an authority constituted by a legal system against which the offence is committed (1959). In this sense, under a framework of state censure, excess harms should not be part of the proportionality analysis since its function serves wider communicative aims about state wrongdoing rather than individual desert related to the offence.

Responses for such wrongdoing can also vary and may include a reduction of sentence. An example can be seen within Canada's context of pre-trial detention which legislatively recognises important credit/reduction for pre-trial detention.[4] Sentencing guidelines can be used to highlight the various degrees of reduction that can be useful and tailored to the specific state wrongdoing.

In brief, this third rationale for incorporating state misconduct in sentencing understands state blame and censure expansively and aims to signal and engage with state blame in contributory harms more dynamically. As such, it allows for greater recognition and responses to state action that produces excessive unforeseeable harms at sentencing and are manifested during the administration of the sentence.

In conclusion, this chapter has outlined different complementary ways in which state misconduct can be a justified consideration at sentencing. These rationales are rooted in communicating functions that are complementary to one another. While some focus on drawing out the impact of state misconduct on individual desert, others are focused on censuring the state for its various forms of misconduct that are relevant within the enterprise of criminal – either by ascribing a more nuanced understanding of responsibility for the offence or by

[3] Within this framework, relevant evidence adduced in sentencing is not meant to include purely subjective experiences of the offender's conditions, such as those highlighted by Kolber 2009 and denounced by Ryberg 2010. Rather, the proposed framework suggests that sentencers should be provided with evidence that can be classified across the objective/subjective spectrum as discussed in Hayes 2018. This rationale proposes a comparative exercise between what is assumed/accepted to be part of the punishment by sentencers and conditions than would be considered excessive harms when compared to what is accepted/assumed by sentencers. The development of sentencing guidelines to delineate what is considered normatively legitimate and proportionate would need to be carved out in more detail than it is currently the case between policy-makers and judges. Additional dimensions created by the state that would exceed the harms assumed/harms would be considered state failures and would need to be communicated and addressed in sentencing.

[4] 719 Criminal Code of Canada; for further discussions on credit/reduction for pre-trial detention, see Manikis and Matheson 2024.

communicating excess harms as state misconduct that relate to the administration of the sentence. These rationales aim to strengthen communicative practices and therefore sentencers would need to be clear about which rationale they are relying on and the aims they are attempting to achieve. The principle of proportionality would also be strengthened. For instance, the first rationale will provide a more accurate sense of the individual's level of blameworthiness by being attentive to the various forms of misconduct that can affect volition. The third rationale will also strengthen proportionality by recognising its limited role within the administration of the sentence. Currently, sentences include several qualitative assumptions and a greater attention to objective components that are considered acceptable within assumed punishments will be important to delineate dimensions that are considered excess harms.

The rationales presented in this chapter are compatible with one another and can form part of different stages within sentencing guidelines. First, state misconduct can feature as part of the analysis of individual moral blameworthiness in step one which aims to censure the individual by relying on the framework of proportionality. Second, state misconduct can feature within a second step that serves to communicate relational blame about the offence. Finally, in determining the sentence, state misconduct can also feature in the analysis about what are foreseeable qualitative conditions of the sanction imposed and taking this evidence into account when sentencing. The sentence review proposed in this chapter suggests that sentencing should not end with a sentence, since punishment and excess harms can take place throughout the administration of the sentence. In this sense, a sentence review process is proposed to consider excess harms that arise during the administration of the sentence.

Finally, the various components of this framework highlight the need for a greater qualitative understanding of sentences, punishment and excess harms along with a more robust introduction of social science research in thinking about responsibility, sentencing and the administration of sentences. In this sense, considering state misconduct in sentencing challenges certain longstanding quantitative assumptions about levels of responsibility and equivalences in punishment/sentences and highlights the need to infuse greater qualitative dimensions, supported by social sciences within our understanding of responsibility and communication of sentences.

12

Police Misconduct and Sentence Mitigation

GABRIELLE WATSON[1]

> 'Get off me. Get off my neck!' A police officer applies pressure with his knee to the neck area of *suspect A*, an ethnic minority, during an arrest and restraint (Independent Office for Police Conduct 2021; Hamilton 2020).
>
> *Suspect B*, a vulnerable woman, is arrested with excessive force and then subject to an illegal strip search in the presence of male officers, receiving no explanation as to why or how the search is to be conducted (Independent Office for Police Conduct 2022).
>
> While *suspect C* is face down and pinned to the ground, a police officer positions the sole of his boot on the suspect's head and stamps on him repeatedly (Independent Office for Police Conduct 2023).

If these cases were to progress through the criminal justice system, and *suspects A*, *B* and *C* were ultimately convicted, should they be entitled to reduced sentences on the grounds that they had been wronged by an agent of the state? After all, these officers not only inflict physical harm, but also flout the values – courage, respect, empathy and public service – on which their authoritative relation to citizens depends (College of Policing 2024; Gardner 2013).

It is no exaggeration to say that policing in England and Wales is in a state of institutional decay (Loader 2023; Harper 2022; Trilling 2023). The high-profile Baroness Casey Review (2023) exposed a series of systemic failings by the Metropolitan Police. Among the most incisive criticisms of the force were its flawed process for resolving allegations of police misconduct, with no clear accountability mechanisms for officers who fail to meet basic standards of ethical behaviour. The force finds itself in a state of crisis and is fast losing its reputation as a legitimate and rights-regarding agency. This is an observable trend not only in England and Wales – Shavisi (2022) insists 'don't call the police' – but internationally, as seen through the activist movement Black Lives Matter (Bestvater et al 2023).

[1] For invaluable commentary and critique, I thank the editors and participants at the State Misconduct seminar at the Institute of Criminology, University of Cambridge (December 2023), and members of the Criminal Law and Criminal Justice Theory Forum at the London School of Economics (January 2024).

No doubt *suspects A*, *B* and *C* were over-policed, and their bodily integrity violated. Such cases raise severe proportionality concerns and imply an urgent need to bring discretionary police power within limits. But should such instances of over-policing become the business of the criminal courts, when traditionally they have been handled by internal police disciplinary procedures or referred to the Independent Office for Police Conduct? It is a normative question to which there is no straightforward answer, and on which remarkably little literature exists (for an exception, see Duda 2021).

This chapter explores the possibility of state misconduct as a new mitigating factor at sentencing – with special reference to the police – to see how far such an argument might extend. The chapter is exploratory in nature – designed to begin a conversation on police misconduct in the sentencing context – and takes the jurisdiction of England and Wales as its primary example. Why focus exclusively on the police? A chapter of this length cannot provide full coverage of every form of state misconduct, but it can identify some powerful instances of misconduct within one of the most visible, morally contested and politically sensitive agencies of the state. The use of force by the police is not new, but their misuse of that power in recent years (Casey 2023) is deserving of sustained attention. As illustrated by the experiences of *suspects A*, *B* and *C*, there is an increasing coincidence in England and Wales of excessive force with sinister signals that make a mockery of the idea that the police are a legitimate expression of state violence (see further Harding 2020).

Loader and Walker lament the 'gradual de-coupling of police and state' in theory and practice and set out to reconstitute and defend a 'positive' connection between the two (2001: 9). After all, the police connection to state is vital to the legitimate application of reasonable force (Independent Office for Police Conduct 2015). This chapter – in exploring police misconduct as one illustration of state misconduct – might be seen as a modest contribution to the larger project that Loader and Walker articulate.

I. Overview

The chapter is organised as follows. First, it contemplates which forms of police misconduct might qualify as mitigating in the sentencing courts of England and Wales. Second, it introduces comparative insights from the common law jurisdiction of Canada, where substantial sentence reductions for police misconduct have already been issued.[2] While the Canadian case law offers one possible approach to quantum – the magnitude of the reduction to be awarded – the issue is far from being resolved conclusively. Third, the chapter considers two possible arguments in favour of state misconduct as a new mitigating factor at sentencing and assesses their normative adequacy. To conclude, the chapter contemplates the question of

[2] *R v Nasogaluak; R v Morris; R v Acheampong.*

institutional redesign, and the possibility of an alternative forum – quite separate from the sentencing court – for addressing police misconduct.

II. First Impressions

A. Police Misconduct

Police officers are granted rights and privileges – such as the right to use physical force – which ordinary citizens are denied,[3] and policing is intrinsically a high-risk profession for corruption (for examples, see Casey 2023). It is important, then, that the police are seen as ethical by the communities they serve, and their behaviour subject to meaningful correction when necessary.

The College of Policing (2023) imposes vague ethical constraints on officers by defining misconduct as 'unacceptable or improper behaviour'. Meanwhile, the Police (Conduct) Regulations 2020 offer greater specificity, defining misconduct as 'a breach of the Standards of Professional Behaviour that is so serious as to justify disciplinary action' and gross misconduct as 'a breach of the Standards of Professional Behaviour that is so serious as to justify dismissal'.[4] That misconduct can come in many forms: from the excessive use of force, forthright instances of racism, sexism and misogyny, the improper use of tasers, tear gas and firearms, to aggressive or coercive investigation methods, abusive language, lying and deception, manipulation, exploitation of vulnerable victims, and the misuse of technology, including social media.

The landmark case of *Nasogaluak*, to which we will return in section III, encouraged a sense of modest realism in our evaluation of police misconduct. The court observed that 'police actions should not be judged against a standard of perfection … police engage in dangerous and demanding work and often have to react quickly … their actions should be judged in light of these exigent circumstances'.[5] While this point is well made, the police are nonetheless street-level officials wielding state authority to respond to social problems: if necessary, they must be called to account and their behaviour subject to moral criticism.

The prevailing policing culture does not set the scene for ethical conduct between state and citizen. The Independent Office for Police Conduct (2022) recently published a report which found instances of bullying, misogyny and aggression following an investigation into the behaviour of 14 police officers based mainly at Charing Cross Police Station. Weeks later, a Freedom of Information request revealed that 129 officers continue to perform their normal duties despite

[3] 'To use physical force only when the exercise of persuasion, advice and warning is found to be insufficient to obtain public co-operation …' Loader, discussing the Peelian Principles (2016) 430.

[4] Regulation 2(1). See also Reg 23, 'Referral of case to misconduct proceedings'.

[5] *R v Nasogaluak* [35].

being accused of sexual abuse, domestic abuse, or both (Evans 2023). Since the brutal murder of George Floyd in Minneapolis in 2020, and in the face of persistent police violence, scholars on both sides of the Atlantic have effectively given up on their attempts to theorise police discretion, conceding that the police too often use their powers in ways that are inherently and unavoidably authoritarian, determining the basic terms of citizens' lives with limited or no consultation, deliberation or review (Thorburn 2024).

Consider stop and search, the controversial status of which is not new. As a common form of adversarial contact between the police and the public, stop and search taps into deep and ingrained tensions between preventive policing, the exercise of coercive state authority, due process and crime control. Perhaps the most incisive criticism of the practice is its disproportionate and discriminatory exercise in relation to minority ethnic groups (Watson 2020).

The utilitarian ethos of stop and search was reaffirmed in the 2015 Supreme Court judgment on section 60 of the Criminal Justice and Public Order Act 1994, which dismissed the argument that stop and search was intrinsically discriminatory, and backed the continued use of 'suspicionless' stop and search powers on the grounds that they 'benefit' young black men.[6] Strikingly, the court assumed this stance despite empirical evidence of police misconduct, including direct and indirect stereotyping and the disproportionate targeting of ethnic minorities (Watson 2020).

An emerging school of thought posits the *real* aims of stop and search to include the assertion of order, the regulation of marginal populations, and the monitoring of those who are 'known' to the police, 'based on who they are, not how they behave' (Bradford and Loader 2016: 257). It should come as no surprise, then, that too often young black men find themselves subject to inadequate policing and are presumptively criminalised when they are in fact victims of a crime or witnesses to it. Although there is no basis in law for the police to use the power in this way, Bowling and Phillips (2007) have long considered these extra-legal practices to be widespread.

Gardner (2010) prompts us to consider what might make someone a police officer *in name only* as opposed to a *real* police officer, one whose actions are morally defensible as a representative member of the police organisation. The role of the police creates 'police-characteristic temptations' (Gardner 2013). When a police officer acts in a way that is violent, sexist or racist, or abuses his legal powers to apply excessive force, his behaviour is at odds with the values of the organisation and is best understood as independent of the police role.

A first step in contemplating state misconduct as a new mitigating factor in the sentencing court, I suggest, would be to sensitise judges to these most troubling aspects of policing practice. Empirical research and academic commentary

[6] *R (on the application of Roberts) v Commissioner of Police of the Metropolis and another* [2] and [41].

on the prevalence and nature of police misconduct could function as a form of awareness education, 'nudging' judges into considering the potential merits and limits of mitigation claims of this kind (on the judicial nudge, see Aharoni et al 2022). Awareness education might begin with the empirical reality that young, black, socially marginalised men are most often and most heavily policed (Vomfell and Stewart 2021). Judges might also be introduced to the records of disciplinary proceedings, past and forthcoming, on the Metropolitan Police website, which offer a penetrating, and largely ignored, perspective on how some officers behave.[7]

B. Police Misconduct at Sentencing

Let us now shift our attention from judicial education to the sentencing court itself. Once a defendant has been convicted of a criminal offence in England and Wales, the court will move to impose sentence. The sentencing judge will consider any mitigating factors which may reduce the overall seriousness of the offence and justify a more lenient penalty. Traditional mitigating factors indicating lower culpability include a greater degree of provocation than normally expected, mental illness or disability, and youth or age where it affects the responsibility of the individual. Other forms of offender mitigation include remorse, admissions to the police in interview and ready cooperation with the authorities (Sentencing Council for England and Wales 2019).

The challenging question arises as to whether the Sentencing Council for England and Wales might legitimately expand its current list of mitigating factors – adopted in 2004 by its predecessor, the Sentencing Guidelines Council – to include state misconduct. Given that a new factor could substantially affect the severity of the punishment imposed, state misconduct would require a clear rationale and set of criteria for its application. In April 2024, the Council introduced pregnancy, childbirth and post-natal care as its newest mitigating factor (Sentencing Council for England and Wales 2024). The normative arguments and empirical evidence in favour of this new form of mitigation were simply overwhelming (see, eg, Minson 2016). By contrast, where state misconduct is concerned, there is much justificatory work to do.

Might it be possible to determine with any precision which forms of police misconduct might qualify as mitigating in the sentencing court? The most obvious ground for mitigation would involve an officer who had, through his discreditable conduct, brought about the conditions for – or, at the very least, exacerbated – an offender's criminal behaviour, affecting his level of culpability. There are circumstances which might be considered aggravating, especially those with a racial

[7] Metropolitan Police, 'Misconduct Hearings', available at www.met.police.uk/advice/advice-and-information/mis/misconduct-hearings.

dimension. In the era of Black Lives Matter (Bestvater et al 2023), it seems more important than ever for courts to denounce a situation involving, for example, two white police officers applying excessive force to an ethnic minority suspect. Courts might also consider inaction by other officers – for example, in failing to ensure the suspect receives timely medical attention for any injuries suffered at the hands of the police – in compounding the harm. CCTV or body-worn camera footage may provide proof of misconduct.

Another possibility is that we treat state misconduct at sentencing as an *extraneous* mitigating factor (Ashworth 2011). In other words, the misconduct need not have a direct bearing on the elements of harm and culpability but may be crucial to the calculation of sentence. Notably, Swedish sentencing law takes precisely this approach: most aggravating and mitigating factors affect the seriousness (or 'penal value') of the offence, but there is a list of other 'equity factors' that are not related to penal value but which a Swedish court is nonetheless expected to consider (Jareborg 1993).

It seems important that the police misconduct be specific to the defendant: sentencing, after all, is a highly individualised exercise, designed to take account of distinctive features of specific crimes and of offenders' personal circumstances and characteristics (Tonry 2016). Offenders belonging to a community disproportionately targeted by the police or otherwise disadvantaged by state agents should not be permitted to claim mitigation on these grounds alone. Adverse circumstances should not confer automatic mitigation; rather, these circumstances would be best situated within a broader framework of diminished culpability mitigation.

Finally, Roberts and Dagan (this volume) rightly contend that the misconduct should be exceptional, in order to prevent an excess of potentially minor claims. But an exceptionality test may not be as straightforward as it first appears, and sentencers would require detailed guidance from the Sentencing Council for England and Wales to limit inconsistency across cases. While a sentence reduction should not be awarded for conduct which amounts to no more than unprofessional behaviour or unsatisfactory performance, how might sentencers draw the line between 'mere' misconduct and gross misconduct of the kind that might be deemed exceptional? Should the focus be on misconduct that causes serious physical harm to the defendant of the kind suffered by *suspects A*, *B* and *C*? How should the court respond to those defendants who experience no physical harm but, rather, a lack of 'respect and courtesy' that the College of Policing *Code of Ethics* (2024) prioritises?

III. Canadian Precedent

In Canada, courts have already reduced sentences in response to claims for mitigation arising from abuse by state actors, including but not limited to the police. Police misconduct featured as a mitigating factor in the landmark case of *Nasogaluak* in 2010.[8] The 2021 case of *Morris* also merits consideration on the issue of causation.[9]

The police arrested Mr Nasogaluak for driving while intoxicated. While attempting to arrest him, the officers pointed a gun at him, pinned him to the ground, and punched him repeatedly. The final two blows were delivered with such force as to break Nasogaluak's ribs and puncture his lungs. Following release, Nasogaluak checked himself into hospital where he required emergency surgery. He subsequently lost his employment due to the injuries he sustained.

Nasogaluak entered a guilty plea to charges of impaired driving and flight from the police. The Supreme Court of Canada affirmed the lower court's decision to mitigate the sentence following unjustified state harm to the offender and approved a heavy discount in the sentencing calculation. It was held that the excessive use of force by police officers in arresting Nasogaluak – compounded by the failure of those same officers to alert their superiors to the extent of the injuries they inflicted on him and their failure to ensure that he received medical attention – not only failed to respect the principles of 'proportionality, necessity, and reasonableness',[10] but was a breach of his constitutional right to security of the person under the Canadian Charter of Rights and Freedoms. LeBel J expressed his support for 'a sentence that both speaks out against the offence and punishes the offender no more than is necessary'.[11]

Yet, in granting a significant sentence discount to Nasogaluak, the Court's rationale for introducing sentence mitigation for police misconduct was not as clearly articulated as it might have been. Sceptics may suggest that the case exposes the need not for a mitigated sentence but for improved police training and more effective disciplinary proceedings for officers instead.

In the 2021 case of *Morris*, a 22-year-old Black man was apprehended by the police having been incorrectly connected to a nearby home invasion. He was, however, in possession of a loaded handgun and later convicted of firearms offences. The court accepted pre-sentence reports detailing the impact of anti-Black racism on Morris's life and actions, including as a victim of overt racism during repeated interactions with police officers since childhood.

The court proceeded to make a revolutionary admission that 'it is beyond doubt that anti-Black racism, including both overt and systemic anti-Black racism, has been, and continues to be, a reality in Canadian society' which must be 'acknowledged, confronted, mitigated and, ultimately, erased'[12] and observed that racism by state agents should be relevant to the purposes and principles of sentencing. The question then arose: from a procedural standpoint, must the offender demonstrate a causal link between systemic racism and his criminal conduct in order to secure

[8] *R v Nasogaluak*.
[9] *R v Morris*.
[10] *R v Nasogaluak* [32].
[11] ibid [42].
[12] *R v Morris* [1].

a sentence reduction? According to the court in *Morris*, the connection need not be causal, but there must be 'some connection' in place.[13] While an offender might adduce evidence linking his background and history to the offending, and courts should be generous in the admission of such evidence, a requirement to demonstrate a causal link would place an undue evidentiary burden on him (Roberts et al 2024). Certainly, proof of a causal link is not required in other circumstances, such as in the case of young offenders or offenders suffering from mental illness.

In entertaining the possibility of a new mitigating factor of state misconduct in England and Wales, should we subscribe to the *Morris* approach to causation? A 'direct causal link' standard may be unrealistic and insurmountable in many cases, not least because of the complexity of contextual and other contributing factors, and the potential for several forms of state misconduct to enter the sentencing calculation. The alternative would be to adopt an all-encompassing approach to mitigation, capturing misconduct occurring before, during, or after arrest. No doubt there would be differences of opinion among judges and sentencing experts, on which the Sentencing Council for England and Wales would be required to take a stance.

A. Sentence Calibration

As the Canadian case law illustrates, if a new mitigating factor of state misconduct were to be introduced in England and Wales, a major challenge would be the calibration of sentence. By precisely how much should a sentence be reduced to reflect misconduct by police officers, and what would it mean to tailor a sentence reduction to the magnitude of the wrong? If the offence warrants a three-year prison sentence, by how much should it be reduced to account for an assault by police officers upon arrest? How much is an illegal strip search 'worth'? How much is abusive language 'worth'? How much is data violation 'worth'? Should the sentence be tailored either to the wrongfulness of the police misconduct or to the harm inflicted on the defendant? No clear guiding principle emerges. The conversion process would depend on subjective judgments about the severity of police misconduct, which would in turn require some scaling from the Sentencing Council for England and Wales.

Many jurisdictions around the world adopt a non-interventionist approach to aggravating and mitigating factors, leaving mitigating factors susceptible to judicial interpretation. This is despite their crucial role at sentencing, particularly in terms of quantum and around the custody threshold. In standard practice, sentencing statutes or guidelines list the relevant factors, and might even group them, but only rarely do they provide guidance as to the relative weight of those factors or the impact they should have on sentence. Consider the implausibility, for example,

[13] ibid [97].

of the Sentencing Council for England and Wales making decisive judgments on weight: that premeditation is worth 25 per cent, remorse worth 15 per cent, and sole carer status worth 10 per cent. Ashworth (2011) concurs, observing that the role of aggravating and mitigating factors at sentencing is usually left 'largely without structure' – and perhaps rightly so. But state misconduct is arguably a special case – not least because of its controversial nature – and has the potential to result in significant sentencing disparity. Judges are unlikely to adjust their sentences without detailed guidance from the Sentencing Council.

How much is too much reductive credit? In *Nasogaluak*, the Court held that state misconduct weighs in favour of a 'measurable reduction' in sentence and left open the possibility of reducing a sentence below a mandatory minimum only in exceptional cases of 'egregious' police misconduct. *Nasogaluak* escaped a six–18-month period of imprisonment, which would normally have been imposed, in favour of a series of conditional discharges and a fine. In *Morris*, upon considering the systemic anti-Black racism that applied both generally and personally to the defendant, the court reduced the sentence from 15 to 12 months. The Crown later appealed the sentence. While it agreed that courts must acknowledge the reality of anti-Black racism and filter it into the sentencing calculation, they maintained that such considerations should not overwhelm the proportionality analysis. The court accepted the Crown's arguments and increased the sentence to two years less a day as well as probation. Meanwhile, in *Acheampong*,[14] a two-year reduction of the proposed 7.5-year term of imprisonment was considered adequate in view of excessive police force. In that case, it was observed that police violence 'need not be extreme' to generate a significant sentence reduction.

So, there is a major stumbling block concerning incommensurability. While a modest but fixed reduction seems appropriate, we must avoid, at all costs, a mitigated sentence which appears to be much less than the offender deserves. We also risk instances of conflict with the principle of proportionality if police misconduct reduces a sentence to a point where it becomes 'disproportionate to the gravity of the offence or the moral blameworthiness of the offender'.[15]

B. Jurisdictional Differences

Despite some powerful Canadian case law, introducing state misconduct as a new mitigating factor may not be the obviously 'correct' approach for England and Wales. Let us not forget that these jurisdictions have remarkably divergent histories where sentencing is concerned (Roberts 2012), especially over the past three decades or so, and that a mitigating factor of state misconduct may not be worth emulating.

[14] *R v Acheampong.*
[15] *R v Suter* [56].

Furthermore, let us not overlook that, in contrast to England and Wales, Canada does not operate formal sentencing guidelines, opting instead for the discretionary style of sentencing found in most common law jurisdictions (Roberts et al 2024). We should be wary, then, of drawing erroneous conclusions following comparisons between arguably dissimilar sentencing regimes. Perhaps we are better off advancing the pluralist view that sentencing differences between jurisdictions can be both justified and normatively desirable. Criminal sentencing is not – and should not – become a uniform body of norms to be applied irrespective of differences in legal structures, criminal justice policies, and sentencing cultures (see further Zimran and Dagan 2023).

IV. Normative Considerations

It is essential that we confront the question of theoretical justification if police misconduct is to be deemed relevant to the sentencing exercise. In this section, I consider two alternative ways of constructing a case for police misconduct as a new mitigating factor at sentencing and assess their normative adequacy.

A. 'Punished Enough'

The first option is to appeal to the notion, developed elsewhere by Husak (1990), that the offender has already been 'punished enough'. On this view, the harm experienced by an offender assaulted by the police during an arrest, for example, might itself qualify as part of his formal state punishment (see also Ewing, this volume).

After all, to over-punish an offender is not only to impose severe dignitary harms on him, but to undermine a foundational principle of retributive theory: namely, that it is morally impermissible to inflict a disproportionate punishment on criminal wrongdoers (see, eg, Walen 2014). In sentencing and criminal justice, proportionality stands as the pre-eminent concept in the long history of efforts to modernise and temper punishment, and to civilise the retributive approach which dominated pre-modern punishment. This it achieves by purporting to bring discretionary power within limits, requiring that there be broad equivalence between the seriousness of the crime and the severity of punishment. Proportionality is grounded in notions of reason, fairness, and justice and any departure from it stands in need of robust defence (Lacey 2021).

Arguably, the retributive principle *necessitates* a corrective approach to sentencing. An offender who is sentenced without regard to the police misconduct to which he has been subject suffers a total amount of state-imposed harm disproportionate to the crime he committed. A mitigating factor of state misconduct, by contrast, would function to reduce – or perhaps preclude altogether – the punishment that ordinarily would have been imposed. Those who have been 'punished enough' receive a form of 'compensation' that reflects the form of the harm: a mitigated state punishment for a state-imposed harm (Duda 2021). A mitigating factor of state misconduct could be said to matter, then, because it functions as public recognition of the misconduct and reaffirms the underlying normative principles for how police-citizen relationships are to be constituted.

B. Preserving Legitimacy and Dissociating the Court

In constructing an argument for the relevance of state misconduct at sentencing, we might appeal to the concept of legitimacy instead. On this view, a mitigated sentence for state misconduct would allow the court to preserve its legitimacy and dissociate itself from misconduct occurring elsewhere in the justice system. The offender, meanwhile, may point to police misconduct not to elude accountability by displacing his culpability onto the state but, rather, to show that his mistreatment by the state threatens to render the court process illegitimate if corrective measures are not applied (on protecting the legitimacy of the criminal process, see also Zimran and Dagan 2023).

Legitimacy is an essential foundation of just state institutions. It is fundamentally important in the context of criminal justice since the sheer monopoly of authority its institutions possess – including their capacity to coerce citizens and impose punishment – demand the highest levels of legitimacy. As the defendant moves through the system, every decision must command legitimacy, since it has major implications for due process. Ultimately, without legitimacy, criminal justice institutions would not achieve their instrumental ends (Lacey 2012).

Legitimacy is broadly defined as the property of being valid or proper, either as set out in law (intrinsic legitimacy) or from the perspective of citizens (perceived legitimacy), or both. On this view, legitimacy has two elements, which may sometimes conflict: institutions must not only be legitimate according to some external standard or benchmark of acceptability but be seen by citizens to be legitimate too. In the context of criminal justice institutions – in this case, the sentencing court – having legitimacy means that all citizens believe that decisions made by judges are in some way 'right' or 'desirable'. Key here is the belief that the sentence passed by the court is 'valid' in the sense that it ought to be obeyed by virtue of who made the decision and how it was made (see, for example, Jackson 2008).

By framing the case for a new mitigating factor in terms of preserving the court's intrinsic and perceived legitimacy, we must take seriously the view that constituent criminal justice agencies are in real terms part of an integrated whole (Duff et al 2007; Holroyd and Picinali 2021). So, the behaviour of one of its representatives – in our case, a police officer – undermines the authority of the court to condemn and punish. While apprehension by the police is instrumental to securing a conviction at trial, the criminal courts can exercise, at best, indirect control over police activities, and only after the fact. On the legitimacy view, the court could apply state misconduct as a mitigating factor and thus have a means of dissociating themselves from the conduct, repudiating it, and preserving judicial integrity. The legitimacy account thus requires us to reject the so-called separation thesis according to which criminal justice agencies are 'isolated' from one another, and courts are justified in overlooking the unethical activities of the police (ibid; Stark 2024).

C. Normative Adequacy

I have argued that we might entertain the possibility of state misconduct as a new mitigating factor in the sentencing court in one of two ways. On the one hand, we might appeal to the view that an offender, having been brutalised by the police, has already been 'punished enough'. On the other hand, we might appeal to the concept of legitimacy: police misconduct threatens to render the court process illegitimate if a remedial measure – such as sentence mitigation – is not applied.

When we juxtapose them, it becomes clear that the accounts of 'punished enough' and 'preservation of court legitimacy' take us in different directions, not least because the first is focused on the individual experience of state punishment, and the second on the institutional matter of dissociating the court from misconduct occurring elsewhere in the system. Neither account seems powerful enough to trump the other, and it seems neither necessary nor desirable to force a choice between them.

Yet this theoretical ambivalence is a problem where criminal justice reform is concerned. If we arrive at a case for sentencing reform via different justificatory routes, then we will hardly be able to bridge the gap between theory and practice with confidence and render state misconduct meaningful as a mitigating factor – still less convince the Sentencing Council for England and Wales of it. Finally, we must be alert to the inherent risk of normative theorising about sentencing and punishment: it may inflate expectations of what criminal justice institutions can realistically accomplish (Watson 2020).

V. Alternative Fora

Despite having identified some promising normative resources with which to construct an argument for the relevance of state misconduct at sentencing, it should not go unnoticed that only convicted offenders would benefit, representing a very small minority of those who have suffered oppressive, abusive or discriminatory treatment at the hands of the state. As a response to state misconduct, sentence mitigation would be severely limited in scope, failing to address those who have been subject to misconduct and convicted of no offence.

Any argument for mitigated punishment in response to police wrongdoing has the potential to be seriously divisive, not least because it risks shifting the focus of the sentencing hearing entirely. It is not the priority of a sentencing judge to hold the criminal justice system accountable for its systemic failures, nor should a sentencing hearing descend into an investigation into the relative culpability of both parties (see also Roberts and Dagan, this volume). It would be mistaken to promote the sentencing court as a site for an unnecessary trade-off: that somehow one individual's wrongdoing can detract from the appropriate punishment of another's. Pointing to state wrongdoing should not be a way of diverting attention away from an offender or shielding him from scrutiny or accountability for his offending.

Perhaps the best we can do is concede that the sentencing court – notwithstanding its status as 'the point in the trial where the aims of punishment are given concrete and public expression' (Henham 2012: 1) – is not the most appropriate forum for addressing police misconduct in England and Wales. A push for alternative fora, then, is understandable. The effectiveness of the existing police disciplinary system has been called into question in several high-profile publications over the past year (see, eg, Casey 2023; Home Office 2023; House of Lords Library 2023). Questions have arisen about the consistency of decision-making at police misconduct hearings, particularly in cases of discrimination; sexual misconduct and violence against women and girls; potential disproportionality in police dismissals; the composition of misconduct panels, including the legal and financial protections in place for panel members; the dismissal process for probationary officers, and the effectiveness of the existing three-tier performance system in communicating to officers what is expected of their rank and role (ibid).

One way forward would be to commit to a bold programme of institutional redesign and introduce a supplementary process of police–citizen accountability entirely distinct from the criminal process (for an analogous dual-process approach to criminal justice for victims and offenders, see Lacey and Pickard 2019). This new accountability process might offer a differentiated space to bring together – and serve the needs and ends of – police officers and citizens they have harmed. In pursuit of meaningful exchange, this forum might offer an attractive way of defusing any difficulties that existing processes present, addressing the distinctive concerns of each party with 'equal concern and respect' (Dworkin 1977). And the gesture of inviting traditionally excluded groups into a process designed to reflect on police misconduct might itself cultivate concern and respect in ways that generate a virtuous circle (Watson 2020).

VI. Conclusion

Let us return to the central question of the chapter. Should *suspects A, B and C*, if convicted in the criminal courts of England and Wales, be entitled to claim mitigation at sentencing on the grounds that they were victims of misconduct by the state (on whose behalf punishment is imposed (Zedner 2016))? Even if a reduced sentence seems in line with our intuitions about fairness towards those who have been doubly disadvantaged by the justice system (see further Elias 2018), in practice, a new mitigating factor would be hardly tenable at this time.

The question moves us into complex and largely unexplored terrain in the field of sentencing and criminal justice. As I hope to have shown, the matter is not only of abstract theoretical interest but is also fiercely pragmatic. Notwithstanding the Canadian case law, especially *Nasogaluak*, the Sentencing Council for England and Wales is unlikely to be persuaded of the need for a mitigating factor of this kind, not least because of the divergent sentencing styles of each jurisdiction (Roberts 2012). While judges would likely disagree on the precise grounds for state misconduct and the magnitude of the reduction to be awarded, these practical challenges are not insurmountable. We stand in need, however, of a stronger theoretical justification than is currently available for the relevance of state misconduct in the sentencing context if such a proposal is to be articulated and defended in practice.

We have been confronted in this chapter with a compelling thought experiment that is unlikely to disrupt the status quo and take effect in the sentencing regime of England and Wales as we know it in the here and now. Without understating the brutal mistreatment suffered by *suspects A*, *B* and *C* at the hands of the police, they would be well-advised to sidestep the sentencing hearing and seek redress in alternative fora.

13

Epistemic Injustice, State Misconduct and Sentence Mitigation

ANDREI POAMA AND MOJCA M PLESNIČAR

Consider the following cases:

(1) *Remorse*: Judge James presides over a jury trial where the defendant, Jackson Jones, a young African American man, is found guilty of aggravated assault and battery. During the sentencing hearing scheduled later that day, and keen to find out whether he repents for his crime, Judge James asks Jones if he has anything to say for himself. Jones silently stares at the table in front of him. He then looks at the judge, and shortly mutters that he is sorry for what happened. To the judge, Jones's tone of voice sounds indifferent, his face looks cold-hearted, and his overall body posture detached. The judge sees his impression confirmed in the eyes of the jurors and other court officials in the room. Finding no trace of remorse and no other mitigatory or aggravating factors, Judge James gives Jones a presumptive sentence of six years in prison. Unbeknownst to Judge James, Jones has experienced deep remorse for his crime but was too confused and intimidated to express it in court. What is more, Jones's behaviour during the sentencing hearing resonates with growing scientific evidence about 'remorse bias' among judicial officials who have been found to be often unreliable in their assessment of offenders' remorse in court, and even less reliable when gauging racial minority offenders' display of remorse.[1]

(2) *Battering*: Judge Joy presides over a bench trial where the defendant, Laura Barber, is accused of second-degree murder. Barber is a middle-aged, working-class woman with four children. At the time of the trial, she had been subject to physical and psychological abuse by her husband for a period of over 10 years. On the day of her husband's death, Barber thought her husband was once again trying to hit her, so she picked up a knife and stabbed him. At

[1] Based on the Bobby Jones case mentioned and discussed in Hanan 2018. For the actual report, see US Department of Justice 1996.

trial, the defence lawyer argues that, given her long battering history, Barber should have her sentence mitigated accordingly. The prosecutor contests this argument and indicates that there is sufficient evidence that Barber is tough and sometimes aggressive both at work and in her relationship with friends – hardly the helpless behaviour that fits the battered woman syndrome criminal courts have rightly admitted as a mitigating factor in other cases. In reply, the defence lawyer presents recent research that helplessness is not a necessary or even typical feature of battering, especially among women from a working-class environment. The lawyer further notes that members of the scientific community increasingly agree that, given its diagnostic limitations, the concept of battered woman syndrome should be replaced with the more adequate concept of battering. Judge Joy is unpersuaded by the plea in mitigation, hence Barber is convicted of second-degree murder, and receives a presumptive sentence of 16 years in prison. One year following Barber's trial, the Department of Justice publishes a comprehensive report which concludes that the term '"battered woman syndrome" is no longer useful or appropriate', recommends battering as a better diagnostic alternative, and notes that that evidence of a person's assertiveness, strength or active search for support does not constitute counter-evidence against battering.[2]

(3) *Accent:* At an annual criminal judges training event, Judge Novak reunites with her old university friend, now a renowned law professor. Over coffee, their conversation meanders from professional updates to academic endeavours, where her friend mentions an interesting PhD dissertation by one of his students. The dissertation's main findings suggest that the accent of witnesses – including defendants and victims – could significantly influence their perceived trustworthiness in criminal court. Intrigued, Judge Novak requests the dissertation, but the document gets buried in her inbox until, one day, she rediscovers and reads it. Upon reading it, Judge Novak comes across a compelling argument backed by robust empirical research. The findings reveal that accents can subconsciously influence court participants' judgements, including her own, in assessing witness sincerity, competence and credibility, in particular when it comes to their sentencing decisions. This leads her to consider a past case where the defendant she sentenced had a strong accent and ponder how that may have affected her decision.[3]

While varying on more than one dimension, these cases are meant to illustrate a distinctive kind of wrong, which can and often does affect whether and how some mitigating factors impact sentencing decisions. The distinctive nature of this wrong can be articulated in epistemic terms, in the sense that the decision to mitigate a criminal sentence (or not) is prima facie wrong because of the evidence and explanations that are either missing from the sentencing process or

[2] Based on the *Leah* case mentioned and discussed in Ferraro 2013.
[3] Based on Drobnjak 2024.

preventing the consideration of other evidence or explanations which matter for that process. Importantly, the improper consideration given to relevant evidence or explanations in these cases is not mere happenstance, but can be tied to foreseeable and at least partly avoidable limitations that affect sentencing practice. Because of this, the cases involve epistemic wrongs, not just epistemically innocent or imminent errors. Simply put, the judges in the cases above *should know better* when considering and evaluating the evidence and explanations relevant for mitigation. Specifically, sentencing judges are in the wrong when they assess the offender's credibility – for instance, when Judge James misreads Jones's remorse – or when they ponder on whether the offender's act is intelligibly consistent with a mitigating factor – for instance, when Judge Joy misinterprets Barber's behaviour as inconsistent with battering *and* reduces battering to the battered woman syndrome (BWS).

In this chapter, we argue that the kind of wrong at play in the cases above can be coherently construed in terms of epistemic injustice. Drawing on recent work in epistemology and political philosophy (Fricker 2007; Kidd, Medina and Pohlhaus 2017; Byskov 2021), we examine how epistemic injustice can work as a recurrent, often socio-economically patterned form of state misconduct that undermines the justification of criminal sentences in general, and sentence mitigations in particular. To anticipate, the argument is that the evidence about actual or potential epistemic injustices at sentencing should prompt state officials – most notably, judges – to either reconsider or be additionally diligent when they evaluate the credibility and intelligibility of the claims made through mitigation pleas, especially when it comes to defendants that belong to disadvantaged or otherwise socio-economically marginalised groups. Our argument is conditional, not categorical: it states that, *if* epistemic injustice occurs or is likely to occur at sentencing concerning a specific mitigating factor, there is a presumption in favour of sentence mitigation that judges should positively rebut if they decide *not* to mitigate. Thus stated, our argument resonates with recent debates about state misconduct in relation to sentence mitigation (see Manikis in this volume) and adds to current analyses of epistemically unjust criminal law practices (Bublitz 2023; Lackey 2023; Medina 2021).

I. Overview

The chapter is structured as follows. In section II, we unpack the concept of epistemic injustice, and substantiate the claim that it amounts to state misconduct. In section III, we explain the rationale behind our epistemic injustice approach to sentence mitigation, and draw on discussions about two central forms of epistemic injustice – testimonial and hermeneutical injustice – to diagnose the epistemic wrongs at play in the three cases introduced above. Based on this diagnosis, section IV concludes by proposing some reforms whereby epistemic injustices that occur or might occur during the sentence mitigation processes can be better addressed.

II. Epistemic Injustice as State Misconduct

In this section, we aim to answer two questions. First, what is epistemic injustice? Second, why and to what extent does epistemic injustice constitute state misconduct and, to the extent that it does, why does this matter for criminal justice practices?

A. What is Epistemic Injustice?

Broadly characterised, epistemic injustices are wrongs that result from the mistreatment of persons considered as epistemic subjects – viz, either in their capacity as knowers or in their opportunity to be known to themselves or others (Fricker 2007; Kidd, Medina and Pohlhaus 2017; Byskov 2021). The list of epistemic injustices identified by recent work in social epistemology and political philosophy has expanded in the last two decades to the point that it is hard to isolate the necessary and sufficient conditions whose satisfaction results in something counting as an instance of epistemic injustice.[4] Even so, there is some agreement that the two forms of epistemic injustice identified by Fricker in her initial analysis of the concept (2007) – namely, testimonial and hermeneutical injustice – are paradigmatic, such that many particular instances of epistemic injustice fall under one of these two categories.

For Fricker (2007), epistemic injustice is often tied to background social injustices broadly understood – viz, morally objectionable and politically contestable class, race or gender inequalities – but they are irreducible to these other injustices, meaning that they are 'distinctively epistemic in kind, … consisting, most fundamentally in a wrong done to someone specifically in their capacity as a knower' (Fricker 2007: 1). Fricker takes testimonial and hermeneutical injustice to be central forms of epistemic injustice: the former 'occurs when prejudice causes a hearer to give a deflated level of credibility to a speaker's word', while the latter 'occurs at a prior stage, when a gap in collective interpretive resources puts someone at an unfair disadvantage when it comes to making sense of their social experiences' (ibid). In short, following Fricker's initial account, testimonial injustices amount to unfair *credibility* deficits, while hermeneutical ones cover unfair *intelligibility* deficits.

B. Testimonial Injustice

To illustrate and analyse testimonial injustice, Fricker takes Tom Robinson's case, the young black male protagonist in Harper Lee's 1960 novel, *To Kill a*

[4] For discussions, see Kidd, Medina and Pohlhaus 2017; Byskov 2021.

Mocking Bird. Robinson is accused of and wrongfully convicted for the rape of a white woman. Because of racist prejudice, Robinson is prevented from communicating the knowledge he has (*qua* direct witness) about the case at hand – for instance, that his running away on the day of the incident was motivated by his attempt to avoid the girl's sexual advances. Fricker argues that Robinson's plight features the primary wrong at play in testimonial injustice – namely, an 'identity-prejudicial credibility deficit' that undermines his capacity to provide others with the knowledge he holds. Testimonial injustice is thus *epistemic* because it indexes the credibility of the testimony on epistemically undeserved prejudice, which is a 'judgment made or maintained without proper regard to the evidence' (Fricker 2007: 33), and it is *unjust* insofar as the hearer systematically gives less credibility than speakers deserve in response to their testimony.

C. Hermeneutical Injustice

With regard to hermeneutical injustice, Fricker focuses on Carmitta Wood's case, a middle-aged woman who decided to quit her job at Cornell University in 1975, after a period of being repeatedly subject to her male supervisor's intrusive sexual behaviour and rude remarks. Following her resignation and the university's refusal to pay Wood's unemployment benefits, a group of women with similar experiences – Working Women United (WWU) – formed to defend her case. In their campaign, WWU articulated the concept of sexual harassment to capture and convey the range of experiences to which they had all been subjected. As a result of the social and discursive pressure set by WWU, the media and other supporting collectives, the US Supreme Court ruled sexual harassment illegal approximately a decade after Wood's resignation (*Meritor Savings Bank v Vinson*). Fricker argues that the time before the introduction of the concept of sexual harassment into conventional discourse marks a period of hermeneutical injustice whereby the subject – in this case, Wood and other sexually harassed women – is 'rendered unable to make communicatively intelligible something which it is particularly in his or her interests to be able to render intelligible (Fricker 2007: 162). Hermeneutical injustice is thus *epistemic* because it covers lacunae in 'hermeneutical resources' – viz, concepts, theories, or communicative styles that can account for existing social experiences – and it is *unjust* because these lacunae result from the social marginalisation of those whose experiences are left misunderstood or underexplained – most notably, by their exclusion from or subordination within mainstream media, political or legal institutions.

While Fricker focuses on cases where epistemic injustices err in a deficiency direction, commitment to a neo-Aristotelian view of virtue, and of the virtue of justice in particular, should keep us *conceptually* open to the possibility that epistemic injustice might also err in the direction of excess.[5] Lackey's (2023) analysis of testimonial injustice in the US criminal justice system resonates with this insight. Lackey identifies cases where speakers are given too much credibility – for instance, when purported crime eyewitnesses' testimony is extracted through deception, manipulation or coercion, and subsequently granted an amount of credibility that these testimony-extractive processes do not warrant. This putatively counts as a case of excessive testimonial injustice.

Similarly, Falbo (2022) considers examples where sentencing judges show more understanding than their interlocutors deserve – for instance, in *People v Turner*, where the offender's portrayal as a 'golden boy' – viz, an exemplary, hard-working athlete whose rape is thereby rendered hardly imaginable – makes his plea for leniency more understandable than it in fact is. Here, hermeneutical injustice errs in the direction of excess.

The extension of a neo-Aristotelian account of virtue ethics to virtue epistemology does not only imply that the vice of epistemic injustice can err in a deficiency or excess direction; it also implies that the *virtue* of epistemic justice occupies an intermediate position between these extremes. But how should we determine the mean of epistemic justice? One (negative) specification strategy works relationally or comparatively: taking the relevant evidential standard as fixed, we ask whether the person to whom we want to give a fair amount of credibility or intelligibility *would* be considered significantly more/less credible or intelligible if their situation varied along the dimensions that are epistemically problematic relative to the evidential standard at hand. In particular, we ask if the person's utterances would be considered more/less credible or their behaviour more/less intelligible if we only varied their gender, race, class or other dimension tracking unjust exclusion and marginalisation patterns. If the answer to that question is negative, then the judgment is *presumably* epistemically just. Thus, to take *People v Turner*, if we agree that the term 'golden boy' lacks epistemic significance, the difference that it makes for the intelligibility of the offender's behaviour should not vary if we change the convicted defendant's race or class.

Another (more positive) specification strategy of the epistemically virtuous mean starts with a general definition of either testimonial or hermeneutical justice. The first is understood as the virtue whereby 'the hearer … neutralises the impact of prejudice in her credibility judgments' (Fricker 2007: 86). The second is defined as the virtue whereby the hermeneutically just person displays 'an alertness or sensitivity to the possibility that the difficulty one's interlocutor is having as she tries to render something communicatively intelligible' (Fricker 2007: 169). This strategy invites us to spell out the virtue of epistemic justice in terms of the mode of *inquiry* one has put into one's credibility or intelligibility assessments, such that enough inquiry of the right kind keeps one within the epistemically just mean.

[5] For discussions of the interpolar structure of *epistemic* virtues (ie, two or more extremes and a mean), see Crisp 2010.

In contrast, insufficient inquiry of the right kind takes one astray in the deficiency direction and surplus inquiry of the wrong kind – viz, responding to epistemically problematic cues or giving uptake to epistemically faulty concepts – moves one in an excess direction.

Finally, a feature that we should expect epistemic justice to have, in addition to being a mean state between two extremes, is that it is political or institutional rather than merely private and personal. Epistemic injustices are often the result of institutions, not just individual actions. In Anderson's (2012: 171) words:

> [I]n the face of massive structural injustice, individual epistemic virtue plays a comparable role to the practice of individual charity in the context of massive structural poverty. Just as it would be better and more effective to redesign economic institutions so as to prevent mass poverty …, it would be better to reconfigure epistemic institutions so as to prevent epistemic injustice from arising.

Conversely, pursuing epistemic justice requires establishing a set of institutions that allow us to avert or, more modestly, correct the vices of testimonial and hermeneutical injustice.

D. Epistemic Injustice and State Misconduct

This institutional dimension of epistemic (in)justice invites our second question – namely, *why, and to what extent, does epistemic injustice constitute state misconduct?* To answer this, we can start with a general definition of state misconduct and ask if there are instances of epistemic injustice that, if committed by the state, would constitute state misconduct. Unfortunately, there is no standard or authoritative definition of state misconduct (for discussion, see Matravers in this volume). However, we can advance a working definition of state misconduct that draws on existing legal statutes and jurisprudence, and views state (or official) misconduct as 'the misconduct of an official in relation to his or her duty as a public servant'.[6] On this broad definition, illegality or criminality are not necessary features of state misconduct, and so violation or disregard for other types of (eg, professional or ethical) standards or norms suffices for state misconduct to be recognised.

While somewhat loose and partly circular, this definition resonates with how state misconduct has been conceptualised in recent criminal justice scholarship. For instance, it coheres with Champion's (2001) characterisation of state misconduct as legally or ethically inappropriate behaviour by criminal justice officials. The definition is also consistent with Manikis's capacious view, which applies to forms of misconduct that 'can be systemic and/or individual and imply various forms of blameworthy conduct notably, intentional, negligent and willful blindness', and

[6] This is one of the clearest (quasi-)legal definitions of state misconduct that we were able to identify; see www.law.cornell.edu/wex/official_misconduct.

allows for diverse forms of state manifestations, such as 'state actors, state institutions, or state decisions/processes that relate to criminalisation, the criminal justice process, and punishment' (see Manikis in chapter 11 of this volume). On this latter view, state misconduct includes both criminogenic state policies and over-criminalising legislation.

But if criminogenic state policies or overcriminalisation constitute state misconduct, so does epistemic injustice, at least in some central cases. On the broad definition, all we need to show to prove that epistemic injustices constitute state misconduct is to identify a relevant norm or standard that such injustices objectionably undermine. At a high level of generality, and stated positively, *truth* represents one such standard: 'the criminal process', notes Weigend (2003: 389), 'is about truth'. The importance of truth in criminal trials is widely recognised across continental and common law systems, albeit with variations in how it is conceptualised and implemented (Langbein 1978). While continental law systems prioritise a more direct search for objective truth through state-led investigation, common law systems focus on procedural integrity and fair competition between the parties involved to reveal the truth (Weigend 2003). Truth-seeking is often balanced with other values, such as efficiency and the protection of rights, and while certain procedures may impair the search for truth, they are often accepted as necessary trade-offs. The overarching goal, however, remains to ensure that criminal sanctions are justly imposed on the truly guilty for the truly relevant reasons. The truth standard can also be stated negatively. We can do so if we understand the aim of criminal law to be *error reduction* (Laudan 2012): we want as few false arrests, wrongful convictions and inappropriate sentences as it is practically possible (see also Kaplow and Shavell, 1992).

However, this conclusion may be too hasty: we do not simply want the truth; we want to get to the truth through a justified procedure. Thus, one of the main guiding standards of criminal law is *knowledge*, construed as justified true belief about the facts that pertain to a decision. When epistemic injustice occurs, the criminal justice system wastes important sources of knowledge – as when it errs in a deficiency direction – or acquires false knowledge when it errs in the direction of excess. If, furthermore, epistemic injustice occurs because of biases or social processes that can be identified and either avoided or reduced by the state and its officials, epistemic injustice constitutes state misconduct.

III. Epistemically Unjust Sentence Mitigation

Existing analyses of epistemic injustice in the criminal process have concentrated on the policing (Lackey 2023), trial (Fricker 2007; Bublitz 2023) or post-sentencing (Medina 2021) stages. This emphasis can be partly explained by the salience that epistemic norms have for the beliefs, judgments and inquiry practices which pertain to suspicions, verdicts and complaints about sentence implementation (eg, prison conditions). But epistemic norms matter for the justification of sentence *imposition* as well, at least if we accept that, in addition to 'trial facts', there are distinctive 'sentencing facts' (Reitz 2011) – for instance, convicted defendants' prior criminal history or their remorse about the offence – which form the subject matter of epistemically evaluable judgments. Here, and given the focus of the present volume, we are examining the sentencing facts and factors that directly bear on sentence mitigation judgments.[7]

When sentence mitigation judgments are epistemically unjust, the unfair credibility or intelligibility judgments that offenders incur are blocking important epistemic resources –evidence, concepts, theories or insights – that could reduce sentences to a level that better coheres with the relevant sentencing facts. On our account, such judgments need to be averted or corrected. This raises a preliminary worry that we want to address from the outset – namely, that construing epistemic injustice in terms of deficits *and* excesses demands that we equally care about sentences that are insufficiently mitigated *and* sentences that are *excessively* mitigated. If so, our account would imply that we should try to avert or correct epistemically excessive mitigations just as much as we try to avert or correct epistemically deficient mitigations. This seems troubling, especially if averting or correcting epistemic excess would further harm offenders who are already unjustly treated across socio-economic lines.

There are at least three replies to this concern. First, and to the extent that we take epistemic injustices to correlate with socio-economic disadvantage generally, the problematic tendency within existing sentencing practices seems to disproportionately err in the direction of epistemic deficiency rather than excess (Xynas et al 2015; Duff 2010). Put differently, there are more reasons to worry that disadvantaged offenders are not being sufficiently heard or understood at the sentencing stage than there are reasons to think that privileged offenders are being heard or understood too much.[8] Second, if we accept that criminal justice institutions should care more about avoiding overly severe than overly lenient punishment (Duus-Otterstrom 2013), the priority should once again be reducing epistemic deficiency rather than excess. Third, the worry neglects that epistemic deficiencies and excesses are relational: there will be cases where tackling epistemic deficiency (eg judgments that unfairly downplay the credibility of the offender's remorse) will coincide with tackling excess (eg judgments that unfairly exaggerate the credibility

[7] This does not imply that sentencing facts are irrelevant for sentence aggravation judgments. If anything, and to the extent that we care about avoiding unjustifiably severe sentences, credibility or intelligibility deficits might in some cases matter more for aggravation judgments than they do for mitigation ones. Note also that there is a class of factors (eg, remorse) that can function both as mitigating (if judged to be convincing) and as aggravating (if judged as missing).

[8] For an analysis and review of some of the relevant empirical literature, see Thomas 2006) This *contextual* focus on deficiency resonates with a neo-Aristotelian account of virtue. For Aristotle, the virtuous mean does not occupy an equidistant position between two (or more) vicious extremes. Rather, it is placed and pulls further away from the extreme that one has a propensity towards (on this, see Groarke 2015).

of the judge's own views and evidence about remorse). In these cases, reducing deficiency also reduces excess, so the scope of the worry shrinks.

The second preliminary point that we want to address before analysing the cases presented in the introduction concerns how, *qua* state misconduct, epistemic injustice *counts* as sentence mitigation. Most current analyses of whether state misconduct mitigates or should mitigate have focused on discussing forms of state misconduct which, if established, would *be* mitigating facts or factors (for defences of this position, see Bergelson, and Manikis in this volume; for sceptical accounts, see Ryberg, and Roberts and Dagan in this volume). Unlike these analyses, but consistent with them, our account focuses on a form of state misconduct that is not, in and of itself, mitigatory, but *stands for* insufficiently examined mitigating facts (eg, remorse) or badly understood mitigating factors (eg, battering). Thus, epistemic injustice should be seen as mitigating in the *indirect* sense: when we have reason to believe that sentencing is epistemically unjust, there is a (positively rebuttable) presumption that a mitigating fact has been discounted or a mitigating factor unappreciated. Put differently, epistemic injustice matters for sentence mitigation because it increases the risk of getting mitigation wrong.

In the rest of this section, we draw on recent work on epistemic injustice to analyse the three cases presented above.

A. Remorse

In *Remorse*, Judge James incorrectly believes that Jones is unremorseful and decides not to mitigate his sentence. At first glance, the case clearly illustrates Fricker's (2007) standard characterisation of testimonial injustice – namely, a credibility deficit that the injustice victim (Jones) incurs because of a social identity prejudice that the hearer (Judge James) holds. Jones's reply to the judge, along with his demeanour and posture, are misread by the judge and mistakenly construed to offer evidence of lack of remorse, partly because of racialised stereotypes about what counts as a genuine expression of remorse.

But testimonial injustice in this case is not solely driven by racial identity prejudices judges tend to more or less implicitly hold about African Americans (*cf* Sweeney and Haney 1992; Yang 2015; Rice et al 2019). The injustice is also enabled by the court setting, within which Judge James elicits Jones's testimony about his remorse: Jones is placed in a highly formal, ritualised and intimidating institutional environment that risks inhibiting clear and convincing expressions of remorse (Hanan 2018; Tata 2020).[9] Moreover, the procedure whereby the judge forms his assessment about Jones's remorse – viz, a quick question about whether the convicted defendant has anything to say for himself – is hardly fit for purpose,

[9] For an ethnographic account of a court setting that is *extremely* epistemically hostile to remorse assessments, see Gonzalez Van Cleve 2020.

and there is no follow-up query or attempt to get more information about Jones's emotional experience of the crime.

Taken together, the court set-up and sentencing procedure seem to subvert Jones's *epistemic agency*, in the sense that they both hinder him from carefully introspecting into his possible feelings of guilt, regret or contrition and prevent him from expressing these feelings (Tata 2020). If so, the testimonial injustice at play in *Remorse* is not fuelled by prior identity prejudice alone; it is also induced by the testimonial context created by court proceedings and the judge's conduct within that context. Drawing on Lackey 2020 and Medina 2021, we can characterise this as an instance of *agential* epistemic injustice whereby convicted defendants' testimony is systematically believed under conditions that undermine their epistemic agency, and discounted under conditions that do not undermine it, or where opportunities for creating such conditions are foreclosed. In such cases, there is not only an unjust credibility deficit that Jones suffers, there is also an unjust credibility *excess* attached to the one-off testimony he offers under epistemically adverse conditions. This claim is neither strictly conceptual nor merely anecdotal. Rather, it can be empirically corroborated and somewhat generalised: there is a non-negligible amount of evidence that sentencing hearings are often structured in a way that obstructs offenders' formation of beliefs or collection of evidence about the mitigating factor at hand (Hanan 2018). This is especially worrisome when it comes to collecting evidence about mitigating factors (eg, remorse) that offenders are in a good position to have.[10]

Here, one might reply that an adverse court context or inadequate judicial procedures could be anticipated and thus (partly or fully) evaded by offenders who take the time to reflect on and prepare statements that persuasively convey their remorse. This reply is problematic in at least three respects. First, it complacently and, if advanced by state officials (eg, magistrates or legislators) complicitly accepts the existing epistemically unjust context as a given. Second, and relatedly, the reply downplays the extent to which disadvantaged or otherwise marginalised offenders are unlikely to afford to prepare their remorse statements and performance in the expected sense, as compared to privileged ones. Third, the reply underestimates the risk of *other* agential testimonial injustices whereby credibility is disproportionately given to heavily formatted and formulaic expressions of remorse, as when judges expect convicted defendants to perform remorse in very specifically scripted ways (Lackey 2023), even if there is no evidence that such performances are particularly reliable indicators of remorse.

There is a further sense in which the testimonial injustice Jones suffers proceeds by way of excess, not only deficit. The excess here attaches to the level of credibility

[10] At this point, we could speculate about cases where other (non-epistemic) forms of state misconduct which precede sentencing (eg, police brutality or prosecutorial intimidation) alienate offenders to the point of them losing trust in judges as well, and so choose to remain silent at the moment of sentencing. Even supposing that defendants *are* guilty in such cases, judges would have reasons to opt for sentencing hearing procedures whereby they can win back offenders' trust, and thus prompt testimonies that might not otherwise be given.

that judges arrogate to their *own* knowledge relative to the knowledge possessed by other parties – for instance, offenders themselves were they to be carefully listened to under improved institutional conditions (eg, less formal court settings, a longer list of follow-up questions) or people that are relevantly connected to the offenders (eg, family, friends, colleagues) that could provide testimonies about the offenders' remorse. Specifically, Judge James grants himself too much credibility in his assessment of Jones's remorse, given the scientific knowledge that he ignores about remorse bias and the epistemic weight he gives to the quick question asked during the sentencing hearing. Given this, it makes sense to view the epistemic injustice at work in *Remorse* as a complex wrong that involves both credibility deficits and credibility excesses.

Two (mutually incompatible) strategies could be considered to address some of the testimonial injustices present in *Remorse*. One strategy is to design a sentencing formula whereby general information about credibility deficits and excess in remorse assessments are calculated and then applied to modify individual remorse-based mitigation decisions. Concretely, this might mean that, if findings about remorse bias become robustly replicated, all offenders would receive an automatic mitigation premium across the board or that disadvantaged offenders could receive a higher premium than non-disadvantaged ones in a way that matches patterned differences in unfair credibility judgments. This accomodationist strategy is doubly problematic. First, the version that focuses on disadvantaged offenders seems unconstitutional, given its potential for deliberately discriminating between offenders across protected characteristics, such as gender, class or race. Second, and closer to our account, neither version of the accommodationist strategy can be grounded in a principled concern for epistemic injustice. This is because, instead of forming judges to *dispositionally* avoid the vices of testimonial injustice in their mitigatory judgments, the strategy entrenches these vices by converting them into acceptable parameters for sentence mitigation.

Another, opposite strategy would be to entirely eliminate remorse as a mitigating factor. Drawing on recent debates about the role of remorse in mitigating sentence severity, this eliminativist strategy holds that, since remorse assessments rendered by jurors (in capital cases) or by judges (in non-capital cases) are both broadly unreliable and inconsistent, and given that differences in reliability and other inconsistencies can and often *do* track already unjust socio-economic differences, avoiding the testimonial injustices that come with remorse bias can be achieved by cutting remorse out from the list of mitigating factors.[11] This strategy is also doubly problematic. First, the formal exclusion of remorse as a mitigating factor does not guarantee that judges or jurors will refrain from implicitly factoring in remorse assessments into their sentencing decisions. Second, eliminating

[11] For the empirical findings on unreliability and inconsistency, see Zhong 2015. For a discussion of how the epistemic quality of remorse assessments varies across socio-economic lines, see Kilty and Weir 2021: 67–96. For a normative defence of the eliminativist stance, see Morse 2014.

remorse is not a wise move if, as indicated at the beginning of this section, we *generally* care more about eliminating unduly severe sentences than we care about eliminating unduly lenient ones.[12] Given this, and assuming that genuine remorse should inform sentence mitigation – for instance, because of its relevance for rehabilitation or prevention – its fully fledged elimination from the list of mitigating factors is guaranteed to increase the number of unjustifiably severe sentences.[13]

The problems surrounding these two strategies raise the question of how testimonial injustices at play in remorse mitigations can and should be addressed. We will return to this in the following section after analysing the two other cases that illustrate epistemically unjust sentence mitigation practices.

B. Battering

In *Battering*, Judge Joy does not fully appreciate the current state of research on spousal abuse, and consequently denies Barber a mitigation claim. Given the temporal set-up of the case, this arguably happens because of a gap in social scientific theories that impedes Judge Joy's mitigation judgment: the sentencing hearing takes place before the publication and circulation of an official report that proposes to replace the BWS with battering.[14] Under *Battering*, Barber has a significantly better opportunity for her sentence to be mitigated; not so under BWS. Given this, Barber's case can be taken to reflect Fricker's (2007) characterisation of hermeneutical injustice – viz, a 'situation [where] the subject is rendered unable to make communicatively intelligible something which it is particularly in his or her interests to be able to render intelligible' (162). This situation is one of 'collective hermeneutical impoverishment' (161) that occurs because of the social marginalisation of the group to which the victims of hermeneutical injustice belong. 'Battering' seems to fit this description neatly: Barber cannot build a persuasive mitigation claim, given the absent concept of battering from the pool of collectively shared hermeneutical resources, and given that the said absence is tied to the marginalisation of a certain group of women (eg, working class) whose behaviour in abuse situations is less likely to match standard BWS symptomatology.

In some jurisdictions, BWS can be used at trial as a component of either self-defence or duress. In cases where these criminal defences fail, BWS can still be presented at sentencing as an imperfect defence that allows judges to

[12] Note that the eliminativist strategy might work for some existing mitigating factors which, on balance, can only increase the risk of unduly severe sentences. This is arguably the case for cooperation of authorities (ie, snitching). There is considerable evidence that, in some jurisdictions, snitching is one of the primary causes of wrongful convictions and, as such, one of the main drivers behind unjustifiably severe sentences (for wrongful convictions, any sentence is unjustifiably severe). For a discussion and critique of snitching, see Natapoff 2022.

[13] For an explicitly eliminativist critique of remorse (genuine or feigned), see Morse 2014.

[14] As indicated in the introduction, the report is US Department of Justice 1996.

mitigate punishment.[15] BWS was first articulated by Walker in her 1979 book, *The Battered Woman*, and further empirically corroborated and theoretically refined throughout the 1980s and 1990s.[16] It is roughly during this period that BWS became increasingly used to either ground existing criminal defences or to directly substantiate sentence mitigation decisions. The BWS profile, as presented by Walker (2016), points to a list of standard symptoms:

> 1. reexperiencing the trauma events intrusively; 2. high levels of arousal and anxiety; 3. high levels of avoidance and numbing of emotions; 4. cognitive difficulties; 5. disruption of interpersonal relationships; 6. physical health and body image problems; 7. sexual and intimacy issues (4).

Central to BWS symptomatology is the strong claim that battered women display learned helplessness and self-destructive behaviour. The BWS profile, then, is predicated on a presumption of passivity, and thus broadly inconsistent with cases where abused women display agency prior to the offence – for instance, by seeking help from or acting violently in relation to others outside of the abusive relationship.

Drawing on 20 years of experience as a US criminal defence lawyer, and on reviews of ongoing research on spousal abuse, Ferraro (2003) shows how, while it has often been successfully used to mitigate the sentences of white, cis-gender, middle- or upper-class women, BWS has also often prevented working class and racially or gender atypical women from constructing successful mitigation pleas based on abuse claims. This is mainly because these women are more likely to behave or be perceived as behaving in a way that displays agency rather than passivity. Specifically, Ferraro notes that 'because most battered women are not passive or helpless and may have done things that make them appear less than 'good,' information about these stereotypes is most frequently used against them, instead of in support of them' (2003: 115). This is not only epistemically regrettable, but also unjustified in a context where other concepts – most notably, the concept of battering – can both sometimes explain inter-partner homicide within abusive relationships *and* make sense of some active behaviours which remain unaccounted for under BWS. Because of this, Ferraro notes that

> although I originally used the language of syndrome in my testimony in accordance with the literature of the time, since 1995, I have described my testimony and expertise as being about 'the effects of battering,' as suggested in the literature and by the National Clearinghouse for the Defense of Battered Women (Ferraro 2003: 111).

If Ferraro is correct about the epistemic limitations and disproportionately negative effects that BWS has on racialised, as well as gender atypical and working-class women, battering does not only instantiate a case of deficit hermeneutical injustice.

[15] For an overview, see Holliday et al 2022.

[16] For a historical discussion of BWS, including its application in trial contexts, see Russell 2014. The latest updated edition of Walker's book is Walker 2016.

It may also instantiate a case of unjust hermeneutical excess. To see why this is so, we need to appreciate the difference that the scientific construction of new concepts and theories, as well as the (full or partial) correction of older ones, can make for whether a particular hermeneutical situation errs only in the direction of deficit, or in the direction of deficit and excess alike. In other words, the temporal nature of epistemic processes matters for how we diagnose any specific hermeneutical injustice.

The period during which BWS is first introduced and before it begins to be more widely applied across various US jurisdictions – namely, at the end of the 1970s and early 1980s – can be plausibly described as one of unjust hermeneutical deficit, the victims of which are all abused women (minority or not), as well as some men and non-binary persons.[17] But the same description is less tenable for the period where BWS is subject to mounting scientific, as well as social criticism, and where alternative concepts and theories – most notably, battering or Post-traumatic Stress Disorder (PTSD)[18] – become available, gain in empirical corroboration, as well as public discourse traction, and can be coherently applied to explain some of the criminal offences committed by abused spouses. For this period – roughly, from the late 1980s to the mid-1990s – it makes more sense to talk about a hermeneutically unjust mitigation practice that errs both in the direction of deficit and in that of excess. We find deficit in a failure to integrate concepts such as battering into the pool of collectively shared hermeneutical resources that convicted defendants can rely on for sentencing mitigation purposes. The excess consists in the epistemically overstated pretensions of BWS as applied by judges, prosecutors or defence lawyers in sentencing mitigation practice – namely, as a factor that purports to explain a significantly larger range of behaviours adopted by abused spouses than it actually does.[19]

Finally, for the period that follows the publication and circulation of the official report that proposes to replace BWS with battering, decisional patterns that tend to apply the former but not the latter are perhaps better described as instances of 'wilful hermeneutical ignorance' (Pohlhaus 2012) whereby state officials – in particular, judges, but also potentially legislators or prosecutors – deliberately maintain their ignorance concerning the explanatory potential of battering and the epistemic limits of BWS by failing to engage with available hermeneutical resources. For these cases, there is considerably less deficit than there is excess.

[17] Of course, the period *prior* to the introduction of BWS can be characterised as one of hermeneutical deficit to which *all* women (not only those belonging to minority groups) are vulnerable.

[18] On PTSD as an alternative to BWS, see Holliday 2022.

[19] This resonates with the excess hermeneutical injustice identified by Falbo 2022, which she presents as an injustice stemming 'from the overabundance of distorting and oppressive concepts which function to crowd-out, defeat, or pre-empt the application of a more accurate hermeneutical resource' (343). The difference between the case on which Falbo focuses – viz, the successful use of the hermeneutically excessive 'golden boy' trope for mitigation purposes – and the BWS case is that there is arguably more excess in the former than in the latter (ie the explanatory pretensions of 'golden boy'-based mitigation decisions are even more ill-founded than the ones which reduce battering to BWS).

The point of identifying the valence (deficit or excess) of different forms of hermeneutical injustice matters because it alerts us to the fact that merely increasing our pool of hermeneutical resources is insufficient if we want to address the full range of hermeneutically unjust mitigations. In other words, if we want to move closer to hermeneutically just mitigation practices, getting rid of gaps is not enough. We also need to consider the surpluses.

C. Accent

In *Accent*, Judge Novak is presented with robust empirical research that identifies circumstances that are linguistically relevant for sentencing. The case includes both hermeneutical and testimonial injustices, and indicates how these two forms of epistemic injustice can trigger and reinforce each other.

The connection between language and credibility assessments in legal settings is not novel idea (Erickson et al 1978; Lind and O'Barr 1979), but recent empirical research on the intersection of extralegal factors with judicial processes has documented both the effect that accent has on its own or in interaction with other factors (eg, race and age) on courtroom perceptions. Studies indicate that accents, particularly those connected to lower social status or deemed non-native, negatively impact the perceived trustworthiness and credibility of witnesses, with implications for both guilt attribution and sentencing outcomes. For instance, witnesses and defendants with regional or foreign accents are often rated less favourably, perceived as more typically criminal, and are more likely to be reaccused, independent of the evidence or crime type presented (Dixon and Mahoney 2004; Frumkin and Stone 2019). Furthermore, the dialect and race of a speaker influence relevant appraisals, with African American vernacular English speakers deemed less professional and educated, negatively affecting their credibility in the eyes of mock jurors (Kurinec and Weaver 2017; Cantone et al 2018). The impact of these biases is both perceptual and practical, and includes harsher sentencing for minority defendants, especially when they exhibit stereotypical accents.

The bias against non-native speakers further complicates this landscape, revealing a 'processing difficulty' that renders non-native speech less credible even in the absence of explicit prejudice (Lev-Ari 2010; Di Dio et al 2011; Romero-Rivas et al 2021). This 'otherness' linguistic effect (Franko 2007) also extends to speakers from socio-economically disadvantaged groups. Moreover, if overcorrected by speakers themselves, the use of 'proper language' is perceived as lacking authenticity and leads to further deficits in trustworthiness assessments (Drobnjak 2024).

Cast in epistemic justice terms, there seems to be a tendency towards an unfair epistemic deficit when sentencers face disadvantaged or disadvantage-adjacent accents, and potentially an excess when exposed to accents they judge as trustworthy. Specifically to our case, Judge Novak is presented with a seemingly pervasive instance of hermeneutical injustice whereby some marginalised offenders are put at a further disadvantage by the way they speak, at least if we compare them to linguistically privileged ones. The hermeneutical injustice in this case is triggered by the differential distribution and integration of accents, dialects and communication styles across criminal justice (and, arguably, other state) institutions. Additionally, as Fricker (2007: 17) notes, accent-based discrimination can also be more immediately tied to testimonial injustices whereby accents might carry 'an epistemic charge' that can result in credibility deficits. Thus, in cases where the defendant speaks with an accent socially tied to untrustworthiness, they risk incurring blatant testimonial injustice: their account is discounted or considered less relevant based solely on the way they speak.

Both types of accent-related injustices can present themselves as mitigation deficits or excesses. The problem lies not in the decision to mitigate or not, but rather in the fact that the decision is based on the perceived trustworthiness, highly impacted by hermeneutical injustice – the discounted notion of accent impact on the assessment of credibility – and/or testimonial injustice – the inexistence of the defendant's opportunity to be perceived as trustworthy based solely on their accent. Given this, *Accent* illustrates a particularly complex case of epistemic injustice that is simultaneously testimonial and hermeneutical.

IV. Addressing Epistemic Injustice at Sentencing

This section considers some policy proposals through which epistemic injustice can be better addressed at sentencing. On our argument, when epistemic injustices occur or are likely to occur at sentencing concerning a specific mitigating factor, there is a presumption in favour of sentence mitigation. Judges should have the option to rebut it, but only if they do so mindfully. Respecting this presumption can already be done informally by individual judges themselves – for instance, by developing decisional habits which remind and alert them to the possibility of biases that can distort their sentences. Unlike current initiatives that try to counter these biases intermittently (eg, via regular but relatively rare implicit bias training), such routines would be directly and continuously integrated within sentencing practice. They could include individual judges developing perspective-shifting or category-switching techniques when interacting with the defendant: the former imaginatively place judges in the offender's shoes, while the latter counterfactually vary offenders' social identity (eg, from working class to middle or upper class) (Galinsky and Moskowitz 2000). Judges could also single-handedly introduce pre-scheduled sentencing hearing feedback breaks designed to receive comments about the quality of their exchange with the defendant or defence from specially assigned court officials. Relatedly, judges could organise frequent professional forums and peer review sessions that allow for candid discussion of sentencing decisions. Taken together, these informal individual and collective initiatives would encourage a culture of self-examination and vigilance toward biases and other related injustices that undermine sentencing quality (*cf* Vidmar 2011).

Moreover, given the institutional dimensions of epistemic justice highlighted in the introduction, there is room for more formal policy innovations. Here, we highlight three such reform initiatives. One type of measure focuses on the amount and structuring of the time allocated to sentence hearings. Drawing on Dzur's concept of 'slow justice' (2012), we support a move toward *slow sentencing*. Dzur's proposal for slow justice focuses on jury verdicts and underlines the importance of sustained deliberation and careful consideration of reasons and evidence. Similarly, slow sentencing would be geared toward a sentencing process that allows for deep deliberation, meaningful participation from relevant stakeholders (eg, defendants, victims, their families, and the community), and a comprehensive evaluation of the circumstances surrounding the cases at hand. Practically, slow sentencing would involve measures such as repeated sentencing hearings, opportunities for adjournment to gather additional evidence or listen to new arguments or considering using alternative sentencing models like sentencing circles. Giving sentencing more time may be politically unpopular as it counters the (academically unpopular) mantra of efficiency. More importantly, however, expeditious sentencing decisions serve both the defendant and the victims by allowing them to move past the crime and the proceedings more swiftly. However, slow sentencing would plausibly render sentence mitigation less epistemically unfair, as compared to the status quo, especially when it comes to dealing with testimonial injustices of the kind at play in *Remorse*. More generally, slow sentencing would arguably better track truth and knowledge norms within criminal justice, and also more closely resonate with the ideal of individualised punishment (Saleilles in Ottenhof 2001). Cleary, a compromise between these different considerations should be sought, possibly something we could refer to as slow-enough sentencing.

Second, the judiciary could self-organise in more centralised ways – for instance, by creating a sentencing monitoring institute tasked with reviewing and signalling erroneous or epistemically faulty sentencing processes or outcomes. This institute could be situated within the judiciary or outside and could play a crucial role in ensuring that overlooked aspects of mitigation are reconsidered, especially by producing reports and memoranda which document new or revising mitigating factors that are being neglected or overestimated by sentence mitigation practice. By so doing, the institute would provide judges with important hermeneutical resources in cases where they have doubts about the application of standard or applicability of *sui generis* mitigating factors of the kind at play in *Battering* and other epistemically similar cases.

Third, and finally, epistemically unjust mitigation practices call for *corrective* measures in addition to the preventive ones outlined above. Here, we plead for an institutionally *sui generis* retroactive sentence mitigation measure. Unlike traditional parole, which primarily assesses the conduct of the convicted individual post-sentencing, retroactive sentence mitigation would allow for a judicial review of sentences in light of new evidence or significant changes in the general understanding of circumstances that were not available or considered at the time of sentencing. Retroactive mitigation also differs from pardons: the latter typically involve an executive act of clemency, often based on mercy considerations, while the former would remain a strictly judicial measure rooted in epistemically coloured ideals of justice.[20] Crucially, retroactive mitigation would offer a more direct pathway for courts to learn from their mistakes.[21] Of course, such a remedy is not without potential drawbacks. Concerns include the risk of undermining the finality of judgments, potentially overburdening the judicial system with requests for re-evaluation, and the challenge of establishing robust criteria for when and how this remedy should be applied.

The proposals outlined in this section do not exhaust the set of policy options needed to eliminate epistemically unjust sentence mitigation practices. Arguably, given the inherent fallibility of state action in general and criminal justice practices in particular, no such set of policy options is ever available. Nonetheless, the unfairly distorted credibility and intelligibility assessments that state officials – particularly judges – deploy through sentence mitigation decisions can be significantly reduced, even if they cannot be fully eliminated. By fostering an environment where individual judges are empowered to challenge their biases and the system is structured to support fair and informed decision-making, significant strides can be made towards rectifying the epistemic injustices that currently undermine the integrity of sentencing decisions. If our argument is convincing, judges could use it to consider and more justly assess mitigation facts and factors, and thus reduce the extent of (broadly construed) state misconduct in the criminal justice domain.

[20] Importantly, the measure would be consistent with the authority of judges in the penal domain, which is an important desideratum for legitimate sentencing. For a recent discussion and defence of judicial sentencing authority, see Poama and Tripkovic 2024.

[21] This measure is inspired by a policy which existed in the Slovenian criminal justice system until 2012, when it was abolished on the (contestable) grounds that it was both redundant and burdensome for the judicial system (Polegek 2011).

14

Unpacking the Recidivist Sentencing Discount from a State Misconduct Perspective

ANTJE DU BOIS-PEDAIN

In the sentencing practices of many jurisdictions there exists a longstanding tension between the sentencing of, on the one hand, multiple offending that comes before the court, and, on the other hand, recidivist offending. As is well known, multiple offending[1] is, in practice, 'discounted' in the sense that when a defendant stands to be sentenced in court for his criminal participation in an incident that is the sole incident before the court, his participation in that incident tends to attract a sanction of greater severity than if that same offending behaviour is being sentenced as one of a multitude of distinct incidents for which the defendant is sentenced on the same occasion in court. This pattern is apparently universal and often further reinforced by prosecutorial practices that permit other similar or less serious offences committed by the same defendant to be treated as wrapped up by the sentence imposed for the offences and incidents for which the defendant is brought to trial.[2]

By contrast, recidivist[3] offending – understood here as a criminal offence committed after the accused had been convicted and sentenced on one or more previous occasions for one or more different criminal incidents – appears to affect the punishment for this subsequent crime in the direction of aggravation.[4]

[1] Multiple offending is in this context understood as the commission of crimes during different incidents, whether or not the crimes committed are of the same or of a different kind, and also whether or not the different incidents are linked through a wider plan or other factor that socially suggests that they should be viewed holistically (such as different occasions of physical abuse of a romantic partner over the course of a relationship or a phase of relationship breakdown).

[2] On the empirical patterns and proposed normative justifications for sentence discounts for multiple offenders, see eg De Keijser, Roberts and Ryberg 2017.

[3] I use this term due to its familiarity but with some misgivings. It appears to me to mark out as somehow special offending that follows a prior criminal conviction and punishment, when it isn't clear whether there are any grounds for viewing it as significantly different from other multiple offending.

[4] Roberts and Harrendorf 2020: 261 fn 3 found only one jurisdiction where sentencing law explicitly stipulates that an offence is not aggravated by the fact that the offender has a previous record: Western Australia (Sentencing Act 1995, s 7(2)).

Sometimes this is achieved mechanistically or formally through sentence grids or binding instructions to judges to treat all (or similar) recidivist offending as an aggravating factor. When the application of such rules is subject to judicial discretion, the best possible outcome from an offenders' perspective is, then, that the recidivist dimension of his behaviour is disregarded for the purposes of sentence – it is sentence-neutral instead of aggravating.[5]

In legal systems where recidivism in the sense defined above is not expressly labelled aggravating, but merely forms part of considerations pertaining to the history and context of the offending behaviour under sentence, there is also an empirically observable tendency that the fact that the offence was committed post-release from prison, or after another type of punishment had been imposed for a crime on a previous occasion, will often be treated by the courts as warranting increased punishment and/or the imposition of a different type of sanction usually understood to be more burdensome than its alternative.[6] It must be stressed, however, that this is not a foregone conclusion. Courts in jurisdictions where substantial sentencing discretion exists not only tend to reward strong but defeated efforts to desist with mitigation,[7] but may also punish less severely in response to other pressures towards reoffending faced by the defendant.[8]

It is not immediately obvious why that chasm exists. Alternatively, any multiplicity of offending incidents could be approached in the same way, whether the sequence was punctuated by intermittent experiences of prosecution, trial, conviction and punishment, or not. (For such an approach based on coherence, see Reitz 2010.) Petter Asp submits that one should approach multiple and recidivist offending with similar sentencing principles tending towards leniency so as to avoid 'attach[ing] too much importance to … the chronological structure' of persistent offending (Asp 2010: 225). When the case for a recidivist discount is in this way based on a combination of the view that bulk offending should be discounted, and that when one judges offenders at different points in a longer criminal career, it should make little difference whether that point follows in temporal sequence upon an earlier conviction and sentence or not, recidivist discounts arise from the consistent application of sentencing principles that support what Nils Jareborg (1998) memorably labels 'bulk discounts' in sentencing.[9] Asp's

[5] For examples of these legal responses to recidivism (taken from the US, UK and German legal systems) see Roberts and Harrendorf 2020. For a concise summary of current UK sentencing law and practice regarding repeat offending, see commonslibrary.parliament.uk/research-briefings/cdp-2022-0116.

[6] Roberts and Harrendorf 2020.

[7] On desistance as a ground for mitigation of sentence see Bunce 2023.

[8] For instance, the German Federal Supreme Court (*Bundesgerichtshof*) has held, in the case of a recidivist frequent offender charged with further offences of drug-possession, that due to the offender's continuing addiction issues it had been wrong of the trial court to take into account the quick speed of relevant reoffending when passing sentence (BGH, Decision of 4 March 2020 – 1 StR 46/20).

[9] Not every recidivist offender might be affected by a bulk offending discount, of course, due to the absence of a bulk offending pattern in their criminal behaviour. This ground of discounting a punishment would have greatest application to prolific property offenders, and similar.

starting point, however, meets opposition from authors such as Bennett (2010), Brand (2022), Lee (2010) and Ewing (2019b), who ascribe enhanced culpability to recidivist offenders based on what they take to be a morally salient difference between *resuming* and *continuing* offending. I will engage with their arguments in section III of this chapter.

Asp is also concerned that 'The recidivist premium will generally speaking hit the underprivileged the hardest' (Asp 2010: 225), and while he does not explain precisely why this supplies a moral case for leniency in the sentencing of recidivist offenders, a possible reason is suggested by Christopher Lewis (2021) when he links recidivism to the criminal justice system's impact on most recidivist offenders, for whom leading a law-abiding life has been made more rather than less difficult by their prior punishment. Lewis suggests that in light of this heightened disadvantage, recidivist offenders are less culpable for their choice to reoffend than otherwise comparable first-time offenders are for their choice to offend. This is a tenable but not, I shall argue, a conclusive argument. It would be difficult, for instance, to apply it to a recidivist offender who has not made any perceptible effort to avoid reoffending. Given the limitations of the culpability-based case for sentence reduction, further argument is required to show why increased disadvantage should be met with a reduced sentence.

I. Overview

What I want to do in this chapter is to strengthen the case for sentence discounts for recidivist offenders through a state misconduct argument. I do not mean to suggest that this is the only way of so doing. A different argumentative path would proceed from a particular theory of punishment – say, a theory of punishment-as-reintegration, or of punishment-without-blame – which would provide an independent normative basis for making punishment less burdensome for (and thereby more helpful to) offenders, the longer their offending behaviour persists. While I find these theories of punishment attractive, my argument in this chapter is designed to address theorists and practitioners who are committed to theoretical justifications of punishment that rely (in whole or in part) on desert or censure.[10]

In section II, I recast the link between prior experiences of criminal prosecution and punishment and recidivist offending as raising an issue of whether and when the prior punishment (either in itself, or on account of its effects on

[10] Due to space constraints I will not be able to address potential utilitarian arguments against recidivist discounts as such. Such arguments would likely point to concerns regarding a depletion of incapacitative and deterrent effects. My response would be to deny the soundness of the factual assumptions underpinning such concerns based on research that has shown no or negligible effects of continued detention of prolific offenders on crime rates, and (with the exception of drink driving) no correlation between increases in sanction severity and increased deterrence.

the offender's self and/or his circumstances) constitutes state misconduct, and argue that prior punishment – which a recidivist offender has, by definition, undergone – amounts to state misconduct if it generates additional burdens or disadvantages that *unjustifiably* leave the punished individual in a worse position for accessing a law-abiding life trajectory than they were in before the hiatus of conviction and punishment. Using this approach and focusing on imprisonment, I identify a range of settings and circumstances where imprisonment constitutes state misconduct. Drawing on what is known empirically about reoffending I then, in section III, first reject a number of arguments that have been put forward to show that a recidivist crime is either more culpable or in other ways more serious per se than an otherwise comparable non-recidivist crime. I then turn to the inverse argument, developed most fully by Lewis, that recidivism is typically associated with reduced culpability levels, and argue that Lewis's case for the recidivist discount is more limited than he takes it to be. Defendants could qualify for such a discount more easily, were it to be granted based on a state misconduct argument. I submit that this kind of sentence discount rests on a quasi-parsimonious foundation that views state misconduct as supplying a non-ideal ground for leniency (what on some theories would amount to under-punishment) at the sentencing stage and offer some observations as to what follows from this conceptualisation for the application of the sentence discount.

II. Understanding Reoffending: The Criminologist's Perspective

In the introduction I referred to Asp's view that a penal system should not 'attach too much importance to … the chronological structure' of persistent offending, including the question whether offending behaviour followed earlier courtroom appearances and criminal sanctions or not. This view makes sense only on the assumption that the commission of a new crime *after* one has been put on trial and punished for an earlier crime, is as such no worse (in ways that should affect sentence severity) than if that same crime had been part of an uninterrupted sequence of criminal behaviour.

This starting point could appear misguided to some, and they might offer an illustrative example along the following lines in support of their objections:

> Imagine George and Susan, who have promised fidelity to each other. After 10 years of marriage, George discovers that Susan has been unfaithful on five different occasions. He finds her betrayals wrong. Contrast that to George discovering one instance of betrayal, discussing it with Susan, moving on, only to have her do it again a second time, followed by another conversation, followed by another betrayal, and so on, until you get to five betrayals. Morally speaking, these two '5× multiplicities' are terribly

different: and it is undeniable that Susan's behaviour in the second case is much more blameworthy.[11]

Broadly speaking, the answer to this challenge which I will develop in this section is that recidivist offending trajectories are (at least typically) not like that. At the end of this section, I will be in a position to specify why the various parallels explicitly and implicitly suggested in this hypothetical – between marital promises and laws, marital unfaithfulness and crimes, discussions between couples and trials, etc – do not hold. As a first step, I will take a closer look at what is known about trajectories of (re)offending. As a second step, I consider how prior state punishment typically affects these trajectories.

A. Offending Trajectories Considered

It is well established that personal-biographical and environmental-social factors interact in criminal offending, including reoffending. The kinds of interactions that occur are theorised in P-O Wikström's Situational Action Theory (SAT) model, which seeks to capture how motivation, outlook, past experience and context co-produce offending (and other) behaviours (see eg Wikström, Treiber and Roman 2024). In Wikström's model, people commit crimes when they operate in life settings that create temptations and opportunities to do so, and when their personal moral outlook and desires converge to interpret these opportunities as worthwhile behavioural options for themselves in the circumstances they are facing.

Fine-grained observational, ethnographic, interview- and lived-experience-based studies suggest that considerable variety exists in respect of pathways to reoffending. Some individuals just slip back into criminal lifestyles or harmful behaviour patterns, eg those linked to addiction or mental illnesses (where harming others and self-harm appear as two sides of the same coin); others are defeated in their efforts to avoid reinvolvement in crime. Sometimes a decision to 'go straight' is eroded by setbacks or in other ways undermined; sometimes direct pressure is exerted by others to resume criminal behaviour; sometimes an individual does not view the criminal behaviours they engage in as deeply wrong but as viable options in certain conditions, or as preferable to the alternatives despite the apprehension risk and the punishment cost. (For summaries of research findings, see eg Payne 2007; Polascheck 2019; Bunce 2023.)

Sociological studies stress that most of those who engage in persistent (re) offending are subject to structural social forces that powerfully discourage commitments to desist from crime, and/or in other ways place obstacles before a crime-free life. Many of these structural social forces consist of patterns of

[11] I thank Leo Zaibert for raising this challenge and providing the hypothetical.

disadvantage and discrimination that make law-abiding life trajectories more difficult to 'access' for some criminal justice-involved individuals than for others who do not appear repeatedly on the criminal justice system's radar screen (see eg Western 2018; Western and Harding 2022). By contrast (although this is less well researched), many of those who don't reoffend after their first conviction and sentence apparently don't need to get onto a different life trajectory in order to lead law-abiding lives. They go about their daily life again, and that life doesn't involve them in more crime. Perhaps they act a little more carefully, monitor their spending better, adjust their habits and lifestyle in some fairly modest way. Easily implemented behavioural modifications already secure non-continuation of the behaviour that led to their criminal justice involvement and explain why they do not return to court. Put differently, some convicted offenders don't need to 'stop offending' in order not to reoffend.

However, the difficulties many offenders face in accessing non-criminal life trajectories mean that, for some of those who do end up in court, not returning to be tried and sentenced for another crime on a subsequent occasion takes conscious – and constant – effort (see eg Nugent and Schinkel 2016; Shapland and Bottoms 2011). This is where the notion of desistance comes in.

Desistance can be understood as a 'process by which an individual begins to reduce their level of offending, terminate involvement in offending, and ultimately maintain a state of non-offending' (Bunce 2023: 4, relying on McCuish et al 2020). Some analyses of individual desistance trajectories suggest that successful desistance requires first and foremost a commitment to desist (see eg Shapland and Bottoms 2011). For some, it may be the experience of being tried, convicted and sentenced that triggers a personal commitment to go straight. For others, it may be a new relationship, a family crisis or simply a point in time when it sinks in that they have to free themselves from the habits of criminal offending because their lives are not working out the way they want (of course, the *n*th – as opposed to the first, second, or third – courtroom appearance can also have this effect). Stops in reoffending are often correlated with life-changing events such as a stable relationship or parenthood (see especially Sampson and Laub 1993 and the voluminous literature on 'turning points'). Whatever the individual pathway, the commitment to stop offending, where it is needed to stop offending, is not enough on its own, but needs to be accompanied by a reshaping of life circumstances (see especially Shapland and Bottoms 2017).

There is also a strong correlation for young people between, on the one hand, attention by social services, and, on the other hand, criminal justice involvement. Bunce summarises findings from Scotland, particularly the Edinburgh Study of Youth Transitions and Crime, showing that 'children who become known to services early on tend to be slower to desist than those who are similarly involved in offending behaviour but do not become known to services', and that 'the deeper a young person enters the criminal justice system, the less likely they are to desist' (Bunce 2023: 8 (original emphasis omitted); for a systematic meta-review of studies finding negative effects of standard criminal justice processing on young persons' subsequent offending behaviour, see Petrosino et al 2019). Especially when contrasted with communities where conviction-avoiding processing of allegations of criminal behaviour, including of fairly serious crimes, is preferred in respect of young persons (for the example of Jersey, see Miles and Raynor 2014; Evans, Raynor and Heath 2022), these findings indicate that record-generating disposals can lock criminal life trajectories into place during the early stages of what, from a developmental perspective, might to some extent even be considered socially normative rule-breaking behaviour. There is agreement among criminologists that offending careers are as much made and shaped by the state's response system to problem behaviours, as they are made and shaped by people who commit offences (see especially Western and Harding 2022).

B. The Culpable State

But how exactly does the state's response influence reoffending? As mentioned above, one of the most important insights to emerge from criminological work on life-course offending and desistance is that avoiding the commission of further crimes requires access to a law-abiding life trajectory. Ex-prisoners' descriptions of re-entry (eg Carey, Grant and Tompkins 2022) often stress that what stands in the way of post-release formation of a law-abiding life are manifold socially stigmatising effects of the offence of conviction and of the period of imprisonment served. These pertain to an ex-prisoner's social reception and employment opportunities offered, to deskilling, to legal restrictions on types of work following a conviction and sentence, to the absence or low quality of educational and training options in prison, and to limited work experience – all of which have negative effects on labour market access and attainment, on income, and on personal achievement and self-perception more generally. Life after release from prison can be cognitively and practically disorienting. Often, tight conditions of early release and parole supervision add to fears of failure rather than providing effective support (see generally LeBel and Richie 2023; Miller and Stuart 2017). These effects are clearly attributable to imprisonment; it is a different question, however, when and why the state should be considered culpable for bringing them about.

Under the definition of state misconduct proposed in section I of this chapter, any authoritative behaviour by state agents that is intended or foreseen to expose its recipient to unjustified social disadvantage of the kind that makes access to a law-abiding life trajectory significantly more difficult, qualifies as state misconduct. Relevant disadvantage can consist of ill-treatment, exclusion from or refusal of services/benefits to that individual, whether by state actors or by other social actors. Punishment in the form of imprisonment unjustifiably and thus culpably increases social disadvantage when such added disadvantage arises from irresponsible neglect of prisoners' interests during their imprisonment.

It is well established that negative post-release outcomes are correlated with bad prison conditions, inadequate resettlement preparation, missed educational or professional development opportunities in prison, and insufficient medical responses, including psychiatric interventions and treatment programmes for problem behaviours, addictions, and physical and mental illness while in prison, or their sudden discontinuance after release (see generally Kazemian and Walker 2018; Visher and Travis 2011; Link, Ward and Stansfield 2019; Drago, Galbiati and Vertova 2011). Many repeat offenders who have slipped into a revolving door pattern find that this pattern is sustained by an already fragile support network breaking down during their imprisonment (see eg Halushka, 2020, Rubio Arnal and McNeill, 2024). Minority ethnic and black ex-prisoners often find themselves at a confluence of various sources of post-imprisonment heightened disadvantage (see eg Kazemian 2020: 212–13; Pager, Western and Sugie 2009; Miller 2021; Western 2018). It is clear also that negative after-effects of a stay in prison (whether of shorter or longer duration) on an offender can be mitigated or even avoided through better prison environments (see generally Kazemian and Walker 2018: 580 and, for recidivism-reducing effects of stays in a particularly impressive Italian open prison, Mastrobuoni and Terlizzese 2021). Steps can also be taken pre-release to increase the receptiveness of a prisoner's social environment post-release, whereas imprisonment without anticipatory post-release preparation will very likely reinforce social impediments to living law-abidingly (see generally Richards and Jones 2004).

Conditions of confinement that constantly violate the dignity of prisoners (such as overcrowding, the absence of privacy for bodily functions), subject them to physical violation, whether by other prisoners or by staff (see Wolff et al 2007), to sensory deprivation or sensory overload, and to prolonged isolation, clearly amount to state misconduct. Such conditions have also been found to have lasting negative effects on the social and mental functioning of ex-prisoners after their release (see especially Haney 2020; Toch 1992). However, conditions in many of the minimally decent standard prisons, where the foregoing violations are avoided, also constitute maltreatment: the boredom, deskilling and infantilisation, and the absence of meaningful occupation, which come with prolonged involuntary confinement, stunt a person's social and intellectual functioning and breed passivity and loss of hope. The additional disadvantages that arise from imprisonment, mainly through its various criminogenic conditions, are unjustified to the extent that they are an avoidable and therefore unnecessary feature of an offender's punishment. The negative effects of living in a 'total institution' (Kolstad 1996: 334) of the kind that most prisons constitute, do on this basis count as state misconduct not only when a person is exposed to them unnecessarily because available non-custodial options were disregarded (as will often be the case with young offenders), but also when the length of time a person spends in prison raises serious concerns that the released prisoner will not be able to build a minimally decent life for himself after release, and no active countermeasures are taken to counteract these risks and consequences of prolonged confinement.

C. Serial Marital Misbehaviour and Reoffending Compared

Before leaving this section, it is important to make explicit how actual trajectories of reoffending differ in crucial respects from Susan's trajectory of extramarital affairs in the hypothetical formulated at the start of this section.

To start with, doubts are warranted concerning the parallel drawn between breaches of marital promises and criminal offending. The hypothetical would, at least to me, appear far less suggestive if we had been invited to consider instead that George had beaten up Susan badly on five different occasions, in one (but not in the other) alternative punctuated by discussions with Susan about his violence towards her. It would then seem (at least to me) that the cases were clearly of comparable seriousness. The reason for this, it would appear to me, is that, when we consider the cumulative weight of multiple occasions of serious physical abuse involving pain and injury, we would immediately focus on the physical and psychological harm suffered by Susan on each of these occasions. Even if, arguably, there were an added layer of disappointment, a further violation of trust, during the later incidents in the alternative where Susan spoke to George about his behaviour after each occasion, this would appear to carry little weight in the overall seriousness assessment of George's recurrent beatings of Susan. What this suggests is that the very appeal of the original hypothetical is importantly linked to the feature that a violation of trust/breach of promise is, in essence, the type of wrong we are being asked to consider. In the original hypothetical, Susan's initial promise to be faithful to George is central to the character of the wrongs she commits: a breach of her promise to George and of George's trust. It is much more plausible that repeating this kind of wrong becomes significantly more serious when interactions aimed at re-establishing trust take place in the interim than when no such interactions take place.

This would also give additional moral weight to any (again, we imagine, actually given) promise not to do it again in Susan and George's 'discussions' of her transgressions – a feature we may struggle to see replicated in the criminal justice context. In response, one might seek to argue that criminal trials and punishments are sufficiently like marital promises of faithfulness that we should analogise the former practices to the latter. Clearly, that would require significant philosophical argument. Such arguments have been attempted in different ways by Lee 2010 and Bennett 2010, and I will engage with them in the next section. In the present context, I merely wish to highlight that the Susan hypothetical obscures the need for such arguments to be provided at all by making us think of actual discussions between the marital partners which leave George satisfied that Susan is committed to desisting from having extramarital affairs in the future.

Lastly, there is no sense in which George's reaction to his discovery of Susan's affair has put Susan into a position in which it has become appreciably more difficult for her to avoid further affairs, let alone that this effect has arisen in a way that lays George open to criticism. Assuming that in the original hypothetical George stands for the state and Susan for the defendant in a criminal trial, the hypothetical would then fail to track what this chapter seeks to establish as the morally salient basis on which mitigation should be granted – that the offender's circumstances have been worsened unjustifiably, in a way that makes compliance more difficult to achieve, by the culpable misconduct of the agent which seeks to call the offender to account.

In short, even if in Susan's case, the '5× multiplicities' were indeed 'terribly different', in most criminal offending scenarios, they are not. That, however, does not yet meet the (implicit) challenge that a recidivist offender's behaviour may, by reason of constituting reoffending, be 'much more blameworthy'. The response to this challenge will be provided in section III.

III. The Sentencer's Perspective: Reoffending as Grounds for Mitigation

What I carry over from the discussion of the Susan hypothetical into this section is the need for further engagement with the assumption that drives it; that there is something especially or additionally blameworthy about recidivist offending compared to non-recidivist offending. This point emerges perhaps more clearly when one compares, not different multiplicities of offending, but recidivist and first-time offending. It is the comparison of, say, the third-time recidivist offender with the first-time offender in respect of the commission of an otherwise comparable crime that has prompted some authors to develop arguments that seek to show that the recidivist's crime is distinctly worse than the non-recidivist's. Since the direct harmfulness of the compared crimes is held constant in these comparisons, it is the culpability of the recidivist's offence that is argued to be aggravated, or an additional wrong is construed to be present when a crime is being committed by a recidivist offender.

In subsection A below, I will rebut arguments which seek to show that the recidivist's crime is – other things being equal – more serious per se than a non-recidivist's crime. I will then, in subsection B, turn to the question how recidivist offending fares under standard culpability assessments, focusing on the argument developed by Lewis 2021 in favour of a recidivist discount, namely, that recidivist offenders, other things being equal, are necessarily less culpable than non-recidivist offenders in light of the after-effects of earlier punishments. While I accept that many of the post-imprisonment disadvantages faced by recidivist offenders can have culpability-reducing effects when an ex-prisoner turns back to crime, I point to various difficulties that can arise in individual cases before a culpability-based sentence reduction would be sufficiently substantiated. In subsection C, I therefore seek to convince readers of the practical value of accounting for punishment-induced unjustified additional disadvantage through a state misconduct argument by showing that it is both easier to establish a sufficient factual basis for misconduct-based sentence mitigation and that such mitigation can shape the sentence in a more profound way than a culpability-based sentence adjustment would likely do.

A. Why Recidivist Offending isn't Worse per se than Otherwise Comparable Non-recidivist Offending

Various scholars have offered arguments that seek to establish that recidivist offenders are typically or presumptively more culpable than first-time offenders in respect of otherwise similar offending occasions (eg Bennett 2010; Lee 2010).

Lee argues that someone who has been tried, convicted and sentenced for an offence is thereby placed under an obligation 'to organise his life in a way that reduces the risk of his reoffending' (Lee 2010: 50). Even if one were to accept this starting point (but see Tonry 2010: 104, who insists that there is no obligation not to offend or reoffend in any event but simply liability to criminal sanction, should one (re)offend), an argument for increased punishments for recidivists is thereby still lacking. To the extent that such an obligation could be used to justify practices such as placing convicted offenders under a duty to participate in treatment programmes offered to them in prison, or have obligations to modify their behaviour in certain specified ways imposed on them as part of custody-avoiding sanctions packages, or in the context of early release, the argument serves to underpin the imposition of certain additional primary duties that can form part of the sanctioning exercise itself. It does not, however, justify imposing additional punishment for the violation of such obligations. This is why it is generally accepted that offenders who refuse participation in treatment programmes in prison cannot for this reason be additionally penalised, and why it is seen as problematic when breaches of behavioural obligations that do not themselves constitute the commission of further offences lead to the revocation of parole. Labelling the non-fulfilment of this obligation an omission does not supply a normative argument why additional punishment would be justified in respect of the commission of a further crime.

From a situational action theory perspective, where offending behaviour continues, it continues because the environment–person interaction is such that the choice to offend is the preferred choice for that particular situated agent. As Wikström and Treiber (2018: 273) explain, 'People's crime propensities are triggered by specific environmental inducements, and environmental inducements are made relevant by people's particular propensities'. Crime propensity is defined as 'the tendency to see and choose crime as an action alternative in response to particular opportunities and frictions' (ibid). The important point that follows from this is that, when an offender has 'learned nothing' from his earlier trial and punishment, he is simply the same irresponsible/indifferent/aggressive anti-social agent going about his life, not a distinctly worse agent, on those subsequent offending occasions. Nor does his reoffending require actual defiance of the criminal conviction's message or heightened criminal energy, just that he hasn't reacted to his prior punishment in the way one hoped he might. This also supplies the answer to Brand's (2022) suggestion that character flaws which recidivist offenders manifest in their recidivist offending should be reflected in enhanced punishments. Even if the commission of a crime reflects a character flaw – as it often might – and even if this flaw perhaps becomes more deep-seated or pronounced with every occasion on which an agent acts on it, it is still the same flaw that continues to be manifested in continuing offending.

Some scholars do, however, argue that it is normatively significant when a recidivist offender hasn't, as I put it in the preceding paragraph, reacted to his prior punishment in the way one hoped he might. For Bennett 2010, who conceptualises ordinary legal punishment as an 'apology ritual', a recidivist offender has 'more to apologise for'. The 'more', I take it, consists of the breach of a promise usually associated with a sincere apology not to misbehave again. This promise is, like the apology, construed rather than real. Since undergoing the court-imposed punishment constitutes the offender's ritual apology, it is therefore appropriate to impose on him an increased punishment. It should be clear from this summary that the argument rests entirely on normative constructions rather than on assumptions about actual communications occurring in a penal setting. This, however, cannot suffice. In my view, there would need to be an empirical docking point that would make the ascription of these meanings plausible, at least as an idealised reconstruction of actual criminal trials and punishments. I do not see, however, how such a docking point could be supplied, given that the courtroom experience does not mimic interpersonal interactions in which we extract apologies and promises from each other.[12]

Ewing 2019b contends that the courtroom experience provides convicted defendants with a 'moral opportunity' to rethink their ways and make efforts to go straight, such that any subsequent return to criminal behaviour should for this reason be considered morally worse than their initial slide into criminal behaviour. This argument, again, would need to be grounded in some empirical evidence that convictions are indeed 'special opportunities' for commitments to avoid a return to crime (leaving aside, for the moment, additional hurdles that a thus-committed individual may face in implementing their commitment). Empirically speaking, however, there is little evidence of this. Even if one follows scholars such as

[12] This is not the place to go into the question whether the courtroom experience should mimic such practices (which I would be uncomfortable with). So long as it doesn't, neither an apology not a promise not to reoffend can be ascribed to defendants.

MacLeod, Grove and Farrington 2012, who assume that convictions are empirically plausible occasions where people decide to go straight, other research on biographical–psychological turning points points to a variety of personal triggers for decisions to refrain from crime (see section II.A above). If moral weight is attached to an offender having missed an opportunity to make a commitment to desistance, therefore, that moral significance would have to be accorded as well to other life events that have been observed to trigger in some offenders a commitment to going straight, such as a new relationship. The very strangeness of the thought that one might consider a crime committed by a recidivist offender who recently acquired a girlfriend *morally worse* by reason of the fact that starting this relationship provided him with a moral opportunity to step away from crime that a recidivist offender who has not found a girlfriend is left without, illustrates the problems with this argument. It cannot rest of any special quality of the courtroom experience. Because of this, it is ultimately no more convincing than the various theoretical constructs of 'reoffending' as morally worse per se than 'offending' that have been put forward.

B. Culpability-based Sentence Reductions for Recidivist Offenders: Preconditions and Limits

Many of the arguments we have considered in the previous subsection suffered from a shared weakness, in that they tended to ascribe meanings and commitments to the behaviour of repeat offenders that are unlikely to find any reflection in the lived experience and psychological reality of the person engaging in such conduct. But not all arguments that make culpability the linchpin of how a sentencer should react to recidivist offending rely on such construed meanings. Some simply suggest that actual cases of recidivism will frequently exhibit indicators of raised or reduced culpability already embedded in the application of standard sentencing principles.

Attention to how the aetiology of recidivist offending relates to established sentencing principles has led some scholars to argue for a culpability-based lesser sentence, insisting that the culpability of a repeat offender (especially when the record is long) will typically be lower than that of a non-prolific or first time offender committing an otherwise similar crime (see eg Lewis 2021; Petersen 2012; Janssen 1991). This, then, turns us to the question how the prior experience of trial, conviction and punishment affects, under standard sentencing principles, the culpability of an ex-prisoner who reoffends.

Situational action theory explains that 'crime results from people's intersections with different settings (their action contexts)' and that these 'may be affected by changes in a person's characteristics and/or changes in the settings to which he or she is exposed, i.e., his or her activity field' (Wikström and Treiber 2018: 281). The experience of imprisonment, in a typical case, affects both factors in a negative direction. The person herself may become a less socially confident and less resilient individual, anticipating mistrust and social rejection from others, hampered by the personality changes and experiences of prolonged imprisonment in their functioning across many social domains. Moreover, many ex-prisoners face a quickly acute lack of money, have no stable living arrangements, and little meaningful occupation – in other words, they operate in settings where crime is more readily 'on the cards' than in other activity fields (see the empirical literature summarised in section II.B above).

Attention to these consequences of imprisonment has prompted Lewis (2021) to base his case for a recidivist sentence discount on what he argues is a recidivist offender's reduced culpability that follows from the criminogenic effects of imprisonment. Lewis contends that there is 'less evidence of ill-will in the recidivist's case' (Lewis 2021: 1247), given that an ex-prisoner's circumstances are such that law-abiding behaviour has become even more difficult for them, in that they now have even fewer alternatives to criminal behaviour and/or face stronger incentives to commit crimes. Lewis's arguments are particularly strong in the American context, where a vast array of disqualifications and restrictions directly block access to many lawful occupations, including some that would otherwise be promising areas in which ex-prisoners might find work. The typical circumstances faced by ex-prisoners give therefore rise to stronger incentives to turn back to crime, which for Lewis conclusively supplies the case for reduced culpability (see especially Lewis 2021: 1259ff).

I agree with Lewis that possible objections based on an argument that ex-prisoners are themselves responsible for the stronger incentives they now face since their past crime generated the need and justification for their past punishment do not bite. My reason for this is that, even if the ex-prisoners were responsible for the added disadvantages they face post-release, there would still be no reason to ignore the fact that affected ex-prisoners would (as a Canadian trial judge put it in respect of other marginalised social groups facing additional strong incentives to turn to crime[13]) be 'virtue tested' to a much greater extent than the average person. And it is this consideration that supplies the basis for allowing stronger incentives to be taken into account in assessing an offender's culpability.

My concern that Lewis's case for the recidivist discount is more limited than he appreciates arises from his equation of stronger incentives with reduced culpability. To my mind, the presence of stronger incentives gives us a reason to consider carefully in every individual case whether and how these stronger incentives have affected the ex-prisoner's reoffending. But I am not convinced that this consideration would necessarily lead to a finding of reduced culpability on standard approaches to culpability assessments at sentencing. The reason why I doubt that

[13] *R v Hamilton* (2003) (Hill J), overturned on appeal *R v Hamilton* (2004). For discussion, see Devlin and Sherrard 2005.

a culpability-based argument would necessarily succeed when a repeat offender has previously experienced criminogenic imprisonment pertains to what is known about how such increased disadvantage does, and does not, play out in individual cases of reoffending. As we have seen in section II, reconviction studies identify a range of factors that make future offending more or less likely. These factors track motivation, skill and social capital. Assuming that an offender has made a commitment to 'going straight', whether he will be able to do so depends to a large extent on whether he is able to find employment or some other structure in his life, has family support, avoids criminal friends, drugs and depression. Behavioural traits that made success or even adequate functioning in standard social contexts difficult, also make avoiding offending difficult.

In practice, courts will frequently encounter recidivist offenders who have not made any perceptible effort to avoid reoffending. Sentencers do not normally take culpability to be reduced by contextual facts that have not affected the offender's decision-making. For objectively greater hurdles to leading a law-abiding life to register in reduced levels of culpability, it would need to be shown that they made a concrete difference to the commission of a criminal act, creating at that moment a level of additional difficulty that made a difference to what happened. This would likely require concrete evidence of some prolonged effort made by the defendant to avoid the commission of further crimes, which were in some traceable way undermined by particular effects of his prior imprisonment. By contrast, when recidivist offenders simply slide back into their former life patterns, without engaging in observable efforts to do things differently, it is difficult to see how the objective context of higher hurdles becomes relevant in a reduced culpability story.

Since I find the effect which a situational context of increased disadvantage has on culpability less clearcut and direct than Lewis does, I am not persuaded that prison's known criminogenic effects provide a strong enough basis as such for reduced culpability findings for recidivist offenders. The nuanced and case-specific considerations which I consider necessary will sometimes fail to establish that a particular ex-prisoner's culpability was reduced through the way in which these contextual factors played out concretely in his case.

C. The Difference that State Misconduct-based Sentence Mitigation Makes to a Sentence

Even if the additional hurdles that the criminogenic effects of imprisonment place before a law-abiding life do not make an ex-prisoner necessarily less culpable for sliding back into criminal behaviour, they do give rise to the question what weight should be given to the fact that the state has voluntarily chosen a penal path that is known to increase the extent to which an individual is exposed to criminogenic activity fields and to diminish the individual's capacity to resist criminal opportunities. As I argued in section II.B, the additional criminogenic disadvantages that arise from imprisonment are unjustified, and therefore attributable to state misconduct, when a person is exposed to them unnecessarily because available non-custodial options were disregarded, and/or when the length of time a person spends in prison raises serious concerns that the released prisoner will not be able to build a minimally decent life for himself after release, and no active countermeasures are taken to counteract these risks and consequences of prolonged confinement. In practice, given the conditions of most (even minimally decent) prisons, this means that many (although not all) ex-prisoners could conceivably rely on a state misconduct-based argument for sentence mitigation.

How, then, should we conceptualise and apply this ground of mitigation? Let us first turn to the appropriate conceptualisation. When the editors write in their introductory chapter to this book that the state, '[having] to some degree directly or indirectly contributed to the offending (or the re-offending) … carries some liability for [the offending]' which it 'can discharge … by awarding mitigation to the offender', their use of such technical legal language suggests that they conceive of misconduct-based sentence mitigation in terms of a remedy for such misconduct. Yet their very next sentence rows back from any such implication when the issue raised by state misconduct is redescribed as being that 'Some of the offender's culpability for the offence is shared with the state, and this needs recognition at the time of sentencing' (Zaibert, Roberts and Ryberg, this volume).

In my view, sentence mitigation based on state misconduct does not constitute a remedy for such misconduct in any technical legal sense; not even a second-order remedy which compensates for an experienced violation (in contrast to first-order remedies that put an end to the violation). This is so because it is not apparent that, or how, sentence mitigation constitutes compensation for the misconduct suffered. (Plausible second-order remedies would be payment of damages, or the moral satisfaction provided by a declaration that the state acted unjustly.) In my view, then, sentence mitigation for state misconduct should be thought of as a third-order reaction; an available non-ideal reaction to state misconduct, something that the court does to mark the misconduct out as significant without claiming to remedy it thereby, and without claiming that it follows from the misconduct with any deductive necessity.

This conceptualisation assists us in answering the second question: how sentence mitigation on a state misconduct basis should be applied. The editors of this book are concerned that 'Without some link between the offence and the misconduct … the appeal for mitigation may become implausibly loose' (Zaibert, Roberts and Ryberg, this volume). What is and what isn't implausibly loose, however, depends importantly on whether or not we take ourselves to be in the business of providing remedies. If one were to approach the recidivist discount subject to the logic of second-order remedies, this would imply that it should be made conditional upon showing a causal or at least potentially causal link between the additional unjustified disadvantage to which the ex-offender was exposed and his subsequent offence. We would then face limitations in the application of the discount that would be similar to the limitations based on a reduction in the culpability of the recidivist ex-prisoner. By contrast, conceptualising the recidivist discount as an acknowledgement of prior state misconduct obviates the need for such a causal connection to be demonstrated. It is enough that the prior imprisonment can be shown to have been highly likely to generate unjustified additional hurdles placed before access to a law-abiding life trajectory. Unless the state can show that it made clear efforts to affect both dimensions identified by Wikström and Treiber (2018: 281) as affecting the pathway to reoffending (the prisoner's characteristics, and his activity fields post-release) in a positive direction, so as to help a released offender avoid reinvolvement in crime, sentence mitigation for ex-prisoners on a state misconduct basis is appropriate.

One implication of my approach is that especially persistent offenders are likely to qualify for the largest discounts in their sentences, if it appears to the court that their opportunities in life were particularly starkly depleted by the cumulative effects of punitive state interventions. Here, it could, for example, justify custody-avoiding disposals even in cases of offenders that constitute 'bad risks' for future reoffending. Another implication is that, in considering whether the discount applies, the court should focus on the question whether the particular ex-prisoner in front of it really did face heightened levels of disadvantage post-release. There could be cases where this assumption is implausible (say, if the ex-prisoner won the lottery while in prison, or for other reasons was released into a privileged environment). Finally, it is important to remember that a sentence discount warranted on a state misconduct basis could be outweighed, in an individual case, by strong indicators of raised culpability. Culpability levels are not increased by the mere fact of recidivism, but there is nothing to rule out the possibility that a particular ex-prisoner's choice to reoffend exhibits well-established grounds for raised culpability, such as extensive prior planning, particular callousness towards vulnerable victims, and the like.

IV. Conclusion

My case for a presumptive recidivist discount is built on appreciating the reality that, as Asp put it, 'The recidivist premium will generally speaking hit the underprivileged the hardest' (Asp 2010: 225), and that this is so in considerable part because imprisonment still works to reinforce and increase systemic disadvantage and personal ineptitude, and too little effort and resources are invested to embed it in structures that are conducive to a crime-free life post-release. This supplies the foundation for the argument made in this chapter that imprisonment itself must be viewed, in very many instances, as a form of state misconduct, which in turn justifies sentence mitigation for recidivist offenders on grounds of such state misconduct.

It is important to see, and accept, that this sentence discount is not for the poster children of the penal system – those who have already made great strides towards turning their lives around, have overcome practical obstacles, formed new bonds, developed marketable skills, invested in a law-abiding future. If ex-prisoners for whom this is true reoffend, sentencers already respond with great sensitivity by taking such efforts into consideration. The recidivist discount argued for in this chapter is, instead, for those who (as von Hirsch 1994: 37 memorably put it) have made 'no effort … to improve [their] lot'. Many of the recipients of such discounted sentences will be perceived as socially unattractive individuals – some will have made no serious or perceptible attempts to desist; others will complain of what life, and prison, did to them but show little concern for what they have done to others. Many of them will be likely to continue to offend. For the case for a recidivist discount to retain traction in the face of such apparent undeservingness, one must accept that the odds were against them after their previous punishment even more so than before, and for reasons that a fair system of punishment would not want to deny responsibility for.

Moreover, I do not wish to suggest that a 'discounted' sentence is in itself a solution to the moral and social challenge of the harms of imprisonment. To punish less, and less harshly, in recognition of exposure to the harms of prior punishment is, at best, a second-best response. It would be better, were the response more ambitious (as Hanafy argues in her chapter in this volume when she demands penal disposals that are intended and able to avoid or counteract such harmful add-on effects). To punish less (while other matters remain unchanged) is an exercise in damage-limitation only.

15

Whataboutism at Sentencing?

BENJAMIN EWING[1]

By all means: let he who is without sin cast the first stone. But should a wrongdoer escape accountability for want of an authority who can impose it with clean hands? In recent years, doubts about some parties' 'standing to blame' (especially unjust states' standing to blame unfairly disadvantaged offenders) have gushed forth in philosophical journals like water from a firehose.[2] It might take a sociologist of knowledge to account for all the forces that have wrought the academic stampede at this moment in time. Yet the allure of challenging others' standing to blame is plain. It tempts us with the promise of a kind of ethical jujitsu: a path to claiming the moral high ground without having to consider other people's criticism of us on the merits.

Even if scepticism of others' standing to blame is not quite the last refuge of scoundrels, it is at risk of constituting a high-brow form of that great evasion of contemporary moral and political discourse known as 'whataboutism': ie, an attempt to deflect legitimate criticism, or evade appropriate accountability for wrongdoing, through countercriticism that, however apt, fails to justify the relief from responsibility one is seeking.[3] For that and other reasons, I have previously expressed serious reservations about the current philosophical vogue for attacks on unjust states' standing to blame disadvantaged offenders (see Ewing 2023b).

[1] For helpful feedback on the ideas developed in this chapter, I thank participants in the workshop held for contributors to this volume at Cambridge University, and colleagues who discussed the chapter at a meeting of the Ottawa Criminal Law Workshop group via Zoom.

[2] For references to some of the important contributions to the literature, with an emphasis on scepticism about unjust states' standing to blame disadvantaged offenders, see Ewing 2023b.

[3] I borrow the term 'whataboutism' from American political discourse, in which use of the term is ubiquitous. Given the strongly negative connotation of 'whataboutism', and in the interest of felicity of expression, my definition and use of the term 'whataboutism' is restricted to a narrow pejorative sense of it. In their recent discussions of 'whataboutism', however, Fischer 2021, Bowell 2023 and Lieblich 2024 all suggest that the term 'whataboutism' might be used in a merely descriptive and not necessarily pejorative way. And they seek to identify kernels of insight or valid argument that might lie beneath 'whataboutism' in the facially neutral sense of responding to accusations with counteraccusations or (in the case of Bowell 2023: 91) 'redirect[ing] attention from the specific case in hand'.

The premise of this book is that if a state has unclean hands because of its own wrongdoing, this might furnish a reason for the state to mitigate the punishment it imposes for crime – at least for some offences or offenders.[4] One reason that might be so is that sentence mitigation might be a way of recognising a state's compromised standing to blame or authority to punish – particularly if the state has *wronged* an offender, and especially if the state has thereby made it more likely the offender would commit her crime. But offenders who have been wronged by the state whose criminal law they violated might make any number of other pleas for mitigation at sentencing. They might allege that the state violated their constitutional rights in the criminal process (see, eg, *R v Nasogaluak*), or entrapped them.[5] Offenders might also claim mitigation as compensation either for an advance payment on punishment they have already borne (owing to prior undeserved suffering somehow connected to their crimes) (see Klein 1990; *cf* Husak 1990), or for distributive injustice done to them (see Chau 2012). Finally, they might submit that the state's wrongdoing deprived them of a fair opportunity to avoid their offences and thus of a fair opportunity to avoid unmitigated punishment for them (see Ewing 2023a).

Although such arguments for mitigation would differ in important ways from one based on scepticism about the state's standing to blame, they would all share with it the supposition that somehow one agent's wrongdoing can detract from the appropriate punishment of another's. And that is a presumptively mysterious and unsettling idea that we must parse and qualify if we are to avoid whataboutism and to construct sound arguments for mitigation. For although in tort law it is common to divide the remedial responsibility of paying damages among multiple tortfeasors, in criminal law additional offenders whose wrongdoing must also be accounted for – such as aiders, abettors, and co-conspirators – do not detract from the responsibility of principal offenders. Though a non-principal party's lesser degree of contribution to a crime is a familiar ground for mitigating her sentence, in the common law world at least it would be odd – and likely legally erroneous – for a sentencing judge to suggest that the blameworthiness or punishment-worthiness of different parties – even to the same crime – should be traded off against one another, such that the greater is one party's fitness for blame or punishment the lesser should be the other's.

[4] I take the category of 'mitigating' factors at sentencing to encompass all appropriate grounds for reducing an offender's sentence – not merely considerations that diminish the offender's culpability. Indeed, I have argued elsewhere that the mitigating factors that lie in mitigation's normative core are neither (a) partial justifications or excuses left to sentencing because they fail to meet thresholds for full defences, nor (b) mere public policy considerations such as harms to innocent third parties that punishment would impose, but rather (c) non-exculpatory claims of fairness to mitigated hard treatment (Ewing 2019a). Possible bases of such claims may include, for instance, an offender's lack of prior convictions, unfairly disadvantaged background, or acceptance of responsibility for his crime.

[5] A finding of entrapment precludes a conviction in the US and Canada. See, eg, Dillof 2004 and *R v Mack*. But there is also precedent in the common law world for entrapment-like conduct to serve as a mitigating factor at sentencing if it does not bar conviction. See Murphy and Anderson 2014.

I. Overview

In this chapter, I survey several ways in which mitigated punishment might be conceptualised as a justified response to state wrongdoing: as a recognition of compromised state standing to blame or authority to punish; as a remedy for the violation of procedural rights; and as compensation for state wrongdoing that led an offender to suffer undeserved misfortune, distributive injustice, or lack of fair opportunity to avoid wrongdoing. I am particularly interested in exploring whether and when these conceptualisations of the mitigating force of state wrongdoing might give rise to whataboutism. Put concretely, which arguments for sentence mitigation divert attention from crimes of an offender to wrongs by the state that, even when real, are irrelevant to, or fail to justify reducing, an offender's sentence? And which if any arguments for mitigation based on state wrongdoing are relevant either to offenders' culpability for their crimes or fair punishment for them?

If the state merits condemnation for misconduct relevant to criminal wrongdoing or the prosecution of it, it may be appropriate or even necessary for the criminal process somehow to acknowledge and address it (see Manikis 2022a). When it comes to the remedy of sentence mitigation, however, I contend that what is of primary importance is neither state wrongdoing as such, nor the state's mistreatment of the offender or standing in relation to her per se, but whether she has been wronged by the state in a way that reduced her culpability for her crime or has threatened to make the unmitigated application of the criminal law procedurally or substantively unfair to her. Perhaps an offender had weaker reason to obey the law, and is less culpable for breaking it, because the state's legitimate authority over her was diminished. Alternatively, perhaps the state engaged in wrongful entrapment-like conduct toward an offender, gained an unfair advantage in prosecuting the offender by violating his constitutional rights in the criminal process, or is responsible for conditions of criminogenic social injustice that deprived him of fair background opportunities in life to fortify himself against manifesting criminally culpable disregard for other people. If so, then the justification for sentence mitigation is both clear and insulated from the charge of whataboutism. For in such cases offenders can point to state wrongdoing not to elude accountability by shifting blame onto the state but, rather, to show that their mistreatment by the state threatens to make their punishment disproportionate to their culpability, or to make unmitigated punishment unfair to them.

II. Recognising the State's Compromised Standing or Authority

Contemporary concern that state wrongdoing may be relevant to criminal justice has frequently manifested itself in scepticism about unjust states' moral standing to blame disadvantaged offenders. The meaning of 'standing to blame' remains less than clear because writing about the topic has emphasised its preconditions rather than its nature.[6] But the basic idea is relatively easy to grasp in negative terms. To say that I lack the standing to blame someone is to say that my relationship to her or her wrongdoing is such that it would be wrong and/or normatively impotent for me to blame her, even if she were blameworthy, and even assuming my blame would be justified in principle, in the sense of appropriately tracking her actual blameworthiness (see Ewing 2023b: 252–56; *cf* Edwards 2019: 456). Yet it is critical to distinguish between standing *to blame* and standing *to hold accountable*. Not all practices of accountability involve blaming people. It is therefore conceivable that one might lack the standing to blame someone while retaining the standing or authority to hold her accountable (see, eg, Ewing 2023b: 252–56; Lacey and Pickard 2021; *cf* Shelby 2016: 244–48). Consequently, we can distinguish two different possible concerns about the standing of an unjust state. On the one hand, it might lack the standing to blame certain offenders, even while retaining the standing to hold them accountable. On the other hand, an unjust state might lack the standing or authority to hold certain offenders accountable at all for their conduct.

Let us first consider scepticism about the state's standing to blame before turning to scepticism about its authority to punish. One reason that an unjust state might lack the standing to blame some offenders but not others is that the state might lack the standing to blame the perpetrators of some types of offences – perhaps those of which the state is also guilty, and which it would be hypocritical for the state to condemn. However, any argument for mitigating punishment of crimes that it would be hypocritical of the state to condemn would appear to prove too much – both because it would entail categorical mitigation for certain types of offences (rather than a subset of their perpetrators) and because the relevant set of offences could easily become the exception that proves the rule (though this would depend on the thorny question of when the 'state' should be deemed to have engaged in wrongdoing sufficiently similar to an offender's). Moreover, offender appeals for mitigation based on state hypocrisy would seem particularly exposed to the charge of 'whataboutism' because they would redirect our attention toward wrongdoing of another (ie, the state) that – however real and similar in type to the offender's – would have no necessary connection to the offender or his crime, and no obvious relevance to a fit sentence for it.

Scepticism of the state's standing to blame stands on sturdier ground when the state has not only done wrong but behaved wrongly in relation to the offender or her offence. As Howard and Pasternak 2023: 44–49 have recently contended, unjust states' moral standing to blame oppressed offenders specifically might be

[6] But see Edwards 2019 and Radzik 2023 for recent efforts to unpack the meaning, respectively, of 'standing to hold responsible' and standing to engage in a broad range of accountability-related practices such as blaming, apologising and forgiving.

'tainted', for instance, if by unjustly depriving them of the democratic influence over the law to which they are morally entitled, the state has made itself unaccountable to such offenders, even as it seeks to hold them fully accountable to it. Drawing on Duff 2010a to defend that view, Howard and Pasternak 2023: 48 argue that 'It is intrinsically disrespectful to hold others to account while simultaneously shielding oneself from accountability to them'. And the problem is compounded if the non-oppressed can 'hold the state to account but the oppressed cannot', leading to 'denial of their equal standing'.

Furthermore, if the state was complicit in an offender's crime – because it created or failed to eradicate unjust criminogenic conditions that made the offence more probable – then the state's wrongdoing relates not only to its relationship to the offender but to her crime specifically, and to a full understanding of the circumstances in which she committed it. I doubt that unjust state complicity, as such, in an offender's crime, is enough to make a strong case for mitigation at sentencing. For if the state enables extreme, unjust inequalities of wealth and power, and those who are enriched and empowered are tacitly encouraged to commit certain crimes by their sense that it will be difficult for the state to hold them accountable, mitigating their punishment would strike me as counterintuitive (see Ewing 2018: 48–51). It would arguably worsen the initial problem. But the argument that a state's complicity in crime erodes its standing to blame appears more plausible if confined to offenders in whose crimes the state was complicit through criminogenic injustice of which the offenders were victims.

There are many different angles from which to approach the arguments that the state might lack the standing to blame because its blame would be: (a) hypocritical; (b) accountability of the offender to the state without reciprocal accountability of the state to the offender; or (c) inappropriate because the state treated the offender unjustly in ways that made her crime more probable. I have elsewhere discussed reasons to think that unjust states either retain the standing to blame unjustly disadvantaged offenders or should continue to condemn their crimes, all things considered, even if the states' moral standing to do so is compromised (see Ewing 2023b).[7] Given the subject of this book and chapter, however, my focus here is on one question in particular: even if a state has compromised standing to blame certain offenders, does this justify mitigating their sentences?

Insofar as an offender is arguing for mitigation on account of the state's lack of standing to blame (rather than on some other ground), the offender is not

[7] If the state's wrongdoing threatens to undercut its standing to blame an offender, plausibly the best thing for the state to do in response is both to condemn the offender and to accept responsibility for its own relevant wrongdoing through public self-criticism. Yet if the state can seemingly 'regain' its standing to blame in that way, did the state ever lose the standing to blame in the first place, or did it simply need to put its blame in appropriate context so that its content would not be morally misleading (Ewing 2023b: 261–65)? Criminal wrongdoing also creates a unique need for authoritative condemnation that only the state can supply, which puts moral pressure on unjust states to continue to condemn the crimes of unjustly disadvantaged offenders, notwithstanding concerns about standing to blame (Ewing 2023b: 265–70).

claiming to be any less guilty of, or culpable for, the crime he committed. He is not disputing his blameworthiness, but only the appropriateness of the state being the one to blame him. The state has already blamed him by allowing a conviction to be entered against him. Why mitigate hard treatment now, as opposed to refraining from entering a conviction against the offender in the first place (which involves blaming him)? And if mitigation is conceived to be a second-best alternative when a conviction has been entered, why would mitigation even be a second-best option? Why not instead try to defuse or side-step concern about the state's standing to blame by de-emphasising the condemnatory aspect of the hard treatment (see, eg, Ewing 2018: 53–55; Shelby 2016: 248), condemning the state alongside the offender, or incorporating the victim and local community into a restorative justice process designed to emphasise that the offender is accountable to them, even if the standing of the state is questionable?[8]

It might be argued that although the condemnation and hard treatment components of punishment can be distinguished in theory (see Feinberg 1970), in practice it is inevitable that materially harder treatment will express more forceful condemnation. If so, and if less forceful condemnation is required when the state has wholly or partially lost the standing to blame, then it seems to follow that if a state is going to punish notwithstanding its lack of standing to blame, it should at least mitigate the hard treatment it imposes. And one can imagine another argument that would be related but distinct. One might contend that the social condemnation involved in punishment is itself a form of hard treatment; hence, if the state's compromised standing to blame makes its condemnation of the offender inappropriately harsh, sentence mitigation might be seen as a way of compensating for that portion of the offender's 'hard treatment' that takes the form of inappropriate blame by the state.[9]

Yet mitigation so justified would strike me as self-defeating in an important sense: it would blur the very distinctions giving rise to its putative justification. The practice of mitigation would be purportedly justified, not because the offender is any less blameworthy or any less fit in principle for hard treatment, but because the state is less well positioned to blame him. And mitigating the offender's hard treatment would send precisely the *wrong* message – namely, that the offender was less worthy of hard treatment and less worthy of it because he was less worthy of blame. And in sending the erroneous message that the state's compromised standing makes the offender less blameworthy, or less fit to face hard treatment as accountability for wrongdoing, such a policy of sentence mitigation would seem to give unjustified credit to an argument guilty of whataboutism: an attempt to use blame of the state unjustifiably to evade appropriate blame and accountability for the offender.

[8] For an ingenious defence of the last of those ideas, see Howard and Pasternak 2023.

[9] *cf* Husak 1990 (tentatively defending, against salient objections, the idea that heavier-than-normal public stigma of an offender might itself constitute a form of punishment and give the offender a credit against otherwise appropriate state punishment).

Finally, let us consider, as an alternative to scepticism of the state's *standing to blame*, doubts about the state's *legitimate authority* over some of its subjects. If certain groups are so badly treated by the state that its legitimate authority over their members is lost or diminished, when the state persists in holding them accountable for crimes they commit, there is an argument that it ought at least to mitigate their punishment. The argument is simple: if one reason to obey the criminal law (over and above the moral wrongfulness of what it prohibits) is its legitimate authority over its subjects, then when such authority was absent or weakened in regard to a specific lawbreaker, she will have had one less reason to obey the law, arguably making her conduct less culpable, or even less grave a wrong (Ewing 2018: 41–45; see also Goran Duus-Otterstrom's chapter in this book).

Although I am sympathetic to this argument – and have suggested that it may have some force in regard to Indigenous offenders in Canada (see Ewing and Kerr 2024) – the claim to mitigation it generates seems to be both: (a) marginal in strength (at least where core, *mala in se* crimes are concerned); and (b) merely a species of a broader genus of partially exculpatory claims to mitigation (based on weaker reasons to obey the law) that need not have any connection to state wrongdoing. Even the victims of grave political injustice, such as colonialism or apartheid, have nearly the same reasons as other members of their societies not to commit ordinary criminal acts of violence or fraud against other people.[10] In any case, what we are imagining here is simply a special case of a claim to mitigation based on diminished culpability owing to weaker reasons to obey the law – not an argument that the state's wrongdoing, or even wronging of the offender, is relevant *as such* to sentencing.

III. Remedying the Violation of Procedural Rights

The US and Canada have well-established frameworks for bringing investigative misconduct to bear upon criminal prosecutions. Evidence obtained unconstitutionally may be excluded at trial, and a conviction will be precluded if the offender was entrapped (meaning, broadly speaking, that the state induced his crime or wrongfully tempted him to commit it). Sentence mitigation could serve as a fallback remedy for constitutional rights violations or entrapment in various circumstances: in jurisdictions unwilling to bar the conviction of an entrapped offender; in cases in which state inducement of a crime does not rise to the level of

[10] Individuals subjected to extremely unjust or illegitimate authority might have significantly weaker reasons to refrain even from familiar *mala in se* offences, however, if their commission of such offences is reasonably calculated to advance a justified political struggle when less harmful means of doing so are foreclosed, or to bring about vigilante justice where the state systematically fails to protect members of groups it oppresses.

legal entrapment; in jurisdictions unwilling to exclude evidence obtained in violation of an accused person's constitutional rights; and in cases in which the state has violated the accused's procedural rights in an investigation or prosecution but found no useable incriminating evidence thereby.[11] To understand the logic of sentence mitigation in such cases, it will help first to consider why legal entrapment might justify preventing the conviction of the offender, and why constitutional rights violations might justify the exclusion of incriminating evidence obtained through them.

Entrapment is often conceptualised as an exculpatory defence. The offender's crime is thought to be non-culpable on account of being wrongfully manufactured by the state. If an offender is subjected to entrapment-like conduct that does not satisfy the strict requirements of the full defence but nevertheless reduces the offender's culpability, then we have a clear and straightforward argument that it should constitute a mitigating factor at sentencing.

But if entrapment were relevant to criminal responsibility primarily by undercutting an offender's culpability, then it would be unclear why the doctrine of legal entrapment should apply only when it is the state specifically – and not a private party – that had a wrongful hand in bringing about the crime.[12] That aspect of the doctrine of legal entrapment implies that the role of the *state* in bringing about a crime matters over and above its impact on an offender's options, incentives, or culpability. Partly for that reason, it is tempting to conceive of entrapment as a non-exculpatory defence.

In Canada, which has adopted a non-exculpatory interpretation of entrapment, the defence leads not to an acquittal or conviction, but to a permanent 'stay of proceedings' for 'abuse of process' (*R v Mack*). The idea is that although the offender is not excused, it would undermine the repute of the administration of justice to allow a conviction for a crime by an offender who was legally entrapped by the state. The thinking here is self-consciously similar to Canada's rationale for excluding evidence 'obtained in a manner' that violated the constitutional rights of the accused. Such evidence is not excluded categorically, but in precisely those cases in which its admission 'would bring the administration of justice into disrepute' in light of an overall assessment of: (a) the gravity of the state's constitutional rights-violating conduct; (b) the severity of its impact on the accused's constitutionally-protected interests; and (c) 'society's interest in an adjudication on the merits' (*R v Grant* [2009] [67]–[86]).

Canada's approach to entrapment and the exclusion of evidence obtained unconstitutionally might seem, therefore, to emphasise state wrongdoing, and to show how it can give offenders distinctive claims in the criminal process not

[11] The Supreme Court of Canada, for instance, has recognised that state misconduct toward an accused in the criminal process – including but not limited to violations of his constitutional rights – can justify sentence mitigation (see *R v Nasogaluak* [39]–[65]).

[12] But see Yaffe 2005 (developing a novel argument for thinking that entrapment by public officials is likely to undermine culpability but private entrapment is not).

dependent on diminished culpability. But before we jump to the conclusion that such doctrines concern themselves with state wrongdoing per se we must stop and register one of their crucial shared features. In neither case is state wrongdoing enough. Rather, in both cases the state must have wronged the offender, specifically. The state might entrap a dozen other offenders in an investigation, but an accused can claim the defence of entrapment only if *she* was entrapped herself. And the state might violate the constitutional rights of many parties in its investigation of a crime, but an accused is eligible to seek to exclude evidence for being obtained unconstitutionally only if it was obtained in a manner violating *her* constitutional rights (*R v Edwards* [45], [51], [55]). That suggests the rationale for precluding the conviction of an entrapped offender and the admission of evidence obtained unconstitutionally is not deterring, punishing, or even compensating for state wrongdoing per se. What is more, Canada's doctrine of entrapment and its exclusionary rule appear to concern themselves only with threats to the repute of the administration of justice caused by procedural unfairness to the accused, specifically – and not by mere violations of the rights of third parties, even if they were instrumental to achieving an accused's conviction.

Anthony Dillof 2004 offers a normative reconstruction of entrapment that illuminates what I have in mind when I suggest that the defence may be grounded in fairness to the accused rather than concern for deterrence, culpability, or even the repute of the administration of justice as such. In Dillof's view, the doctrine of entrapment is justified because 'For society to impose criminal sanctions on an entrapped person would be to place on her a disproportionate share of the cost of general crime prevention and control, violating … distributive justice' (Dillof 2004: 831).[13] As I have suggested elsewhere (see Ewing 2023c), criminal justice may be seen as, at least in part, a problem of distributive justice: ie, justice in the distribution of security against crime and punishment. When the state entraps an offender, although this does not justify or excuse his offence, arguably it deprives him of a fair opportunity to avoid his crime and punishment for it.[14]

[13] American states have tended to conceive of entrapment as an exculpatory defence and to withhold it from accused persons who were predisposed to commit their offences anyway absent the state's intervention (see, eg, Yaffe 2005: 6–7; Dillof 2004: 831–35). By contrast, Canada, which conceives of entrapment as a non-exculpatory defence, does not preclude predisposed offenders from claiming it (see *R v Mack*). Yet while barring predisposed offenders from claiming entrapment may seem appropriate if the defence is focused on offender culpability, and inappropriate if the defence is focused on state culpability, the justification of entrapment to which I am attracted lies neither in offender culpability nor state culpability per se. It emerges rather from the way in which entrapment threatens to make application of the criminal law unfair to the accused absent a remedy for it. In my view, whether such a theory would suggest that a predisposed offender should or should not be allowed to claim entrapment is a tricky further question. The fairness of the criminal process is arguably still undermined by entrapment even when the accused was predisposed to commit the crime. Hence, I am tentatively inclined to favour the Canadian position, which does not bar the predisposed from claiming entrapment. But Dillof 2004: 889–92 offers a thoughtfully conflicted perspective, and I am not yet prepared to take a stand one way or another.

[14] One might wonder whether the doctrine of entrapment could be justified on the theory that through entrapment the state negates or diminishes its standing to blame. See, eg, Howard 2016: 44–45

Suppose that what justifies us in estopping the state from convicting an entrapped offender or proving an offender's guilt through evidence obtained in violation of his constitutional rights is the importance of ensuring that conviction and punishment occur only at the conclusion of a criminal process that is fair to the accused. If that is our justification of the entrapment defence and the exclusion of evidence obtained unconstitutionally, can it justify *sentence mitigation* as an alternative remedy to a permanent stay of proceedings or the exclusion of evidence? If a conviction has been precluded because of entrapment, sentencing will not arise. And if an accused has been convicted despite the exclusion of evidence obtained unconstitutionally, then his guilt has not been proven through procedural unfairness to him. But what if a jurisdiction refuses to bar conviction on account of entrapment, or the state has engaged in entrapment-like conduct falling short of the legal standard for entrapment? And what if the state does not have an exclusionary rule for evidence obtained unconstitutionally, it has violated the accused's constitutional rights in the criminal process but garnered no incriminating evidence in so doing, or it has found incriminating evidence through unconstitutional conduct but excluded it at trial?

Arguably the central interest we are seeking to protect by insisting on fairness in the criminal process is the fairness of our opportunity to avoid criminal conviction and punishment. It therefore strikes me as eminently appropriate to resort to mitigation at sentencing, as a fallback remedy, if an accused subjected to entrapment or entrapment-like conduct has nevertheless been convicted, and the question of a fit sentence has arisen. If entrapment compromises the fairness of the criminal process by depriving its victims of a fair chance to avoid their crimes and punishments for them, then by mitigating the sentences of entrapped offenders, we will at least approximate more closely (than we otherwise would) the ideal of ensuring that punishment is conditioned upon a fair opportunity to avoid it. Moreover, if an entrapped offender has been deprived of a fair opportunity to avoid his crime and punishment, and the fairness of people's opportunities to avoid crime and punishment comes in degrees, then sentence mitigation also seems justified in the case of entrapment-like conduct that unfairly diminished the quality of an offender's opportunity to avoid wrongdoing but insufficiently to satisfy the strict requirements of the entrapment defence.

Similarly, if the state gained an unfair advantage over the offender in the criminal process by violating his constitutional rights, and this has not otherwise been adequately remedied, then mitigation at sentencing might be justified

(raising but not seeking to resolve the question of whether the state lacks the standing to blame and punish offenders it has entrapped). But it is highly doubtful that lost or diminished standing to blame could explain Canada's approach to entrapment. The defence of entrapment is assessed after the elements of the crime have been proven (see *R v Mack* [972]). So rather than precluding punishment by preventing the state from blaming the offender, arguably Canada's doctrine of entrapment allows public condemnation of a sort (through a finding of guilt) but simply precludes formal conviction and punishment.

as a way of ensuring that the state's wrongdoing does not unfairly diminish his opportunity to avoid punishment by unfairly increasing his odds of conviction. Violations of an offender's constitutional rights might unfairly ease an investigation or prosecution in other ways than by yielding incriminating evidence against an accused. Such rights violations might also play a role in helping to locate and detain a suspect who might otherwise elude apprehension. Exclusion of evidence would not be available as a remedy, but sentence mitigation could be justified as one. And in a jurisdiction lacking an exclusionary rule, if the state obtains evidence through the violation of an accused's rights, sentence mitigation would be an attractive alternative way of diminishing the unfair disadvantage in the criminal process that an offender suffers. In some cases, sentence mitigation would not be as good a remedy for the accused as an exclusionary rule (ie, when such an exclusionary rule would have the practical consequence of thwarting a prosecution). In other cases, sentence mitigation would be better (ie, when the accused would end up convicted anyway, despite the exclusion of evidence obtained through the violation of the accused's rights).

Furthermore, exclusion of evidence and mitigation of sentence should not necessarily be seen as mutually exclusive remedies. We can see this if we observe that when an accused's constitutional rights are violated but no evidence is obtained as a result, the situation is arguably similar to one in which evidence obtained unconstitutionally is excluded. In each case the accused's rights in the criminal process are violated, but this does not give the state useable evidence against the accused. Even if no evidence is obtained by an unreasonable search, arbitrary detention, or excessive use of force, or the impact of evidence obtained is neutralised by its exclusion at trial, there are likely to remain wrongful harms to the accused not fully remedied – eg, setbacks to her interests in privacy, liberty, or bodily integrity.

Insofar as an unreasonable search, arbitrary detention, or excessive use of force has not helped to facilitate the criminal investigation or prosecution of an offender but has simply set back other interests of the offender (such as to privacy, liberty or bodily integrity), it is somewhat more difficult to justify sentence mitigation as a remedy. For arguably the state has gained no unfair prosecutorial advantage that it would be necessary to neutralise, and the offender has faced no unfair disadvantage in his opportunity to avoid punishment that would need to be remedied. On the other hand, it would still be plausible to see the situation as involving wrongdoing or unfairness to the accused in the criminal process, such that conviction and punishment would not be founded upon full procedural fairness to the accused. Mitigation might therefore still be conceptualised as a means of more closely approximating the ideal of conditioning punishment upon the conclusion of a criminal process that is fair to the accused. We would clearly risk whataboutism were we to make criminal sentencing an occasion to adjudicate any and every legitimate grievance an offender might have against her state, irrespective of whether (or how closely) it might be connected to her crime, its circumstances, or the fairness of the criminal process. But perhaps it is enough to justify sentence mitigation if state misconduct injects into the investigation or prosecution of an offender's crime a wrongful harm to the accused – even if such wrongful harm does not undercut the offender's interest in a fair opportunity to avoid punishment.

IV. Compensating for Background Injustice or Lack of Fair Opportunity

In reflections on the potential significance of social injustice for criminal justice over the past half-century, a handful of theorists have suggested that unfair or undeserved disadvantages that an offender previously suffered (which might be traceable to injustice or wrongdoing by the state) might function as a credit against the punishment that would otherwise be deserved or justified. Several decades ago, moral philosopher Martha Klein 1990: 76–84 argued that emotional deprivation contributing to an offender's wrongdoing might be conceptualised as a kind of 'payment-in-advance' and credited against the burdensome blame an offender would otherwise deserve for wrongdoing. Almost two decades before her, Jeffrie Murphy 1973: 228–29, 240, 242 contended that if one accepts a retributive justification of punishment according to which an offender deserves punishment because of the wrongful advantage he has taken of society, then perhaps an offender's desert of punishment is undermined if it is his society that has, on the whole, taken wrongful advantage of him across his life. More recently, Peter Chau 2012 has argued for mitigating the punishment of offenders who have faced undeserved poverty, on the opportunistic basis that doing so will bring about a marginal improvement in overall distributive justice in society.

Such arguments for sentence mitigation as compensation for social injustice (for which the state might be deemed responsible) vary somewhat in their structures. But they are all vulnerable to the charge that they may constitute diversionary whataboutism – on the theory that the state wrongs to which they point, even if real, do not appropriately bear upon the fitness of criminal sentences. For each asks a sentencing judge to show lenience to unjustly disadvantaged offenders neither because they are less culpable nor because they have lacked a fair opportunity to avoid their punishments, but only because they have suffered a distinct form of background injustice.[15]

[15] If we conceive of the criminal justice system as partly a functional substitute for, and thus somewhat continuous with, the welfare state, then it might seem wrong to restrict mitigation to factors that bear on 'criminal justice,' narrowly understood. I thank Benjamin Berger for a helpful comment that prompted me to reflect on that possibility. In my view, however, precisely because criminal justice systems are poor and ineffective as substitutes for systems designed to help the deviant and downtrodden manage social problems, my inclination is to resist, and not lean into, a model of criminal sentencing as generic social welfare management.

To be sure, sentence mitigation can be conceptualised as compensation for other wrongful harm an offender previously suffered. And insofar as the state itself was responsible for the background injustice, sentence mitigation can be seen not only as compensation but as a form of corrective justice – insofar as the state that caused wrongful harm is the same agent offering compensation for it. But none of these arguments contain a convincing explanation of why such compensation should take the form of sentence mitigation specifically. If the prior wrongful harm an offender suffered took the form of subjection to social injustice or undeserved suffering, why compensate specifically by intervening in the dispensation of criminal justice – which is a unique 'sphere of justice' (*cf* Walzer 1983) subject to its own distinctive rules, principles, and norms? And as George Sher 1987: 84–85 fn 24 has argued in response to Jeffrie Murphy, even if an offender's society has taken wrongful advantage of him by subjecting him to background social injustice, this does not necessarily mean that he has been taken wrongful advantage of within the sphere of criminal justice (as might be the case, for instance, if he were systematically deprived of protection against criminal victimisation). Without a clear justification for making criminal justice the site of compensation, we are also left with the sense that although there is a reason for compensation, the offender is not entitled to such compensation as a matter of criminal justice itself. Although she is entitled to compensation for the background unjust harm she previously suffered, if such compensation does not occur in the form of sentence mitigation, she will not have been subjected to an unfairness or injustice in the application of criminal law itself.

Yet as I have argued at length in other work (see especially Ewing 2023a), there is another way in which social injustice to which an offender has been subjected (for which the state is likely to bear substantial responsibility) may give him a claim of fairness to mitigation at sentencing: by having deprived the offender of a fair opportunity to avoid his crime.

Fair opportunity to avoid wrongdoing is most often thought of as a precondition of culpability, such that lack of fair opportunity to avoid wrongdoing is an excuse (or a partial excuse, if a person lacks fair opportunity to avoid wrongdoing only to some degree) (see, eg, Brink and Nelkin 2013; Brink 2021). In unjust states, people living in unfairly disadvantageous social conditions may be more likely to confront circumstances that excuse prima facie criminal conduct, in whole or in part: eg, duress or necessity, or coercive or exigent circumstances that mitigate culpability even if they fail to constitute defences to liability. The exculpatory force of such conditions is easy to explain if we conceptualise criminal culpability as the manifestation of insufficient concern for other people's rights and interests (see especially Alexander 2000; Alexander and Ferzan (with Morse) 2009: 23–68; Sarch 2017). If I engage in prima facie criminal conduct because it is my only means of defusing a threat of death or bodily harm proportional in significance to the harm I am inflicting or risking, the duress or necessity under which I act changes my reasons for action, diminishing if not negating the inadequacy of regard for other people that my conduct manifests. If I drive the getaway car to aid a bank robbery because of an imminent lethal threat I cannot otherwise avoid, I am not so much improperly devaluing the rights and interests of the bank and its depositors as I am properly weighing my own right to life and continuing interest in it.

It is important to notice, however, that unfair social disadvantages can make it more challenging and burdensome to avoid crime in another, different way than by changing people's reasons for action and thereby diminishing the inadequacy of concern for other people their crimes manifest (see Ewing 2023a). The victims of social injustice may find it unfairly difficult or costly to avoid acting culpably (ie, in a way that manifests truly inadequate regard for others). Failures to show sufficient concern for others' rights and interests are often triggered, at least in part, by garden-variety pressures, such as quotidian slights and provocations, temptations, economic constraints, psychological compulsions, and the influence of alcohol or drugs. Such factors usually do little if anything to diminish criminal culpability, because they largely trigger rather than mitigate inadequate regard for other people's rights and interests. We also expect all moral agents to take proactive steps to guard against such pressures, as part of a continual process of what Jeffrey Howard 2017 has helpfully labelled 'moral fortification'. Yet unjust social disadvantages can make the process of moral fortification systematically more difficult and costly in a way that I have argued can be unfair (see Ewing 2023a). Owing to clusters of factors such as poverty, lack of educational opportunity, racism and intergenerational trauma passed down through abuse or neglect, the deeply disadvantaged may find it harder to develop their moral capacities and dispositions to recognise and respond to moral reasons, and to structure their choice environments to minimise temptations and other pressures to commit crimes that show insufficient regard for others. The kind of 'fair opportunity to avoid wrongdoing' on which culpability depends may be a function only (or at least primarily) of conditions that are *synchronic* or contemporaneous with acts of crime. But I contend that the kind of 'fair opportunity to avoid culpability' or 'fair moral opportunity' (see Ewing 2023a) that is necessary for unmitigated punishment to be fair is *historical* in nature.[16]

Even if an offender is culpable for her crime (in the sense that it shows genuinely inadequate regard for other people's rights and interests), if she has lacked a fair opportunity in life to fortify herself against failing to give other people their due, then she has not had a fair opportunity to avoid the punishment to which her culpability presumptively makes her morally liable. If the fairness of an offender's opportunity to avoid punishment was diminished, reducing her sentence will bring it closer to a level of punishment that she had a fair opportunity to avoid. Indeed, sentence mitigation for lack of fair moral opportunity is best conceived not as 'compensation' for prior harm but as simply a way of tailoring punishment

[16] I draw the terms 'synchronic' and 'historical' from Brink 2021: 116, who views conditions of responsibility as synchronic and not historical.

to the fairness of an offender's opportunity to avoid it, to safeguard fairness in the application of the criminal law. To trace that pathway from state wrongdoing to the mitigation of a criminal offender's sentence is not to engage in a form of whataboutism, but to identify a specific type of state wrongdoing that can compromise the fairness of the criminal law if it is not acknowledged and remedied.

V. Avoiding Whataboutism at Sentencing

State wrongdoing is not, as such, a mitigating factor at sentencing. It is one thing for the state to have done wrong, another thing for it to have wronged an offender. And even state mistreatment of an offender does not, in and of itself, justify mitigating her sentence. Some forms of state misconduct may, however, diminish an offender's culpability, undermine the fairness of the criminal process, or otherwise make unmitigated punishment unfair to an offender.

As we have seen, for instance, a state's wrongdoing might diminish the legitimacy of its authority over an offender, weakening one of the reasons for her to obey the criminal law. States may also engage in entrapment-like conduct that falls short of a criminal defence, violate an offender's constitutional rights in a way that compromises the fairness of an accused's opportunity to avoid punishment, or fail to eradicate conditions of criminogenic social injustice that deprive people of a fair opportunity to avoid resorting to crime. In such cases, there are relatively clear, principled bases for sentence mitigation.

On the other hand, if the state has wrongfully harmed an offender in a way that is irrelevant to his culpability and would not appear to compromise the fairness of unmitigated punishment, the state would have a more tenuous basis for mitigating his sentence. Doing so would be one of many possible ways to compensate the offender. Yet the question would arise: if sentence mitigation can be an appropriate form of compensation for this wrongful harm, then what if any legitimate grievance of the offender against the state is *not* appropriate to raise at sentencing in a plea for mitigation – and why? There is a danger here that arguments for mitigation based on state wrongdoing will devolve into whataboutism. And as we saw earlier, that risk is particularly acute when it comes to arguments for sentence mitigation grounded in the theory that, through wrongdoing or injustice of some kind, the state has lost its moral standing to blame an offender. Even if the state *has* lost its standing to blame, it is hard to see how sentence mitigation, specifically, would be an appropriate remedy.

As weak hypothetical arguments for sentence mitigation based on scepticism of the state's standing to blame show, whataboutism has the potential to be worse than mere moral deflection or evasion. If, in responding to accusations with countercriticism, we aspire to turn the tables – ie, to make the best 'defence' a good 'offence' – then we thereby raise the moral stakes. We risk doubling our error by not merely seeking to avoid appropriate accountability but self-righteously demanding a form of accountability from our critics that is inappropriate and unjustified. In addition, we threaten to intensify and harden an antagonism between us and those who rightly seek to hold us accountable for wrongdoing.

The whataboutist tactic of making one thing about other things also threatens to make one thing about everything. Guarding against whataboutism at sentencing is thus partly a matter of ensuring that the offender's adversarial response to a criminal conviction stays within appropriate bounds. It may therefore seem to involve a grudging and unsympathetic attitude toward offenders. Yet it is worth remembering that whataboutism can, and often does, ricochet back in cycles of recrimination. Unsurprisingly, liberal criminal law theorists have long sought to limit the scope of the state's adversarial posture against offenders – for example, by restricting it to the prosecution and punishment of discrete, seriously wrongful acts or omissions proscribed in advance, and by placing constraints, even at sentencing, on the role that offenders' bad character can play. Moreover, as Bill Stuntz 1997: 27–35 eloquently taught us, when we add more things for defendants to contest in the criminal process, we risk widening the gap between the rich and the poor in their protection against punishment. While a few privileged defendants are well positioned to make full use of the adversarial tools at their disposal, most ordinary defendants are not.

In sum, state wrongdoing sometimes justifies sentence mitigation. But neither the state nor offenders would be well served by turning criminal sentencing into an adjudication of every legitimate grievance between them.

16

State Misconduct and Sentence Mitigation: Final Reflections

NICOLA PADFIELD

At first glance, perhaps, many people might not take this book very seriously: give someone less punishment simply because the state had let them down? Liberal nonsense; surely not. And yet we don't have to dig very deep to discover that the question is a good one: to what extent does the state's misconduct towards an individual or a group of individuals justify mitigation in the sentence imposed on them for committing a criminal offence?

Indeed, there are many compelling arguments for taking state misconduct very seriously and for arguing that it should reduce the 'amount'[1] of penalty an offender suffers. It is particularly obvious when you look at the sentencing of indigenous people whose ways of living were so devastated by white invaders. There are excellent and devastating examples from the US, Australia and New Zealand (see, in particular, here, Bergelson, this volume and Anthony 2013). In this afterword I shall explore some of the arguments presented in this book – and raise some others. I have not focused on the chapters in a balanced way, but, having read the whole book, I became something of a bee, landing a little randomly on those parts which happened to catch my attention, when other parts might have offered even more nectar. I apologise to the authors of those chapters for which I do not provide a complete review.[2]

I am a lawyer (academic yet practical!), sceptical of theories which have no relevance to the 'real world'. Yet the discussions here, largely philosophical and theoretical, are fascinating, revealing the many challenges of sentencing 'justly'. I was somewhat chastened by Zaibert's repeated, 'this is true but perfectly uninteresting!' – well, I found his questions interesting. And I was encouraged by Ryberg's assertion (to me) that the purpose of engaging in and developing ethical theories is to provide practical guidance. But then even Ryberg concludes that his discussion

[1] I put the 'amount' in inverted commas because I am not convinced that we can measure 'punishment' in terms of quantity or weight very accurately.

[2] Where I mention an author without citing a reference, I am referring to their chapter in this book.

still leaves us without a practical theory. How to proceed? What is 'interesting', and what's so difficult about practical guidance? What sort of guidance is useful?

I. State Misconduct

Let us start by considering the extent of the 'state misconduct' we are discussing. One of the challenges in this book is the vast reach of state misconduct. The chapters largely separate out state misconduct in terms of states which treat (or have treated) some people or groups of people unfairly (long-term social and economic deprivation, for example), from state misconduct in individual cases (where, for example, the police beat up a suspect or break the rules on gathering evidence). But there are many sub-categories. For example, Poama and Plesnicar interestingly distinguish criminogenic state policies from over-criminalising legislation. Other contributors struggle to distinguish state indifference from wilful neglect, or to identify which state actions create or exacerbate criminogenic risk factors. This is no easy topic.

These discussions made me reflect on peace researcher Johan Galtung's work on structural violence.[3] Huge amounts of harm are done to people through unfair social, political, and economic structures and institutions. This leads to systemic discrimination which directly disadvantages and oppresses (does violence to) members of certain groups. The impact of current prison conditions in the UK is a case in point. Du Bois-Pedain provides a hard-hitting account of the negative impact of imprisonment, particularly in the reality of most UK prisons today. This leads to the astonishing but convincing (to me) argument that recidivists might deserve a discount, rather the usual 'uplift' if the defendant's criminal record 'generates additional burdens or disadvantages that *unjustifiably* leave the punished individual in a worse position for accessing a law-abiding life trajectory than they were in before the hiatus of conviction and punishment'. She also makes the astute point that many theoretical justifications for punishment are 'unlikely to find any reflection in the lived experience and psychological reality of the person engaging in such conduct'. Indeed, let's get real! She concludes that

> the additional criminogenic disadvantages that arise from imprisonment are unjustified, and therefore attributable to state misconduct, when a person is exposed to them unnecessarily because available non-custodial options were disregarded, and/or when the length of time a person spends in prison raises serious concerns that the released prisoner will not be able to build a minimally decent life for himself after release, and no active countermeasures are taken to counteract these risks and consequences of prolonged confinement.

The implications of this argument for the real world are huge.

[3] My thanks to David Baker of Liverpool University for a stimulating conversation on this.

Bergelson's homeless man, destitute because of the state's failure to provide him with his fair share of public goods, is another wonderfully controversial example – to what extent does the state owe its members any 'distributive justice'? She struggles brilliantly with the question whether this distributive injustice makes the defendant less (subjectively?) culpable or his lawbreaking less (objectively?) wrong. But it feels more convincing to me to argue that this is not about him or his culpability or his lawbreaking: what has happened is that the 'state' has diminished its authority to punish. A state which is completely outrageous loses all right to punish. Can a state which lets its citizens down, but less outrageously, lose the right to impose the whole punishment that is considered 'just'? I was reminded here of von Hirsch's undergraduate lectures in Cambridge when for many years he would discuss a 'squeegee merchant', someone who wipes your windscreen at a busy road junction in the hope of money. Should they get a discount on their sentence for stealing cars, he would ask, because the likelihood of them ever earning enough money legitimately to buy an expensive car is nil. If the nearest they will get to owning an expensive car legitimately is when they clean windscreens, how should the sentencer respond? Another example of possible state misconduct which should lead to mitigation (or leniency?) not much discussed in this book is the thorny problem of the disadvantage caused by the state's imprisonment of offenders to their families. It is well known that imprisonment causes harm to the families of prisoners. The state could do so much more to support the children of prisoners and indeed it would be sensible if it did so if it wanted to break the 'cycle' of disadvantage. Should it also refuse to imprison parents, or at least mitigate the length and/or weight of their punishments?

Let us turn to state misconduct when the state breaks the rules of criminal justice. State misconduct here includes not just systemic disadvantage and indirect discrimination (discounts for guilty pleas, for example, well known in the UK to be accepted by/given to white offenders much more frequently than by Black offenders), but also individual acts of misconduct – should you get a discount if the police beat you up, or if the courts lose some of your documentation? We may need another distinction here – when the state leads you to commit a crime, or when the state just acts very badly (illegally?) in investigating crime. Zaibert suggests that 'if the improper functioning of a certain aspect of the state's functioning contributes to someone committing a crime, then this state is simply not just in the broad sense'. What does this 'contribute' mean?

Roberts and Dagan also explore what they argue might be the necessary links: they ask whether there is a conceptual distinction between state misconduct which occurs prior to the commission of the crime and unlawful acts committed after the crime. Like Zaibert, they seem to want to take a narrow approach, to limit mitigation, by requiring a 'link' between the misconduct and the crime. But the need to find a causal link between the state misconduct and the crime seems unnecessary to me. English law is surely right to recognise that shocking misconduct results in an 'abuse of process', which means that a prosecution cannot be continued, whether or not the misconduct led to the commission of the offence. One example is the illegal extradition of a suspect from one country to another.[4] A huge concern in England today is the appalling unlawful actions of undercover police officers (see the long-running public inquiry, set up in 2015, and far from completion).[5] The law on abuse of process is understandably complex – there is a tension between the desire to punish those who break the law, and the need to stop the agents of justice from breaking it. There are many inconsistent rulings in English law. In *R v Grant* [2005] [57], the Court of Appeal (rightly) resoundingly disapproved of the police eavesdropping on conversations between prisoners and their lawyers:

> We are quite clear that the deliberate interference with a suspect's right to the confidence of privileged communications with his solicitor, such as we have found here, seriously undermines the rule of law and justifies a stay on the grounds of abuse of process, notwithstanding the absence of prejudice consisting in evidence gathered by the Crown as the fruit of police officers' unlawful conduct.

But this decision was 'disapproved' by more senior judges in *Warren et al v AG for Jersey* [36]:[6]

> [T]he particular circumstances of each case must be considered and carefully weighed in the balance. It was obviously right to hold on the facts in *Grant* that the gravity of the misconduct was a factor which militated in favour of a stay. But as against that, the accused was charged with a most serious crime and, crucially, the misconduct caused no prejudice to the accused. This was not even a case where the 'but for' factor had a part to play. The misconduct had no influence on the proceedings at all. In these circumstances, surely the trial judge was entitled to decide in the exercise of his discretion to refuse a stay and the Court of Appeal should not have held that his decision was wrong.

The law is even more confusing when we move from 'abuse of process' to consider when the courts will exclude improperly or illegally obtained evidence from a trial. Generally speaking, they are readier to exclude evidence where the authorities deliberately flouted the rules than when they accidentally broke them.[7] And although 'big' breaches sometimes matter more than little ones, the worse the crime, the less the courts seem to be inclined to exclude vital evidence because of the way it was obtained.[8] I was surprised that some of the contributors to this book appeared more resistant to sanctioning misconduct than the courts. But that's the point. Many of the authors would doubtless want to sanction state misconduct

[4] Which happens – see *R v Horseferry Road Magistrates' Court, ex p Bennett* for a 'classic' example.

[5] www.ucpi.org.uk.

[6] Was it really OK to put a listening device in the car of a suspect who was about to drive through France and Germany, without bothering to get the permission of the French and Dutch authorities to use listening devices on their national territory (indeed, knowing that they would refuse permission)? Not a good decision!.

[7] A good example is *R v Mason*. Mason's conviction was quashed because the police deliberately lied to him and to his solicitor in order to gain a confession – is it true that deceiving the solicitor as well as the suspect somehow made the lying worse?.

[8] *Attorney General's Reference (No 3 of 1999)*; see also *Warren v AG of Jersey*.

severely, but may not want to benefit the defendant by either throwing out the case or giving a discount on their sentence. The question remains: what is the right sanction or remedy? Is it excluding evidence (in practice, not allowing a trial to proceed) or mitigating sentences, or neither?

Even if some state misconduct is so bad that you can't even be prosecuted, it is difficult to identify the line which is crossed when less serious misconduct might still result in a kind of 'partial prosecution'. There is no such thing, of course. Either you are prosecuted, or you are not. So, can there be scope for a half-way measure, a sentence discount? If a sentence discount is justified, the challenge to the judge of calibrating the level of mitigation is a nightmare, to which we shall return in the next section of this chapter.

Roberts and Dagan confront the specific problem of the claims for mitigation arising from wrongful acts by state actors (such as police or prison officers) which harm the offender. By 'misconduct' they mean unlawful acts; conduct by state officials which rises to the threshold of an offence or which violates a professional code of conduct. This is the conundrum. Of course, the state should not blatantly break the rules, but should it lead to sentence mitigation? This is Watson's concern, too: she argues that the bad police officer is acting 'independently' of their police role (a bit like vicarious liability?). But how does this help us decide whether their actions should mitigate sentence, and where exactly to draw the line between conduct which might mitigate and that which should not?

I would suggest that it is helpful in discussing sentencing (or at least the role of the judge at sentencing) to recognise the role played by other 'players' in the process – here, the discretion of prosecutors to decide whether or not to prosecute. In most common law jurisdictions, the prosecution has the duty to throw out cases which should not be prosecuted. So, some of the ethical problems discussed in this book are not necessarily sentencing problems. They should never reach the sentencing stage. As with many other contributors, Hanafy wisely asks why the remedy for state misconduct should be found in sentencing. Ewing too asks whether sentence mitigation can be a 'remedy' for misconduct. He seems to urge caution: 'neither the state nor offenders would be well-served by turning criminal sentencing into an adjudication of every legitimate grievance between them'. Of course, mitigating the sentence is a curious remedy for state misconduct. It benefits a person who has done wrong. There are obviously much better answers – stop police corruption, make the world a fairer place – but I'm with Matravers (and others) who seems to conclude that although this is all very difficult, 'in the absence of wholesale change, mitigation be better than nothing'. Throwing cases out before they reach the courts may often be even better. So ignoring the role of the discretion to prosecute may limit the debate on sentence mitigation? And it deserves greater philosophical consideration.

The question of 'punishing' the state 'effectively' for breaking the rules is one core issue. The 'right' remedy would often be, as Hanafy points out, to improve a state's policies in the socio-economic sphere, redistributing resources, improving conditions of material welfare, and reversing harmful policies. In practice, the exclusion of evidence at trial will often hit home: police officers are dismayed when they learn that their crafty way of gathering evidence was actually so wrong that the suspect can't be tried. The disciplining of individual bad 'apples' is also clearly essential. 'Punishing' the state by mitigating a sentence raises important questions about how the state and its institutions learn – the criminal justice process does not seem to be a good 'learning opportunity'.

What if state misconduct involves the judge? Judges certainly make mistakes. For example, a judge should reduce the 'just' sentence where an equally guilty accomplice has been sentenced more recently in error.[9] Poama and Plesničar's fascinating discussion of 'epistemic' injustice explores what judges are doing when they misunderstand issues such remorse, battering or accent, for example. Their conclusion is to encourage not only better judicial training, but also a sentence-monitoring institute and retroactive sentence mitigation to deal with this problem of judges getting things wrong. There are many examples of judicial errors, which can be defined as misconduct. But as ever, it is difficult to know how to draw the line between sufficiently serious misconduct and that which is 'acceptable'. And what about the judge who knows that the sentences she imposes increase the likelihood of reoffending? That happens all the time.

Ryberg convincingly separates the question whether an offender who has been 'exposed to severe social deprivation' deserves that to be a mitigating factor from the question whether a state that has maltreated its citizens, or not done what it should to alleviate the plight of citizens living in poverty, has the standing to hold offenders accountable for their misdeeds. They are surely different. And both can (sometimes) be answered to benefit the 'offender'. The state's right to punish is dependent on it being a responsible state. (Is this a right or a duty? I would say surely merely a right – I can't imagine living in a system where the state did not have a discretion not to prosecute.)

Some authors focus more on the state's moral responsibility than do others. Duus-Otterstrom focuses on the broad philosophical question whether a state's lack of legitimate authority *ought* to count as a mitigating factor at sentencing. For him, legitimate authority refers to a state's *moral* right to rule. Some states are so bad that the person should not be convicted in the first place. Bergelson's argument is also a strong one based on the individual's right to demand mitigation as a matter of justice. Matravers has a marvellous section on the duties of the state to facilitate the living of non-criminal lives.

Before we move to questions of mitigation, there is one final problem with state misconduct. Who has to prove what? The question of mitigation for the disadvantaged is not simply a question of working out how much disadvantage is enough to justify a discount. From my perspective, most of the people I have met in prison

[9] Walker and Padfield 1996 cite *R v Reeves*, where a man had been convicted of receiving stolen property and was sentenced to nine months' imprisonment. His accomplice had been tried separately and fined, although he had a previous conviction for a similar offence. The Court of Criminal Appeal (rightly?) quashed his sentence of nine months and ordered his immediate release.

over many years have been incredibly unlucky in their life chances. We know that many prisoners grew up in care – and that the care system was not 'careful'. Lots of prisoners have had really traumatic lives. Many have mental and physical illnesses and addictions which they have not really been supported to address. If the defendant raises any form of 'misconduct' should it be for the state to disprove it? We return to questions of the burden of proof in the next section.

II. Sentence Mitigation

So far I have been discussing the problems associated with state misconduct. Even more difficult are the questions of sentence mitigation. This book makes a powerful case for the inter-connectedness of penal policy and social policy (though not always explicitly). Perhaps Lippke's chapter does this most clearly, focused on the 'unjust' disadvantages suffered by so many citizens. He worries that it is difficult to argue that judges should recognise this in sentencing when we live in societies in which politicians, and the public generally, do not seem concerned by this social and economic inequality. It is unsurprising that he is left sceptical about sentence mitigation as a remedy for state failures. Matravers seems to agree, arguing that there are better ways to reduce the burdens on the disadvantaged than by simply lessening their punishments. But the justice gap is very real. Let's return to structural violence. Billingham and Irwin-Rodgers 2022 argue convincingly (to me) that inequality and the social harms suffered by young people drive violence. Social harms blight the lives of many young people who, they argue, are 'structurally' harmed by institutions, policies and services. They argue that 'emphasising individual responsibility does not advance the cause of reducing violence very far' (2022: 230).

Judges cannot, of course, provide a solution to socio-historical factors of discrimination and inequality. But is there anything wrong with them recognising, for example, the huge stigma which is attached to poverty and which means that some young people seek alternative ways to matter? Anthony 2013 is convincing (to me, again) in her depressing indictment of the way indigenous Australians have been treated by the judges who sentence them. She argues that there was a 're-imagining of Indigeneity since the late 1990s' with a sharp swing of the pendulum 'from judicial sympathy to judicial disregard or condemnation'. Whether the pendulum will swing again in Australia in the direction of what she calls a 'transformative justice paradigm' remains to be seen. But her careful analysis of sentencing remarks should encourage much greater self-consciousness, more critical self-awareness, from judges everywhere.

But, of course, the judge is but one player in a complex system. There are, for me, two main problems when we consider the question of sentence mitigation. One is how one justifies any sentence, which is where a workable theory of punishment comes in handy. The second is the role of the individual judge in finding the 'right' sentence.

First, a workable theory of punishment. One difficulty is that most of the contributors seem to accept that sentence mitigation suggests a discount, which suggests a tariff. This requires more reflections on the concept of mitigation. Does mitigation means reducing the severity of a sentence, focusing on traditional justifications for sentencing, and discussing how state misconduct might reduce the sentence according to these traditional justifications? Many jurisdictions seem to have become hung up in recent times with questions of consistency, which has led in many countries to guidelines, and in some places, grids. Of course we all want consistency, but we need to recognise that sentencers can be consistently wrong as well as consistently right.

Manikis works hard to justify making state misconduct a mitigating factor from a desert perspective. For her, the key is about censure and the degree of 'moral impairment' that this state misconduct has had on the individual's volition. Perhaps this is true of criminogenic state misconduct, but as we have seen, not all state misconduct which might be taken into account is strictly speaking provable as criminogenic. She argues first that state misconduct can feature as part of the analysis of individual 'moral blameworthiness' in 'step one' which aims to censure the individual by relying on the framework of proportionality. Secondly, she argues that state misconduct can feature within a second step that serves to communicate relational blame about the offence. Finally, in determining the sentence, state misconduct can also feature in the analysis about what are foreseeable qualitative conditions of the sanction imposed and taking this evidence into account when sentencing. Manikis's step-by-step process echoes current English guidelines. She recognises the limits of these steppe processes in proposing a sentence review mechanism. Indeed, sentencing should not end with the imposition of a sentence. Not only do judges get it wrong, but Manikis goes much further: a sentence review process is proposed to consider excess harms that arise during the administration of the sentence. That would be wonderful!

Zaibert makes much of the difference between distributive injustice and retributive injustice, arguing that a state can be just in a retributive sense without being just in a distributive sense (and vice versa). But where does that take us? I think Zaibert is arguing that because 'we are complex meaning-seeking creatures', we have 'prima facie reasons for welcoming modifications to retributive justice resulting from (seemingly unrelated) deficiencies within distributive justice'. He values retributive justice for its own sake, identifying 'the intrinsic goodness of retributive justice'. I have never understood this argument for retributive justice. What is so good about punishing people, unless we think we may be achieving something useful with it? And, what's more, the 'anchoring points' seem inevitably fluid and liable to being hijacked by punitive states to ever-increased levels of punitiveness. Zaibert would, I think, argue that just because people getting what they deserve is intrinsically good does not mean that they should necessarily get that – other things which are good (intrinsically and otherwise) may trump the importance of the intrinsic goodness of deserved punishment.

Yet many of the contributors to this volume appear to accept a retributivist framework, focusing on arguments of 'moral desert'. As an old-fashioned utilitarian, who grew up at the feet of Nigel Walker (in a manner of speaking!), I don't understand this rejection of the more utilitarian arguments for penal discounts. And they certainly merit discussion. One important question is whether 'discounts' generate, or undermine, respect for the criminal law. Brooks usefully justifies a reduction in sentencing for state misconduct in discussing how sentence guidelines commonly accept what he calls 'penal pluralism' in supporting multiple purposes for justifying punishment. Brooks's contribution is also particularly helpful in pointing out that we are here talking about factors external to the offender, recognising, for example, that systematic discrimination does not impact the gravity of an offender's crime. What it does is mitigate the degree of responsibility the offender has for the crime. (Even Brooks, though, seems to believe that the mere fact of deprivation or unemployment is not enough – the discriminatory conduct needs to have a 'contributory connection' to the offence.)

Secondly, I turn to the role of the judge in finding the 'right' sentence. Du Bois Pedain, despite her arguments about the state's 'misconduct' in creating criminogenic prisons, gives the judge a let-out clause: she argues that 'in practice, courts will frequently encounter recidivist offenders who have not made any perceptible effort to avoid reoffending'. This raises questions about 'the burden of proof' at sentencing. Who has to prove what? I would suggest that the courts (ie judges) are not very good at looking for the efforts that many offenders have made to lead good and useful lives. Nor do court processes facilitate this. I have interviewed prisoners going through parole hearings who have poured out to me the efforts they have made, but do not mention any of this in the parole hearing. The parole hearing is terrifyingly important to them, and they only speak when asked direct questions. In a more relaxed interview, they can shape the way the discussion goes and can control the agenda. A sentencing hearing in court is even more difficult than a parole hearing – the defendant is often, in England, in a glass box at the back of the court, seemingly the invisible object of a sentencing decision, not a participant in the discussion. This raises another difficult question: the role of the defence lawyer. For me they are, ideally, there to help the prisoner make his case, to advise, assist and support, but not simply to make his case for him. I would happily make the argument for both a barrister (an advocate) and a solicitor (an advisor), but legal aid becomes ever less generous, in practice. I wonder what the philosophers think. Another book?

This book leads me to argue for more understanding and empathy from judges. Why do we, when sentencing, focus almost exclusively on the offender (the offender's conduct and his culpability)? During the 14 years I sat as a part-time judge, I often reflected when sentencing on the variety of people and institutions who were culpable, who were part of the problem which resulted in this particular crime being committed at that particular time. Sometimes, the blame might be shared by the defendant's friends and family – the social context is important and should be taken into account. Much is understood in the criminological literature about the interaction between the offender and their environment (see eg Wikstrom et al 2012). In 'real life', the role of 'community' is often intriguing, and perhaps blameworthy. A criminal offence is never an 'isolated event' (see Ryberg). A man thumps his drug dealer and kills him. Why was he not helped more to address his addiction and his mental health? A previously convicted sex offender rapes a child. Why did that woman leave her child in his care, when she went out dancing, knowing his record?[10] Why did those responsible for his supervision in the community not worry a bit more about his relationships in the community? There is much to be said for society putting up its hands and admitting to its responsibilities and failures. Other examples clearly reflect state culpability. I have dealt with cases of benefit fraud where the state made no effort to verify the fraudulent documentation: if only someone from the benefits agency had gone round to visit a fraudulent claimant at home, they would have easily discovered that she had a resident partner. Such frauds are often easily detectable, but due to inefficiency, lack of resources, or worse, someone's fraudulent debt is allowed to grow over 10 years, making prison an inevitable consequence (given the guidelines). And that's before we look at the criminogenic effects of imprisonment. Are people solely to blame for many of their crimes?[11]

It is attractive to think that any mitigation is not to do with the offender, or their culpability, but all about the nature and terms of the state's authority (as Hanafy argues). The state's authority must be 'legitimate'. Perhaps one can argue that this counts as personal mitigation: perhaps the defendant has already suffered enough? Hanafy points out in a straightforward way that the increased likelihood of offending caused by poverty and social deprivation does not necessarily absolve individuals from responsibility for their crimes. As we have seen, she argues that the appropriate remedy has to engage with the reasons that created the deficit in the first place. The 'right' remedy would be to improve a state's policies, redistributing resources, and reversing harmful policies. But Hanafy also argues that a 'sentencer should be strongly encouraged to mitigate the sentence from a custodial to a non-custodial sentence to support the offender's desistance in recognition of the deprivations that this individual has suffered due to the state's policies'. But she recognises that this does not happen because the sentencer is well aware of the 'prevalence of the state's functional failures towards millions of individuals and the criminogenic impact of these functional failures'. So?

The judge is surely not there just to measure harm and culpability; to come up with a figure and then to dilute it for personal mitigation. The role is surely more complicated and more 'human' than that. Zaibert very usefully addresses the tension between the values of justice and the values of mercy (and forgiveness and

[10] I am aware that this is outside the scope of 'state misconduct', but perhaps part of the wider context of offending that the judge might want to consider when dealing with 'mitigation' in its widest sense, or at least might want to exclude from 'mitigation'. The term 'mitigation' itself might need greater analysis.

[11] An extreme version of this argument may be adopted by the followers of Robert M Sapolsky's Determined: A Science of Life Without Free Will (Bodley Head, 2023) – if we really understand someone's background, how can we punish them at all?.

humanity). Walker (1995) asked 'whether mercy is a fictitious animal, or merely an endangered species'. It has become a lot more endangered since 1995. Compassion and empathy are not encouraged in systems based on sentencing guidelines, which too easily over-simplify the sentencing exercise, reducing it to an exercise in numbers, and where defendants do not play a central role in their court hearing. Judges should surely recognise when the state has let someone down badly. Is it justice or mercy to deal leniently with those who have been victims of state misconduct? I'm not sure, but unfortunate people deserve empathy, and sometimes mitigation. Being lenient is sometimes right, or to use, Zaibert's word, attractive.

Sentencing-by-numbers also means that there is a problem in measuring the size of any discount. Lippke discusses Bagaric's 25 per cent rule, but if one accepts that there is no right'number in the first place, the precise size of the discount becomes less crucial. Judges can and should individualise a sentence as long as they can explain their reasoning to their many audiences, ie defendant, victims, media, appellate courts.

Victims too are given little space in this book, but perhaps they deserve some more. Lippke recognises the victim-affirming aspect of sentencing. But we have to recognise that offenders and victims are often the same people. It is well recognised that many people in prison, particularly women, have been victims of much more serious offences than those they are accused of committing. Shockingly, most women go to prison to serve a sentence for a non-violent offence. Yet most have also suffered domestic violence and experienced emotional, physical or sexual abuse as a child (see Prison Reform Trust 2024). Many men have been victims too, of course.

Another area which I find surprisingly absent from this book is international criminal justice. Here the issues can be even more stark. Look at the prosecutions of men at the Special Court for Sierra Leone, set up in 2002 to prosecute those who bore the greatest responsibility for the dreadful humanitarian violations committed during the lengthy civil war in Sierra Leone. Large numbers of children had fought in that war. Should the Court have taken into account that they were brutalised as children when imposing sentence?[12] The issue was raised more recently in the case of Dominic Ongwen, a former commander in the Lord's Resistance Army in Uganda. In December 2022 the International Criminal Court refused his appeal, upholding his conviction and 25-year prison sentence for 61 war crimes and crimes against humanity. In mitigation, it had been argued that he had suffered brutally as a child: when he was abducted, his parents were murdered and his initiation into the LRA was breathtakingly inhumane. What impact should this background have have had on the sentence? Was it grounds for mitigation?[13]

[12] I thoroughly recommend the documentary film by Rebecca Richman Cohen, *War Don Don* (2010). This is a powerful investigation into the trial of Issa Sesay, a former rebel leader in Sierra Leone.

[13] Indeed, should he have been prosecuted before the ICC? The Acholi Religious Leaders Peace Initiative (2015) contrast 'the Court system, which is punitive or retributive, promotes polarisation that only leads into ultimate alienation on both sides' with the 'cultural justice system of Mato Oput', with its focus on healing and reconciliation.

It certainly feels like serious state misconduct which led to the brutal kidnapping of children. Does this mitigate the appropriate sentence? Is there an appropriate sentence?

III. Conclusion

It seems to me right, having reflected on this book, that, not only is the state's right to punish compromised if it engages in misconduct, but that this misconduct can and indeed should be taken into account in sentencing. The concept of 'misconduct' is so broadly conceived that initially I felt that it would be too difficult to draw any conclusions. But, at the end, I am a little clearer that there is a difference between factors which mitigate the sentence, and factors which might reduce the seriousness of the offence or the culpability of the offender. I am still confused about what the state is doing when it punishes – does it have a duty to punish those who break the law, or is it just a right?

Most of all, this book underscores the challenges that face a 'just' judge having to impose a 'just' sentence in an 'unjust' world. Let's recognise that in this country the prison population has doubled in recent years and is still rising fast. Many prisoners spend long periods of time in deeply unpleasant prisons. Prison is often a cruel punishment. Despite (or because of?) sentencing guidelines, the average length of sentences is growing. We are often overdosing offenders with the weight of punishment. This book has confirmed my view that there is too often a focus (particularly under a guideline system, mentioned in passing by several contributors), too much emphasis, on a judge getting it 'right'. I don't want to abolish guidelines and guidance, of course, and inconsistent sentences have to be justified, but judicial education should include much more emphasis on what works to reduce reoffending (community support, money, accommodation, education or training, health care, etc). While there may be 'wrong' sentences, there is no such thing as a 'right' sentence. Several of the contributors to this book acknowledge this, calling for greater flexibility on appeals and reviews. Sentencing is always a deeply difficult moral exercise. The state's misconduct towards an individual or a group of individuals justifies judicial sympathy, even if 'mitigation' is not quite the right word.

BIBLIOGRAPHY

Acholi Religious Leaders Peace Initiative (2015) 'Statement on the Position of ARLPI on Ogwen Dominic, former LRA Commander', drive.google.com/file/d/0BwyHGIEA97AyQVBydUNndVhvbmM/view?resourcekey=0-v3XamDHNAA1LCNiT3-hdBA.

Ackerman, B, *Social Justice in the Liberal State* (New Haven, Yale University Press, 1980).

Aharoni, E, Kleider-Offutt, HM, Brosnan, SF and Hoffman, MB 'Nudges for Judges: An Experiment on the Effect of Making Sentencing Costs Explicit' (2022) 13 *Frontiers in Psychology.*

Aiyer, SM et al, 'Exposure to Violence Predicting Cortisol Response During Adolescence and Early Adulthood: Understanding Moderating Factors' (2014) 43 *Journal of Youth Adolescence* 1066.

Alexander, L, 'Insufficient Concern: A Unified Conception of Criminal Culpability' (2000) 88 *California Law Review* 931.

Alexander, L and Ferzan, KK (with Morse, SJ), *Crime and Culpability: A Theory of Criminal Law* (Cambridge, Cambridge University Press, 2009).

Alexander, M, *The New Jim Crow: Mass Incarceration in the Age of Colorblindness* (New York, The New Press, 2012).

Allam, L, Wahlquist, C and Evershed, C, 'The 147 Dead: Terrible Toll of Indigenous Deaths in Custody Spurs Calls for Reform' *The Guardian* (27 August 2018).

American Law Institute, 'Model Penal Code, Tentative Draft No.1.' (Philadelphia, American Law Institute, 1985).

—— 'Model Penal Code and Commentaries (Official Draft and Revised Comments 1980–1985)' (Philadelphia, American Law Institute, 1985).

Amnesty International, 'Hong Kong: Arbitrary arrests, brutal beatings and torture in police detention revealed' (2019), www.amnesty.org/en/latest/press-release/2019/09/hong-kong-arbitrary-arrests-brutal-beatings-and-torture-in-police-detention-revealed.

—— 'Life Detained: Politically-Motivated Arbitrary Detentions Continue in Venezuela AMR 53/7077/2023' (2023), www.amnesty.org/en/documents/amr53/7077/2023/en.

Andersen, SN and Skardhamar, T, 'Picking a Number: Mapping Recidivism Measures and Their Consequences' (2015) 63 *Crime & Delinquency* 613.

Anderson, ES, 'What Is the Point of Equality?' (1999) 109 *Ethics* 287.

Anselm, 'Proslogion' in T Williams (ed) *Anselm: Basic Writings* (Indianapolis, Hacket, 2007) 75–98.

Anthony, T, *Indigenous People, Crime and Punishment* (London, Routledge, 2013).

Applbaum, A, 'Legitimacy Without the Duty to Obey' (2010) 38 *Philosophy & Public Affairs* 215.

Arendt, H, *The Origins of Totalitarianism* (Harmondsworth, Penguin, 2017).

Ashworth, A, *Principles of Criminal Law*, 6th edn (Oxford, Oxford University Press, 2009).

—— 'Re-evaluating the Justifications for Aggravation and Mitigation at Sentencing' in JV Roberts (ed), *Mitigation and Aggravation at Sentencing* (Cambridge, Cambridge University Press, 2011).

—— *Sentencing and Criminal Justice*, 6th edn (Oxford, Oxford University Press, 2015).

—— 'Culpability, Consequences, and Sentencing' in M Manikis and G Watson (eds), *Sentencing, Public Opinion, and Criminal Justice: Essays in Honour of Julian V Roberts* (Oxford, Oxford University Press, 2025).

Ashworth, A and Kelly, R, *Sentencing and Criminal Justice*, 7th edn (Oxford, Hart, 2021).

Ashworth, A. and Roberts, JV (eds), *Sentencing Guidelines: Exploring the English Model* (Oxford, Oxford University Press, 2013).

Asp, P, 'Previous Convictions and Proportionate Punishment Under Swedish Law' in JV Roberts and A von Hirsch (eds), *Previous Convictions at Sentencing. Theoretical and Applied Perspectives* (Oxford, Hart, 2010).

Bagaric, M, 'Rich Offender, Poor Offender: Why It (Sometimes) Matters in Sentencing' (2015) 33 *Law and Inequality* 1.

Baldus, D, Woodworth, G, Zuckerman, D, Weiner, N, Neil, A and Brofit, B, 'Racial Discrimination and the Death Penalty in the Post-Furman Era: An Empirical and Legal Overview, with Recent Findings from Philadelphia' (1998) 83 *Cornell Law Review* 1638.

Banks, R and Harris, L, *Banks on Sentence*, 8th edn, vol 2 (self-published, 2013).

Barnett, RE, *The Structure of Liberty: Justice and the Rule of Law* (New York, Oxford University Press, 1998).

Barry, B, *Culture and Equality* (Cambridge, MA, Harvard University Press, 2001).

Bazelon, DL, 'The Morality of the Criminal Law' (1976) 49 *Southern California Law Review* 385.

Beade, G, 'Who Can Blame Whom? Moral Standing to Blame and Punish Deprived Citizens' (2019) 13 *Criminal Law and Philosophy* 271.

Beetham, D, *The Legitimation of Power*, 2nd edn (London, Bloomsbury Publishing Plc, 2013).

Bennett, C, '"More to Apologise For": Can We Find a Basis for the Recidivist Premium in a Communicative Theory of Punishment?' in JV Roberts and A von Hirsch (eds), *Previous Convictions at Sentencing. Theoretical and Applied Perspectives* (Oxford, Hart, 2010).

Bergelson, V, *Victims' Rights and Victims Wrongs: Comparative Liability in Criminal Law* (Stanford, Stanford Law Books, 2009).

Berman, M, 'Modest Retributivism' in K Ferzan et al (eds), *Legal, Moral, and Metaphysical Truths: The Philosophy of Michael S. Moore* (Oxford, Oxford University Press, 2016).

Bestvater, S, Gelles-Watnick, R, Odabaş, M, Anderson, M and Smith, A, *#BlackLivesMatter Turns 10: Social Media, Online Activism and 10 Years of #BlackLives Matter* (Washington DC, Pew Research Center, 2023).

Bezdek, B, 'Silence in the court: Participation and subordination of poor tenants' voices in legal process' (1991) 20 *Hofstra Law Review* 533.

Billingham, L and Irwin-Rogers, K, *Against Youth Violence: A Social Harm Perspective* (Bristol, Bristol University Press, 2022).

Bird, C, *An Introduction to Political Philosophy* (Cambridge Introductions to Philosophy (Cambridge, Cambridge University Press, 2006).

Blackmon, DA, *Slavery by Another Name: The Re-Enslavement of Black Americans from the Civil War to World War II* (New York, Anchor Books, 2008).

Blackstone, W (1765) *Commentaries on the Laws of England* (Oxford, 1765).

Booker, C, 'Booker, Durbin, Armstrong, Jeffries Announce Re-Introduction of Bipartisan Legislation to Eliminate Federal Crack and Powder Cocaine Sentencing Disparity' (2023), www.booker.senate.gov/news/press/booker-durbin-armstrong-jeffries-announce-re-introduction-of-bipartisan-legislation-to-eliminate-federal-crack-and-powder-cocaine-sentencing-disparity.

Boonin, D, *The Problem of Punishment* (New York, Cambridge University Press, 2008).

Bottoms, A and Tankebe, J 'Beyond procedural justice: dialogic approach to legitimacy in criminal justice' (2012) 102 *Journal of Criminal Law and Criminology* 119.

Bowell, T, 'Whataboutisms: The Good, the Bad, and the Ugly' (2023) 43 *Informal Logic* 91.

Bowling, B and Phillips, C, 'Disproportionate and Discriminatory: Reviewing the Evidence on Police Stop and Search' (2007) 70 *Modern Law Review* 936.

Bradford, B and Loader, I, 'Police, Crime and Order: The Case of Stop and Search' in B Bradford, B Jauregui, I Loader, and J Steinberg (eds), *The SAGE Handbook of Global Policing* (California, SAGE, 2016).

Brand, J, 'Character and Repeat-Offender Sentencing' (2022) 35 *Canadian Journal of Law and Jurisprudence* 59.

Bremner, JD, 'Traumatic Stress: Effects on the Brain' (2006) 8 *Dialogues in Clinical Neuroscience* 445.

Brink, DO, *Fair Opportunity and Responsibility* (Oxford, Oxford University Press, 2021).

Brink, DO and DK Nelkin, 'Fairness and the Architecture of Responsibility' in D Shoemaker (ed), *Oxford Studies in Agency and Responsibility*, vol 1 (Oxford, Oxford University Press, 2013).

Brooks, T, 'Retribution and Capital Punishment' in MD White (ed), *Retributivism: Essays on Theory and Practice* (Oxford, Oxford University Press, 2011) 232–45.

—— *Climate Change Ethics for an Endangered World* (London, Routledge, 2021a).
—— *Punishment: A Critical Introduction*, 2nd edn (London, Routledge, 2021b).
—— 'Why should guilty pleas matter?' in JV Roberts and J Ryberg (eds), *Sentencing the Self-Convicted: The Ethics of Pleading Guilty* (Oxford, Hart, 2023) 127–50.
Brown, G, *Criminal Sentencing as Practical Wisdom* (Oxford, Hart Publishing, 2017).
Bublitz, JC, 'When is Disbelief Epistemic Injustice? Criminal Procedure, Recovered Memories, and Deformations of the Epistemic Subject' (2023) *Criminal Law and Philosophy*, link.springer.com/article/10.1007/s11572-023-09695-3.
Buchanan, A, 'Political Legitimacy and Democracy' (2002) 112 *Ethics* 689.
Bull, M, *Mercy* (Princeton, Princeton University Press, 2019).
Bunce, A, *Desistance and Sentencing. A Review of Research* (London, Sentencing Academy, 2023).
Byskov, MF, 'What makes epistemic injustice an "injustice"?' (2021) 52 *Journal of Social Philosophy* 114.
Callamard, A, 'Investigation of, accountability for and prevention of intentional State killings of human rights defenders, journalists and prominent dissidents: Report of the Special Rapporteur on extrajudicial, summary or arbitrary executions.' A/HRC/41/36, https://digitallibrary.un.org/record/3853356?v=pdf.
Campagna, G, *The Constitution of Mercy* (PhD dissertation, University of Cambridge, 2023 on file with Leo Zaibert).
Campbell, L, Ashworth, A and Redmayne, M, *The Criminal Process* (Oxford, Oxford University Press, 2019).
Cantone, JA, Martinez, LN, Willis-Esqueda, C and Miller, T, 'Sounding guilty: How accent bias affects juror judgments of culpability' (2019) 17 *Journal of Ethnicity in Criminal Justice* 228.
Cardoso, T, 'Bias behind bars: A Globe investigation finds a prison system stacked against Black and Indigenous inmates' *The Globe and Mail* (24 October 2020), www.theglobeandmail.com/canada/article-investigation-racial-bias-in-canadian-prison-risk-assessments.
Carey, L, Grant, A and Tompkins, S, 'Swinging Doors: An Autoethnographic Look at the Challenges Faced by Previously Incarcerated People in the USA and Australia' (2022) 30 *Journal of Prisoners on Prisons* 38.
Carter, DA, 'To Catch the Lion, Tether the Goat: Entrapment, Conspiracy, and Sentencing Manipulation' (2009) 42 *Akron Law Review* 135.
Casey, Baroness, 'The Baroness Casey Review Final Report: An Independent Review into the Standards of Behaviour and Internal Culture of the Metropolitan Police Service' (London, Metropolitan Police, 2023).
Champion, DJ, *Police Misconduct in America: A Reference Handbook* (ABC-CLIO, 2001).
Chan, G, 'Remedial Minimalism under Section 24(1) of the Charter' (2010) 51 The *Supreme Court Law Review* 349.
Chau, P, 'Poverty, Distributive Justice, and Punishment' (2012) 25 *Canadian Journal of Law and Jurisprudence* 39.
Chiao, V, 'What Is the Criminal Law For?' (2016) 35 *Law and Philosophy* 137.
Child, JJ, Simester, AP, Spencer, JR, Stark, F and Virgo, GJ, *Simester and Sullivan's Criminal Law: Theory and Doctrine* (Oxford, Hart Publishing, 2022).
Chow Pok Yin S, 'Reconsidering Sentencing Principles in Cases of Civil Disobedience: Cuadrilla Bowland Ltd and Others v Persons Unknown and Others' (2022) 85 *Modern Law Review* 1062.
Clair, M, 'Being a Disadvantaged Criminal Defendant: Mistrust and Resistance in Attorney-Client Interactions' (2020) 100 *Social Forces* 194.
Clear, TR, *Imprisoning Communities: How Mass Incarceration Makes Disadvantaged Neighborhoods Worse* (New York, Oxford University Press, 2009).
Clutton-Brock TH and Parker, GA, 'Punishment in Animal Societies' (1995) 373 *Nature* 209.
Coca-Vila, I and Irarrázaval, C, 'A Criminal Law for Semicitizens' (2022) 39 *Journal of Applied Philosophy* 56.
Cohen, GA, *Rescuing Justice and Equality* (Cambridge, Mass, Harvard University Press, 2008).
Cohen, L (1988) 'Everybody Knows', *I'm Your Man* (Columbia Records).

College of Policing, 'Guidance on Outcomes in Police Misconduct Proceedings' (2023).
—— 'Code of Ethics' (24 January 2024).
Coppola, F, *The Emotional Brain and the Guilty Mind: Novel Paradigms of Culpability and Punishment*, 1st edn (Oxford, Hart Publishing, 2021).
Criddle, EJ, 'The Case Against Prosecuting Refugees' (2020) 115 *Northwestern University Law Review* 717.
Criminal Cases Review Commission, 'CCRC Annual Report' (2020).
Crisp, R, 'Virtue ethics and virtue epistemology' (2010) 41 *Metaphilosophy* 22.
Crown Prosecution Service, 'Confessions, unfairly obtained evidence and breaches of PACE' (2022), www.cps.gov.uk/legal-guidance/confessions-unfairly-obtained-evidence-and-breaches-pace.
Dagan, N and Roberts, JV, 'Retributivism, Penal Censure, and Life Imprisonment without Parole' (2019) 38 *Criminal Justice Ethics* 1.
Dagger, R and Lefkowitz, D, 'Political Obligation' in E Zalta (ed), *The Stanford Encyclopedia of Philosophy* (2014), plato.stanford.edu/archives/fall2014/entries/political-obligation.
De Beauvoir, S, 'An Eye for an Eye' in M Simons et al (ed), *Philosophical Writings* (Chicago, University of Illinois Press, 2004).
De Keijser, J, Roberts JV and Ryberg, J (eds), *Sentencing for Multiple Crimes* (Oxford, Oxford University Press, 2017).
Death Penalty Information Centre, 'Race and the Death Penalty by the Numbers' (2024), deathpenaltyinfo.org/policy-issues/race/race-and-the-death-penalty-by-the-numbers.
Delgado, R, 'Rotten Social Background: Should the Criminal Law Recognize a Defense of Severe Environment Deprivation?' (1985) 3 *Law and Inequality* 9.
Demleitner, N, Berman, D, Miller M, and Wright, RF, *Sentencing Law and Policy: Cases Statutes & Guidelines* (Boston, Aspen Publishers, 2013).
Devlin, RF and Sherrard, M, 'The Big Chill?: Contextual Judgment after R. v Hamilton and Mason' (2005) 28 *Dalhousie Law Journal* 409.
Di Dio, C, Schulz, J and Gurd, J, 'Foreign Accent Syndrome: In the ear of the beholder?' (2006) 20 *Aphasiology* 951.
Dillof, AM, 'Unraveling Unlawful Entrapment' (2004) 94 *Journal of Criminal Law and Criminology* 827.
Dixon, J and Mahoney, B, 'The Effect of Accent Evaluation and Evidence on a Suspect's Perceived Guilt and Criminality' (2004) 144 *The Journal of Social Psychology* 63.
Dore-Horgan, E, 'Do Criminal Offenders Have a Right to Neurorehabilitation?' (2023) 17 *Criminal Law and Philosophy* 429.
Drago, F, Galbiati, R and Vertova, P, 'Prison Conditions and Recidivism' (2011) 13 *American Law and Economics Review* 103.
Drobnjak, M, *The Role of Speech Perception in the Evaluation of Testimony Credibility* (PhD dissertation, University of Ljubljana, 2024).
Dubber, MD, *Victims in the War on Crime* (New York and London, NYU Press, 2002).
—— 'Toward a Constitutional Law of Crime and Punishment' (2004) 55 *Hastings Law Journal* 509.
—— *An Introduction to the Model Penal Code*, 2nd edn (Oxford, Oxford University Press, 2015).
Duda, MD, 'Remedying Police Brutality Through Sentence Reduction' (2021) 107 *Virginia Law Review* 99.
Duff, RA, *Trials and Punishments* (Cambridge, Cambridge University Press, 1986).
—— 'Law, Language, and Community: Some Preconditions of Criminal Liability' (1988) 18 *Oxford Journal of Legal Studies* 189.
—— 'Punishment, Communication, and Community' in M Matravers (ed), *Punishment and Political Theory* (Oxford, Hart Publishing, 1999).
—— *Punishment, Communication, and Community* (Oxford, Oxford University Press, 2001).
—— 'I Might Be Guilty, but You Can't Try Me: Estoppel and Other Bars to Trial' (2003a) 1 *Ohio State Journal of Criminal Law* 245.
—— *Punishment, Communication and Community* (Oxford, Oxford University Press, 2003b).
—— 'Punishment, Communication and Community' in D Matravers and J Pike (eds), *Debates in Contemporary Political Philosophy* (London, Routledge, 2005).

—— 'Blame, Moral Standing and the Legitimacy of the Criminal Trial' (2010a) 23 *Ratio* 123.
—— 'A criminal law for citizens' (2010b) 14 *Theoretical Criminology* 293.
Duff, RA, Farmer, L, Marshall, S and Tadros, V, *The Trial on Trial Vol III: Towards a Normative Theory of the Criminal Trial* (Oxford, Hart Publishing, 2007).
Dugas, MC, 'Committing to Justice: The Case for Impact of Race and Culture Assessments in Sentencing African Canadian Offenders' (2020) 43 *Dalhousie Law Journal* 03.
Duus-Otterstrom, G, 'Why Retributivists Should Endorse Leniency in Punishment' (2013) 32 *Law and Philosophy* 459.
—— 'Weighing Relative and Absolute Proportionality in Punishment' in M Tonry (ed), *Of One-Eyed and Toothless Miscreants* (Oxford, Oxford University Press, 2020).
—— 'Fair-Play Obligations and Distributive Injustice' (2021) 20 *European Journal of Political Theory* 167.
Duus-Otterstrom, G and Kelly, E, 'Injustice and the Right to Punish' (2019) 14 *Philosophy Compass* e12565.
Dworkin, R, *Taking Rights Seriously* (Cambridge, MA, Harvard University Press, 1977).
—— *Sovereign Virtue: Equality in Theory and Practice* (Cambridge, Mass, Harvard University Press, 2000).
Dzur, AW, *Punishment, Participatory Democracy, and the Jury* (New York, Oxford University Press, 2012).
Edmundson, W, 'Legitimate Authority Without Political Obligation' (1998) 17 *Law and Philosophy* 43.
Edwards, J, 'Standing to Hold Responsible' (2019) 16 *Journal of Moral Philosophy* 437.
Elias, S, *Fairness in Criminal Justice: Golden Threads and Pragmatic Patches*. The Hamlyn Lectures (Cambridge, Cambridge University Press, 2018).
Ellis, A, 'A deterrent theory of punishment' (2003) 53 *Philosophical Quarterly* 337.
Erickson, B, Johnson, BC, Lind, EA and O'Barr, 'WM Speech style and impression formation in a court setting: The effects of "powerful" and "powerless" speech' (1978) 14 *Journal of Experimental Social Psychology* 266.
Escobar, N, 'One author's controversial view: In defense of looting' (2020), www.npr.org/sections/codeswitch/2020/08/27/906642178/one-authors-argument-in-defense-of-looting.
Evans, M, 'Almost 130 Met police officers being investigated for sexual abuse are still working' *The Telegraph* (4 November 2023).
Evans, J, Raynor, P and Heath, B, 'Locality, Legitimacy and the Limits of Diversion: Reviewing Youth Justice in Jersey' (2022) 61 *Howard Journal of Criminal Justice* 367.
Ewing, B, 'Recent Work on Punishment and Criminogenic Disadvantage' (2018) 37 *Law and Philosophy* 29.
—— 'Mitigating Factors: A Typology' in L Alexander and KK Ferzan (eds), *The Palgrave Handbook of Applied Ethics and the Criminal Law* (Cham, Palgrave Macmillan, 2019a).
—— 'Prior Convictions as Moral Opportunities' (2019b) 46 *American Journal of Criminal Law* 283.
—— 'Criminal Responsibility and Fair Moral Opportunity' (2023a) 17 *Criminal Law and Philosophy* 291.
—— 'Do Unjust States Have the Standing to Blame? Three Reservations About Scepticism' (2023b) 43 *Oxford Journal of Legal Studies* 249.
—— 'Mass Incarceration as Distributive Injustice' in MC Altman (ed), *The Palgrave Handbook on the Philosophy of Punishment* (Cham, Palgrave Macmillan, 2023c).
Ewing, B and Kerr, L, 'Reconstructing *Gladue*' (2024) 74 *University of Toronto Law Journal* 156.
Fabens-Lassen, B, 'A cracked remedy: the anti-drug abuse act of 1986 and retroactive application of the fair sentencing act of 2010' (2015) 87 *Temple Law Review* 645.
Falbo, A, 'Hermeneutical injustice: Distortion and conceptual aptness' (2022) 37 *Hypatia* 343.
Feinberg, J, 'The Expressive Function of Punishment' in *Doing and Deserving: Essays in the Theory of Responsibility* (Princeton, Princeton University Press, 1970).
—— 'Noncomparative Justice' (1974) 83 *The Philosophical Review* 297.
Ferraro, KJ, 'The words change, but the melody lingers: The persistence of the battered woman syndrome in criminal cases involving battered women' (2003) 9 *Violence Against Women* 110.
Fischer, JM, 'How We Argue Now' (2021) 94 *Philosophers' Magazine* 30.

Flanders, C, and Hoskins, Z (eds), *The New Philosophy of Criminal Law* (London, Rowman & Littlefield, 2015).

Fortas, A, *Concerning Dissent and Civil Disobedience* (New York, Signet Books-New American Library, 1968).

Franko, K, *Globalisation and crime* (London, Sage, 2007).

Frase, R, *Just Sentencing: Principles and Procedures for a Workable System* (New York, Oxford University Press, 2013).

Frase, RS, *Just Sentencing: Principles and Procedures for a Workable System.* (Oxford, Oxford University Press, 2013).

Freer, EA, *Sentencing: New Trajectories in Law* (New York, Routledge, 2021).

Freixo, I, 'Colloquium Report: Sentencing/Strafzumessung-Comparative Insights' (2019) 30 *Criminal Law Forum* 473.

Fricker, M, *Epistemic Injustice. Power & The Ethics of Knowing* (Oxford, Oxford University Press, 2007).

Frumkin, LA and Stone, A 'Not all eyewitnesses are equal: Accent status, race and age interact to influence evaluations of testimony' (2020) 18 *Journal of Ethnicity in Criminal Justice* 123.

Galinsky, A and Moskowitz, G, 'Perspective-taking: decreasing stereotype expression, stereotype accessibility, and in-group favoritism' (2000) 78 *Journal of personality and social psychology* 708.

Gardner, J, 'Justification under Authority' (2010) 23 *Canadian Journal of Jurisprudence* 71.

—— 'Criminals in Uniform' in RA Duff, L Farmer, SE Marshall, M Renzo and V Tadros (eds), *The Constitution of the Criminal Law* (Oxford, Oxford University Press, 2013).

Gibbons, F et al, 'The Impact of Early Racial Discrimination on Illegal Behavior, Arrest, and Incarceration among African Americans' (2020) 75 *American Psychologist* 952.

Gonzalez Van Cleve, N, 'Crook County: Racism and Injustice in America's Largest Criminal Court' (Stanford, Stanford University Press, 2020).

Goulian A, Jauffret-Roustide M, Dambélé S et al, 'A cultural and political difference: comparing the racial and social framing of population crack cocaine use between the United States and France' (2022) 19 *Harm Reduction Journal* 44.

Gray, D, 'Punishment as Suffering' (2010) 63 *Vanderbilt Law Review* 1617.

Green, L, 'The Authority of the State' (Oxford, Oxford University Press, 1988).

Groarke, L, 'Aristotle's contrary psychology: the mean in ethics and beyond' (2015) 69 *The Review of Metaphysics* 47.

Halushka, J, 'The Runaround: Punishment, Welfare, and Poverty Survival after Prison' (2020) 67 *Social Problems* 233.

Hamilton, F, 'Officer suspended after police filmed kneeling on man's neck' *The Times* (17 July 2021).

Hampton, J, 'A New Theory of Retribution' in RG Frey and CW Morris (eds), *Liability and Responsibility: Essays in Law and Morals* (Cambridge, Cambridge University Press, 1991).

—— 'The moral education theory of punishment' (1984) 13 *Philosophy and Public Affairs* 208.

Hanan, ME, 'Remorse bias' (2018) 83 *Missouri Law Review* 301.

Haney, C, 'The Science of Solitary: Expanding the Harmfulness Narrative' (2020) 115 *Northwestern University Law Review* 211.

Harding, J, 'Unreasonable Force' *London Review of Books* blog (1 December 2020).

Harper, T, *Broken Yard: The Fall of the Metropolitan Police* (Hull, Biteback Publishing, 2022).

Hart, HLA, 'Prolegomenon to the Principles of Punishment' (1959) 60 *Proceedings of the Aristotelian Society*1.

Hayes, D, 'Proximity, Pain, and State Punishment' (2018) 20 *Punishment and Society* 235.

Heinkel-Wolfe, P, 'Is it a crime to sleep in the park after dark? A U.S. appeals court says no' *Denton Record Chronicle* (22 September 2018).

Henham, R, *Sentencing and the Legitimacy of Trial Justice* (Abingdon, Routledge, 2012).

Herbert, S, 'Coercion, Territoriality, Legitimacy: The Police and the Modern State' in KR Cox, M Low and J Robinson (eds), *Handbook of Political Geography* (London: Sage, 2008).

Hessick, CB and Berman, DA, 'Towards a Theory of Mitigation' (2016) 96 *Boston University Law Review* 161.

Holliday, JR, McNiel, DE, Morris, NP, Faigman, DL and Binder, RL, 'The Use of Battered Woman Syndrome in US Criminal Courts' (2022) 50 *The Journal of the American Academy of Psychiatry and the Law* 373.

Holroyd, J, 'Punishment and Justice' (2010) 36 *Social Theory & Practice* 78.

Holroyd, J and Picinali, F, 'Excluding Evidence for Integrity's Sake' in C Dahlman, A Stein and G Tuzet (eds), *Philosophical Foundations of Evidence Law* (Oxford, Oxford University Press, 2021).

Horton, J, *Political Obligation*, 2nd edn (Houndsmills, Palgrave Macmillan, 2010).

Hoskins, Z, *Beyond Punishment?: A Normative Account of the Collateral Legal Consequences of Conviction* (New York, Oxford University Press, 2019).

House of Lords Library, *Police Standards and Culture: Restoring Public Trust* (London, House of Lords, 2023).

Howard, JW, 'Moral Subversion and Structural Entrapment' (2016) 24 *Journal of Political Philosophy* 24.

—— 'Punishment as Moral Fortification' (2017) 36 *Law and Philosophy* 45.

Howard, JW and Pasternak, A, 'Criminal Wrongdoing, Restorative Justice, and the Moral Standing of Unjust States' (2023) 31 *Journal of Political Philosophy* 42.

Hume, D, *A Treatise of Human Nature*, 2nd edn (Oxford, Oxford University Press, 1978).

Husak, D, *Overcriminalization* (Oxford, Oxford University Press, 2008).

Husak, DN, 'Already Punished Enough' (1990) 18 *Philosophical Topics* 79.

Independent Office for Police Conduct, 'Learning for Met officer over Finsbury Park arrest' (29 July 2021).

—— 'Operation Hotton: Learning Report' (2022).

—— 'Met Police officer given final written warning relating to strip search of woman' (21 December 2022).

—— 'West Yorkshire Police officer struck man's head with his boot during arrest' (21 September 2023).

Independent Police Complaints Commission, 'Police Use of Force' (2015).

Jackson, J, 'Norms, Normativity, and the Legitimacy of Justice Institutions: International Perspectives' (2008) 14 *Annual Review of Law and Social Science* 145.

Jacobs, J, 'From Bad to Worse: Crime, Incarceration, and the Self-Wounding Society' in S Farrall, B Goldson, I Loader and A Dockley (eds), *Justice and Penal Policy* (Abingdon, Routledge, 2016).

Jacobson, J and Hough, M, 'Personal Mitigation: An Empirical Analysis in England and Wales' in J Roberts (ed), *Mitigation and Aggravation at Sentencing* (Cambridge, Cambridge University Press, 2011).

Jannsen, B, 'Probleme der Strafzumessung bei Rückfalltätern' (1991) *Zeitschrift für Rechtspolitik* 52.

Jareborg, N, 'The Swedish Sentencing Law' (1993) 2 *European Journal on Criminal Policy and Research* 67.

—— 'Why Bulk Discounts in Multiple Offence Sentencing?' in A Ashworth and M Wasik (eds), *Fundamentals of Sentencing Theory: Essays in Honour of Andrew von Hirsch* (Oxford, Oxford University Press, 1998).

Kagan, S, *The Geometry of Desert* (New York, Oxford University Press, 2012).

Kant, I, *The Philosophy of the Law: An Exposition of the Fundamental Principles of Jurisprudence as the Science of Right* (trans W Hastie) (Edinburgh, T. & T. Clark, 1887).

Kaplow, L and Shavell, S, 'Accuracy in the Determination of Liability' (1992) 37 *The Journal of Law and Economics* 1.

Kazemian, L and Walker, A, 'Effects of Incarceration' in DP Farrington, L Kazemian, and AR Piquero (eds), *The Oxford Handbook of Developmental and Life-Course Criminology* (Oxford, Oxford University Press, 2018).

Khoriaty, DJ, 'Criminal Law – Government Conduct That Breaches a Plea Agreement in the Third Circuit' (1992) 37 *Villanova Law Review* 1014.

Kidd, IJ, Medina, J and Pohlhaus Jr, G (eds), *The Routledge Handbook of Epistemic Injustice* (New York, Routledge, 2017).

Kilty, JM and Weir, C, 'Temporary irresponsibility, foolish mistakes, and outright villains' in S Tudor, R Weisman, M Proeve and K Rossmanith (eds), *Remorse and Criminal Justice: Multi-Disciplinary Perspectives* (New York, Routledge, 2021).

Klein, M, *Determinism, Blameworthiness, and Deprivation* (Oxford, Oxford University Press, 1990).

Kleinig, J *Punishment and Desert* (Martinus Nijhoff, The Hague, 1973).

Knowles, D, *Political Obligation* (London:, Routledge, 2010).

Kolber, A, 'The Subjective Experience of Punishment' (2009) 109 *Columbia Law Review* 182.

Kolstad, A, 'Imprisonment as Rehabilitation: Offenders' Assessment of Why it Does Not Work' (1996) 24 *Journal of Criminal Justice* 323.

Krinsky, M. and Komar, L 'Victims' Rights and Diversion: Furthering the Interests of Crime Survivors and the Community' (2021) 74 *Southern Methodist University Law Review* 527.

Kurinec, CA and Weaver III, CA, 'Dialect on trial: use of AAVE influences juror appraisals' (2019) 25 *Psychology, Crime & Law* 803.

Lacey, N, 'Principles, Policies, and Politics of Criminal Law' in L Zedner and JV Roberts (eds), *Principles and Values in Criminal Law and Criminal Justice: Essays in Honour of Andrew Ashworth* (Oxford, Oxford University Press, 2012).

—— 'Getting Proportionality in Perspective: Philosophy, History, and Institutions' (2021) 50 *Crime and Justice* 77.

—— 'Criminal Justice and Social (In)Justice' (LSE International Inequalities Institute, 2022) Working Paper 84, eprints.lse.ac.uk/116949/1/Lacey_criminal_justice.pdf.

Lacey, N and Pickard, H, 'A Dual-Process Approach to Criminal Law: Victims and the Clinical Model of Responsibility without Blame' (2019) 27 *The Journal of Political Philosophy* 229.

—— 'Why Standing to Blame May Be Lost but Authority to Hold Accountable Retained: Criminal Law as a Regulative Public Institution' (2021) 104 *Monist* 265.

Lackey, J, *Criminal Testimonial Injustice* (Oxford, Oxford University Press, 2023).

Lambert, EW, 'A Way out of the "Rotten Social Background Stalemate: "Scarcity" and Stephen Morse's Proposed Generic Partial Excuse' (2018) 21 *University of Pennsylvania Journal of Law and Social Change* 297.

Langbein, J, The Criminal Trial Before the Lawyers (1978) 45 *University of Chicago Law Review* 263.

Laub, JH and Sampson, RJ, 'Understanding Desistance from Crime' (2001) 28 *Crime and Justice: A Review of Research* 1.

Laudan, L, 'Truth, error, and criminal law: an essay in legal epistemology' (Cambridge, Cambridge University Press, 2006).

LeBel, TP and Richie, M, 'Prisoner Re-entry and the Life Course' in AD Redlich and JA Quas (eds), *The Oxford Handbook of Developmental Psychology and the Law* (Oxford, Oxford University Press, 2023).

Lee, Y, 'Repeat Offenders and the Question of Desert' in JV Roberts and A von Hirsch (eds), *Previous Convictions at Sentencing. Theoretical and Applied Perspectives* (Oxford, Hart, 2010).

—— 'Mala Prohibita, the Wrongfulness Constraint, and the Problem of Overcriminalization' (2022) 41 *Law and Philosophy* 375.

Lev-Ari, S and Keysar, B, 'Why don't we believe non-native speakers? The influence of accent on credibility' (2010) 46 *Journal of Experimental Social Psychology* 1093.

Lewis, C, 'The Paradox of Recidivism' (2021) 70 *Emory Law Journal* 1209.

Lieblich, E, 'Whataboutism in International Law' (2024) 65 *Harvard International Law Journal* 343.

Lind, EA and O'Barr, WM, 'The social significance of speech in the courtroom' in H Giles and R St Clair (eds), *Language and Social Psychology* (Oxford, Blackwell, 1979).

Link, N, Ward, J and Stansfield, R, 'Consequences of Mental and Physical Health for Reentry and Recidivism: Toward a Health-Based Model of Desistance' (2019) 57 *Criminology* 544.

Lippert-Rasmussen, K, *The Beam and the Mote: On Blame, Standing, and Normativity* (Oxford, Oxford University Press, 2024).

Lippke, R, 'Some Surprising Implications of Negative Retributivism' (2014) 31 *Journal of Applied Philosophy* 49.

—— 'Parsimony and the Sentencing of Multiple Offenders' in J Ryberg, J Roberts and J Keijser (eds), *Sentencing Multiple Crimes* (New York, Oxford University Press, 2018).

Lippke, RL, 'Diminished Opportunities, Diminished Capacities: Social Deprivation and Punishment' (2003) 29 *Social Theory and Practice* 459.

—— 'Social Deprivation as Tempting Fate' (2011) 5 *Criminal Law and Philosophy* 277.

—— 'Chronic Temptation, Reasonable Firmness, and the Criminal Law' (2014) 34 *Oxford Journal of Legal Studies* 75.

—— 'Remorse, Dialogue, and Sentencing' (2022) 16 *Criminal Law and Philosophy* 611.

Loader, I, 'In Search of Civic Policing: Recasting the "Peelian" Principles' (2016) 10 *Criminal Law and Philosophy* 427.

—— 'A Fair Cop: The Charge Sheet Against the Metropolitan Police' *Times Educational Supplement* (30 June 2023).

Loader, I and Walker, N, 'Policing as a Public Good: Reconstituting the Connections between Policing and the State' (2001) 5 *Theoretical Criminology* 9.

Locke, J, *Second Treatise of Government* (New York, Classic Books, 2009 [1689]).

Macaulay, TM Baron, 'Speeches and poems, with the report and notes on the Indian penal code' (New York, AC Armstrong, 1874).

MacLeod, JF, Grove, PG and Farrington, DP, *Explaining Criminal Careers: Implications for Justice Policy* (Oxford, Oxford University Press, 2012).

Manikis, M, 'Recognising State Blame in Sentencing: A Communicative and Relational Framework' (2022a) 81 *The Cambridge Law Journal* 294.

—— 'The Principle of Proportionality in Sentencing: A Dynamic Evolution and Multiplication of Conceptions' (2022b) 59 *Osgoode Hall Law Journal* 587.

Manikis, M and Doiron, N, 'Solitary Confinement as State Harm: Reimagining Sentencing in Light of Dynamic Censure and State Blame. Punishment and Society' (2023) 26 *Punishment & Society* 72.

Manikis, M and Matheson, A, 'Communicating Censure: The Relevance of Conditions of Imprisonment at Sentencing and During the Administration of the Sentence' (2024) 87 *Modern Law Review* 570.

Manson, A, *The Law of Sentencing* (Toronto, Irwin Law (Essentials of Canadian Law), 2001).

Markovits, D, *The Meritocracy Trap* (New York, Penguin, 2019).

Maruna, S, 'Reentry as a Rite of Passage' (2011) 13 *Punishment & Society* 3.

—— 'The Locked Up Living Podcast [Desistance or Desistence?]' (23 June 2021).

Maslen, H, *Remorse, Penal Theory and Sentencing* (Oxford, Hart Publishing, 201).

Mastrobuoni, G and Terlizzese, D, 'Leave the Door Open? Prison Conditions and Recidivism' EIEF Working Paper 21 (Einaudi Institute of Economics and Finance, 2021).

Matravers, M, '"Who's Still Standing?" A Comment on Antony Duff's Preconditions of Criminal Liability' (2006) 3 *Journal of Moral Philosophy* 320.

—— 'Remaindered Culpability: Comment on Fundamentals of Criminal Law' (2021) 23 *Jerusalem Review of Legal Studies* 138.

—— 'Living Non-Criminal Lives: What Role for the State?' in AE Bottoms and J Jacobs (eds), *Criminology As a Moral Science* (Oxford, Hart Publishing, 2023).

—— 'Punishment and Social Injustice' in J Ryberg (ed), The Oxford Handbook of the Philosophy of Punishment (Oxford, Oxford University Press, 2025).

Maynard, R, *Policing Black Lives: State Violence in Canada from Slavery to the Present* (Black Point, Nova Scotia, Fernwood Publishing, 2017).

McCuish, E, Lussier, P and Rocque, M, 'Maturation beyond Age: Interrelationships among Psychosocial, Adult Role, and Identity Maturation and their Implications for Desistance from Crime' (2020) 49 *Journal of Youth and Adolescence* 479.

Medina, J, 'Agential epistemic injustice and collective epistemic resistance in the criminal justice system' (2021) 35 *Social Epistemology* 185.

Meixner, JB Jr, 'Modern Sentencing Mitigation' (2022) 116 *Northwestern University Law Review* 1397.

Mervyn, J and Ashton, S, 'Trauma-Informed Neurobiology and Criminal Behaviour' in S Hassan, D Lett and L Ballantyne (eds), *Introduction to Criminology* (2023).
Miles, H and Raynor, P, *Reintegrative Justice in Practice: The Informal Management of Crime in an Island Community* (Farnham, Ashgate, 2014).
Miller, RJ, *Halfway Home: Race, Punishment, and the Afterlife of Mass Incarceration* (Chicago, Little, Brown & Company, 2021).
Miller, RJ and Stuart, F, 'Carceral Citizenship. Race, Rights and Responsibility in the Age of Mass Supervision' (2017) 21 *Theoretical Criminology* 532.
Minson, S, 'Mitigating Motherhood: A Study of the Impact of Motherhood on Sentencing Decisions in England and Wales' (London, Howard League for Penal Reform, 2016).
Monaghan, N, *Law of Evidence* (Cambridge, Cambridge University Press, 2015).
Monchalin, L, *The Colonial Problem: An Indigenous Perspective on Crime and Injustice in Canada* (Toronto, University of Toronto Press, 2016).
Moore, M, *Placing Blame: A Theory of the Criminal Law* (Oxford, Oxford University Press, 2010).
Moraro, P, 'On (Not) Accepting the Punishment for Civil Disobedience' (2018) 68 *The Philosophical Quarterly* 503.
Morris, H, 'Persons and Punishment' (1958) 52 *The Monist* 475.
Morse, S, 'Deprivation and Desert' in W Heffernan and J Kleinig (eds), *From Social Justice to Criminal Justice* (Oxford, Oxford University Press, 2000).
—— 'Commentary: Reflections on Remorse' (2014) 42 *Journal of the American Academy of Psychiatry and the Law* 15.
Morse, SJ, 'The Twilight of Welfare Criminology: A Reply to Judge Bazelon' (1976) 49 *Southern California Law Review* 1247.
—— 'Excusing and the New Excuse Defenses: A Legal and Conceptual Overview' (1998) 23 *Crime and Justice: A Review of Research* 329
—— 'Diminished Rationality, Diminished Responsibility' (2002) 1 *Ohio State Journal of Criminal Law* 289.
Muller, C and Wildeman C, 'Punishment and Inequality' in J Simon and R Sparks (ed), *The SAGE Handbook of Punishment and Society* (London, SAGE Publications Ltd, 2013).
Murphy, B and Anderson, J, 'After the Serpent Beguiled Me: Entrapment and Sentencing in Australia and Canada' (2014) 39 *Queen's Law Journal* 621.
Murphy, J, 'Marxism and Retribution' (1973) 2 *Philosophy and Public Affairs* 217.
Nagin, DS, 'Deterrence and Incapacitation' in M Tonry (ed), *The Handbook of Crime and Punishment* (New York, Oxford University Press, 1998).
Narveson, J, *The Libertarian Idea* (Philadelphia, Temple University Press, 1988).
Natapoff, A, 'Misdemeanors' (2012) 85 *Southern California Law Review* 1313.
—— *Snitching. Criminal Informants and the Erosion of American Justice*, 2nd edn (New York, NYU Press, 2022).
Nathanson, S, 'Does It Matter if the Death Penalty is Arbitrarily Administered?' (1985) 14 *Philosophy and Public Affairs* 149.
National Council of Welfare, 'Justice and the Poor' (2000).
National Inquiry into Missing and Murdered Indigenous Women and Girls, 'Reclaiming Power and Place: The Final Report of the National Inquiry into Missing and Murdered Indigenous Women and Girls' (2019).
National Registry of Exonerations, 'Government Misconduct and Convicting the Innocent: The Role of Prosecutors, Police and Other Law Enforcement' (2020), www.law.umich.edu/special/exoneration/Documents/Government_Misconduct_and_Convicting_the_Innocent.pdf.
Norris, P and Inglehart, R, *Cultural Backlash: Trump, Brexit and Authoritarian Populism.* (Cambridge, Cambridge University Press, 2019).
Nozick, R, *Anarchy, State and Utopia* (New York, Basic Books, 1974).
Nugent, B and Schinkel, M, 'The Pains of Desistance' (2016) 16 *Criminology & Criminal Justice* 568.
Nussbaum, M, 'Equity and Mercy' (1993) 2 *Philosophy and Public Affairs* 3.

Odudu, O, 'Retributivist Justice in an Unjust Society' (2003) 16 *Ratio Juris* 416.
Office for Victims of Crime, 'U. S. Resource Map of Crime Victim Services and Information', www.ovc.gov/map.html.
Osterweil, V, *In Defense of Looting: A Riotous History of Uncivil Action* (New York, Bold Type Books, 2020).
Ottenhof, R, *L'individualisation de la peine. De Saleilles à aujourd'hui.* (Erès, 2001).
Pager, D, Western, B and Sugie, N, 'Sequencing Disadvantage: Barriers to Employment Facing Young Black and White Men with Criminal Records' (2009) 623 *The Annals of the American Academy of Political and Social Science* 195.
Parekh, B, 'A Misconceived Discourse on Political Obligation' (1993) 41 *Political Studies* 236.
Payne, J, *Recidivism in Australia: Findings and Future Research* (Canberra, Australian Institute of Criminology, 2007).
Perry, S, 'Pardons' in D Sobel and S Wall (eds), *Oxford Studies in Political Philosophy*, volume 8. (Oxford, Oxford University Press, 2021) 215–44.
Petersen, TS, 'Less for Recidivists? Why Retributivists Have a Reason to Punish Repeat Offenders Less Harshly than First-time Offenders' in C Tamburrini and J Ryberg (eds), *Recidivist Punishments: The Philosopher's View* (Lanham, MD, Lexington Books, 2012).
Petrich, DM, et al, 'Custodial Sanctions and Reoffending: A Metal Analytic Review' (2021) 50 *Crime and Justice.*
Petrosino, A, Petrosino, C, Guckenburg, S, Terrell, J, Fronius, TA and Choo, K, 'The Effects of Juvenile System Processing on Subsequent Delinquency Outcomes' in DP Farrington, L Kazemian and AR Piquero (eds), *The Oxford Handbook of Developmental and Life-Course Criminology* (Oxford, Oxford University Press, 2018).
Poama, A, 'Social Injustice, Disadvantaged Offenders, and the State's Authority to Punish' (2021) 29 *Journal of Political Philosophy* 73.
Poama, A and Tripkovic, M, 'Collateral Legal Consequences and the Power to Punish' (2024, online first) *Journal of Applied Philosophy*.
Polaschek, DLL, 'The Psychology of Desistance' in DLL Polaschek, A Day and CR Hollin (eds), *The Wiley International Handbook of Correctional Psychology*, 1st edn (Chichester, John Wiley & Sons Ltd, 2019) 315.
Polegek, B, 'Izredna omilitev kazni: Odprava ali prenova?' (2011) 30 *Pravna praksa* 17.
Prison Reform Trust, 'Bromley Briefings Prison Factfile: February 2024', prisonreformtrust.org.uk/publication/bromley-briefings-prison-factfile-february-2024.
Proeve, M and Tudor, S, *Remorse: Psychological and Jurisprudential Perspectives* (New York, Routledge, 2016).
Public Inquiry into the Administration of Justice and Aboriginal People, 'Report of the Aboriginal Justice Inquiry of Manitoba' Vol 1 (1991).
Rachels, J, 'Punishment and Desert' in H LaFollette (ed,) *Ethics in Practice* (London, Blackwell, 1997).
Radzik, L, 'Standing and Accountability' (2023) 68 *American Journal of Jurisprudence* 153.
'Raising of America: Early Childhood and the Future of our Nation' Documentary series (2015) produced by California Newsreel.
Rawls, J, 'Two concepts of rules' (1955) LXIV *Philosophical Review* 5.
—— *A Theory of Justice* (Cambridge, Mass, Harvard University Press, 1971).
—— *A Theory of Justice* (Oxford, Oxford University Press, 1999a).
—— *A Theory of Justice*, revd edn (Cambridge, MA, Harvard University Press, 1999b).
Raz, J, *The Morality of Freedom* (Oxford, Oxford University Press, 1986).
Reitz, K, 'Proof of Aggravating and Mitigating Facts at Sentencing' in J Roberts (ed), *Mitigation and Aggravation at Sentencing* (Cambridge, Cambridge University Press, 2011).
Reitz, KR, 'The Illusion of Proportionality: Desert and Repeat Offenders' in JV Roberts and A von Hirsch (eds), *Previous Convictions at Sentencing. Theoretical and Applied Perspectives* (Oxford, Hart, 2010).
Rice, D, Rhodes, H and Nteta, T, 'Racial bias in legal language' (2019) 6 *Research & Politics*.

Richards, SC and Jones, RS, 'Beating the Perpetual Incarceration Machine: Overcoming Structural Impediments to Re-entry' in S Maruna and R Immarigeon (eds), *After Crime and Punishment: Pathways to Offender Reintegration* (Cullompton, Willan, 2004).
Ristroph, A, 'Conditions of Legitimate Punishment' in C Flanders and Z Hoskins (eds), *The New Philosophy of Criminal Law* (London, Rowman & Littlefield, 2016).
Rivers III, L, Gibbs, C and Paternoster, R, 'Integrating Criminological and Decision Research Theory: Implications for Understanding and Addressing Crime in Marginalized Communities' (2017) 38 *Deviant Behavior* 74.
Roach, K, *Canadian Policing: Why and How it Must Change* (Toronto, Delve Publishing, Irwin, 2022).
Roberts, JV, *Punishing Persistent Offenders: Exploring Community and Offender Perspectives* (Oxford, Oxford University Press, 2008).
—— 'Punishing, more or less: exploring aggravation and mitigation at sentencing' in JV Roberts (ed), *Mitigation and Aggravation at Sentencing* (Cambridge, Cambridge University Press, 2011).
—— 'Structuring Sentencing in Canada, England and Wales: A Tale of Two Jurisdictions' (2012) 23 *Criminal Law Forum* 319.
—— 'Complying with Sentencing Guidelines' in A Ashworth and J Roberts (eds), *Sentencing Guidelines: Exploring the English Model* (Oxford, Oxford University Press, 2013).
Roberts JV and Dagan, N, 'The Evolution of Retributive Punishment: From Static Desert to Responsive Penal Censure' in A Du Bois-Pedain and A Bottoms (eds), *Penal Censure: Engagements Within and Beyond Desert Theory* (Oxford, Hart, 2019).
—— 'Rewarding Virtue: An Ethical Defence of Plea-Based Sentence Reductions' in JV Roberts and J Ryberg (eds), *Pleading Guilty: Ethical Perspectives on Sentencing the Self-Convicted* (Oxford, Hart Law, 2020).
Roberts, JV and Harrendorf, S, 'Criminal History Enhancements at Sentencing' in K Ambos et al (eds), *Core Concepts in Criminal Law and Criminal Justice* Vol. 1 (Cambridge, Cambridge University Press, 2022).
Roberts, JV and Gazal-Ayal, O, 'Sentencing Reform in Israel: An Analysis of the Statutory Reforms of 2012' (2013) *Israel Law Review* 46, 455–479.
Roberts, JV and Ryberg, J (eds), *Sentencing the Self-Convicted: The Ethics of Pleading Guilty* (Oxford, Hart, 2023).
Roberts, JV and von Hirsch, A (eds), *Previous Convictions at Sentencing: Theoretical and Applied Perspectives* (Oxford, Hart Publishing, 2010).
Roberts, JV, Watson, G and Hester, R, 'Sentencing Members of Minority Groups: Problems and Prospects for Improvement in Four Countries' (2024) 52 *Crime and Justice* 343.
Robinson, P, *Intuitions of Justice and the Utility of Desert* (New York, Oxford University Press, 2013).
Romero-Rivas, C, Morgan, C and Collier, T, 'Accentism on Trial: Categorisation/Stereotyping and Implicit Biases Predict Harsher Sentences for Foreign-Accented Defendants' (2022) 41 *Journal of Language and Social Psychology* 191.
Rosett, A, 'The Negotiated Guilty Plea' (1967) 374 *Annals of the American Academy of Political and Social Science* 70.
Ross, A et al, 'Impact of residential schooling and of child abuse on substance use problems in Indigenous Peoples' (2015) 51 *Addictive Behaviors* 184.
Ross, L, 'The Intuitive Psychologist and his Shortcomings' (1978) 10 *Advances in Experimental Social Psychology* 173.
Rubio Arnal, AR and McNeill, F, 'Exploring Social Re/habilitation and Developing a New Conceptualisation of Re/integration' in F Coppola and A Martufi (eds), *Social Rehabilitation and Criminal Justice* (London, Routledge, 2024) 251.
Russell, BL, *Battered woman syndrome as a legal defense: History, effectiveness and implications* (Jefferson, NC, McFarland, 2014).
Ryberg, J, *Proportionate Punishment: A Critical Investigation* (Dordrecht, Kluwer Academic Publishers, 2004).
—— 'Punishment and the Measurement of Severity' in J Ryberg, and JA Corlett (eds), *Punishment and Ethics: New Perspectives* (London, Palgrave Macmillan, 2010).

—— 'Punishing Adolescents: On Immaturity and Diminished Responsibility' (2014) 7 *Neuroethics* 327.
—— *Neurointerventions, Crime, and Punishment* (New York, Oxford University Press, 2020a).
—— 'Proportionality and the Seriousness of Crimes' in M Tonry (ed), *Of the One-Eyed and Toothless Miscreants: Making the Punishment Fit the Crime* (New York, Oxford University Press, 2020b).
—— 'Retributivism and the (lack of) Justification of Proportionality' (2021a) 15 *Criminal Law and Philosophy* 447.
—— 'The Ethics of Punishment and the Impact Assumption – Reconsidering the Role of Penal Ethicists' (2021b) 40 *Criminal Justice Ethics* 235.
—— 'Guilty Plea Discounts and Retributivism' in JV Roberts and J Ryberg (eds), *Sentencing the Self-convicted: The Ethics of Pleading Guilty* (Oxford, Hart Publishing, 2023).
—— 'How Should We Work as Penal Ethicists?' in J Ryberg (ed), *The Oxford Handbook of the Philosophy of Punishment* (New York, Oxford University Press, 2025).
Ryberg, J, Roberts, JV and De Keijser, JW, *Sentencing Multiple Crimes* (Oxford, Oxford University Press, 2018).
Sampson, RJ and Laub, JH, *Crime in the Making: Pathways and Turning Points through Life* (Cambridge, MA, Harvard University Press, 1993).
Sandel, M, *The Tyranny of Merit: What's Become of the Common Good?* (New York, Penguin, 2021).
Sarch, A, 'Who Cares What You Think? Criminal Culpability and the Irrelevance of Unmanifested Mental States' (2017) 36 *Law and Philosophy* 707.
Scheck, B, Neufeld, P and Dwyer, J, *Actual Innocence: Five Days to Execution and Other Dispatches from the Wrongly Convicted.* (New York, Bantam, 2000).
Scheid, DE, 'Constructing a Theory of Punishment, Desert, and the Distribution of Punishments' (1997) 10 *The Canadian Journal of Law and Jurisprudence* 441.
Schepers, D, 'Causes of the causes of juvenile delinquency: social disadvantages in the context of situational action theory (2017) 14 *European Journal of Criminology* 143.
Sen, A, *Inequality Reexamined* (Cambridge, Mass, Harvard University Press, 1992).
Seneca, 'On Mercy' in JF Procopé and JM Cooper (eds), *Seneca: Moral and Political Essays* (Cambridge, Cambridge University Press, 1995) 117.
Sentencing Council for England and Wales, 'General Guideline: Overarching Principles' (1 October 2019).
—— 'Sentencing Pregnant Women and New Mothers' (1 April 2024).
—— 'Aggravating and mitigating factors' (2024), www.sentencingcouncil.org.uk/explanatory-material/magistrates-court/item/aggravating-and-mitigating-factors.
Sentencing Guidelines Council, 'Guideline Judgments Case Compendium' (2005).
Sered, D et al, Young Men of Color and the Other Side of Harm: Addressing Disparities (Vera, 2014).
Shahvisi, A, 'Don't Call the Police' *London Review of Books* blog (21 March 2022).
Shapland, J, 'Personal Mitigation and Assumptions about Offending and Desistance' in Roberts, J (ed), *Mitigation and Aggravation at Sentencing.* (Cambridge, Cambridge University Press, 2011).
Shapland, J and Bottoms, AE, 'Reflections on Social Values, Offending and Desistance among Young Adult Recidivists' (2011) 13 *Punishment & Society* 256.
—— 'Offending and Offence Patterns in the Early Stages of Desistance: A Study of Young Men in England' in AAJ Blokland and V Van Der Geest (eds), *The Routledge International Handbook of Life-Course Criminology* (London, Routledge, 2017) 301.
Shelby, T, *Dark Ghettos: Injustice, Dissent, and Reform* (Cambridge, MA, Belknap Press, 2016).
Sher, G, *Desert* (Princeton, Princeton University Press, 1987).
Simmons, AJ, *Justification and Legitimacy* (Cambridge University Press, 2001).
Simmons, AJ, *Moral Principles and Political Obligations* (Princeton, Princeton University Press, 1979).
Stark, F, 'Standing and Pre-trial Misconduct: Hypocrisy, "Separation", Inconsistent Blame, and Frustration' (2024) 18 *Criminal Law and Philosophy* 327.
—— 'Standing and Pre-Trial Misconduct: Hypocrisy, "Separation", Inconsistent Blame, and Frustration' (2024) 18 *Criminal Law and Philosophy* 327.

Starr, SB, 'Sentence Reduction as a Remedy for Prosecutorial Misconduct' (2009) 97 *The Georgetown Law Journal* 1509.
Steffensmeier, DJ, Allan, EA, Harer, MD and Streifel, C, 'Age and the Distribution of Crime' (1989) 94 *American Journal of Sociology* 803.
Stewart, F and Freiberg, A, 'Provocation in Sentencing: A Culpability-Based Framework' (2008) 19 *Current Issues in Criminal Justice* 283.
Stuntz, WJ, 'The Uneasy Relationship Between Criminal Procedure and Criminal Justice' (1997) 107 *Yale Law Journal* 1.
—— 'Race, Class, and Drugs' (1998) 98 *Columbia Law Review* 1795.
Sweeney, LT and Haney, C, 'The influence of race on sentencing: A meta-analytic review of experimental studies' (1992) 10 *Behavioral Sciences & the Law* 179.
Tadros V, 'The Characters of Excuse' (2001) 21 *Oxford Journal of Legal Studies* 495.
—— 'Poverty and Criminal Responsibility' (2009) 43 *Journal of Value Inquiry* 391.
Tasioulas, J, 'Mercy' (2003) 103 *Proceedings of the Aristotelian Society* 101.
Taslitz, A 'The Rule of Criminal Law: Why Courts and Legislatures Ignore Richard Delgado's Rotten Social Background' (2011) 2 *Alabama Civil Rights and Civil Liberties Law Review* 79.
Tata, C, *Sentencing: A Social Process* (London, Palgrave Pivot, 2020).
Ten, CL, *Crime, Guilt, and Punishment* (Oxford, Clarendon Press, 1987).
Thomas, KA, 'Beyond Mitigation: Towards a Theory of Allocution' (2006) 75 *Fordham Law Review* 2641.
Thompson, F 'State of Fear: Arbitrary Arrests, Torture, and Killings' (Human Rights Watch, 2015), www.hrw.org/report/2015/09/17/state-fear/arbitrary-arrests-torture-and-killings.
Thorburn, M, *Punishment and Public Authority. Criminal Law and the Authority of the State* (Oregon, Hart Publishing, 2017).
—— 'Criminal Punishment and the Right to Rule' (2019) 70 *The University of Toronto Law Journal* 44.
—— 'What Kind of Order do we Want? Policing, Governance, and the Public Point of View' (All Souls Criminology Seminar Series, University of Oxford, 2024).
Toch, H, *Mosaic of Despair: Human Breakdowns in Prison*, rev edn (Washington, DC, American Psychological Association, 1992).
Tonry, M, *Malign Neglect: Race, Crime and Punishment in America* (New York, Oxford University Press, 1995).
—— 'The Questionable Relevance of Previous Convictions to Punishments for Later Crimes' in JV Roberts and A von Hirsch (eds), *Previous Convictions at Sentencing. Theoretical and Applied Perspectives* (Oxford, Hart, 2010).
—— 'Equality and Human Dignity' (2016) 45 *Crime and Justice* 459.
—— *Doing Justice, Preventing Crime* (New York, Oxford University Press, 2020).
Trilling, D, 'Not Much Like Consent' (2023) 45 *London Review of Books*.
Tuckness, A and Parrish, JM, *The Decline of Mercy in Public Life* (Cambridge, Cambridge University Press, 2014).
United Nations, 'UN Human Rights Committee publishes findings on Egypt, Panama, Peru, Sri Lanka, Turkmenistan and Zambia' Press release (24 March 2023), www.ohchr.org/en/press-releases/2023/03/un-human-rights-committee-publishes-findings-egypt-panama-peru-sri-lanka.
United Nations Human Rights Council, 'Report of the Special Rapporteur on extreme poverty and human rights on his mission to the United States of America' A/HRC/38/33/Add.1 (2018), digitallibrary.un.org/record/1629536?v=pdf.
—— 'Visit to the United Kingdom of Great Britain and Northern Ireland. Report of the Special Rapporteur on Extreme Poverty and Human Rights' A/HRC/41/39/Add.1 (2019), digitallibrary.un.org/record/3806308?ln=en&v=pdf.
—— 'Visit to the European Union – Report of the Special Rapporteur on Extreme Poverty and Human Rights' A/HRC/47/36/Add. (2021), www.ohchr.org/en/documents/country-reports/ahrc4736add1-visit-european-union-report-special-rapporteur-extreme.

United Kingdom Government, 'Discrimination: your rights' (2024), www.gov.uk/discrimination-your-rights.

United States Attorney's Office, Northern District of Oklahoma, 'A homeless sex offender pleads guilty to rape' (2023), www.justice.gov/usao-ndok/pr/homeless-sex-offender-pleads-guilty-rape.

United States Department of State, '2022 Country Reports on Human Rights Practices: North Korea' (2022), www.state.gov/reports/2022-country-reports-on-human-rights-practices/north-korea.

Unites States Sentencing Commission, 'Analysis of Penalties for Federal Rape Cases' (1995), www.ojp.gov/pdffiles1/Digitization/155367NCJRS.pdf.

—— 'Overview of Federal Criminal Cases' (2022), www.ussc.gov/sites/default/files/pdf/research-and-publications/research-publications/2022/FY21.

—— '2023 Guidelines Manual Annotated' (2023a), www.ussc.gov/guidelines/2023-guidelines-manual-annotated.

—— 'Aggravating and mitigating role adjustments' (2023b), www.ussc.gov/guidelines/primers/aggravating-and-mitigating-role-adjustments.

US Department of Justice, 'The Validity and Use of Evidence Concerning Battering and its Effects in Criminal Trials, Report Responding to Section 40507 of The Violence Against Women Act' (1996), www.ojp.gov/pdffiles/batter.pdf.

Vidmar, N, 'The Psychology of Trial Judging' (2011) 20 *Current Directions in Psychological Science* 58.

Visher, CA and Travis, J, 'Life on the Outside: Returning Home after Incarceration' (2011) 9 *The Prison Journal* 102S.

Vomfell, L and Stewart, N, 'Officer Bias, Over-Patrolling and Ethnic Disparities in Stop and Search' (2021) 5 *Nature Human Behaviour* 566.

von Hirsch, A, 'Proportionality in the Philosophy of Punishment' (1992) 16 *Crime and Justice* 55.

—— *Censure and Sanctions* (Oxford, Clarendon Press, 1993).

—— 'Sentencing Reform: Its Goals and Prospects' in RA Duff, S Marshall, RE Dobash and RP Dobash (eds), *Penal Theory and Practice. Tradition and Innovation in Criminal Justice* (Manchester, Manchester University Press, 1994).

—— *Deserved Criminal Sentences* (Oxford, Bloomsbury Publishing, 2017).

von Hirsch, A and Ashworth, A, *Proportionate Sentencing* (Oxford, Oxford University Press, 2005).

Walen, A, 'Retributive Justice' in EN Zalta and U Nodelman (eds), *The Stanford Encyclopedia of Philosophy* (2023).

—— 'State Standing to Blame and Punish' (2024), papers.ssrn.com/sol3/papers.cfm?abstract_id=4730859.

Walker, LE, *The Battered Woman Syndrome*, 4th edn (New York, Springer, 2016).

Walker, N, 'The Quiddity of Mercy' (1995) 70 *Philosophy* 27.

Walker, N and Padfield, N, *Sentencing: Theory, Law and Practice*, 2nd edn (Oxford, Butterworths, 1996).

Walzer, M, *Spheres of Justice: A Defense of Pluralism and Equality* (New York, Basic Books, 1983).

Warner, K, 'Equality before the Law: Racial and Social Background Factors as Sources of Mitigating at Sentencing' in JV Roberts (ed), *Mitigation and Aggravation at Sentencing*. (Cambridge, Cambridge University Press, 2011) 124–45.

Washington Post Editorial Board, 'A Prison Overreacts to a Book' *The Washington Post* (3 October 2011) A16.

Wasik, M, *A Practical Approach to Sentencing*, 5th edn (Oxford, Oxford University Press, 2014).

Wasik, M and von Hirsch, A 'Section 29 Revisited: Previous Convictions in Sentencing' (1995) *Criminal Law Review* 409.

Watson, Gabrielle, 'Respect and Legitimacy at Sentencing: Current Research and Future Priorities' (Sentencing Academy, 2021).

—— *Respect and Criminal Justice* (Oxford, Oxford University Press, 2020).

Watson, Gary, 'A Moral Predicament in the Criminal Law' (2015) 58 *Inquiry* 168.

—— 'Responsibility and the Limits of Evil: Variations of a Strawsonian Theme' in G Watson, *Agency and Answerability* (Oxford, Clarendon Press, 2024).

Weigend, T, 'Is the criminal process about truth? A German perspective' (2003) 26 *Harvard Journal of Law & Public Policy* 157.
Western, B, *Homeward: Life in the Year After Prison* (New York, Russell Sage Foundation, 2018).
Western, B and Harding, DJ, 'Careers in Criminalization: Reentry, Recidivism, and Repeated Incarceration' (2022) 51 *Crime and Justice* 435.
Wikström, P-O, 'Individuals, Settings, and Acts of Crime: Situational Mechanisms and the Explanation of Crime' in P-O Wikstrom and RJ Sampson (eds), *The Explanation of Crime* (Cambridge, Cambridge University Press, 2006).
Wikström, P-O and Treiber, K, 'Social Disadvantage and Crime: A Criminological Puzzle' (2016) 60 *American Behavioral Scientist* 1232.
—— 'The Dynamics of Change: Criminogenic Interactions and Life-Course Patterns in Crime' in DP Farrington, L Kazemian and AR Piquero (eds), *The Oxford Handbook of Developmental and Life-Course Criminology* (Oxford, Oxford University Press, 2018).
Wikström, P-O, Oberwittler, D, Treiber, K and Hardie, B, *Breaking Rules: the social and situational dynamics of young people's urban crime* (Oxford, Clarendon Studies in Criminology, 2012).
Wikström, P-O, Treiber, K and Roman, G, *Character, Circumstances, and Criminal Careers: Towards a Dynamic Developmental and Life-Course Criminology* (Oxford, Oxford University Press, 2024).
Wolff, N, Blitz, CL, Shi, J, Siegel, J and Bachman, R, 'Physical Violence Inside Prisons: Rates of Victimization' (2007) 34 *Criminal Justice and Behavior* 588.
Wolff, RP, *In Defense of Anarchism*, 2nd edn (Berkeley, University of California Press, 1998).
Working Group on Arbitrary Detention, 'Report of the Working Group on Arbitrary Detention' A/HRC/54/51 (2023), documents.un.org/doc/undoc/gen/g23/144/26/pdf/g2314426.pdf?token=wJeH2pen8CuVxZzbNi&fe=true.
Wringe, B, 'Punishing Noncitizens' (2021) 38 *Journal of Applied Philosophy* 384.
Xynas, L, Bargaric, M and Lambropolous, V, 'Excessive Criminal Punishment Amounts to Punishing the Innocent' (2015) 57 *South Texas Law Review* 1.
Yaffe, G, '"The *Government* Beguiled Me": The Entrapment Defense and the Problem of Private Entrapment' (2005) 1 *Journal of Ethics and Social Philosophy* 1.
Yang, C, 'Free at last? Judicial discretion and racial disparities in federal sentencing' (2015) 44 *Journal of Legal Studies* 75.
Yost, B, 'Standing to Punish the Disadvantaged' (2023) 17 *Criminal Law and Philosophy* 711.
Zaibert, L, 'Mercy' in J Ryberg (ed), *The Oxford Handbook of Punishment Theory and Philosophy* (Oxford, Oxford University Press, 2024).
—— *Punishment and Retribution* (Aldershot, Ashgate, 2006).
—— 'The Instruments of Abolition, Or Why Retributivism is the Only Justification of Punishment' (2013) 32 *Law and Philosophy* 33.
—— *Rethinking Punishment* (Cambridge, Cambridge University Press, 2018).
—— 'Figuring Things Out (Morally Speaking)' (2021) 96 *Philosophy: The Journal of the Royal Institute of Philosophy* 553.
Zedner, L, 'Penal Subversions: When is a Punishment not Punishment, Who Decides and on What Grounds?' (2016) 20 *Theoretical Criminology* 3.
—— 'Security Against Arbitrary Government in Criminal Justice' in A du Bois-Pedain, M Ulväng and P Asp (eds), *Criminal Law and the Authority of the State* (Oxford, Hart, 2017).
Zhong, R, *Judging remorse* (2015) 39 *NYU Review of Law & Social Change* 133.
Zimran, A and Dagan, N, 'Retributivism, State Misconduct, and the Criminal Process' (2023) 42 *Criminal Justice Ethics* 20.

INDEX

www.ingramcontent.com/pod-product-compliance
Ingram Content Group UK Ltd.
Pitfield, Milton Keynes, MK11 3LW, UK
UKHW020135290926
15471UKWH00003B/504

9 781509 975648